CRACKS IN THE EMPIRE

CRACKS IN THE EMPIRE

STATE POLITICS IN THE VIETNAM WAR

Paul Joseph

NEW YORK
COLUMBIA UNIVERSITY PRESS
1987

Columbia University Press Morningside Edition   1987

Columbia University Press
New York   Guildford, Surrey
Copyright © 1981 by Paul Joseph
Preface to the Morningside Edition copyright © 1987 by Paul Joseph

Library of Congress Cataloging-in-Publication Data

Joseph, Paul, 1948–
    Cracks in the Empire.

Reprint. Originally published: Boston : South End Press, 1981.
    Includes index.
        1. Vietnamese Conflict, 1961–1975—United States.
    2. United States—Politics and government—1963–1969.   I. Title.
DS558.J67   1987   959.704′33′73   87-13212
ISBN 0-231-06635-X (pbk.)

This edition is published by arrangement with the author.

To my parents

PREFACE TO THE
MORNINGSIDE EDITION

This book elaborates divisions among U.S. policymakers during the war with Vietnam. The governing elite shared a broad consensus about the importance of trying to keep (South) Vietnam non-Communist. And they were also willing to expend enormous resources in that ultimately unsuccessful effort. But significant disagreement developed over vital issues such as the bombing of the North, the method of deploying ground troops, and managing domestic dissent. *Cracks in the Empire* elaborates both themes: consensus over ends and disagreement over how to grapple with obstacles to secure those ends.

One cannot avoid the conclusion that the overall orientation of United States policymakers toward the efforts of the Vietnamese to secure their national independence and carry out genuine social and economic reform was extremely hostile. Nonetheless, the differences among the policymakers that did emerge were significant. In particular, one orientation toward the war would have produced far less bloodshed and would have altered the social fabric of both the United States and Vietnam in a positive direction. While the precise content of this "reformist" or "left" current changed during different periods of United States intervention, in general its adherents recognized the strength of the Vietnamese revolution and that military force, especially conventional tactics and use of air power, would not, by itself, permit the United States to prevail. In fact, they understood that it was impossible for Washington to dictate terms. The only issue was how to minimize the loss of credibility that gradual withdrawal from Vietnam would, in their terms, produce. Some in the reformist current also wanted

vii

to preserve as much United States influence as possible in Indochina following the cessation of hostilities.

This book argues that the existence of this policy orientation cannot be understood on its own terms, but only as a reflection of the tenacity of the Vietnamese revolution and the strength of opposition to the war within the United States. The willingness of some decision-makers to consider a more realistic policy was not internally generated, but reflected instead these two very different but nonetheless interrelated social movements.

There are two moments where it appeared that Washington might actually follow the tenets of the reformist position. The first was between April and November 1968. The bombing over the north was halted, a ceiling was placed on the number of ground troops, and significant progress was made in the Paris negotiations with the Vietnamese. The election of Richard Nixon over Hubert Humphrey ended that experiment. The second was the first year of the Carter administration. For a brief time the prospects for normalized relations with Vietnam were bright. The overall ascendancy, however, of National Security Adviser Zbigniew Brzezinski over Secretary of State Cyrus Vance ended that period.

From 1978, Washington has attempted, with renewed determination, to punish Vietnam. This time the tools are not the direct deployment of military force, but the use of proxy armies, most notably the Khmer Rouge, and economic, political, and diplomatic isolation. The United States is still waging war, albeit indirectly, against Vietnam. The assumptions guiding policy remain fundamentally the same as those molding our policy over the postwar period.

It is unlikely that Washington's latest effort to impose its own terms will work. The United States was never able to use war to force the Vietnamese to their knees. Less direct means will not be successful either, although they may inflict costs. Vietnam's self-confidence, its ability to sacrifice, and its record of postwar development, however modest that may be, all dictate the conclusion that Hanoi will resist all efforts to impose control. Nonetheless, Washington's hostile stance carries great costs for the Vietnamese: it restricts economic development and forces Hanoi toward a dependency relationship with the Soviet Union.

Washington's current policy carries costs at home as well. The continued attempt to punish Vietnam interferes with efforts to understand our original motivations to intervene and to draw the appropriate lessons from our mistakes. Images of the war and its aftermath become dominated by the simplistic images of *Rambo*. It is hard to have a more realistic discussion. In addition, normalized relations with Vietnam would bring concrete benefits. These include an opportunity to research the impact of dioxin on both Vietnamese and U.S. citizens, and a chance for Vietnamese veterans to make peace with what frequently is an unhappy set of memories. Our government made a mistake in Vietnam and should begin to remedy it. In the process, we can confront the legacy of our own history as well!.

ACKNOWLEDGMENTS

I would like to express my thanks to the friends, family and colleagues who helped me with this book. The suggestions, criticisms, and support of the following people were especially helpful: Michael Albert, Fred Block, Carl Boggs, Peter Dreier, Lou Ferleger, Banning Garrett, Andrei Joseph, Joe Joseph, Ralph Miliband, Martin Murray, members of the *Socialist Review* and South End Press collectives, and Sigmund Schiffman. I owe a special debt to Franz Schurmann who directed my attention toward the politics of national security bureaucracies. In addition, three friends deserve special mention. Peggy Somers and Bob Wood contributed detailed criticisms and warm support. And David Plotke gave the entire manuscript a close reading, sending exhaustive and valuable comments. Taken together these people made the project take much longer, but the final version is much better.

The University of California at Berkeley provided financial support enabling me to conduct interviews with some of the decision makers of the Johnson Administration.

The contributions of my wife, Linda Schiffman, were invaluable, ranging from generously permitting me the time necessary to do a proper job to understanding and sympathy when progress was not as rapid as I wanted. She helped with many of the necessary and important tasks along the way including transcribing interviews, typing, and proof-reading. She encouraged me and reacted to my ideas when I got stuck. Without her the emotional demands of this project would have been much harder to bear.

That is quite a lot of people and quite a lot of assistance. I trust *Cracks in the Empire* reflects their collective contributions.

—Paul Joseph

CONTENTS

TABLES AND CHARTS

GLOSSARY

ABM	Anti-Ballistic Missile
ARVN	Army of the Republic of Vietnam (South)
ASEAN	Association of Southeast Asian Nations
CINCPAC	Commander-in-Chief, Pacific
COMECON	Soviet-led trading bloc
COMUSMACV	Commander, U.S. Military Advisory Command, Vietnam
CPC	Communist Party of China
DMZ	Demilitarized Zone
DRV	Democratic Republic of Vietnam (North)
ICBM	Intercontinental Ballistic Missile
MACV	Military Advisory Command, Vietnam
MAD	Mutual Assured Destruction
MIG	Soviet-built fighter plane
MIRV	Multiple Independently Targeted Reentry Vehicle
NLF	National Liberation Front
NSAM	National Security Action Memorandum
NVN	North Vietnam
OSS	Office of Strategic Services
PCF	Communist Party of France
POL	Petroleum, Oil, Lubricants
PRC	People's Republic of China
ROLLING THUNDER	U.S. Bombing Campaign Against North Vietnam
SEATO	Southeast Asia Treaty Organization
SVN	South Vietnam

INTRODUCTION

CONSIDER FOR A MOMENT that you are the President of the United States. Your military forces have just suffered a humiliating set-back on the battlefield. The overburdened economy shows signs of cracking under the strain of meeting your promise of providing both "guns and butter." Bankers are complaining about rising gold prices, the drain on American gold reserves, and the weakening position of the dollar. Recently they met their foreign counter-parts to establish a two-tier system of Special Drawing Rights. "Bretton Woods is dead" they say, and everyone blames you. Another "piss-ant" country besides Vietnam is on your mind. The North Koreans have captured one of your spy ships. Two F-111's, planes that you counted on to penetrate the North Vietnam air defenses and bomb in the most inclement weather, have either been shot down or crashed. It is hard to know which is worse. Your Saigon government is showing signs of irresponsibility again. This time their call to "march to the North" is met by editorial rebuke from major U.S. newspapers. Congressional criticism seems to have reached an all-time high. Not only the liberals, but your old pals from the Hill days, are demanding a reduction in your Great Society programs before passing a much needed tax increase. Your own commission on racial rebellions is advocating a huge job and housing program. Because of the War there isn't the slightest chance that even a small percentage of the recommendations will be adopted. Another Great Society program, this one providing better health care, has been reduced, again because the War is draining available funds.

The *New York Times* has leaked a story of your general's request for a huge troop increase; this time one that would necessitate a call-up of reserves and an additional ten billion dollars. The Governors

1

say "Don't call up the reserves. We need them for the expected race riots this summer." Everyone seems to be against the troop increase except Abe and Walt — and everyone laughs at them. You have had to fire McNamara, a man who you once said was the best of them all. Now your new Secretary of Defense, an old friend you trusted to hold the line in that suddenly dovish Pentagon, has also turned on you. A meeting of Wall Street and national security types who only a couple of months ago gave a big OK to the war now say "forget it." United States casualties in Vietnam pass the Korean War mark.

It is a Presidential election year. Your ranking on public opinion polls drops to the lowest point since entering office. You used to carry them around in your pocket and show them to visitors; now you can't bear to look at them. The newspapers hate you. In the very first primary you have been embarrassed by a dove not known for his mass appeal, and in a conservative state. Much more serious, Robert Kennedy has just announced that he will run for the Presidential nomination. He might win too. Your probable Republican opponent has announced a secret plan for peace. The newspapers seem to lap it up. Those hippies in the street have been joined by parents, teachers, trade unionists and others. Their antiwar demonstrations might mushroom into something even worse. And all this has happened in just the last month.

It's enough to make you want to quit.

In 1973 Nixon and Kissinger signed a peace treaty with the Vietnamese which resulted in the withdrawal of U.S. troops, the return of POWs, and an electoral procedure to determine the political future of the southern part of Vietnam. Nixon made secret assurances to the Saigon government that the U.S. would reintervene if President Thieu's rule was threatened. But, in the temporary turmoil of Watergate, Congress passed a War Powers Act which expressly prevented the President from using U.S. military forces in Indochina without consulting Congress.

Before launching the Final Offensive in the spring of 1975, the North Vietnamese Political Bureau met and debated for eleven days the following question: did the Watergate crisis so handicap the executive branch that reintervention by U.S. military force would be impossible? Would the Congressional War Powers Act stand up? The Political Bureau agreed that the opportunity for finally liberating the south was present, but they also agreed that renewed U.S. military involvement could spell disaster. Even when they at last decided that the crisis of legitimacy within the U.S. was sufficient to prevent another intervention, the Vietnamese carefully tested their conclusion with a series of small scale attacks. Only when Congress continued to vote against Administration requests for large increases in military aid was the Final Offensive launched.

Politics. The politics of war. How are we to understand it? What was the Vietnam War all about?

Prevailing interpretations of the Vietnam War claim that it was all a mistake. In this view Washington's intentions — to save democracy from Communism — are held to be honorable. But somewhere along the way the decision-making process broke down, we lost sense of the scale of our commitment, and the result was an ineffective, but nonetheless costly, intervention. The U.S. failed to understand Vietnam. We were ignorant of that country's language and cultural traditions; we failed to appreciate the tenacity of the anti-colonial struggle. Washington was blinded by an outdated anti-communist ideology. Optimism designed to gain public support congealed into a mythology that hampered effective policy formulation. Government agencies fought one another, not the Communists. Government officials were more interested in furthering their own careers than securing the national interest. Presidents were given misleading information and made bad decisions as a result. In this view, economic interests do not play a major role in explaining U.S. behavior in Vietnam. The morality of U.S. intervention in the Third World is not examined or is assumed to be beyond reproach. The Vietnam War was an accident, an abberation in postwar U.S. foreign policy. Bureaucracy is the culprit, not capitalism.

Cracks in the Empire offers a different explanation of U.S. intervention in Vietnam. It takes as its starting-point the thesis that the Vietnam War was not an accident but a logical outgrowth of the principles and interests guiding U.S. foreign policy. American decision-makers have consistently attempted to maintain the dominant position of the U.S. in the world arena by: preserving access to important raw materials located in the Third World; combatting the spread of socialism in underdeveloped countries, or even movements attempting to secure genuine independence from the economies of the West; erecting a vast military apparatus, including nuclear weapons, counter-insurgency capabilities, and training programs specifically designed to strengthen the repressive resources of client regimes; managing, through international agencies, the world economy in a manner that preserves the dominant role of multinational corporations; and coordinating economic, political and military policies with Japan and Europe to minimize the growth of leftwing social movements in the more industrialized countries. American decision-makers have not always been successful in the pursuit of these principles. The U.S. is not omnipotent. Opposition forces can win. Mistakes and miscalculations can occur. Yet these principles form the basis of U.S. foreign policy. The capitalist class within the U.S. has been the main beneficiary of these policy priorities.

The specific history of the Vietnam War raises a number of crucial theoretical issues regarding the conduct of U.S. foreign and military policy. What was the role and influence of the capitalist class in formulating, approving, or disapproving that policy? What was the impact of other classes in the U.S.? Stated another way, how much autonomy did the state have from the directives of the most powerful economic class and from public opinion? Within the state itself, what was the role of divisions such as those between the civilian and military leadership, or between contending bureaucratic power bases? Did Presidential ambitions and interests affect policy outcomes? Was the decision-making process fundamentally rational or irrational? And by what criteria should rationality be judged? What about other nations, especially the Soviet Union and China: did their rivalry affect U.S. decisions in Vietnam?

The main purpose of *Cracks in the Empire* is to link these theoretical issues surrounding the nature of power and the political process in the U.S. with a specific history: the details of American intervention in Vietnam between August 1967 and March 1968. To fully grapple with the determinants of Washington's policy towards Vietnam an analysis of the full domestic and international context is provided. The TET Offensive, the air war over North Vietnam and the seige at Khe Sanh are analyzed. We also stop in Moscow and Peking to consider the interests of the leading socialist powers and the relationship of the Sino-Soviet dispute to Vietnam decision-making. We stop in Madison, Wisconsin and Manchester, New Hampshire to consider the role of presidential politics. We stop in Wonsa, North Korea to examine the possible significance of the capture of the *Pueblo*, a U.S. spy ship. We stop in Stockholm and the Pentagon to measure the role of visible protests over the war. We stop in Memphis, Tennessee for a march led by Dr. Martin Luther King to examine the mood created by the racial crisis and its effect on Vietnam. We stop in Basel, New York and Paris to analyze the growing crisis in the international monetary system and its relationship to Vietnam decision-making. We stop on Wall Street to consider business opinion concerning the economic impact of Vietnam War spending. We also explore the connection between the strategic arms balance with the Soviet Union, including the then controversial anti-ballistic missile system (ABM), on Vietnam. We explore as well efforts to manipulate the press, the quality of intelligence assessments made by the national security apparatus, the role of interservice rivalries, and the tactics of bureaucratic warfare.

U.S. policy-makers disagreed with each other. Not over the morality of U.S. intervention; nor over fundamentals such as the "right" of U.S. based multinationals to penetrate and exploit the economies of other nations. Yet they did disagree. And understanding the disagreements among policy makers is crucial to understanding how the system operates. One of the principal themes of this book is that an adequate theory must harmonize two realities. The first is the history of calculated intervention in Vietnam in pursuit of the basic principles of foreign policy. The second reality is the disagreement, conflict, and even chaos that exists within the state.

U.S. policy-makers entertained different ways of exercising American power in Vietnam. Each different method of fighting the Vietnam War nonetheless shared an identity molded by the position of the U.S. as the leading capitalist nation in the world arena. Each position wanted to stop the advance of socialist forces. Each was immoral in its disregard for the human consequences of intervention. Each stance tried to make the Vietnam Revolution an example of the hopelessness of attempting economic and political development outside of the Western web of control. This much the state managers had in common. Yet there were important differences as well. Should the United States bomb North Vietnam in such a way that direct intervention from the Soviet Union or China might be provoked?

Should U.S. ground troops invade the "sanctuaries" of Laos and Cambodia or restrict themselves to safe enclaves on the South Vietnamese coast? Should the federal government increase taxes in order to manage better the economic costs of the Vietnam War? Should the strategic reserve within the U.S. be mobilized in order to rally patriotic fervor behind the war effort? Was Vietnam as an example of movements for national liberation a greater threat than the Soviet Union? The answers to these and other questions are analyzed in *Cracks in the Empire* under the concept of policy currents. Policy currents is the theoretical tool in which issues such as the relationship between the capitalist class and the state, divisions or cleavages within the state, and the influence of domestic opposition on policy are analyzed.

U.S. policy makers illustrated both commonality in purpose and disagreement over particulars. The concept of policy currents attempts to bring these two levels together. Thus *Cracks in the Empire* starts with the radical interpretation of the principles and interests that have guided U.S. foreign policy and offers a theoretical perspective capable of investigating the specific history of U.S. intervention in Vietnam.

Any author must establish limits to their subject matter. *Cracks in the Empire* focuses on the factors influencing decision-making in the national security apparatus, not the history and structure of the Vietnamese Revolution. This particular angle, taken by itself, is misleading. The Vietnam War is first and foremost the story of the heroic resistance of a poor country against the efforts of the U.S. to control it, politically and economically. The reader should be aware that the particular history to be analyzed, including the details of Washington's deliberations, stems from the strength of the Vietnamese, and from the effectiveness of their battle against U.S. hegemony.

The Vietnam War is also about domestic dissent within the U.S. The type and quality of that dissent varied, but its total impact on U.S. policy makers was powerful: the American public effectively constrained the imperative to control.

Thus the main history of the Vietnam War is that of the Vietnamese struggle and opposition within the United States. The project of this book is to present a second history: tracing the impact of "people making history" within secret deliberations conducted in the interests of the powerful.

Writing this book, an analysis of the details of U.S. policy in Vietnam, has required a partial suspension of moral outrage. *Cracks in the Empire* focuses on differences among state managers who were engaged in a common barbaric exercise. The Senate Subcommittee on Refugees estimated the civilian casualties alone from American intervention in Vietnam at 400,000 dead, 900,000 wounded and 6.4 million refugees.[1] In oblique form, American policy makers occasionally recognized that they were fighting a popular movement which commanded the respect and support of the Vietnamese population. We heard statements such as "essentially we are fighting Vietnam's birthrate," or the U.S. "must step up refugee programs deliberately aimed at depriving the VC of a recruiting base" or the "greatest asset the NLF has is the people" — statements made in support of programs aimed at Vietnamese society itself.[2] Washington became locked into a situation in which vast military resources were expended, not against an equivalent army, but against a nation. Yet disagreements among the state managers were never made on moral grounds. No top decision-maker ever said, "Wait a minute, we're intervening where we have no right to be, we're killing Vietnamese by the thousands, we're on the wrong side, we should get out as fast as possible." Elite opposition was based on pragmatic grounds. "Our policy is self-defeating" would be the argument. On the human costs, to both Vietnamese and Americans, there was terrible silence.

I have found it necessary to temporarily quell my anger in order to treat the differences among the state managers with the importance that they deserve. On occasion I found myself unable to live up to this standard. The reader is asked to excuse the well-deserved blast that results. Do not mistake the dispassionate tone that sometimes marks the text for academic neutrality. My project is to contribute to our knowledge of how the system works in order to change it.

It would be useful to define some of the terms used in *Cracks in the Empire* at the outset.

(1) The *national security apparatus* is the bureaus and departments within the executive branch that are responsible for collecting, analyzing, and presenting foreign affairs and defense information to the state managers. The national security apparatus is also responsible, within certain limits, for implementing decisions made by the state managers. The national security apparatus includes the Central Intelligence Agency; the State Department; the Pentagon, including the civilian staff of the Secretary of Defense and intelligence divisions of the armed forces; the staff of the President's Special Assistant for National Security; and, in the case of Vietnam, the U.S. Embassy in Saigon and the military commands in Honolulu and Saigon. Among those excluded from the national security apparatus are the heads of each of the agencies listed above, the semi-civilian "think-tanks" such as RAND, the economic elite, and special representatives of business sentiment such as the Committee for Economic Development.

Two important theoretical issues concerning the national security apparatus are (a) the degree to which self-interest (careers, self-preservation, larger budgets, etc.) can conflict with the conduct of policy, and (b) the quality of information and intelligence assessments supplied to the state managers.

(2) the *state managers* or top officials of the national security apparatus are a very small group (about fifteen people) responsible for determining and directing the major foreign and defense policy decisions. They include the President; the Secretaries of Defense and State; their closest aides; the Joint Chiefs of Staff; the director of the Central Intelligence Agency; the Special Advisor to the President on National Security Affairs; and, in the case of Vietnam, the Ambassador to South Vietnam, the Commander-in-Chief of the Pacific (CINCPAC), and the Commander of the United States Military Advisory Command in Vietnam (COMUSMACV). The small size of the group reflects the extreme centralization of significant decision-making.

Three important theoretical issues concerning the state managers are (a) the extent to which they are drawn from the capitalist class; (b) the degree to which the content of their decisions differ from the interests of the capitalist class (regardless of whether or not they are drawn from the capitalist class); and (c) the role of internal divisions such as those falling along civilian-military or other lines.

(3) the *capitalist class* are the owners of the most powerful economic institutions in the country. Their ownership is based on stockholdings. The capitalist class comprises approximately one half of one percent of the population.

Two important theoretical issues concerning the capitalist class are (a) its degree of control over state policy either directly, through individual ties or through private consensus-reaching groups, or indirectly, through withdrawal of support from policy that appears to deviate from perceived interests; and (b) the degree of unity among the capitalist class.

(4) the *economic elite* are the board of directors and top management of the largest five hundred corporations, financial institutions, and leading law firms. Most of the economic elite are drawn from the capitalist class, but it is possible to enter this group through a managerial career which is secured through the acquisition of stock at favorable prices. In either case the economic elite is responsible for managing the most powerful economic institutions.

The most important theoretical issue concerning foreign policy is whether members of the economic elite attempt to maximize the shortrun position of their individual firm or the longrun interests of the capitalist class as a whole.

The organizational structure of *Cracks in the Empire* is one method of grappling with the inevitable tension between theoretical analysis and narrative history. PART ONE is largely theoretical, with Chapter One outlining five different perspectives on the Vietnam War. Chapter Two delves more deeply into the discussion of radical theories of the capitalist state and presents the main theoretical concept of the book — that of policy currents. Chapter Three begins to flesh out that concept through an analysis of U.S. intervention in Vietnam from World War II to 1967. This chapter also establishes an historical background against which the detailed analysis of the August 1967-March 1968 events can be viewed.

Policy currents largely emerge from various kinds of opposition to U.S. hegemony. Each chapter in PART TWO examines a particular policy cost or opposition to U.S. intervention in Vietnam. Chapter Four focuses on the relationship among Moscow, Peking and Hanoi: it argues that the Sino-Soviet dispute, while posing a genuine threat to the Vietnamese and generating tensions which later exploded into war between China and Vietnam, did not prevent necessary military and economic assistance from reaching the Vietnamese. Washington found that no matter how it bombed the industrial and military structures of the north, compensatory aid from China and the Soviet Union was forthcoming. Chapter Four also assesses the impact of expenditures on the Vietnam War on the nuclear balance with the Soviet Union and examines the arguments of those who disliked the war because it led to defense spending for conventional rather than strategic forces. Chapter Five examines the influence of dissent within the U.S. on Vietnam policy. Chapter Six looks at the economic impact of the Vietnam War — and the reaction of the capitalist class and economic elite.

Theory and history are brought together in PART THREE, a detailed examination of U.S. policy between August 1967 and March 1968. Chapters Seven and Eight apply the policy currents approach, first to efforts to escalate the Vietnam War in the Fall of 1967 and immediately following the TET Offensive, and then to the search for another policy with lower political and economic costs. Chapter Nine returns to the theoretical level, drawing out from the preceding analysis the crucial implications for the nature of the capitalist state and the conduct of U.S. foreign policy. An Economic Appendix supplies added detail on the economic impact of the Vietnam War.

PART I: THEORETICAL AND HISTORICAL BACKGROUND

I: FIVE INTERPRETATIONS OF U.S. INTERVENTION IN VIETNAM

Why did the U.S. intervene in Vietnam? Was our national interest at stake? Was Washington's effort to defeat the National Liberation Front completely immoral? Could the U.S. have won the war by adopting a different strategy?

In the international arena: did the war affect the position of the U.S. in the world economy and its relationship with Europe? What was the impact of the Sino-Soviet dispute and the triangular relationship among Hanoi, Peking and Moscow on U.S. policy? What was the specific impact of U.S. intervention upon neighboring countries and on movements for national liberation elsewhere in the world? Did policy-makers believe their own rhetoric concerning the domino theory?

Within the national security bureaucracy itself: did rightwing pressures produce a higher level of escalation than preferred by the leading state managers? Did quasi-conspiracies exist, some reflecting the interests of the Southern Rim, or even of organized crime? Were specific subagencies of the Central Intelligence Agency closely tied to specific corporate centers of power? Were significant internal interests developed to the point where the underlying rationale of the war became self-aggrandizement? Did the bureaucracy become a source of irrationality? Did political divisions among the state managers handicap the war effort? What was the impact of the threatened use of nuclear weapons in Indochina? Did some U.S. officials place a higher priority on countering the deteriorating strategic balance *vis a vis* the Soviet Union than on winning the war in Vietnam?

What about the impact of the war at home? Was it responsible for the inflation, unemployment and deteriorating competitiveness of

13

the U.S. economy? Did it encourage a drain of research and development funds and top-flight scientists and engineers from the civilian to the military sector? How, exactly, did the war affect the capitalist class? What was their response? Was competition between different segments of the economic elite intensified? What impact, precisely, did the antiwar movement and public opinion have on decision-makers? What role did Presidential ambitions play in foreign policy? Were the media willing partners in government deception or did they serve as increasingly effective critics?

The answers to these questions can be divided into different schools or interpretations of the American role in Vietnam. This chapter outlines five: radical, state intervention, quagmire, "the system worked," and conservative. Additional differences exist within each and I shall attempt to be as clear as possible in distinguishing between general positions that mark one school off from another and more specific positions that produce shadings within each school.

My own views conform more closely to the radical perspective for it provides the most convincing explanation of the tenacity and duration of the U.S. effort to defeat the Vietnam Revolution. Radicals situate, better than any other position, the history of U.S. intervention within a specific array of economic, political and class forces. The horror of U.S. involvement in Vietnam is incomprehensible without a level of analysis focusing on American capitalism as a system.

The weakest element of the radical approach is a comparative failure to analyze political developments within the state itself, tending to reduce state policy to external social forces. In fact, many of the issues surrounding the actual exercise of political power are posed more forcefully by the other schools. Thus this chapter is not just an exercise in comparing five different perspectives. An argument that elements of the other interpretations of the Vietnam War need to be incorporated into a radical perspective of politics is made as well. Specifically, the state intervention perspective helps focus our attention on the importance of the national security bureaucracy and the significant interests that are contained within it. The quagmire perspective carries a description of the bureaucratic environment that comes closer to reality than that offered by radicals (although competing policy preferences are a better *explanation* of these machinations than organizational imperatives). Advocates of the "system worked" approach address the critical difference between winning and not losing the Vietnam War. And, in their frustration, the conservatives capture, perhaps better than any other approach, the constraints and limits on U.S. intervention in Vietnam.

These schools or interpretations are composite positions. Individuals located within a particular school cannot be expected to agree with every aspect of the general positions presented below.

I. The Radical View
("It Was a War in the Interests of Capitalism")

For radicals the Vietnam War was not an accident, an aberration or an outgrowth of bureaucratic or personal failure. Nor did the war reflect the national interest. The thirty years of U.S. intervention in the political and economic affairs of Vietnam was an illegitimate attempt to impose a system of control closely tied to the priorities of the most powerful capitalist nation in the world.

Harry Magdoff, an editor of the socialist periodical *Monthly Review*, has provided a Marxist formulation of this position.[1] Magdoff argues that Vietnam served as the key to the control and influence of the future of Southeast Asia. The attraction lay in raw materials and markets (potential as well as actual) for both the United States and Japan. Preserving access to tin, rubber, iron ore, rice, copra and oil was a fundamental premise of American policy considerations. Magdoff accepts the domino theory, offered by policy-makers as an explanation of intervention, as an accurate statement of self-interest.[2] A secure South Vietnam could serve as an important military base for the accumulation of supplies and equipment, help to contain Chinese influence, and provide a jumping-off point for possible land wars elsewhere in Asia. For Magdoff, the vast expenditures of the Vietnam War are not explained by local concerns alone, but by the economic importance of the entire region.

Differences within the radical camp stem from the relative weight assigned to the economic, political and military components of American policy. Those stressing economic motivations behind

U.S. intervention generally cite the "Pacific Rim" concept by which American and Japanese economic priorities determine Southeast Asia's role in an international division of labor.[3] From the U.S. standpoint, the goal is to prevent the emergence of a regional economy capable of competing with American interests. The Pacific Rim includes the West Coast of both North and South America as well as the arc reaching from Alaska to Australia. The U.S. and Japan stand at the apex of the hierarchy, drawing resources from and selling goods to the middle tier, composed of Australia, Canada and New Zealand, and dominating the economies of those at the bottom. These lower levels supply raw materials, cheap labor, and serve as tax havens for the multinationals based in the more "advanced" countries. A small number of countries in this latter category may experience modified forms of "economic growth," but only of a type sculptured to the priorities of the powerful states that coordinate the activities of the entire Rim. Vietnam would have been one of these countries since one consequence of massive military intervention was a modern industrial infrastructure including deepwater ports, airfields, highways and a new communications system. The tenacity, if not the origins, of U.S. intervention in Vietnam are explained by the potential gains from this economic system. The presence of substantial oil deposits, for example, does not explain the original decisions of the nineteen-fifties for the discoveries were made later on. But the prospect of exploiting these reserves becomes an increasingly important factor in the calculus of policy-makers from the mid-sixties.

Other radicals, while agreeing that Washington's intervention in Vietnam was calculated to secure the international position of the U.S. and the interests of the capitalist class, place comparatively less emphasis on the possibilities of profit, present or future. American commercial interests were certainly present in Vietnam. But they followed, and for the most part fed upon, the ever increasing military commitment. Felix Greene argues, for example, that economic explanations were primarily a rationale aimed at the American public. The driving forces behind U.S. intervention were the political containment of China and an "imperialist urge for control."[4] Doug Dowd sees U.S. intervention in Vietnam as a method of stabilizing the entire world capitalist system.[5] The U.S. supported the French in the years immediately following World War II as a *quid pro quo* for the reduction of obstacles to German participation in postwar Europe. Later, Washington attempted to find a secure role for Japan in Southeast Asia, thus limiting the need of the defeated power to seek better economic relations with China or other Left governments.[6] In this view Vietnam provides a chance for Washington to demonstrate its anticommunist commitment on behalf of the entire capitalist world.

Only a few radicals have attempted to explore the cultural dimensions of the war. Among these Francis Fitzgerald's *Fire in the Lake* stands out.[7] Her subtle interpretation focuses on the inability of the Americans to win the hearts and minds of the Vietnamese. Her skill and her contribution lie in the capacity to demonstrate, through the recounting of a number of day-to-day encounters, the structure underlying the frustration of even the best-intentioned American efforts to win Vietnamese loyalty and legitimacy. American and Vietnamese attitudes are compared along the entire intellectual landscape. Fitzgerald captures, perhaps better than any other English-language writer, the fundamental revolutionary character of the Vietnamese resistance. The tactics of counter-insurgency, American aid, support for the Saigon government, even efforts to achieve land reform, were all hopelessly inadequate. At the same time the NLF displayed a remarkable capacity to adapt a modern ideology, that of Marxist-Leninism, to the rich tradition of Vietnamese resistance to foreign invaders. The Vietnamese peasantry understood, embraced, and, in the final analysis, became the NLF. Washington never understood that it was fighting a movement that, in purely national terms, had already won.[8]

Radicals also see Vietnam as an enforcement of the "rules of the game" governing small nations that attempt to gain political and economic independence from a global system of control. Gabriel Kolko has stated this view succinctly:

> That Vietnam itself has relatively little value to the United States is all the more significant as an example of America's determination to hold the line as a matter of principle against revolutionary movements. What is at stake, according to the domino theory with which Washington accurately perceives the world, is the control of Vietnam's neighbors, Southeast Asia, and ultimately Latin America.[9]

Here Vietnam becomes a test case for future wars of national liberation. The political and strategic importance of Vietnam is calculated against the benefits to be derived from the entire Third World. Revolutionary and socialist movements are to know that the fight to gain liberation will be resisted and that victory can only come at the highest cost.

Finally, the war served as a vast training arena for counter-insurgency programs preparing for the next Vietnam.[10] The war permitted the U.S. to build up a string of bases in Asia and to hone the tactics and weaponry to be deployed against guerilla movements. Vietnam became a testing ground for a variety of military doctrines designed to compensate for a previous over-reliance on nuclear weapons. Chomsky and Herman, for instance, stress the determination of U.S. policy-makers to supply military aid, training advice and torture devices to bolster "subfascist" regimes in the Third World.[11]

The Vietnam War helped to preserve U.S. power in several important ways: the Sino-Soviet split deepened; greater political stability for a Washington-supported dictatorship was achieved in Indonesia, in large measure through the massacre of hundreds of thousands of Communists and other political opponents of neo-colonialism; and Third World movements entertaining new relations with the West had to consider the devastation that the U.S. left in Indochina. Yet the huge expenditures on the war, its drain on the American economy, the declining influence and legitimacy of the U.S. in the world arena, and the final humiliating forced withdrawal all raise the question of the irrationality of Washington's policy in Vietnam — even when this irrationality is measured against the standards of capitalism. As Kolko has argued:

> Ultimately, as many in Washington well realize, the major cost of Vietnam will not be its impact on gold and trade balances, but the weakening of U.S. resolve and ability to interfere in the domestic affairs of nations everywhere, making both increasingly possible and plausible to others the revolutionary path, one that even the greatest intervention in history by the strongest against the weak could not bar.[12]

Radicals have been comparatively quiet on the self-defeating aspects of Washington's own intervention. How could a policy taken by a state loyal to the interests of the dominant class ultimately undermine American power? Radicals generally offer two kinds of answers, neither of which is really satisfactory.

One method of explaining the irrational aspects of the war is to focus on the pervasiveness of ideological influences, originally conceived as a defense of the international role of the U.S., but now at least somewhat out of control. William A. Williams, for example, attributes the distortions, failures and mistakes in judgment that marked an overvaluation of Vietnam to the attitudes and analysis that are part of the maturation of the "corporate political economy."[13] Noam Chomsky notes that the U.S. was "spending more on the war than it (could) possibly hope to gain in return" and traces the sources of this self-destructive impulse to "an anti-communist crusade that cannot be turned on or off at will." Chomsky adds that even when the "dominant segments of American society decide that the war is no longer a paying proposition, there is no guarantee that they will be able to bring this particular case of anti-communist aggression to an end."[14]

The other approach is to explain the stubborn persistence of U.S. efforts in Vietnam by a struggle between competing factions of the capitalist class. These divisions are either defined regionally, for example Northeast versus Southern Rim, or by a conflict between different industries such as those desiring peaceful international trade versus defense contractors.[15]

The final argument distinguishing the radical position is an appreciation of the impact of domestic dissent, and especially the antiwar movement, on policy-makers in Washington.[16] The movement succeeded in checking a variety of possible aggressive actions in Vietnam including an intensified bombing program of the North, a greater number of ground troops in the South, and even the use of nuclear weapons. Washington's reluctance to use these measures did not reflect the decision-makers' own morality, but was imposed on them by the fear of the domestic and international consequences of their actions. Radicals also stress the subservience of the press to the state, particularly a reluctance to question the ideological assumptions guiding foreign policy.[17] Newspaper editorials, elite pressure groups, politicians, and the media may have begun to turn away from the war. But the form of their criticism tended to be pragmatic rather than principled: they accepted the major premises of U.S. foreign policy and based their opposition on either the inability of the U.S. war effort to secure the anticommunist commitment within a promised time period, or on the rising economic costs of the war. This pragmatic criticism only emerged after the earlier and more intensive opposition marked by campus disturbances, draft protests, growing labor opposition, and resistance within the armed forces. The anticipation of provoking even greater hostility led to a reluctance on the part of the state managers to adopt economic measures which would have reduced the war's impact — such as raising taxes or cutting back on social programs. Thus the radical position sees even elite opposition as an outcome of the antiwar and other social movements of the sixties.

II. State Intervention
("The Military-Industrial Complex Was Responsible")

Members of the state intervention perspective share with radicals a fundamental belief that the U.S. intervention in Vietnam was illegitimate.[18] Unlike the radicals, they locate the power behind the Vietnam War and the interests served by it in the state, especially the executive branch and the Pentagon, and in particular branches of industry, especially defense contractors. Radicals see the Vietnam War as an attempt to extend the economic interests of the entire capitalist order. The state intervention position contrasts the comparatively peaceful impulses that emanated from business and international trade with the imperative towards war that derived from the Pentagon, its supplying companies, and the "imperial Presidency." By shifting research and development funds, skilled labor, and engineers out of the civilian sector and into the military-industrial complex the Vietnam War actually hurt the multinational corporations and industrial firms.[19] Vietnam encouraged inflationary tendencies and restricted improvements in productivity. In this respect, the state intervention perspective dovetails with a school of thought, often identified with the views of C. Wright Mills, concerning the distribution of power in the U.S. This school emphasizes the increasing influence of the military, the centralization of power in "institutional command posts" (which include both large economic units and bureaucracies in the state), and the declining influence of public opinion over the direction of foreign affairs and national security policy.[20]

Radicals may examine periods where the costs of maintaining countries within the capitalist orbit outweigh the benefits — but they rarely do an adequate job of explaining how and why such periods occur. The state intervention perspective elevates the cost over benefit calculus to the center of its analysis. In Vietnam, and in U.S. foreign policy in general, a great deal of money is spent to create and protect a particular political environment. This huge investment is unlikely to generate a commensurate return: it serves the power of the Pentagon and the profit picture of some defense contractors but little else. Seymour Melman, for example, maintains that government does not regulate business: rather, *government is business*.[21] Melman focuses on the centralization of political and economic power in the Departmant of Defense (and not in either the board rooms of Lockheed — the defense sector — or General Motors — the industrial sector). The Department of Defense becomes the "new imperialism" with a budget larger than any other government in the world.

Due to their connections with the Pentagon, defense industries enjoy a number of competitive advantages over the rest of the economy. Defense industries do not have to compete with each other. They enjoy the relative security of supplying a large and permanent customer. Defense contractors are paid on a cost-plus basis. (Although Melman argues that cost-plus contracts are more important as a lever of control for the Pentagon than as a source of profit.) The guaranteed flow of capital enables defense contractors to out-bid civilian industries for top managerial and technical talent. One result is the gradual depletion of the civilian sector and a decline in civilian technology. As examples Melman cites the poor quality of the American railroad system, the advanced age of the U.S. merchant fleet, the fact that the U.S. operated, in 1968, an old stock of metal-working equipment, and the trend towards increased imports of machine tools. Unlike the civilian sector, the industries controlled by the state-management do not require economic stability. For example, for the civilian sector inflation is a source of worry. For defense industries inflation merely adds resources. In the civilian sector cost overruns result in a loss; in the defense sector cost overruns merely accelerate the stockpiling of capital.

Unlike the radical appreciation of the restraining influence of the antiwar movement on the state managers, the state intervention approach stresses the ability of the executive branch to deceive the American public and manipulate their opinions on a fairly consistent basis. The actual and potential political influence of the middle and lower levels of society are treated under the rubric of "mass society."[22] Opinions are easily manipulated because the leaders control mass communications. The lowest layers of society project onto foreign affairs the low quality and insecurity of their daily lives. They react emotionally to international events; many are attracted to and dazzled by the power of the President and follow wherever he leads. Foreign policy is further insulated from public pressure by the secrecy of decision-making, especially the practice of refusing information on the basis of protecting "national security." The soon-to-be-discussed quagmire perspective, on the other hand, asserts that secrecy within the national security apparatus derives from the tendency of particular government agencies to hide information from one another, not the public. The state intervention advocates also argue that the Pentagon and armed forces possess huge public relations facilities which help to impose their views on a relatively misinformed, passive, and apathetic public.

The influence of the military stems from the vast weight of its organizational apparatus including an enormous budget, access and control over sophisticated technology, an atmosphere of secrecy, and the public relations offices at its command. Moreover, the system of checks and balances has broken down. The decline of the State Department, Foreign Service, and Congressional control over the military has left a "power vacuum" in the conduct of international affairs, and the Pentagon has filled it. The distribution of government funds available for research and development and the research priorities of the largest universities now reflect the interests of the military-industrial complex.

The national security bureaucracy is thus a special concentration of organizational power undreamed of by the radical focus on the privately-owned economy. It follows that U.S. intervention in Vietnam is less the result of class interests than of the "technology of intervention" (once the weapons and techniques of counter-insurgency are created the pressure to use them becomes more powerful) and of a "bureaucratic compulsiveness" to control as much of the world political environment as possible.[23] Vietnam is of little importance economically. Policy makers may cite the importance of containing China and defeating a revolution that could encourage insurgency elsewhere. But these political factors are only intellectual justifications to conceal the true motivation: perpetuating the state's own interests and power.

In some instances the descriptions of bureaucratic behavior offered by the state intervention perspective come close to the theme of organizational irrationality presented by the quagmire approach. Both recognize a degree of self-deception. And, in both, the myths originally propagated to sustain the power of the state can influence and handicap internal decision-making. The existence of "scenarios" complete with multiple options helps spread the illusion of certain success. But there is a critical tone to the state intervention approach that is missing in the quagmire explanations of the war, particularly in the refusal to absolve high government officials from responsibility. Bureaucratic culture is dangerous and promotes fear and insecurity, factors which help to explain the tendency towards intervention. In some cases, the state intervention approach links the need to demonstrate "toughness," to advocate "hardnosed" policies, and to associate concessions with weakness with prevailing definitions of masculinity in the U.S. In some versions, the combination of the culture of bureaucracy and concentration of resources leads to an "arrogance of power" or "the illusion of American omnipotence."[24]

Strongly implied in the state intervention approach is the need for a major effort to check the power of the military-industrial complex. Dramatic reductions of the military budget can be made without seriously threatening our national security. Conversion of military installations to civilian uses will mitigate the economic effects of the new priorities. We must control the independence of the national security apparatus by making covert operations more difficult to mount and installing more effective Congressional "watchdog" measures. In this way the narrow goals of one section of the state will no longer dominate foreign policy.

Franz Schurmann offers a unique interpretation of U.S. intervention in Vietnam that contains elements of the radical, state intervention, and quagmire perspectives.[25] As such it defies easy classification, although it falls closest to the state intervention position. Schurmann shares with radical and state intervention schools an implacable hostility to the massive effort to control Vietnam. Like the state intervention school, Schurmann sees a fundamental split between the interests of the corporate class and the state. The former are committed to the preservation of capitalism and the expansion of trade, investments and markets. Capitalism is peaceful. The state, however, organizes a much more violent imperialism which contains powerful impulses towards war. Intervention in Vietnam was primarily engineered by the state, not the corporate class. Like the quagmire approach, Schurmann recognizes the importance of divergent bureaucratic centers of power within the national security apparatus. In contrast to the administrative rationality assumed by the radicals, he describes the normal state of affairs among the different agencies as "warfare." Overlapping the bureaucratic battleground (and thus departing from the quagmire school) is a more fundamental conflict among alternative policy orientations towards Communist states. Substantial influence is attributed to rightwing forces and the military, at least in their ability to force important concessions from the President. Schurmann is especially concerned with nuclear weapons which contribute to the centralization of executive authority. The war becomes a very complex affair in which different policy orientations battle with each other as much as with the Vietnamese. To maintain control over policy fundamentals and over strategic doctrines covering the use of nuclear weapons, Presidents are sometimes forced to make concessions to different bureaucracies. Presidents can usually win on any issue that they consider important. But they can't win every time. Vietnam becomes a conflict among a variety of different bureaucratic centers with the President struggling to maintain control over policy. Disputes over the use of nuclear weapons and the influence of rightwing political forces lurk ominously in the background.

III. The Quagmire Position
("The War Was a Mistake")

Viewed in the context of U.S. foreign policy since World War II, the "quagmirists" maintain that Washington's intervention in Vietnam was an accident, an aberration, and a classic example of the "politics of inadvertence."[26] The metaphors favored by the quagmirists — Vietnam as a "morass," or a "tarbaby" — evoke the image of a sticky mess into which no one would walk willingly and from which one cannot get free.[27] U.S. policy in Vietnam became a failure, not in intent or purpose, but in its inability to produce a consistent program due to numerous compromises among competing individuals, agencies and political factions. Policy outcomes did not confront the weaknesses of the Saigon regime, adequately address the sources of strength of the Vietnamese Revolution or resolve the severe internal differences among American decision-makers.

Members of the quagmire perspective differ among themselves over the precise location of the irrationality of U.S. intervention in Vietnam. For some, it is the special prejudices and interests of the field analyst and his immediate superior. Others examine the imperatives built into the nature of bureaucracy and organizational routines.[28] The momentum of existing policy and the pressure to produce supporting intelligence is yet another source for distortion. All advocates of the position share the view that bureaucracies contain limits on "organizational intelligence."[29] But some are more likely to root the failure in bureaucracy itself, while others point towards the mistaken judgment of the Cabinet level officials, leading advisors and even the President himself. A final version focuses on mutual misperception of motives and interests by Washington and Hanoi.[30] The Vietnam War, in this view, was unwanted by both sides. It happened for psychological reasons such as those revolving around basic human fears and emotions. In the general focus on the failure of bureaucracies, the quagmire critique parallels the popular notion of large scale organizations as lumbering, rule-ridden mechanisms incapable of decisive, coherent action.

Advocates of the quagmire position who focus on the bureaucracy itself complain that the national security apparatus did not possess a significant number of Vietnamese or Indochina experts while the fundamental decisions determining U.S. involvement were made. As a result, the top decision-makers based their choices on preconceptions and applied false analogies — for example, that Vietnam required the same response to "aggression" as Munich.

Both information from the field and intelligence assessments in Washington were systematically (and falsely) biased towards optimism. Ambitious career officers determined to impress their superiors filed glowing progress reports that misled the top managers of the national security bureaucracy. Disputes between competing agencies also led to distortions. Their intelligence estimates were more likely to reflect parochial interests than events on the battlefield. Agencies sought favored status by overestimating their own success. Other features of the bureaucratic environment that generated optimistic assessments during the Vietnam War included:

- the reporting system which was set up so that assessments of the effectiveness of policy were made by those responsible for implementing policy
- the tendency of subordinates to tell their superiors what they thought they wanted to hear
- the American ethic, which is to get the job done
- the tendency of optimism to breed optimism
- the classification of good news as a job well done and bad news as personal failure[31]

Intelligence agencies normally suffer from a glut of ambiguous data and from information overload from a high volume of field reports, statistics, and analysis; as well as from firsthand information garnered from spies, satellites, captured documents, and other sources. Too much information actually increases the possibility for preconceived notions to govern the selection of policy options.[32] Those connected to operational agencies tend to sift out the most optimistic. Those connected to the comparatively detached analytic divisions produce more pessimistic appraisals. And the leader committed to a particular policy normally selects those assessments closest to his own viewpoint.

Those who stress organizational imperatives underline a variety of problems: the intractability of bureaucratic environments and irrationalities emanating from the permutation of "discretionary

Chart 1.1
Comparison of Five Interpretations of U.S. Intervention in Vietnam

	Key Features of U.S. Intervention	Role of Economic Interests	Role of Domestic Political Forces	Rationality of Decision-Making Process
Radical	Defense of the world capitalist system; completely illegitimate; test case of "war of national liberation"	Capitalist class is main beneficiary	Antiwar movement an effective restraint on escalation; dissent spreads to other elements of society	Rational in the interests of the capitalist class
State Intervention	Extending the resources of the military-industrial complex; completely illegitimate	Defense companies benefit; Pentagon and intelligence agencies receive larger budgets	Not generally considered influential	Process of decision-making biased to increase resources of military-industrial complex
Quagmire	Intervention the culmination of small, poorly thought out decisions; general anti-communist commitment not questioned	Not considered to be influential	Not usually considered	Bureaucratic bungling and organizational imperatives lead to very bad decisions
The System Worked	Anticommunist consensus; U.S. tries to "not lose" rather than "win"	Not considered to be influential	Decisions reflect the conflict among different political groups	Presidents know what they are doing; intelligence is accurate but does not determine final decisions
Conservative	U.S. could have won with a stronger effort from the start; intervention was in national interest	Private sector not influential; overall economic costs could have been reduced with full use of U.S. power	Dissent was a factor; a more decisive policy would have swung majority of Americans behind war effort	Civilians should have listened to professional military judgment

gaps" throughout the organization (the compounding effect of the failure of subordinates fully to understand and subsequently to behave on the basis of directives from their superiors); the "tyranny of the routine" (in which established procedures may arbitrarily lock out relevant information); competing goals (with some officials pursuing personal goals such as advancement up the organizational ladder, regardless of whether these activities help to secure the overall goals of the organization); and the more or less deliberate distortion of information on the part of officials in order to advance favored policies or their personal fortunes.

Other members of the quagmire position blame a closer circle of Presidential advisors or the so-called "best and the brightest." In this view, the roots of the anticommunist commitment are less bureaucratic than "Presidential," deriving specifically from the domestic climate perceived by each President and from the personal values and intellectual baggage that each brought to the White House. While the recognition of continuity of U.S. policy through six Presidents is somewhat at odds with the overall quagmire tendency to view the U.S. commitment as the product of incremental steps, this version shares with the others a fundamental view that the specific prosecution of the war was irrational. "Facts are elusive in Vietnam," writes Richard Holbrooke in an essay generally emphasizing the continuity of American commitment, "but today we can see that the assessments were based on dangerously self-promoting report cards. A pyramid of self-deception was created."[33] The importance of the President is stressed except for two mitigating factors: the President does not make his decisions in a vacuum — the information must come from somewhere — and once policy is formulated somebody must carry it out. In both cases bureaucratic influences become critical.

Quagmirists also complain of an overly secretive environment within the national security bureaucracy and its disastrous effect on achieving smooth coordination.[34] Incomplete information causes some agencies to work at cross purposes. The media also play a crucial role in the quagmire interpretation. To improve their own position within the national security bureaucracy and to gather general support for administration policy, various agencies leak reports of progress to the press. Presidents and other official spokesmen are reluctant to jar public optimism. They cannot really criticize their own policies. They join in the chorus and false optimism begins to feed upon itself. The leading decision-makers are victimized by their own system. No President, for example, would willingly choose the high cost military stalemate faced by Johnson in late 1967. Each President merely inherited the commitments of his predecessors and was fooled into making an additional step. The decision-making process was not marked by deliberation or protracted consultation. Neither the President nor the top civilian managers are to blame. In the words of Arthur Schlesinger, one of the leading quagmire theorists, "It is not only idle but unfair to seek out guilty men. . . . The Vietnam story is a tragedy without villains."[35] Thus the political implications of the quagmire position are that better information, more rational methods of processing and better analysis will improve U.S. foreign policy. The approach dovetails with a postwar tradition of criticism of the national security bureaucracy, a tradition that has attempted to improve the procedures governing decisions while leaving the fundamental premises of those decisions unexamined.[36]

IV. The System Worked
("Don't Lose South Vietnam, but Don't Win Either")

One of the more intriguing perspectives on U.S. intervention in Vietnam asserts that Presidents deliberately chose a military stalemate. Developed independently by Leslie Gelb, director of the Defense Department study of decision-making in Vietnam that became known as the "Pentagon Papers," and by Daniel Ellsberg, the man who eventually released that study to the press, the perspective emphasizes that a consensus existed among generations of policy makers that South Vietnam should not be permitted to "go communist."[37] Both Gelb and Ellsberg point to the continuity of that commitment over thirty years and six Presidents. They reject the concept of "crucial turning points" (where Washington seriously entertained withdrawal). Ellsberg and Gelb see decision-makers faithfully acting on the basis of a general anticommunist consensus that has dominated U.S. foreign policy since 1947. For Gelb, this consensus "is embodied in doctrine and acquires the character of a political imperative."[38] Participants in internal deliberations never posed the issue of withdrawal, but only attempted to determine the level of commitment necessary to prevent a Communist victory. Internal differences were limited to tactical issues. The leaders knew what they were doing. The system worked, at least in the narrow sense that accurate information passed through the national security apparatus to the state managers and the President.

This much comes close to the radical perspective, but Ellsberg, and especially Gelb, differ from that orientation in three important respects.[39] For them, the source of the commitment to a "non-Communist South Vietnam" is rooted in a broader range of political interests than the capitalist class isolated by the radicals. The influence of "domestic constraints" on decision-making is extended beyond the antiwar movement. And, most importantly, Ellsberg and Gelb argue that instead of trying to "win," that is adopt a strategy designed to eradicate the National Liberation Front from South Vietnam, the decision-makers followed a logic of "not losing." Rather than trying to defeat the NLF, they knowingly took actions that only prevented a "loss." As a result, the war turned out to be an ever escalating military stalemate. The anticommunist commitment ended only in 1975 when Watergate and a unique Congressional mood changed the political balance within the U.S. A shifting constellation of domestic pressures temporarily weakened those centers of power which had sustained the "don't lose" imperative over the postwar years.

The focus on stalemate appears to bring Gelb and Ellsberg towards the quagmire perspective and its stress on irrationality. But both authors argue that intelligence assessments were remarkably accurate and the top policy-makers were well informed about the consequences of their decisions. After all, the U.S. succeeded in maintaining the anticommunist commitment over the entire postwar period. At times Gelb appears to agree with the quagmire description of bureaucratic pressures that operate within the intelligence community.[40] But these machinations do not control policy; they are not in themselves decisive. In his view, the crucial point is this: Presidential decisions are *not* the product of false or misleading information provided by jealous, competing or self-interested bureaucratic fiefdoms. The quagmirists see Presidents duped into irrational decisions from below. The failure of "organizational intelligence" absolves them from moral responsibility. Gelb and Ellsberg see Presidents *willingly* choosing a stalemate that is the product of competing political pulls, not misleading information. Much more than Gelb, Ellsberg holds the President responsible for the enormous costs that this pattern of decisions has for this country and especially for the Vietnamese. Ellsberg is not the least sympathetic; Gelb's views did not prevent him from holding an important position in the first years of the Carter Administration.[41]

What is the nature and source of the commitment to strike, not for victory, but against defeat, in South Vietnam? Presidential ambitions figure prominently. Each President feared that the consequences of withdrawal would affect his chances for reelection disastrously. Rightwing political groups, especially the "China lobby," would claim that the Administration was "soft on communism."[42] And European allies would claim that Washington does not keep its international commitments. For Gelb, Congress, public opinion and newspaper editorials are part of a wide variety of pressures that channel Presidential decisions and reinforce the anticommunist consensus. The need for a consensus is also rooted (but very vaguely) in a distinctively American tendency to "reject things alien." Nothing is more alien than communism. Thus the roots of the anticommunist commitment are located within U.S. society as a whole. Ellsberg, on the other hand, has come closer to the radical position in his recent stress on the connection between the interests of the economic elite and the anticommunist commitment.

The anticommunist consensus is thus solid. But Presidents cannot commit sufficient resources to guarantee a win. Following the Korean War, substantial segments of U.S. opinion, including a part of the military, became opposed to the use of American troops in an Asian land war. While U.S. G.I.s were used in Vietnam, political and economic restrictions combined to make the number of troops less than the level determined by advisors as that necessary to "produce a win." Other possible ways of attempting a win policy, including the use of nuclear weapons and invading North Vietnam, were ruled out by anticipated international repercussions and domestic constraints, although never without some debate.

Ellsberg originally described this pattern of Presidential decision-making governing U.S. intervention in Vietnam in a simple, yet elegant, two-rule model.[43] The first rule is *do not lose South*

Vietnam to Communist control before the next election. Truman, Eisenhower, Kennedy, Johnson, Nixon and Ford inherited the commitment of their predecessors, and added the men and resources necessary to stave off the Vietnamese Revolution, but not defeat it. Why? Because of a second rule to *minimize the level of military commitment in Vietnam*, especially the use of U.S. ground troops, insofar as this is consistent with Rule I.

More recently Ellsberg modified his position.[44] Rule I is still "don't lose South Vietnam," although the pressures on the President to maintain this commitment are now located more narrowly in the economic elite than in Presidential fears of a general rightwing backlash. Rule II remains essentially the same: if a low cost stalemate is available — take it. Rule II governed Presidential decisions in Vietnam from World War II to 1965 and from 1973 to 1975. Rule III is *if a win appears to be available — go for it.* Ellsberg argues that Johnson's increase of ground troops from 100,000 to 500,000 between 1965 and 1968 approached a win policy. Nixon and Kissinger also thought that their "secret plan to end the war" — heavily intensified and secret bombing of North Vietnam and Cambodia, aid to Thieu, management of U.S. public opinion through phased withdrawal of U.S. troops, and leverage on Hanoi through Moscow and Peking — would produce a win. Rule IV is that *if the consequences of attempting a win become disastrous, only representatives of the capitalist class can reel a President in.* Ellsberg suggests that an incumbent can acquire a large stake in defending a win policy — even past the point where it serves the interests of the economic elite. The conflict that then emerges between the President and the business community is resolved in favor of the latter, and the basic "don't lose" pattern is reestablished. In March 1968, analyzed in detail later in this book, representatives of industrial and financial power vetoed Johnson's plans to escalate the war.

Ellsberg and Gelb also argue that the "don't lose/no win" pattern required Presidents to lie to the public. Promises of early success were made, even while Presidents committed men and resources at levels that made this outcome next to impossible. To cite just one example: President Johnson told the nation in a April 7, 1965 speech at Johns Hopkins University that bombing North Vietnam would "slow down aggression, at least limit further infiltration of men and supplies, and demonstrate our resolve and determination to Hanoi."[45] Two months earlier, Johnson had been told privately by McGeorge Bundy, his Assistant for National Security, that the odds for success of a program of sustained reprisals through bombing were not good, probably somewhere between twenty-five percent and seventy-five percent. Bundy went on to argue "that even if it fails the policy will be worth it. At a minimum it will damp down the charge that we did not do all that we could have done, and this charge will be important in many countries, including our own."[46]

For the "don't lose/no win" argument there are two significant features of Bundy's position: realistic pessimism regarding the effectiveness of the chosen policy, and recognition of domestic political pressures on Johnson. Unless he took actions consistent with the anticommunist commitment Johnson would be held responsible for the "loss" of South Vietnam.

In contrast to the radical focus on the domination of the corporate upper class and the impact of the antiwar movement, Ellsberg, and especially Gelb, divide the domestic political spectrum into a more loosely defined system of cleavages and interest groups that comes closer to the pluralist model. Neither the public as a whole nor the antiwar movement is seen as critical or even influential when compared to the power of organized interest groups of both "hawkish" and "dovish" tendencies. Unlike the radical's appreciation of the antiwar movement, mass opposition to the war is described by Gelb as neither principled nor "ideological." The public just "got tired," or didn't understand the war; the anticommunist commitment itself was never rejected.

The "don't lose/no win" perspective is located at the left fringe of the foreign policy establishment. To create its early image of a new orientation, the Carter Administration hired several supporters of this position, including Leslie Gelb. Ellsberg, needless to say, was not among them. His "disloyalty" in distributing the Pentagon Papers and zeal in pointing out the inhumane consequences of a wilfully chosen stalemate made him ineligible. In the meantime, it is not at all clear that the new mavericks have enjoyed any success in blocking the rightward slide of U.S. foreign policy, let alone in establishing any significant new directions.[47]

V. The Conservative Position
("We Could Have Won It")

The conservative retrospective on the Vietnam War is now being conducted with an ever increasing pace.[48] Its conclusion — that Washington could have won — is significant not only for history's sake but for the future position of the U.S. in world affairs. The conservative attack is aimed at least as much at conventional or liberal interpretations of the war as at radicals. Its implication is that the U.S. should not shy away from the future use of military force; that dissent, both from the public and within government itself, is dangerous; and that the international arena, particularly the Sino-Soviet split, can be exploited to much greater advantage.

Washington fought a brutal war. It cost over a hundred and fifty billion dollars, millions of Vietnamese were killed, wounded, or left homeless. Fifty thousand American lives were lost. More bombs were dropped than in all of World War II. And the ecology of the region has been fundamentally altered. Yet the war was fought within limits and had definite rules. During the Johnson Administration, U.S. armed forces could not invade North Vietnam, Cambodia, or Laos; or bomb the North in such a way that might provoke a reaction from China or the Soviet Union; or commit a sufficient number of ground troops (over a million Americans would have been required) to actually defeat the NLF.

The conservatives argue that these constraints were self-imposed by timorous and vacillating liberals, and that greater latitude in the use of armed force was possible. The conservative mistake is to project the easing of some of the limits, particularly those on the bombing of the North and the invasion of the sanctuaries along the Cambodian and Laotian borders — that were obtained during the Nixon Administration — back to the Johnson Administration. LBJ, they argue, should not be burdened with the responsibility for U.S. intervention. He merely inherited the policies of four previous Presidents. But because of his unwillingness to pursue a more offensive campaign, Johnson does deserve blame for the defeat.

The conservatives focus on the uncertainty of U.S. objectives.[49] Formal public statements and private policy reviews restricted U.S. goals in Vietnam to the containment of socialist forces within South

Vietnam. South Vietnamese generals who threatened to "march to the North," thus threatening North Vietnam, were told to shut up. Yet support for a rollback policy against North Vietnam could be found in the national security bureaucracy, especially in the early sixties. The formal chain of command prevented full discussion of these views. Instead, the right submerged their strategic preferences in particular tactical options.[50] If adopted by top officials these options would have implicitly signalled a more ambitious purpose to U.S. intervention in Indochina. Thus disputes over tactics sometimes carried with them a much larger debate over the very nature of the war itself.

The conservatives argue that different objectives and a different strategy would have brought victory. At the extreme lie those who argue that the U.S. should have pursued a rollback strategy against the North, even that such a strategy was the only possible way of gaining a victory in the South.[51] More "moderate" examples of the conservative stance restrict their complaints to the following themes: air power wasn't used to its fullest advantage, U.S. policy permitted the "enemy" the use of sanctuaries in Laos and Cambodia, and the U.S. was twice on the verge of winning (in 1968 and 1972) only to withdraw. Had the civilian advisors listened to the advice of the "professionals," U.S. force would have been used more effectively, the NLF would have been completely decimated, and the NVN soundly defeated. For the conservatives the irrationality of U.S. intervention in Vietnam lay in its "retreat from victory."[52]

Consider the following comment from Admiral U.S. Grant Sharp, Commander in Chief of the Pacific (CINCPAC) during much of the Johnson Administration:

> We could have won the war long ago — perhaps by the end of 1967. We could have achieved victory with relative ease, and without using nuclear weapons or invading North Vietnam. All that we had to do to win was to use our existing air power — *properly*.
>
> We had tremendous air power within easy striking range of North Vietnam — on aircraft carriers in the Gulf of Tonkin and South Vietnam. Yet never in the entire course of the war have we used our air power to its full advantage. This tragic failure to do so, is in my opinion, perhaps the most serious error we have made in all of American military history.[53]

The liberals responsible for the management of the war usually argued that the escalatory measures called for by the rightwing would have provoked the Soviet Union and China. Moscow would have made a countermove in Berlin, Iran, or the Middle East. Peking would have sent ground troops to the aid of the Vietnamese.

The right now argues that the liberals were overly cautious in their judgment of the degree of commitment that Moscow and Peking were making to the Vietnamese. The U.S. could have escalated further, taken more risks, without provoking a response from Vietnam's allies. Since 1962, some conservatives claim, the fundamental premise of Soviet foreign policy has been to avoid confrontations. They also argue that many of the possible Soviet counter moves anticipated by the liberals were logistically infeasible, and that the U.S. could have adopted stronger measures. For conservatives, the recent China-Vietnam war illustrates that Peking was also not interested in making any major sacrifices to aid the Vietnamese in their anti-imperialist battle with the U.S. Sir Robert Thompson, a British advisor to several Presidents on counter-insurgency, now argues that American bombs could have killed a hundred, or even five thousand, Chinese working in Vietnam without causing Peking to "blink an eye."[54] Rightwing interpretations of the factional disputes within the Chinese leadership during the mid-sixties conclude that the friction between Peking and Hanoi was greater than Johnson and McNamara realized, that Mao Tse-tung was actually quite tolerant of the U.S. position in Southeast Asia, and that more aggressive U.S. action against the North was possible. The "China card" could have been played even then, although against the Vietnamese rather than the Soviet Union.[55]

The rightwing argues that Washington missed many other opportunities. Analyzing 1968, Drew Middleton maintains that "the war was de-escalated at the moment when most soldiers and airmen believed the Communist losses in the TET Offensive offered the U.S. and South Vietnam an opportunity to resume the offensive with a good chance of success.[56] TET became a classic example of winning the military battle but losing the political war.

Thompson tries to make a similar point about 1972 and the impact of B-52 bombing of North Vietnam and the sanctuaries in Laos and Cambodia:

Hanoi could see the situation coming by the end of 1972. Their rear bases were really under attack and the South Vietnamese rear bases, at the same time, were in good shape. In my view, on December 30, 1972, after eleven days of those B-52 attacks on the Hanoi area, *you had won the war. It was over!* They had fired 1,242 SAMs; they had none left, and what would come overland from China would be a mere trickle. They and their whole rear base at that point were at your mercy. They would have taken any terms. And that is why, of course, you actually got a peace agreement in January, which you had not been able to get in October.[57]

Many conservatives worry about the impact of the Vietnam experience on American resolve to use military force in the future. Americans should not feel guilty about Vietnam Guenter Lewy asserts:

> To a large number of Americans the Vietnamese war represents not only a political mistake and national defeat but also a major moral failure. The catalog of evils with which the United States is burdened includes the indiscriminate killing of civilians, the assassination and torture of political adversaries, the terror-bombing of North Vietnam, duplicity about it all in high places and much else. For many younger people, in particular, America and Vietnam stands as the epitome of evil in the modern world; this view of the American role in Vietnam has contributed significantly to the impairment of national pride and self-confidence that has beset this country since the fall of Vietnam.
>
> . . . the sense of guilt created by the Vietnam war in the minds of many Americans is not warranted and the charges of *officially condoned* illegal and grossly immoral conduct are without substance. Indeed, detailed examination of battlefield practices reveals that the loss of civilian life in Vietnam was less than in World War II and Korea and that concern with minimizing the ravages of war was strong.[58]

Unlike the quagmire and the "system worked" approaches, the conservative position is much more likely to appreciate the impact of domestic dissent. Unlike the radical view that this opposition was based on the fundamental injustice of Washington's actions and on the record of government duplicity, the conservatives think that the opposition was "soft" and that its constraining influence could easily have been reversed. Americans were basically loyal, they assert, but do not like long, inconclusive wars. Americans are impatient. Yet with a more aggressive policy the "silent majority" could have been swung around, the antiwar movement isolated. Paul Nitze, for example, reduces that movement to an attempt on the part of "the brightest boys" to restore their masculinity (which was threatened by their own strenuous efforts to avoid the draft).[59] Had there been no "erosion of will at home" the U.S. would have won. Better "management of the domestic front" would have brought victory. Control over inflationary pressures could have been achieved through an increase in taxes. Public support for the war could have been mobilized by calling up reserves. And procedures for drafting Americans could have been more equitable. The depth and influence of public opposition is therefore recognized, but the conservatives argue that the fluidity of that opposition left open the possibility of its reorientation behind the war effort.

Conclusion

On the main issues of the Vietnam War, including the funda-mental immorality of U.S. intervention and the class interests that were served, the interpretation offered by this book falls squarely inside the radical approach. Within that school, the importance of defending the "rules of the game" governing the behavior of Third World countries is a better explanation of Washington's policy than the economic motivations contained in the Pacific Rim inter-pretation. The Vietnam War was a conflict between a socialist movement conducting a war of national liberation and a country responsible for defending capitalism on a world scale. The purpose of the war was to protect the international interests of the capitalist class. The American people were not served well.

Radicals have described and analyzed the world capitalist system and demonstrated that it works to the advantage of some countries over others and in the interests of particular classes over others. But radicals have been comparatively unable to develop theoretically informed interpretations of the actual exercise of policy. Important theoretical consequences flow from a focus on the process of policy formation instead of on the structure of the world capitalist system. Radicals may grant, more often in conversation or in a footnote than in the main part of an analysis, that a broad range of influences affect policy-making, or that class interests or system-wide priorities do not fully explain specific decisions. But these references are more rhetorical than genuine. The significance of these observations are not usually followed theoretically. Leftwing theory, especially Marxist variants, is notoriously weak in its ability to analyze the more immediate influences on decision making and the political process itself.

Cracks in the Empire takes the fundamentals of the radical interpretation of U.S. intervention in Vietnam as a starting-point. But the radical perspective is not exhaustive. Each of the other interpretations offers a level of analysis, a particular method of focusing on the U.S. role in Vietnam, that needs to be incorporated into a radical explanation capable of examining the decision-making process itself. The state intervention school, for example, in its stress on the vast organizational resources within the national security apparatus, forces us to focus on the possible conflict between the interests of the state managers and those of the capitalist class. Radicals, on the other hand, generally assume that dominant economic interests were served by the war *and* that representatives of those interests, drawn from the economic elite itself, were directly responsible for formulating policy. By 1968 it appears that substantial segments of business opinion had become extremely critical of the Vietnam War. The inflation rate was up, the stock market and productivity down. Leading businessmen testified in Congress against the war. Yet Washington persisted for another seven years in an ultimately vain effort. Why? The answer requires examining political developments that cannot be reduced to a calculus of interests based on class alone. Furthermore, advocates of the state intervention perspective force us to focus on the possible influence of the military itself. What impact did the armed forces have on policy? Radicals tend to dismiss the issue.

Many journalistic accounts of the Vietnam War (David Halberstam's *Best and the Brightest* is a good example) provide a glimpse of a Vietnam decision-making process studded with factional disputes and bureaucratic clashes — factors that the quagmire critique wrongly elevate into the main explanation of the U.S. intervention. Radicals normally assume that the state administers a coherent policy in relatively smooth fashion. The state faithfully implements that which the capitalists direct. But the radical view of the internal operation of the state is too simple. Extensive disagreement existed among policy-makers during the Vietnam War. *Cracks in the Empire* accepts the quagmire description of internal differences among the state managers and tries to demonstrate that these conflicts reflect strains between alternative policy orientations, not bureaucracy *per se*.

The "system worked" interpretation is especially tuned to the impact of domestic politics and Presidential ambitions on foreign policy. Where radicals see a straightforward attempt to defeat socialist forces in Vietnam, advocates of the "system worked" position argue that the U.S. followed a policy of not losing — which is a big difference. My approach is to isolate distinct policy currents within the national security apparatus. Some state managers argued for an all-out win policy, others claimed that the U.S. should not lose. Still a third group argued that the U.S. should do all that was possible to win within a variety of limits, imposed in part by domestic politics. The clash among these positions is imperfectly reflected in the quagmire description of bureaucratic politics. Disagreements certainly occured but these were not grounded in organizational imperatives. The "system worked" approach demonstrates that the state managers *knew* what they were doing even while most advocated policies that fell short of victory.

The conservatives assert that the U.S. could have won the war. For a radical, their arrogant proposals which reject international law, display no human decency and border on genocide are completely distasteful. Yet the conservatives obliquely capture the fact that the U.S. could have done far worse. The American record in Vietnam was appalling. The devastation and anguish left by our intervention stands as a major blot in world history. In the final analysis, though, Washington was forced to fight in a way that enabled the Vietnamese to win. The conservatives capture, indirectly, the point that the U.S. could have done far worse.

The radical analysis of policy offered in the rest of this book attempts to weigh the priority of protecting the capitalist system against other aspects and determinants of the decision-making process. These include: the executive power and organizational weight of the state itself, the existence of significant disagreement between not losing and winning, and Presidential ambitions and domestic policies not necessarily revolving around class. "Capitalism" explains U.S. intervention in Vietnam. But "capitalism" did not determine the specific form of that intervention. Washington could have done less. There is nothing about capitalism *per se* that dictates a thirty-year, one hundred and fifty billion dollar failure. And Washington could have done more (although the historical record admittedly makes this difficult to appreciate). There is nothing about capitalism that prevents a nuclear war from developing out of a limited war. It is important, needless to say, to understand why Washington eventually ended up doing what it did.

The next chapter addresses the theoretical tension that has been established between the state as a *capitalist* state, and the state as the center for policy decisions which are not fully explained by capitalism *per se*, that is, by capitalism as a system. At stake here is the knotty and perplexing problem of the Marxist theory of politics, and in particular the relationship between the capitalist class and state managers. It is to this subject that we now turn.

II: POLICY CURRENTS AND THE CAPITALIST STATE

Many political theorists, particularly Marxists, have argued that the state in capitalist society is little more than the passive instrument of the capitalist class. In the *Communist Manifesto,* Karl Marx and Frederick Engels wrote that the "state is nothing more than the executive committee of the ruling class." Yet in the *18th Brumaire of Louis Bonaparte* Marx also wrote that the "extraparliamentary mass of the bourgeoisie...declared unequivocally that it longed to *get rid* of its own political rule [the parliamentary system] in order to get rid of the troubles and danger of ruling."[1] The first quotation states that the ruling class more or less directly controls the state. The second quotation implies that the ruling class does not wish to be responsible for control over the state—at least in particular historical circumstances. These two contrasting views run through the whole of Marx's work. Theoretical works such as *Capital* or the *Critique of Political Economy*, where economics and not politics is of primary concern, contain comparatively deterministic statements stressing the base-superstructure model and the impact of production relations on class relations, although they also contain warnings against simplistic, reductionist determinism. Historical works such as *The Civil War in France* or *The 18th Brumaire* on the other hand rest upon a much more flexible concept of determination. In them, culture, ideology and politics are granted a high degree of autonomy from production relations. In this respect the contrast between Marx's economic and his historical writings, especially those concerning France, is thus remarkable. *Capital,* for the most part, employs a four-class model: bourgeoisie, petty-bourgeoisie, proletariat and lumpenproletariat. But *The 18th Brumaire* contains references to over twenty classes. The theoretical works on political economy situate class in the social relations of production. In the historical works Marx explicitly refers to a class, the republican bourgeoisie, which is formed by its attachment to nationalistic ideologies rather than by its economic position. In the theoretical works the state is either ignored or is seen as an instrument of the ruling class; in the historical works the state is active, worthy of analysis in itself, its role structured by the intensity and direction of class conflict.

This contrast can be overdrawn. In the final analysis Marx's theoretical works are not determinist. The historical writings contain brilliant examples of the impact of production relations on social class and political behavior. So what's the point? That Marx was occasionally inconsistent or that he needed a better editor? No. The difference stems from the inherent difficulty of applying an abstract theoretical analysis of the essential features of capitalism to the particular events and social forces that make up historical circumstances. No theory can be expected to explain every daily event. Marx's theoretical purpose was to illuminate underlying patterns, not everyday contingencies. Relatively microscopic analysis of historical events may result in new generalizations which are somewhat at odds with previous theoretical formulations. The tension, often creative, between deductive theory and theory that derives from historical analysis can be seen in Marx's treatment of state and class. It is also present in the ongoing debate concerning the relationships of class to power, specifically state power, in capitalist society.

This chapter has several purposes. One is to introduce the reader to the main themes in the discussion of political power and the capitalist state which is now being conducted with vigor by radicals and Marxists. That discussion is so wide-ranging and complex that adequate treatment of it in a single chapter is next to impossible. References for those wishing to follow up are provided. Another purpose is to show the relevance of this sometimes abstract debate by drawing out its implications for the interpretation of the Vietnam War. But the main goal of this chapter is to suggest a way of extending the radical interpretation of the *structure and organization* of political power in the U.S. so as to permit the investigation of the political *process* within the state itself. To do so this chapter introduces a crucial concept called policy currents.

Direct Control of the State by the Capitalist Class

There is clearly some relationship between the capitalist class and the state in capitalist society, but there are different views as to the nature of that relationship. According to one, the capitalist class more or less directly controls the state. The state merely administers a policy consensus that has been hammered out in the corporate sphere. The state apparatus either generates no significant interests of its own or subordinates whatever interests it has to those of the capitalist class. Gabriel Kolko, arguing from this point of view, states that the state bureaucracy acts "purely as an instrumentality reflecting class interests. A bureaucracy that has no independent power base and nowhere to find one is one of the distinguishing qualities of the American power structure."[2] This view in effect plays down the importance of examining the political process itself. Kolko thus argues that "to study *how* rather than *why* political power operates in class society, a formalism that Max Weber contributed to conservative social analysis, is to avoid the central issue of the class nature and function of the modern state."[3]

This view of the state and politics in capitalist society is often made to rest on two arguments: first, that there is considerable individual mobility between positions of economic power and powerful political command posts; and second, that state managers, whether or not they have a corporate background, make policy within the framework of a corporate-defined ideology. Each of these propositions is based on considerable evidence.

A number of studies have demonstrated that leading state officials are drawn disproportionately from the capitalist class. Gabriel Kolko studied horizontal mobility between business and government for key American foreign policy makers between 1944 and 1960.[4] Of 234 individuals studied, a mere thirty, drawn from law, banking and investment firms, accounted for twenty-two percent of all positions. Almost sixty percent of the posts were filled by corporate executives, investment bankers and corporation lawyers, with a select number of Wall Street firms (including Sullivan and Cromwell; Dillon, Read; Carter, Ledyard and Milburn; and Coudert Brothers) contributing disproportionately. The composition of the very top positions—Secretaries and Undersecretaries of State and Defense, Secretaries of the three military services, Chairman of the Atomic Energy Commission and Director of the Central Intelligence Agency—is even more skewed towards corporate power. Of the ninety-one individuals who held these posts between 1940 and 1967, seventy were drawn from the ranks of big business or high finance.[5] A Brookings Institution study found that eighty-six percent of the Secretaries of the Army, Navy and Air Force between 1933 and 1965 were either businessmen or lawyers.[6] Most of the special Presidential commissions convened to advise the government on selected foreign policy issues are also dominated by businessmen.

These patterns support the proposition that holders of key government positions serve the foreign policy interests of an internationally-oriented capitalist class. Adherents of this view argue further that policy formulation occurs in business-dominated organizations such as the Committee for Economic Development, the Council on Foreign Relations, or more recently, the Trilateral Commission and the Business Roundtable. Within these organizations important political divisions may exist. But through financial contributions and key personnel, the views of the largest corporations dominate, while other groups such as labor or small agricultural interests play only a minor role. In the Council on Foreign Relations, for example, fifty-five percent of the general membership is drawn from the capitalist class, whereas among Council directors and officers the proportion increases to eighty-four and ninety-three percent respectively.[7] The CFR has, not unexpectedly, played a major role in defining a conception of the national interest which dovetails with that of business.

There is also considerable evidence for the argument that even in those areas where members of the capitalist class do not occupy key positions, state decision-making goes on within a business-defined ideology. A number of contemporary radical historians have stressed the long-standing importance to U.S. foreign policy of the "open door" principle, that is of the "right" of U.S. companies to participate in the economies of other nations.[8] Throughout this century U.S. political and business leaders have defined prosperity and the "American way of life" (formal democratic freedoms, apparent class harmony and a consumer-oriented society) in terms of the expansion abroad of U.S. investment and trade. Continued economic growth has been tied to "multilateralism," or the abolition of colonial restrictions on trade, of special access rights, of protective tariffs and other barriers to full American participation in the world's markets. Further, political stability has been explicitly linked with economic growth, as in Dean Acheson's testimony before Congress in 1943: "We cannot expect domestic prosperity without constantly expanded trade with other nations...To keep prosperity, levels of employment, production and income...we shall have to find increasing markets for our production and increasing investment outlets for our capital." You could "fix it so that everything produced here would be consumed here," the future Secretary of State continued, "but that would completely change our Constitution, our relations to property, human liberty, our very conception of law."[9]

The rhetoric of the campaign for the "open door" and against colonialism added a special quality—zealous, quasi-religious—to the ideal of a "pax Americana." Beneath the fervor lay the pragmatic realization that conditions of equal competition would permit the U.S. to use its enormous economic strength to dominate. And while the apparent ideal may have been peaceful, the harsh reality is that the U.S. world role over the last hundred and fifty years has been the most militaristic of any country.[10]

Several scholars have applied the view that the capitalist class directly controls the state to the history of U.S. intervention in Vietnam. Laurence Shoup's study of the Council on Foreign Relations focuses on the influence of the corporate upper class in defining U.S. national interests in Southeast Asia.[11] Of twenty-five key government decision-makers on American policy in the region since World War II, eighteen, or seventy-two percent, were members of the CFR at some point in their careers. As measured by indicators such as stock ownership, the background of these state managers was overwhelmingly (eighty percent) corporate upperclass. From 1940 to 1963 Council planners stressed the economic and strategic importance of the region: raw materials, falling dominos, and future markets dominated their thinking. In 1964, as the direct military role of the U.S. grew more visible, the Council approved Washington's policy of transforming Vietnam into a test of American will and prestige. Council members rejected the advice of Undersecretary of State George Ball, who was an early critic of Johnson's Vietnam policy.[12] But by 1968 the Council reluctantly recognized the incapacity of the by-then huge U.S. involvement to bring about a military victory. According to Shoup the mechanism for communicating this shift of views to the state managers was a Special Senior Advisory Group on Vietnam composed of some of the most influential men of the corporate world. Twelve of the fourteen members of the group, or "Wise Men" as they were sometimes called, were CFR members. Their initial role was to receive top-level government briefings on Vietnam and to give their stamp of approval. Once the TET Offensive had shattered the official picture of progress, the Advisory Group reversed the policy endorsement it had made only four months before. Council members hastened to construct a new consensus, and the results were framed in a peace proposal " 'rigged' to favor the (Saigon) government."[13] The proposal was carried with "all the pomp and circumstance accorded a communication from private government" to Undersecretary of State Elliot Richardson and Special Assistant for National Security Affairs Henry Kissinger. The 1973 "peace settlement" was the outcome. At each stage, Shoup concludes, government policy closely paralleled the position of the Council on Foreign Relations. Vietnam policy was the result of direct class rule.

Richard DuBoff's study on the National Security Council and Vietnam also stresses the salience of business influence, with one further refinement.[14] DuBoff focuses on the "transmission belts" which convert the structure of corporate economic privilege into complementary political and economic decisions. He argues that key foreign policy institutions in government, such as the Departments of Defense and State, either are run directly by individuals from the economic elite or share and implement an ideology consistent with the interests of the capitalist class. The reorganization of the national security bureaucracy carried out under the National Security Act of 1947, and especially the creation of the National Security Council, limited the influence of the military and "strengthened the bond between the formal policy-making apparatus culminating in the Presidency and the enormous business-banking sector of the external society."[15] Shared ideological concerns permit the virtual fusion of business interests with a particular definition of the national interest. DuBoff maintains that "American policy-makers exercise both functions at once: they represent the economic elite and the national interest as traditionally understood in a *Machtpolitik* terms. Bound up in a seamless relationship, these two functions cannot be segregated by any neat boundary."[16] Business defined the significant ideological components of U.S. foreign policy which were subsequently applied to Vietnam. Washington defended the rules of the game which integrates underdeveloped countries into a U.S. dominated network of control. U.S. propaganda exaggerated and distorted the Communist "threat" in order to lubricate the growth and expansion of U.S. business in the Third World. Washington refused to Third World countries the right to set successful examples of reform and independent behavior. The Vietnam Revolution threatened each of these elements of foreign policy and a long, ferocious intervention resulted.

Conspiracy Theories

Conspiracy theories of the Vietnam War are an extreme form of the perspective stressing direct control of the capitalist class over state decisions. Conspiracy theories come in a number of different variants.[17] Perhaps the most detailed is Peter Dale Scott's exploration of the links between the intelligence community, especially the CIA, and a small number of corporate chieftans. After his close analysis of crucial incidents of U.S. intervention in Indochina, Scott "suggests a sequence of related conspiracies to deceive, not only the U.S. public, but the Congress of the U.S., and at times even recalcitrant elements within the Administration itself."[18] The precise composition, motivation, and direction of the conspiracy remain rather murky. Scott goes on to describe a network of Wall Street influentials working at times with figures from the world of organized crime, and intelligence officials who distort information to their own advantage. Pervasive economic interests, including opium smuggling from Laos, are part of the background of intelligence operations. Yet Scott also argues, in explicit contrast with the position discussed above, that no single ruling class exists.[19] The conspiracy he sees is not a matter of a unified class controlling the entire state but of a small coterie of CIA, Wall Street and Mafia types who manipulate government institutions to their own advantage.

A few examples will help illustrate his argument. In August 1964 North Vietnam allegedly attacked U.S. ships patrolling in international waters. Scott maintains that the subsequent "Gulf of Tonkin incident" was blown out of proportion in order to obtain Congressional legislation to widen U.S. commitments in Indochina.

Scott's own close examination of fragmentary and often contradictory bits of intelligence leads him to conclude that the North Vietnamese attack on the *USS Maddox* never took place. He argues that the U.S. patrol ship attempted to provoke Hanoi into actions which were never taken, but were nevertheless used as a pretext to respond with already planned escalatory measures. The whole incident, in his view, was devised by certain officials of the CIA (but the entire agency is not implicated) and of the military command of the Pacific, with Wall Street financiers with long experience in intelligence operations standing somewhere in the background.

Scott argues that the "Pueblo incident"—North Korea's 1968 capture of the *Pueblo*, another vessel dispatched on an electronic listening mission—was also a war conspiracy. In this case the Pacific military command deliberately sent the spy ship to Korean waters. The military and the rightwing members of the intelligence community hoped that a public uproar following the *Pueblo*'s seizure would dissolve civilian objections to the mobilization of reserves for use in Vietnam, as well as easing political restraints on U.S. air and ground operations in Indochina.

Intelligence reports describing the nature of NLF command posts provided the pretext for the invasion of Cambodia by American troops in 1970. Scott argues convincingly that such headquarters, at least in the usual sense of a fixed installation with facilities for thousands of men, never existed. He explains the motivation for invasion in terms of close interlocks among the rightwing American Security Council, Richard Nixon, intelligence personnel, and Pacific-oriented oil companies whose bureaucratic, personal, and economic interests were aided by the operation.[20]

Scott also contends that the *New York Times* version of the *Pentagon Papers* was deliberately edited in a fashion that preserved the reputation of the CIA. Only accurate and dovish Agency assessments were included while the numerous examples of mistaken predictions or hawkish proposals by the Agency were omitted.[21] He maintains that this selective editing and misrepresentation of key documents is yet another example of the manipulation of intelligence in order to influence government policy and public opinion, and to keep the intelligence-business network invisible to Congressional scrutiny.

For Scott then, certain corporate interests are served covertly by certain intelligence officers and military leaders who in turn influence U.S. foreign policy. He specifically links some members of the capitalist class with some officials of the Central Intelligence Agency, the members of a rightwing think tank, and some military officers in a conscious conspiracy. His theory is quite different from one which emphasizes the control of the capitalist class as a whole over the entire state, an influence based on overlapping representation and ideology rather than specific interest, and expressed in terms of coherent policy rather than conspiracy.

The Concept of Policy Currents

Marxists have tended increasingly over the last decade to come to the conclusion that a theory stressing the direct control of the state by members of the capitalist class is by itself inadequate. Without denying the importance of decision-makers' social background, of corporate policy groups, or of business ideology, recent theorists have argued that the interests of capital are served best when the "capitalist class does not participate directly in the State apparatus, that is to say when the *ruling class* is not the *politically governing class.*"[22]

The reasons for this theoretical shift are compelling. The ability of the capitalist class to develop national policy on its own is reduced by capitalists' internal divisions and their overriding preoccupation with sectional and short-run economic considerations. Consequently the state must play a more independent role in formulating policy than the orthodox Marxist view generally admits. In some instances state managers, operating on the basis of self-interest, may adopt a course of action that conflicts with that preferred by the capitalist class. Some argue that the state is capitalist by its very structure and that the stress on individual links with the capitalist class is an inadequate conceptualization of power. The state is also better adapted and more sensitive than the capitalist class to the need of coopting or repressing demands posed by working-class organizations and other oppositional social movements.[23] The concept of policy currents emerges from this theoretical perspective which recognizes the inability of the capitalist class to rule directly.

Policy currents can be defined as alternative conceptions, found among the capitalist class, state managers, and other defenders of the capitalist order, for exercising U.S. power within the limits imposed by different oppositional forces.

The concept of policy currents brings out the importance of alternative conceptions of how to exercise U.S. political, military and economic power.[24] Each policy current supports capitalism against socialism and seeks to maintain and strengthen the position of the U.S. in the world arena. But each policy current represents a different strategy for accomplishing these common aims.

Policy currents are bridges linking the capitalist class and state managers together with other representatives of the capitalist order. No unidirectional flow between the capitalist class and the state is implied. For example, policy currents do not simply reflect the divergent interests of fractions of capital, or some other form of determinism emanating from different economic conditions. Rather, a policy current is composed of common positions which can be traced among the capitalist class and leading state officials. Journalists, academics, and personnel of foundations and think-tanks also participate in the elaboration of policy currents although they exert less influence in the immediate decision-making process.

Different policy currents do reflect distinct sets of economic interests within the capitalist class and different sets of bureaucratic interests within the state. But policy currents are not reducible to these economic and bureaucratic interests.

Policy currents express long-standing political tendencies within the ruling coalition. They derive from two sources: the challenges from oppositional forces, whether in the form of revolutionary movements, competing forms of capital, or domestic opposition; and the history of the capitalist class and its state representatives of favoring different kinds of responses, such as military force, foreign aid, or covert intelligence operations.

The rest of this chapter elaborates the concept of policy currents further, illustrating theoretical points with examples from the Vietnam War.

(A) Divisions Within the Capitalist Class and State Managers

The policy currents approach shares the position of recent radical discussions of power and the state that emphasize that a variety of internal divisions weaken the ability of the capitalist class to rule directly.[25] The existence of specific class fractions, each based in different conditions of production, may weaken the unity and cohesiveness of the capitalist class.[26] For example, in developed countries financial and industrial capital may quarrel over government monetary or tax policy.[27] In underdeveloped countries national and comprador fractions of capital may be in conflict over government policies toward foreign multinational corporations.[28] Watergate has been interpreted as a conflict between different wings of the capitalist class over the state.[29] Some students argue that different state agencies act on behalf of particular fractions of capital, whereas others maintain that political power is exercised by several different fractions of capital organized in a "hegemonic bloc" which controls the key state agencies. Still others hold that the state acts as the "ideal collective capitalist" or that state managers synthesize diverse viewpoints into a coherent policy that reflects the long-range, general interests of the capitalist class.[30] In still another version intraclass differences are situated regionally: the Northeast (or Snowbelt) competes with the Southern Rim (or Sunbelt) over federal funds, new capital investment, and population, each region attempting to control the state on its own behalf.

The prolongation of the Vietnam War has been explained by both fractional and regional conflict. It has been argued that financial and industrial capital welcomed the expansion of the war in 1964 as an economic stimulus, but that induced inflationary tendencies provoked a change of heart by 1968. Nevertheless fractions of capital dependent on military expenditures successfully pressed for renewed commitment in Vietnam. The regional argument is that "Yankee" capitalists in the Northeast were hurt by the Vietnam effort whereas the "Cowboys" of the Southern Rim benefitted.[31]

Conflict between policy currents (over alternative directions for foreign policy) is general, but each policy current also represents specific interests which conflict with other specific interests that stand to benefit from alternative policies. While contributing, at times very audibly, to the cacophony of contending policies, specific interests do not normally determine political outcomes. Policy currents contain but can not be reduced to the specific interests which are found in corporations that stand to profit from a particular policy, in state agencies administering a policy, in departments of the armed forces that benefit from allocations associated with a given policy, or among Congressmen who evaluate a policy in terms of its impact on their constituencies.

Capitalism sets firm against firm, industry against industry, and sector against sector. Corporation owners and managers are concerned with securing immediate advantages in this competition, and it is ordinarily on behalf of these short-term business interests that they seek to influence government. The normal corporate "influence channels" including lobbying, favors and campaign contributions are not effective avenues for expressing general class interests. Businessmen are sometimes subjected to exhortations from class-conscious representatives such as David Rockefeller to be more active, to "get more involved in politics." Individual capitalists may agree in theory that they should try to achieve the "greatest good for the greatest number of capitalists," but American businessmen tend to oppose greater state intervention even when such action may be on their own behalf.[32] Participants in "consensus-reaching" discussions generally go back to making decisions that maximize their individual interests. For example, the capitalist class has a common interest in maintaining the strength of the dollar in international transactions. But individual multinational corporations demonstrate few inhibitions over participating in speculations that weaken the U.S. currency. Capitalism is an irrational system—even for capitalists! Future survival, expansion and profit remain rooted in the maximization of available short-run opportunities. Only the state can attempt to compensate for the narrow and parochial behavior that results. The capitalist class is incapable of ruling itself.

Specific interests are of course also present within the state. For example, interservice rivalry between the Air Force, Navy and Army complicate the policy formation process. Each service lobbies government to increase its budget. Each service commands large public relations staffs, ample funds, and political allies in Congress in order to influence policy decisions.[33] In the case of Vietnam a number of specific organizational interests acquired a stake in the war. The military wanted to demonstrate that it could defeat a war of national liberation. The Foreign Service had to prove that it could bring about political stability in Saigon and "build a nation." The CIA had to prove that pacification could work. AID had to prove that millions of dollars in assistance and advice could bring political returns.

The state's capacity to achieve a consensus in the general interests of the capitalist class is thus limited by two kinds of divisions: first, by the policy splits that develop within the capitalist class and among the state managers; and second, by the competition among specific interests. As a result the orthodox Marxist concept of the state acting in the "general interest of the capitalist class" becomes difficult to sustain. Significant disagreement exists within that class, even among those attempting to develop a systematic viewpoint. It is difficult to measure the performance of the state against the general interests of the capitalist class when defining the general interest in any concrete sense becomes problematic. It is far more helpful to focus on the debate between different orientations (each of which is in some ultimate sense "capitalist") without assigning one or the other the status of "correct" policy. To imagine a cohesive group of state managers ("ideal capitalists") which makes policy for a divided capitalist class would be to understate drastically the policy differences which exist within the state itself. On the other hand, to explain policy by linking specific state agencies to specific fractions of capital would be far too simplistic. Political divisions within the state do not always correspond to specific fractions of capital, and conflict may exist within state agencies as much as between them.

Despite these divisions some degree of cohesiveness in state policy-making is achieved as a result of several factors. Many special interests cannot lobby on grounds of self-interest without jeopardizing their legitimacy. At some point they must couch their appeal in terms of a policy valuable for the country as a whole. Further, special interests are often associated more or less permanently with other special interests as political allies. It is also true that established policy itself acts to define and build interests, causing individuals and groups in similar circumstances to perceive their interests in different ways. Finally, the state is obliged to present its policies to the public in coherent and persuasive terms, terms that supposedly operate in the interests of the nation as a whole.

Thus, the state tries to implement a policy distilled out of short-run, narrow and competing specific interests. An attempt is made to protect capital from its own internal conflicts, to correct the mistaken versions of capital's own needs and to integrate the plurality of isolated interests into a single class policy. But the state never fully succeeds in synthesizing competing specific interests and contending general priorities. The state in capitalist society may reduce the anarchy of economic production and the tensions of class rule, but it never truly eliminates them.

(B) Ideological Bridges

Rather than emphasize the direct influence of capitalists on the state apparatus, the concept of policy currents includes the notion of ideological bridges linking the capitalist class with the state. The expression "ideological bridges" indicates a particular approach to the question of the autonomy of the state. According to the theory of "relative autonomy" of the state, political space between the capitalist class and the state is necessary in order to permit formulation and implementation of policies that maximize the long-run collective interests of the capitalist class. On the other hand, some strong connections are equally necessary. In this respect those writers stressing connections between the capitalist class and the state are right on target. Members of the capitalist class do "change hats" and participate directly in the state, bringing their ideas and policies with them. But more important than the presence of actual representatives of capitalist interests within the state are the policy battles fought between rival "consensus-seeking groups." Here the stress is on divisions within the capitalist class and among the state managers. Policy currents form links between parts of the capitalist class and the sectors of state which are based on different ideological principles or perceptions of how the world should be managed in the "national interest and security" of the U.S. Such links or ideological bridges effectively organize the various defenders of the capitalist order *vis a vis* foreign policy issues.

Where do policy currents come from, if not from economic or bureaucratic interest narrowly defined? What is their social location?

(C) The Social Location of Policy Currents

Policy currents have two sources: the forces that oppose capitalism and the tendency of capitalists to disagree over the best way to respond to those forces of opposition.

Policy currents are a response to the forces which limit the economic expansion and political power of U.S. capital in the world arena. The concept of policy currents may seem to apply exclusively to elite politics because of its focus on internal struggle between state managers and within the capitalist class. But the approach also presupposes that oppositional forces and popular movements ultimately structure foreign policy. Without opposition, policy currents would not emerge.

Diverse policy currents also arise when defenders of the capitalist order disagree over the best method of responding to these movements. Politics are never the passive reflection of external forces. The capitalist class and state managers must actively grapple with the forces of opposition. Policy currents derive from the fact that capitalism faces opposition and that capitalists have different ways of combatting that opposition. Capitalism is not omnipotent and capitalists are not omniscient.

1. Forces of Opposition

The policy currents approach does not assert that the capitalist class directly controls the state. The capitalist class influences the state to a great degree but other classes can also exert influence. Capitalists or their representatives may be directly responsible for decision-making. But the content of the resulting policies reflects pressures from domestic forces of opposition. The state in fact absorbs and deradicalizes demands emanating from below. The influence of the subordinate classes varies over time, and is often difficult to detect and measure. But the main point is that although the capitalist class is dominant in capitalist society, its power is always constrained and restricted by that of other classes and social groups. Struggle between social classes continuously affects state policy, even in non-revolutionary times. Consequently many Marxists, following Nicos Poulantzas, have abandoned the concept of the state as an instrument of capitalist rule and have come to view the state as "the condensation of class struggle."[34] State policy in their view is not the will of one class but the outcome of class struggle. In the case of the Vietnam War this insight can be documented on two levels. Chapter Five discusses restrictions on U.S. intervention imposed by domestic opposition. Chapter Six examines a more subtle phenomenon, namely that fear of arousing domestic opposition prevented state managers from imposing such economic controls as are normally used during wartime.

Instances in which the state, under pressure from below, acts contrary to the immediate directives of the capitalist class may even further the long-run stability of capitalism.[35] By continually forcing capitalism to modernize, working-class demands for a shorter working day, better working conditions, and public education both reinforce the economic dynamism of capitalism and improve overall living standards. The New Deal is the outstanding example in U.S. history of the state's ability to improve the conditions of capital accumulation by undertaking major reforms in response to working-class pressure. When it responds to pressures from below, the state performs a more complex ideological function than when it simply enacts policies reflecting capitalist aims. The state can only enjoy legitimacy insofar as it presents itself as acting not in the interest of the capitalist class but in the interest of the nation as a whole. The existence of genuine conflict between the state and at least some segments of the capitalist class reinforces the state's ideological claim to be a neutral arbiter among all interest groups in society. The projection of the state as the disinterested coordinator, which becomes more plausible when there really are cases of limited conflict between capitalists and state managers, is essential to what Antonio Gramsci called "ideological hegemony," or the exercise of social control through commonly accepted cultural assumptions.[36]

External obstacles to U.S. capitalism and the range of policy responses take many different forms. Are *competing national capitalisms*, such as those of Japan or the European Common Market, to be understood as an unmitigated threat to the American economy, or as a necessary evil that helps absorb U.S. exports? Do *radical nationalist* movements in underdeveloped countries such as Iran simply benefit the Soviet Union, or are they a legitimate third force in world politics? What policy stance should be taken toward the *officially socialist countries* of the Soviet Union or

Eastern Europe? Or towards more recent *revolutionary regimes* such as Cuba, Vietnam or Nicaragua? Should Washington establish contact with oppositonal movements like the Italian Communist Party or should it attempt to isolate them? What are the dangers of prolonged instability in a nation such as Turkey where the immediate prospects for socialism are dim? Obviously these quesions do not all lie on the same terrain. Tariff negotiations with Japan, SALT talks with the Soviet Union and Marxist movements in Angola are quite different kettles of fish. The concept of policy currents calls attention to the fact that in regard to each there are perceptible differences within the U.S. ruling elite.

Appreciating the impact of domestic and foreign opposition on state decisions evolves on two levels. First, oppositional movements *force all policy-makers* to take account of the influence of different centers of power. Policy reflects the variety and strength of different forms of pressure against capitalism. Policy-makers cannot always do what they want. Second, different policy currents *favor different strategies*, different ways of countering these oppositional forces. The responses favored by competing policy currents are triggered by different readings of history, by different "historical lessons."

2. Historical Lessons

State managers tend to apply the lessons of conducting foreign policy in one period to what seems to be a similar situation in another period. This appears simple enough—only they disagree over the choice of the appropriate lesson. One such disagreement concerns the use of force. The principle that "force should not be exercised until all avenues of diplomacy have been exhausted" lay behind Adlai Stevenson's recommendation to President Kennedy that the U.S. use the United Nations as a forum to pressure the Soviet Union into removing its missiles from Cuba in 1962. A competing principle, the one that has dominated postwar foreign policy, is that "aggression can only be counteracted with force." Another version of this second principle is that "the United States is the strongest country in the world, but only if it acts that way." Kennedy's decision to establish a naval blockade around Cuba expressed his adherence to the second principle. The first principle expresses faith in negotiation and diplomacy; the second, the desire to flex American muscle through symbolic and actual use of military force.

A clear clash between the two tendencies occurred during the Potsdam Conference at the end of World War II.[37] Secretary of War Henry Stimson, representing the diplomatic current, petitioned against the use of an atomic bomb against Japan. Stimson maintained that the combined threat of Soviet, Chinese, U.S., and British troops and of even more destructive weaponry would produce a negotiated settlement. Americans would suffer little loss of life, Japanese property would be preserved, and only paper concessions to the Emperor would be necessary. Moreover, the way would be eased for "responsible" Japanese participation in the postwar economy. Stimson was overruled by President Truman and Secretary of State James Byrnes, who wanted a dramatic show of force and a decisive victory before the Soviet Union could swing the bulk of its armies around to the East. The bomb was meant to impress the Soviet Union in the context of an already hardening Cold War. In the words of Byrnes, the bomb "was meant for Europe," to scare the Soviet Union into more compliant behavior. Underlying the dispute over the bomb lay broader differences over methods of confronting socialism and the relative strength of economic and military postures. Stimson's faith in diplomacy reflected a deep respect for property and a feeling that encouraging participation in the world arena dominated by the West would be the best way to control the Soviet Union. Behind the Truman-Byrnes show of force lay a desire to control the Soviet Union through economic isolation and military threat.

Opposing sets of notions also exist with respect to movements of national liberation and can be illustrated by attitudes toward the National Liberation Front during the Vietnam War. Rightwing currents interpret Third World movements for national liberation as parts of a grand design led by either Moscow or Peking. According to their view Vietnam was a "proxy war" and the U.S. should have attacked China directly and forced the Soviet Union to cut off aid to guerilla movements. President Johnson's public statement that "we seek no wider war" symbolized the dominant current: a desire to avoid a *direct* confrontation with either China or the Soviet Union, while focusing more on the threat of the national liberation movement itself. The official State Department "White Paper" on the Vietnam War was called "North Vietnam's Attempt to Conquer South Vietnam." Had the rightwing controlled policy the document might have been called "China's Attempt..." or "Communism's Attempt..." A "left" current within the national security apparatus would have focused on conditions within South Vietnam and might have written a paper called "A Program of Economic and Political Reform to Undercut the Vietcong (NLF)." In subsequent chapters the history of U.S. intervention in Vietnam will be described in terms of conflicts between left, center, and right policy currents.

Diverse views regarding the use of force are linked with different economic strategies. Henry Stimson's opposition to the use of the atomic bomb, for example, can be tied to notions that economic relations are the most effective means of deradicalizing revolutionary regimes. So can the views of Joseph Davies, the American Ambassador to the Soviet Union during the late-thirties. Davies' personal diary reflects his faith that human nature is capitalist:

> Mrs. Davies and I have often talked about these flower shops and perfume shops. It is one of the significant directions of the drift of this government away from the principles of Marxist Communism. Here were shops owned by the state selling flowers in baskets, at prices ranging from $2 in gold value to $15 in gold value. Fifteen dollars was the equivalent of two weeks' wage to the average workman. A capitalistic profit was being made out of the sale of an article, which found its demand in the fundamental instincts of human nature. The male youth of the country, under the biological urge, all wanted to prove to his particular lady love that he was bigger and better than his rival. To the degree that he could send her better flowers—to that degree he was competitively demonstrating his greater desirability. He therefore had to make more money. He could do so only through the application of the profit motive, the bane of pure Communism. The very essence of Communism, moreover, is a classless society. Here was a stimulus to create a class society, based upon a situation that stimulated the profit motive, because of a state business in a commodity that was desired because of a very primary human instinct.[38]

Even more compelling is a section of a report Davies filed with President Roosevelt following an extended trip throughout the industrial regions of the Soviet Union:

The communist principle has in actual fact been abandoned. 'From everyone according to his abilities and to each according to his needs is gone. They get what they earn. The profit motive and self-interest are the mainspring. From top to bottom production is stimulated by premiums and extra wage for service above the 'norm.' This applies to management, engineers, and workers. The plant itself is required to make a profit and does, generally ranging from five to thirty percent, which goes to the Central Government. This system, they found, was necessary for success. It is a socialistic enterprise based upon capitalistic principles of profit and self-interest, which they had come to, to make the machine function.[39]

People like Davies feel little reluctance to develop close ties with socialist states. In their view, an inevitable and extremely compelling pull toward market mechanisms and material incentives will ultimately transform any alternative economic arrangement. Their seeming tolerance and flexibility—Davies was a great admirer of the accomplishments of the Bolshevik Revolution—conceals a deeper arrogance towards the capacity of people to transform their social nature.

With respect to socialist movements in foreign nations, policy currents differ on the following issues:

· ● preferred location of the opposition movements in the political spectrum (integration into existing or reformed political institutions vs. isolation);

● preferred method of consolidating the power of favored classes (carrying out necessary reforms which would undercut the opposition vs. delivering unambiguous support for existing power elites);

● preferred tactics regarding the use of force (cooptation vs. repression);

● manner of using aid (economic to encourage capital accumulation and to lure movements away from militaristic and possible disruptive policies vs. greater reliance on military aid to shore up preferred leadership);

- views of the relationship between oppositional movements and other socialist states (possible tension that a proper policy can exploit vs. close collaboration and coordination);

- views of the proper U.S. response to success on the part of oppositional movements (minimizing the "loss" by tempering militancy and radicalism vs. overt aggression or isolation).

Debate within the national security apparatus over the appropriate response to revolutionary settings as diverse as Vietnam, Southern Africa, Europe, Iran and postwar China involves remarkably similar policy configurations.

The State As A Capitalist State

If the limits upon the capacity of the capitalist class to rule directly are so strong, what is there to ensure the capitalist orientation of state decisions? Which specific mechanisms insure that state decisions reinforce class rule—even while the dominant class is effectively handicapped from exercising power on its own behalf? It has already been argued that members of the capitalist class are over-represented in the state decision-making apparatus and that state managers tend to make decisions which are consistent with a business-defined ideology. Two more answers deserve close consideration. The first is the importance for the state of maintaining business confidence.[40] The state depends directly upon revenues from taxation which increase with the economy's performance. A declining economy is characterized by unemployment, dislocation, and increased levels of public criticism and opposition. Since key investment decisions remain in private hands the capitalist class is able to maintain an effective veto over the state. State managers entertain various options (policy currents) but know that policies unacceptable to capitalists will be met with lower levels of investment. The state consequently will only undertake programs that do not greatly lower business confidence.

In itself business confidence is not particularly astute—at least politically. Capitalists pay attention to their own economic concerns; perhaps they even demonstrate consciousness of certain common class interests. But making decisions on the basis of explicit policy remains the responsibility of the state. The level of business confidence is more likely to be based on the prospects for stability than an explicit calculation of the long-range interests of capital. So it continues to be the responsibility of the state managers to take the political reins. But they constantly check their saddles to make sure that the economic cinch is properly fastened.

U.S. intervention in Vietnam bolstered business confidence in two distinct ways. First, capitalists were reassured about the security of their overseas investments. As the Vice-President of Chase Manhattan Bank in charge of Far Eastern operations noted in 1965:

> In the past, foreign investors have been somewhat wary of the overall political prospect for the region. I must say that the U.S. actions in Vietnam this year—which have demonstrated that the U.S. will continue to give effective protection to the free nations of the region—have considerably reassured both Asian and Western investors. In fact I see some reason for hope that the same sort of economic growth may take place in the free economies of Asia that took place in Europe after the Truman Doctrine and after NATO provided a protective shield. The same thing also took place in Japan after the U.S. intervention in Korea removed investor doubts.[41]

Secondly, state spending on the war improved the domestic business climate. U.S. business magazines welcomed the 64-66 military build-up both on political grounds and as an economic stimulant. As already mentioned, many members of the business community began to argue by 1967 that Vietnam had become an economic albatross. While continuing to agree with the political goal of a non-communist Vietnam, some of the most influential leaders of the corporate class began to lobby discreetly for a change in policy that would alleviate the economic impact of the war. Details of this shift in business confidence on Vietnam decision-making are described and analyzed in Chapter Six.

Another answer to the question of why the state remains capitalist focuses on the social relations, organizations, and institutions that form the structure of capitalist society. In this "structuralist" view, institutionalized capitalist class relations themselves determine historical outcomes, over and above the consciousness of individuals. Capitalism is a system of production marked by exchange, the treatment of labor as a commodity, a drive for profit, the private appropriation of surplus by members of the capitalist class, and a tendency toward global integration through a world market.[42] These imperatives are an intangible, yet real, determinant of behavior. Structuralists argue that no matter what their social origins or political views, individuals only act out their position or role in the structure of power. The basic logic of capital "works behind the backs" of particular actors and the ultimate consequence of a decision may be far different than originally intended. It is not individual members of the capitalist class, but rather a deeper set of social relations that determines power. Nicos Poulantzas has argued this position:

> The *direct* participation of members of the capitalist class in the State apparatus and in the government, even where it exists, is not the important side of the matter. The relation between the bourgeois class and the State is an *objective relation*. This means that if the *function* of the state in a determinate social formation and the *interests* of the dominant class in this formation coincide, it is by reason of the system itself: the direct participation of members of the ruling-class in the State apparatus is not the *cause* but the *effect*, and moreover a chance and contingent one, of this objective coincidence.[43]

The policy currents perspective attempts to strike a balance between structuralism and a more fluid sense of determinism which recognizes that managers do choose among a range of options. Each policy current has a fundamental capitalist identity, but there is meaningful conflict and disagreement. Each policy current aims ultimately to preserve capitalism as a social system—but each would do so in a different way.

How does the capitalist state limit the range of options so that the capitalist system is protected? Structuralists argue that the internal organization of the state effectively excludes anti-capitalist tendencies. The state is not in itself neutral: capitalist imperatives preserve class rule even when reformist governments enter office. Claus Offe, for example, outlines four "selective mechanisms," constituting part of the structure of the capitalist state, which filter out policies that could lead to a critical assault against capital.[44]

"Structural" mechanisms, or the specific configuration of political institutions, make it difficult for the interests of the dominated classes to be adequately represented. "Ideological" mechanisms determine which issues are viewed as problems to be solved and which are excluded more or less automatically. "Procedural" mechanisms create a decision-making process that favors some interests over others. "Repressive" mechanisms use force or other forms of coercion to eliminate threatening policies. Each of these mechanisms filters out potentially anti-capitalist alternatives that others may allow to slip through. Taken together they provide an effective class bulwark. A political implication of this scheme is that socialist movements seeking a revolutionary transformation must do more than receive enough votes to attain political office; they will have to restructure the state as well.

An example from the Vietnam War will help to illustrate this "negative filter" function of the state. There is nothing about "capitalism" *per se* which forced the U.S. to intervene in Vietnam. But once Washington had made a major commitment in lives and resources, unilateral withdrawal could be seen as a potentially "anti-capitalist" course of action. Unilateral withdrawal served as an "ideological tripwire," clearly demarcating the boundary between acceptable and unacceptable disagreement. If the U.S. turned tail and ran, other national liberation movements would be encouraged. Control over the underdeveloped world as a whole would be weakened should the U.S. appear to be a "paper tiger." Indeed, unilateral withdrawal would weaken the very structure of international capitalist power. As a result of such assumptions, advocacy of withdrawal became taboo, even among critics of Vietnam policy who belonged to the policy-making elite. The possibility of withdrawal was not ruled out entirely—in fact, withdrawal was finally *forced* on Washington in April 1975 by the military success of the Vietnamese—but it was ruled out of the context of "normal" decision-making. The reader of the *Pentagon Papers* will search in vain for evidence of serious discussion of unilateral withdrawal. Let's look at some examples.

National security officials who advocated withdrawal were removed from office. In the spring of 1963, some Washington officials conspired to overthrow Ngo Dinh Diem, then head of the South Vietnamese government. The goal of the coup was to replace

Diem with a leader who would carry out administrative reforms, gain the support of the peasantry and build a social and political base capable of fighting the NLF effectively. Paul Kattenburg, head of the Interdepartment Working Group onVietnam, argued that no leader in South Vietnam could carry out these tasks. If Diem was permitted to remain in power, Kattenburg argued, the "United States would be thrown out of the country in six months."[45] Since there was no leader capable of replacing Diem and carrying out the necessary tasks, Kattenburg concluded that the American effort was hopeless and that the U.S. should withdraw. At this point Secretary of State Dean Rusk laid down some ground rules. A fundamental assumption in all subsequent discussion would be "we will not pull out of Vietnam until the war is won." Secretary of Defense Robert McNamara and then Vice-President Lyndon Johnson quickly moved in to support Rusk's position. Kattenburg was subsequently removed from his post.

President Johnson later made it clear that his closest advisors would be permitted only a narrow margin of disagreement. George Ball later described his own policy dissent as follows: "What I was proposing was something which I thought had a fair chance of being persuasive...if I had said 'let's pull out overnight' or do something of this kind, I obviously wouldn't have been persuasive at all. They'd have said 'the man's mad'."[46] Even the role of devil's advocate played by Ball did not include advocacy of unilateral withdrawal.

In the summer and fall of 1968 Secretary of Defense Clark Clifford's rapidly deepening doubts on Vietnam led him to consider unilateral withdrawal. He eventually expressed this desire publicly in an article published in *Foreign Affairs* during the summer of 1969.[47] But his actual decisions as Secretary of Defense were never made on the basis of withdrawal. Instead, Clifford's efforts to strengthen ARVN (the South Vietnamese Army) simply served as a prelude to Vietnamization. There are several reasons why Clifford failed to lead the Pentagon toward withdrawal, in spite of his private preference for that route. They include a political environment in which the Secretary of Defense becomes ineffective if he appears "too soft" or if he fails to carry his case with the President (as would have happened had Clifford taken the issue up directly with Johnson). Deputy Secretary of Defense Paul Nitze also played a role in temporarily convincing Clifford that Vietnam could be stabilized at a lower level of fighting with U.S. aid. Paul Nitze later told an interviewer:

> From that point on [after the March 31, 1968 partial bombing halt] Clifford and I were on opposite sides. He wanted to get out right away. He came to the conclusion that if he couldn't get a quick end to it by virtue of an intensification of the war, then the thing to do was to get out absolutely...cut and run. I felt, for God's sake, let's try to do the things that are necessary so you can get out while protecting our general interests in the situation. My view was that we put such a degree of effort into this thing that to get out, to cut and run, would undermine everything we'd tried to do in the past.[48]

Another example of exclusion of possibilities perceived as anti-capitalist involves Richard Nixon. After the 1968 election and before the inauguration, then national security advisor Daniel Ellsberg was directed to draft a set of questions which would bring out the different options in Vietnam available to the incoming Administration. The answers to these questions were brought together in a document known as NSSM-1. Ellsberg listed five options, one of which was withdrawal. Presented with this possibility Nixon drew a heavy blue line through it declaring "that's out."[49]

Documentation of the "negative filter" role of the state does not exhaust the analysis of actual policy formation. Once "anti-capitalist" options have been put aside, how is it that one policy comes to be preferred over another? What is the source of the range of options that exist within capitalism? Structuralists tell us that the state is capitalist but their formulations are of limited use when analyzing the actual exercise of power. The goal of protecting the "social relations of capitalism" remains at a fairly high level of abstraction. The concept of policy currents helps us to examine the political and historical roots of the policies that are chosen, as well as to understand the fate of policies that potentially threaten the stability of capitalism.

A structuralist approach is, on the other hand, implied in the concept of policy currents in a certain sense. Policy currents are institutionalized; a current is more than the powerful individuals who represent and articulate it. Individuals and specific interests can come and go without the current itself disappearing. A particular current may lose influence but later gain advocates. Policy currents are located in oppositional forces and historical lessons, not individual preferences. The reemergence of a particular form of opposition, such as a national liberation movement, will reactivate old policy currents. Old arguments about whom to support, how to use aid, or the consequences of defeat will be heard again, and old "historical lessons" will be reapplied. Policies thus become institutionalized into specific bureaucratic structures, interests, perceptions and practices. Outdated policies persist, in part due to the influence of specific interests, but more basically because of the inherently ambiguous project of "reading history" and drawing the appropriate lessons. Supporters of policy currents now held to be "wrong" can often muster arguments with sufficient plausibility that their permanent rejection from debate is difficult to obtain. Policy currents recur; they are a comparatively permanent part of the political landscape.

Conclusion

A brief summary is in order. We started with a perspective which focuses on control of the state by the capitalist class, achieved through consensus-reaching groups, direct participation in government of representatives of capital, and an all-pervasive business-defined ideology which leads state managers to define the national interest in terms consistent with the interests of the capitalist class. According to the "relative autonomy" view which we examined next, the capitalist state plays a more active role. Given the divisions within the capitalist class, the state is forced to take primary responsibility for general political and economic coordination, for defusing or repressing class struggle, and for maintaining social cohesion through ideological forms of control. According to this view, the state is neither subjected to the direct control nor motivated exclusively by the short-term interests of the capitalist class. But it is still a capitalist state: key agencies are controlled by fractions of the capitalist class organized into a hegemonic bloc, the confidence of the capitalist class must be retained, the state channels class struggle into forms that rationalize capitalism, anti-capitalist structural filters operate, as do imperatives springing from the social relations of capitalism. By implication, then, the state acts as the "ideal collective

Chart 2.1
A. Origins of Policy Currents

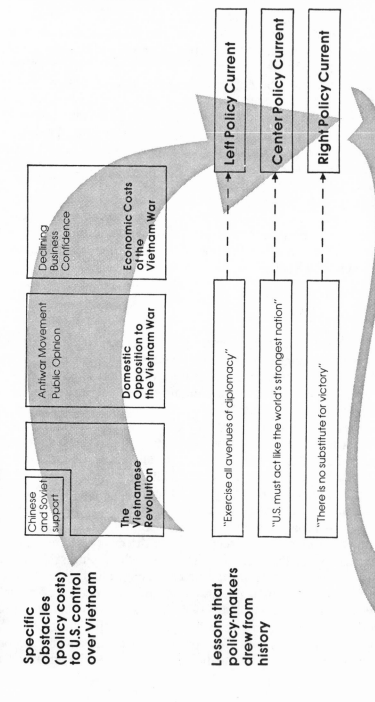

Specific obstacles (policy costs) to U.S. control over Vietnam

Chinese and Soviet support

Antiwar Movement Public Opinion

Declining Business Confidence

The Vietnamese Revolution

Domestic Opposition to the Vietnam War

Economic Costs of the Vietnam War

Left Policy Current

Center Policy Current

Right Policy Current

Lessons that policy-makers drew from history

"Exercise all avenues of diplomacy"

"U.S. must act like the world's strongest nation"

"There is no substitute for victory"

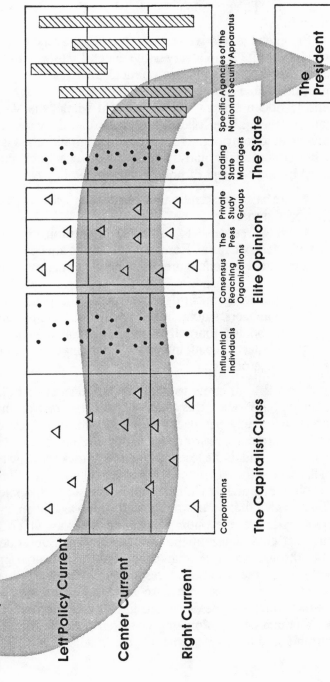

B. Composition of Policy Currents

Left Policy Current

Center Current

Right Current

Corporations

Influential Individuals

The Capitalist Class

Consensus Reaching Organizations

The Press

Private Study Groups

Elite Opinion

Leading State Managers

Specific Agencies of the National Security Apparatus

The State

The President

capitalist." The state takes over where the capitalist class cannot function.

But even the relative autonomy concept overstates the degree to which the state simply serves the general interests of the capitalist class. Because of intraclass political divisions and because of the insurmountable difficulties of melding contradictory elements of a tension-ridden system into a coherent whole, the state can never constitute a final consolidation of class rule. Even the concept of the relative autonomy of the state from the capitalist class is too abstract to be very useful for analysis of actual politics. Such analysis can be aided by the concept of policy currents. Policy currents:

- are basic prescriptions governing the role of the U.S. in the world arena;
- are a response to forces of opposition on the part of defenders of capital. Forces of opposition are both foreign and domestic. Responses are often justified in terms of historical lessons;
- are ideological bridges between the capitalist class and state managers, (including, as well, officials of private policy-making bodies, journalists and influential academics);
- embrace special interests which influence but do not determine policy.

Chart 2.1 attempts to capture the concept of policy currents graphically. A look at this chart will help readers to orient themselves in the theoretical perspective that is used in the rest of the book. Policy currents are rooted in specific obstacles, or forces of opposition, and in the lessons that policy-makers draw from history. In the case of the Vietnam War the obstacles include the Vietnamese Revolution, aided by Chinese and Soviet support; domestic opposition of which there are two types, the antiwar movement and public opinion; and the economic costs of the war which undermined business confidence in the Administration. Subsequent chapters (four through six) will detail each of these forces of opposition and will outline the alternative responses favored by different policy currents. These responses are also based on specific historical lessons which will be discussed in the next chapter.

Vietnam decision-making was characterized by three different currents which, for convenience, are labelled "left," "center," and "right." Taken in their entirety, of course, the range of these views, the arc of the spectrum, is biased towards the right. Unilateral withdrawal, for example, was never considered seriously. Nonetheless, the differences among the three positions remains significant. These policy currents can be traced within the capitalist class, elite opinion, and among the state managers. Despite a predilection to favor a particular current, the actual decisions of the president, for reasons which will be outlined later, shift between different currents, especially during periods of crisis. Specific state agencies do not "belong" to one or another current; during the Vietnam War policy disagreements occurred both between and within agencies of the national security apparatus, especially the Pentagon. Hence the chart shows the president standing "outside" policy currents. Specific interests within the capitalist class can also be located but, as argued above, policy currents are not determined by these interests.

Chapter One discussed five different interpretations of U.S. intervention in Vietnam. This chapter has focused on the organization of power and class influence in capitalist society and introduced the concept of policy currents. That concept helps us to explore significant political differences that develop within the capitalist class and the state. The next chapter applies the concept of policy currents to the actual history of U.S. intervention in Vietnam from 1943 to 1967.

III: POLICY CURRENTS AND THE U.S. IN VIETNAM: 1943-1967

The end of World War II left the United States as the dominant world power. The German, Italian, and Japanese regimes had collapsed. The British, French, and Dutch colonial systems were severely weakened. The United States was the only world power to emerge stronger, its economy revitalized by the demand for armaments, and its productive apparatus expanded and developed by huge scientific and technological advances. In the world arena the United States monopolized nuclear weaponry. And the Bretton Woods Conference established the dollar, like gold in an earlier era, as the international standard of value. With this power came a new responsibility for the organization and overall direction of the global system of capitalism.

In attempting to manage that global system U.S. policy-makers focused on economic priorities: new markets for exports, raw materials, cheap labor, and more profitable investment of capital. In addition, as Nguyen Khac Vien, the editor of *Vietnamese Studies*, has pointed out, U.S. policy emphasized "world counter-revolution," or leadership in the attempt by the capitalist nations to contain the spread of socialism.[1] According to the Vietnamese scholar, under certain conditions the priority of "colonial exploitation" (that is, the extraction of raw material, utilization of cheap labor, etc.) could be subordinated to the worldwide priority of counter-revolution. Despite the importance of new markets, raw material, cheap labor, investment, and controlling areas of future growth in the elaboration of U.S. policy in general, Washington's involvement in Vietnam was characterized by comparatively minimal economic exploitation and by the importance of an ever more expensive policy of counter-revolution. Corporate investment was negligible, although some state managers did measure the economic importance of Vietnam within the context of the entire Pacific Rim.[2] Many references to raw materials, particularly during the nineteen-fifties, can be found in the *Pentagon Papers*, the official Department of Defense study of U.S. decision-making in Vietnam. But this stress reflects the sweeping geopolitical thinking of the Eisenhower Administration as applied to Indochina. Raw materials as such did not serve as a "pull" on foreign policy: tin, tungsten, and rubber were simply government enticements to line up business behind the counter-revolutionary commitment in Southeast Asia. The state pulled the capitalist class along.

In the nineteen-sixties, the war rhetoric of the Kennedy and Johnson Administrations sought to display in Vietnam a model of "enlightened foreign policy." The myth asserted that the United States would "build a nation" and undertake a "Third World New Deal." But most of the capitalist class saw no direct profit for itself in all this and the state was compelled to shoulder the burden alone. Elaborate plans for economic development, such as Eugene Black's Mekong River project, were drawn up, but private capital failed to implement them. In desperation, the CIA even secretly funneled capital to the Japanese as an inducement to invest in Vietnam.[3] Oil was discovered off the coast, but only *after* a major and costly commitment had been made. Toward the end of the war, the inadequate growth of the South Vietnamese economy and the failure of U.S. firms to play a leading role forced Washington to turn to the World Bank as a means of bolstering the Saigon regime.[4] Even in April 1975, as the United States was booted out of Vietnam, direct investment still totaled less than thirty million dollars—roughly the amount needed to build one moderate-sized skyscraper in an American city.[5]

So the Vietnam War entailed costs. U.S. intervention met strong resistance, first by the Vietnamese themselves, and later by the majority of citizens at home. No significant economic considerations were at stake—at least immediately. And the war, unlike most other wars, did not help the U.S. economy. These costs were mostly carried by the Vietnamese and American people. But the capitalist class paid as well, albeit in dollars rather than lives. These features of U.S. intervention help to explain why policy-makers, even while generally agreeing on the importance of combatting socialism, disagreed over many of the specific issues of U.S. involvement. The stakes became more political than economic, counter-revolutionary more than protecting investment; the costs of the military intervention easily outweighed any future economic benefit. And the level of conflict among state managers seeking to manage capitalism increased as a result.

This chapter has two goals: The first is to simply introduce or remind the reader of the history of U.S. intervention in Vietnam. That history reflects a broad consensus among state managers concerning the goals of U.S. policy. These goals included containing the spread of socialism, maintaining an "open door" that preserved the "right" of capitalist investment to expand into other nations and organize its productive activities, and the political and regional organization of other states in a manner that benefits the U.S. These general goals led to a set of specific objectives in Vietnam: the imposition of a client regime in Saigon, the defeat of the National Liberation Front as a test case against wars of national liberation, and the eventual integration of Vietnam into the world capitalist system.

The effort to achieve these goals confronted several obstacles and these obstacles produced severe policy costs. The obstacles included: the strength of the Vietnamese revolution and its capacity to resist the U.S. and its client regimes in Saigon; military aid and economic assistance from the USSR and China; opposition forces within the U.S.; and the economic reverberations of military intervention in Vietnam throughout the international and domestic economy. At first U.S. policy "only" had to grapple with the Vietnamese. That is a big "only" for in purely national terms the Vietnamese revolution won state power in 1945. At first the French, and then U.S., prevented a program of socialist reconstruction by military force alone. In the meantime the strength of other obstacles grew. By 1968 domestic opposition and the economic costs of the Vietnam War assumed major proportions. The focusing of these varied forces of opposition into specific policy costs, in combination with the state managers' own proclivities to favor different strategies, led to conflict among different policy currents.

The second goal of this chapter is to trace the history of internal disagreement among the state managers within the overall context of the counter-revolutionary consensus. Two stories are being told: one a pattern of continuity behind U.S. intervention, taken by the U.S. to secure the stability of world capitalism; the other a pattern of conflict among the state managers over how to accomplish that goal.

The analytic history that follows is divided into different stages. Each stage contains a theme of policy consensus: countering socialist revolution. The specifics of each historical stage contains an important subtheme: that of differences among the state managers. By focusing on the interplay among different policy currents this chapter attempts to treat both aspects of decision-making in Vietnam.

Stage One, 1943-1947: Multilateralism versus Containment

Even in the midst of World War II, Washington policy-makers understood and grappled with the problem of building a postwar order that would avoid another Great Depression and combat the spread of socialism.[6] One answer, preferred by members of the multilateral policy current, was expanding exports. Free trade would provide a stimulus to the American economy. Trade would be unencumbered by the parochialism of colonial trading blocs. Multilateralism presented itself with anticolonial rhetoric aimed at eliminating bilateral trading agreements, special access rights, and the other privileges of colonial systems based on direct administration by the colonizing nation. The new policy called for a universal "open door," since under conditions of equal competition, the vast economic strength of the U.S. would surely predominate. For Vietnam, the implication of this current would be U.S. support for political independence following World War II with no special privileges or considerations for French economic interests. Roosevelt was inclined in this direction although, as a President who tolerated and even encouraged considerable debate within his Administration, his decisions were not consistently multilateral. In 1943 President Roosevelt backed a policy of United Nations trusteeship for the French colonies of Indochina. To encourage anti-Japanese resistance and to build a political force against the return of the French, the Office of Strategic Services (the wartime predecessor of the Central Intelligence Agency) maintained a liaison with the Vietminh, the Vietnamese revolutionary movement, and parachuted limited supplies into the liberated mountain areas of northern Vietnam.[7] The U.S. was not the only country to dabble with self-interested opposition to French colonialism. Chinese warlords, who had captured Ho Chi Minh during the war, released the Vietnamese leader hoping, like Washington, to inspire anticolonial resistance and create a power vacuum that could be used to their own benefit.

Developing alongside the multilateral policy current, and growing stronger as the war came to an end, was the containment policy current. The advocates of this position subordinated immediate economic expansion into Asia, Africa, and Latin America to a strategic consideration: they wished to form a United States— Western Europe alliance to isolate the Soviet Union. Both currents recognized the importance of overseas economic expansion to the health of the American economy; both were opposed to the spread of socialism. But the containment advocates called for a much more militaristic posture towards the Soviet Union while the multilateral current wanted to co-opt the Soviet Union with economic measures, including aid. By the end of 1945 the containment approach gained the ascendant position, where it has remained ever since. American policy at Yalta and Potsdam contained a mixture of both currents; yet it was decidedly more multilateral at Yalta, and at Posdam emphatically more containment.

The multilateral current continued to exercise some influence until the end of the nineteen-forties. The success of the Chinese Revolution in 1949 and the outbreak of the Korean War in 1950 created a more controlled political atmosphere within the national security apparatus. As a result, significant policy debate among the top state managers virtually ended. The multilateral current re-emerged among the state managers during the Kennedy Administration.[8]

The multilateral current and its vision of a single world unified by international trade floundered on one particularly imposing reef: the absence of foreign economies healthy enough to absorb American exports. It became increasingly clear that political stability on American terms could not be secured by economic measures alone. A more direct role for the state, and a policy that elevated political and military priorities, was necessary. Meanwhile, the U.S. occupied Japan and South Korea and built military bases in other countries with borders on the Soviet Union. In Iran the U.S. began to replace the British and attempted to eliminate Soviet influence and undermine popular forces. In each case individuals representing the multilateral position argued the effectiveness of more subtle forms of control, especially through economic ties and political reform, but were defeated by representatives of the containment position. Even Roosevelt was forced, before his death, to compromise his goal of international trusteeship for Indochina. Some of the pressure came from his allies. DeGaulle promised to improve conditions in the region if the French were granted special access, and Churchill feared the repercussions on the British Empire of American support for trusteeship. At home, the Navy and War Departments were concerned that the multilateral principle would jeopardize their desire to claim several Japanese islands for U.S. security purposes.[9] And the State Department straddled the fence with the European desk favoring a French return to Indochina and the Southeast Asia desk favoring its eventual independence. Secretary of State Cordell Hull reflected this ambivalence, arguing that "if France were prepared to restore her own popular institutions and to deal properly with the colonies, I favor the return of Indo-China, with France's pledge of eventual independence as soon as the colony became prepared for it, along the lines of our pledge to the Philippines."[10] By restricting aid to French troops in the area and refusing to transport additional forces, Roosevelt attempted to follow a *de facto* multilateral policy. But his formal policy statements took a more ambivalent tone. FDR told one advisor that "if we can get the proper pledge from France to assume for herself the obligation of a trustee, then I would agree to France retaining these colonies with the proviso that independence was the ultimate goal."[11] Roosevelt's death and Truman's rise to the presidency only accelerated the swing towards containment.

Facing a Congress with isolationist tendencies and a public that continued to see the Soviet Union as an "ally," the Truman Administration began a campaign of anticommunism and anti-Sovietism in order to mobilize support behind its program of restoring capitalism to Europe through the Marshall Plan.[12] Washington dispensed economic aid with the primary intention of weakening the European left and only secondarily of stimulating American exports. Rightwing regimes in Turkey and Greece were bolstered by military aid supplied under the Truman Doctrine. McCarthyism helped galvanize a reluctant public to support this effort. In 1949 the Soviet Union successfully tested an atomic bomb. This development would have far-reaching repercussions for national liberation movements, which could now move under a protective umbrella. For the moment, Washington merely used the event, and the "loss of China" occurring in the same year, to propagandize further for additional aid to meet the "Communist threat."

In the immediate postwar period Southeast Asia was placed on Washington's backburner, leading some analysts to conclude that the United States had "no" policy for the region. The Vietminh took advantage of the temporary power vacuum following Japan's surrender to liberate the entire country. Ho led a triumphant march, which was accompanied by a few OSS officers, into Hanoi in August 1945 and established the Democratic Republic of Vietnam on September 2. Ho wrote several letters to Washington expressing his desire for peaceful relations. The Communist Party was formally disbanded and parts of the new constitution were modeled after the American Declaration of Independence.[13] But the immediate future of Southeast Asia was being decided in Europe and the United States. The prevailing containment current wanted political stability in France and an end to French opposition to a more active role for Germany in Europe. Its tacticians saw that to achieve these aims the U.S. would have to support the French effort to retake their former colonies in Indochina—despite Washington's anticolonial rhetoric. The multilateral current would have preferred to make political independence for former colonies a consistent principle. It would not be the last time that U.S. policy-makers disagreed over the applicability of global priorities to Vietnam itself.

Stage Two, 1947-1954: Support for the French

A note from the American Ambassador in Paris to Premier Ramadier, delivered in early 1947, expressed Washington's commitment to restore France's position in Indochina:

> In spite of any misunderstanding which might have arisen in minds French in regard to our position concerning Indochina they must appreciate that we have fully recognized France's sovereign position in that area and we do not wish to have it appear that we are in any way endeavoring to undermine that position, and French should know it is our desire to be helpful and we stand ready to assist any

appropriate way we can to find a solution for Indochinese problem. At same time we cannot shut our eyes to fact that there are two sides this problem and our reports indicate both a lack of French understanding of the other side (more in Saigon than in Paris) and continued existence dangerously outmoded colonial outlook and methods in area. Furthermore, there is no escape from fact that trend of times is to effect that colonial empires in XIX century sense are rapidly becoming thing of the past. Action Brit in India and Burma and Dutch in Indonesia are outstanding examples of this trend, and French themselves took cognizance of it both in new Constitution and in their agreements with Vietnam. On other hand we do not lose sight fact that Ho Chi Minh has direct Communist connections and it should be obvious that we are not interested in seeing colonial empire administration supplanted by philosophy and political organizations emanating from and controlled by Kremlin.[14]

The United States decided to support the French for two important reasons. The first concerned France's role in a revitalized Europe. French participation in the formation of the European Defense Community (later NATO) was greatly desired, but had been made contingent on Washington's willingness to underwrite the French effort in Vietnam.[15] The United States wanted to conserve the strength of the French army and avoid any undue drain on the French economy. Washington hedged its support for the French by supplying aid through the neocolonial regime of Bao Dai, rather than directly to Paris, and by establishing a military advisory mission in July 1950 that increasingly took charge of the war against the Vietminh. As France regained its economic strength, Washington hoped to reimpose the "anticolonial" stance as a method of "opening the door" for future direct American participation in Southeast Asia. But as the Cold War hardened, Washington became increasingly reluctant to push Paris to modify its essentially colonial stance.

The U.S. also backed the French as part of its global commitment to counter-revolution. The Cold War dictated that every nation choose sides between Washington and Moscow. Third World countries that attempted to follow a neutral course were increasingly viewed as a Soviet instrument. Despite a lack of evidence, Washington continued to perceive the anti-French struggle as something inspired and directed from the Soviet Union. For example, in the cable to Premier Ramadier cited above, the American ambassador steadfastly (and falsely) maintained that the Vietminh was a movement whose "philosophy and political organization emanated from and was controlled by the Kremlin."[16] Yet American intelligence had tried, and failed, to substantiate the existence of controlling ties between Moscow and Ho Chi Minh. A State Department cable to the U.S. Ambassador in China read "the department has no evidence of [a] direct link between Ho and Moscow but assumes it exists..."[17] Thus the Vietnam conflict was seen in Washington as a test case where the West had to stop the spread of "Moscow controlled and directed communist aggression." The multilateral current would have been more likely to appreciate the indigenous roots of the Vietnam resistance. By 1947, however, advocates of this position were without significant influence.

Another policy current, this one seeking actually to "rollback" Communism, also operated within U.S. foreign policy, especially in the Pacific. The advocates of containment wanted to halt the spread of socialism and to isolate the Soviet Union and China through a combination of economic, political and military measures. Members of the multilateral current wanted to excise the revolutionary fervor from socialism by offering participation in a capitalist-dominated world economy. Supporters of rollback wanted to physically "liberate" those countries which had "fallen" to socialism. Pacific-oriented, with strong roots in the Republican Party, some sections of the capitalist class and the Navy, the representatives of rollback established close connections with rightwing leaders such as Chiang Kai-shek and Syngman Rhee.[18] The Korean War in 1950-53 illustrated the conflict between the containment and rollback policy currents. Truman, representing the dominant containment position, wanted to halt the spread of socialism at the 38th parallel. The field commander, General Douglas MacArthur, wanted to use the Korean War as a method of engaging the Chinese directly and rolling back the "Peiping regime." Truman desired containment but did not want war with China or the Soviet Union.

Policy currents emerge from the obstacles to U.S. control, the costs that particular policies engender, and from the lessons that different state managers draw from the history of foreign policy. The containment current accepted the support of China and the Soviet Union in Korea as an effective policy constraint; the supporters of rollback did not. This pattern would be repeated in Vietnam.

The Korean War helped to reinforce anticommunism and rationalize a much larger defense budget.[19] After the immediate post-World War II boom subsided, the American economy had shown signs of tailing off towards a recession or even another depression. Deepseated resistance to government spending in both Congress and the majority of the business community plagued Truman's efforts to stabilize the economy. The economic impact of the Korean War taught business leaders to appreciate the stimulating impact of military spending. A harbinger of Johnson's Vietnam policy, Truman's method of fighting the Korean War, a stalemated ground war with high casualties, entailed severe political costs at home. Mac-Arthur, on the other hand, wanted to use nuclear weapons. As the prospect of full scale war with China loomed, Truman decided to fire MacArthur.[20] But the President's policy became steadily more unpopular with the American people. In another preview of 1968, Democratic candidate Adlai Stevenson lost the 1952 election to Dwight Eisenhower who ran as a "peace candidate." Meanwhile MacArthur returned to the U.S. and was able to draw enthusiastic support. Some state managers drew a specific historical lesson from these events: never commit American troops in an Asian ground war unless you're willing to use nuclear weapons. Those holding to this lesson became known as the "never-again school" and later argued in Vietnam that the U.S. should place less emphasis on ground troops and take the wraps off its air power.[21] Advocates of this position combined a racist view of the effectiveness of American G.I.'s ("we fight well but get chewed up by hordes of Asians who care little about dying") with a determination to "strike at the source of aggression," that is, to escalate bombing even to the point of risking direct confrontation with China or the Soviet Union. MacArthur announced another lesson that would be followed by rightwing forces in Vietnam: that there is no substitute for victory.

Secretary of State Dean Acheson expressed a different perspective. A representative of the containment current, Acheson told Anthony Eden that "it would be disastrous to the position of the Western powers if Southeast Asia were lost without a struggle," but that "on the other hand, the Americans were determined to do nothing in that area which would provoke a third world war."[22] For members of the containment current the struggle itself, the continued commitment and desire to fight was almost as important as the outcome. Rollback was founded on the premise that if you fight you might as well use everything you have and try to win. Those in the multilateral current preferred diplomacy and inclusion in the world community to transform socialism so that it became safe for capitalist trade and investment—thus deferring the need to fight at all.

The Korean War also hardened the American commitment in Vietnam. By 1954, American aid reached three and a half billion dollars, roughly three-quarters of the French expenditure. Despite this aid, or perhaps because of it, Washington had little control over actual French operations in Indochina.[23] Nonetheless the French suffered a decisive defeat at Dien Bien Phu on May 8, just as the Geneva Conference opened. The French had flown into a remote mountain valley hoping to establish a base camp from which they could send out "search-and-destroy" missions against the Vietminh. But they themselves were hopelessly trapped instead. Washington considered direct intervention at the time, but some sections of the armed forces (led by Army Chief of Staff General Matthew Ridgway) scotched a recommendation for a ground invasion and the British failed to provide additional support.[24] Admiral Arthur Radford, Chairman of the Joint Chiefs of Staff and a supporter of rollback, proposed a massive airstrike against the Vietminh, hoping to provoke a military reaction from Peking and a war between China and the U.S.[25] Secretary of State Dulles offered French Foreign Minister George Bidault two atomic bombs for the defense of Dien Bien Phu, but the British and French refused to go along, and consequently so did Eisenhower. The plan's rejection reflected the strength of the Vietnamese, the nuclear capacity of the Soviet Union, and worldwide horror of any further use of atomic bombs.[26] On July 20, 1954, the French settled with the Vietnamese at Geneva, on terms Washington considered a "disaster" despite evidence that the Vietminh gained less than their superior battlefield position warranted.[27]

Stage Three, 1954-1960: Containment

The consolidation of the Geneva Conference is of central importance. The signatories recognized the integrity, sovereignty, and territorial unity of Vietnam; ordered the withdrawal of French troops; prohibited the introduction of other foreign troops and military personnel; banned the construction of military bases; established an International Control Commission to oversee the cease-fire; and finally provided for free national elections under secret balloting within two years. The U.S. did not sign the final agreement, but issued a statement affirming its basic principles and pledging to "refrain from the threat or the use of force to disturb the agreement."[28] Yet Eisenhower told the press that the U.S. did not feel "bound by the accords," and a month later Washington established a Southeast Asia military bloc (SEATO) to provide formal cover for further American intervention in Indochina.

During the mid-fifties, members of the containment current, now dominating Washington decision-making, favored two additional methods for preserving global control. Each was applied in Vietnam. The first, covert interference in the internal affairs of other nations, had been used previously, particularly in Italy during the 1948 elections. But covert interference was now being used with new vengeance. The CIA overthrew Mossadegh in Iran in 1953; Arbenz in Guatemala in 1954. The CIA sponsored covert raids against the Chinese mainland from Taiwan. And in Vietnam, by June 1954, before the Geneva Accords were signed, the CIA's Colonel Edward Lansdale moved his team of agents for "paramilitary operations" and "political-psychological" warfare from Saigon to the North. Lansdale's team busied itself printing and distributing leaflets containing false information, sabotaging railroad lines, and pouring sand in the oil supply of Hanoi's buses. Eventually the CIA's role in Vietnam ranged from training teams to engage in covert operations against the North to political assassination in the South.

The CIA also participated in the selection of Ngo Dinh Diem, a former official in the Bao Dai government, as the new leader in the South. Diem had managed to avoid too close an identification with the French by entering the United States and staying there until early 1954. To the consternation of the French, the U.S., with the aid of the Catholic Church and the China lobby, installed Diem as the new

Premier of the South in June 1954. While Walt Rostow later claimed that "Ho Chi Minh couldn't be elected dog-catcher," others were more realistic. Speaking on the Senate floor in April 1953, then Senator John F. Kennedy argued that "Despite any wishful thinking to the contrary, it should be apparent that the popularity and prevalence of Ho Chi Minh and his following throughout Indochina would cause either partition or a coalition government to result in eventual domination by the communists."[29] Eisenhower later noted that it "was generally conceded that had an election been held, Ho Chi Minh would have been elected Premier."[30] In his memoirs, the President said he had "never talked or corresponded with a person knowledgeable in Indochinese affairs who did not agree that had an election been held at the time of the fighting (1954), possibly 80 percent of the population would have voted for the Communist Ho Chi Minh as their leader rather than Chief of State Bao Dai."[31] When it became apparent that Ho would receive an overwhelming majority Washington backed Diem's refusal to hold the 1956 elections called for by the Geneva Accords. Instead, in violation of the Geneva Agreements, 350 men were added to the U.S. Military Advisory Command. Over half a billion dollars bolstered the covert support for an increasingly repressive and dictatorial Diem regime. By 1959, the amount of military aid alone to the Diem regime reached 1.17 billion.[32]

The containment current also relied on nuclear weapons as political blackmail. The Eisenhower Administration was concerned that too large a defense budget would produce inflationary pressures in the U.S. economy. This conservative economic thinking led to a reliance—an over-reliance some would later say—on the threatened use of very powerful nuclear weapons to control world politics. From 1945 to 1949 the U.S. enjoyed a nuclear monopoly. The doctrine covering the use of these weapons was called "massive retaliation." If a major war with the Soviet Union broke out, nuclear weapons would be used immediately and extensively. But then the Soviet Union acquired nuclear weapons and an atomic war could now cost the U.S. dearly. The purpose of nuclear weapons was no longer "victory" but "deterrence"—at least for the containment current.[33] Washington felt that stockpiling to the point of overkill would not only deter the Soviet Union from war with the U.S. and Western Europe, but would limit Moscow's political thrusts in Africa, the

Middle East and Asia. The Soviet Union would avoid direct nuclear confrontation *and* be less likely to counter U.S. deployment of conventional military strength. Accordingly, there would be no nuclear war, no land war in Europe, and, in the key point for Vietnam, little chance of Soviet response to American intervention in the Third World. Other state managers, particularly those in the rollback current thought that the U.S. should aim for a "first-strike" capability—the ability to launch an attack with enough severity to eliminate virtually all missiles and bombers, and thus avoid "unacceptable damage" from Soviet retaliatory forces. A bureaucratic dimension entered this policy conflict as well. An increasing proportion of the military budget was allocated to nuclear forces, primarily under the aegis of the Air Force; the other services, especially the Army, were hurt by the stress on atomic weaponry.

As an attempt to control political developments in the Third World, the strategy of nuclear deterrence was a failure. During the Quemoy and Matsu crises, the rollback advocates wanted permission to attack the Chinese mainland. The containment supporters wanted to avoid nuclear war but found themselves with inadequate military capability for "limited war"—that is warfare in which strategic nuclear weapons would not be used. Deterrence did not prevent the Cuban Revolution either, and the Batista regime was overthrown in 1959. Some defense intellectuals and high military officers, particularly Army Chief of Staff Maxwell Taylor, began to reassert the need for military programs that would permit the U.S. to fight conventional wars. This group complained that the U.S. had few military options between all-out nuclear war and "surrender." The critique claimed that the U.S. did not have sufficient nonnuclear military capacity.[34] Members of the containment current wanted greater flexibility, a larger range of military options. Among the most alarming was the emergence of scenarios involving nuclear weapons that asserted that the use of these weapons need not culminate in unacceptable damage.[35]

By the end of the fifties American power became weaker on several fronts. The economy grew sluggish and the balance of payments slid into permanent deficit. The Soviet Sputnik dramatized the end of American scientific and military predominance. Khrushchev visited the U.S., symbolizing the first stage of what later came to be called "detente." The containment current recognized the necessity of "coexistence" with the Soviet Union, a political development always resisted by the supporters of rollback. At the same time, general interest in the domino theory, in tactical nuclear weapons, and conventional military capability all reflected the need to stabilize the underdeveloped world. Vietnam became a testing ground for new methods of countering revolutionary movements. The need was great for in 1960, in response to the abolition of village elections, population relocation, and still greater efforts to control political life, the anti-Diem insurgency in the South became organized under the National Liberation Front.

Stage Four, 1960-1964: Counterinsurgency

The Kennedy Administration introduced new dedication and structure to the U.S. commitment to counter-revolution. Kennedy was particularly concerned with developing a strategy for combatting movements for national liberation. Military strategy was shifted from sole reliance on nuclear weapons for deterrence to "flexible response." Flexible response combined continued nuclear strength with renewed capacity to fight limited wars and conduct counterinsurgency operations. It became the new strategy to secure the containment current. Under the leadership of Secretary of Defense Robert McNamara the military budget was expanded. The U.S. had to be prepared to fight "two and a half wars:" major wars in Europe and Asia and half a war elsewhere. Vietnam, in this thinking, was only "half a war." Kennedy created the Special Forces, designed for counterinsurgency. The Air Force and Navy were ordered to develop logistic capabilities for sending the Army and Marines to every corner of the world on short notice. And as the Cuban missile crisis showed, Kennedy did not shy away from the arena of nuclear confrontation with the Soviet Union.

Members of the rollback current, such as General Curtis LeMay of the Air Force, opposed these changes in military posture, notably the establishment of the Special Forces. They argued that movements for national liberation were little more than conspiracies controlled by Moscow and "Peiping." They felt that the United States should strike at the "source of aggression" in the Soviet Union and China rather than be dragged into limited wars elsewhere. For the dominant containment current, however, flexible response was a strategy aimed at countering the growing strength of revolutionary movements while avoiding nuclear confrontation with Moscow.

Kennedy's first crucial decision in Indochina came in 1961. At that time Laos, not Vietnam, was the focal point. The new President had just experienced the failure of the Bay of Pigs invasion and a number of danger signs were looming in Berlin. In a pattern typical of the postwar period, the general atmosphere of crisis was used to implement a change in policy. When the Laotian crisis erupted in late April, the Joint Chiefs alerted the Commander of the Pacific Fleet, Admiral Harry Felt, an advocate of the rollback current, "to be prepared to undertake air strikes against North Vietnam and possibly southern China."[36] Washington temporarily accepted a neutralist solution in Laos but resolved to make a firm stand elsewhere. A Pentagon task force meeting recommended that 3,600 men be sent to Vietnam and additional troops alerted for duty in Laos. Kennedy realized that the Diem regime was unstable (as demonstrated by the abortive coup in the summer of 1960). A national intelligence estimate also told him that more than half of the entire rural region south and southwest of Saigon was under strong Communist influence. Some of these areas were closed to any government authority that was not backed by substantial armed force. The report also noted that the NLF had encircled Saigon and was beginning to move closer to the city.[37] Under these circumstances, and pushed by the crisis, Kennedy responded with 400 Special Forces troops and 100 "advisors." At that time the American military mission in Saigon had a 685-man limit. Those in the containment current attached great importance to "commitment" and "meeting international responsibilities." Hence the new troops signaled a deeper involvement than the actual numbers indicate. Kennedy also ordered renewed clandestine warfare against the North under the direction of the CIA. Later in the year General Maxwell Taylor and Walt Rostow visited South Vietnam. Impressed with the strength of the NLF, they urged Kennedy to commit six to eight thousand American ground troops. Taylor warned that "greater troop commitments were likely in the future." Kennedy feared a hostile response at home and adopted Taylor's recommendation that the troops be deployed under the guise of flood control efforts.[38]

From seven hundred Americans in Vietnam when he assumed office, Kennedy deepened U.S. involvement to 3,200 by the end of his first year, and then more than tripled that figure to 11,300 by the end of 1962. U.S. soldiers started getting killed with regularity. American pilots flew combat missions against the NLF.[39] These commitments, less than the level recommended by some as necessary to achieve victory, were undertaken against the background of greater NLF success. Kennedy knew that the immediate chances of victory were slim but that deeper involvement was necessary to stave off defeat. As always the containment current calculated the impact of these decisions in global terms. "The U.S. should commit itself to the clear objective of preventing the loss of South Vietnam to Communism," read one critical position paper, and "the loss of South Vietnam...would not only destroy SEATO but would undermine the credibility of American commitments elsewhere."[40]

By mid-1963 Kennedy faced a major dilemma: the American program of forcing political, social and administrative reform on the Diem regime had failed. While Kennedy's "New Deal" reformers in Vietnam talked of winning the hearts and minds of the peasants, aid to the Saigon government really benefitted the landlords, provided additional spoils for the corrupt system to divide, and helped establish a political base for Diem. As actually carried out, administrative reform only strengthened the repressive apparatus of Diem's regime. Paradoxically, the more aid Washington delivered to Diem the less leverage it was able to exert.[41] An evaluation by Maxwell Taylor later illustrated Washington's awareness of the strength of the NLF. The report said in part that "the ability of the Viet Cong to continuously rebuild their units is one of the mysteries of this guerilla war... Not only do the Viet Cong units have the recuperative powers of the phoenix, but they have an amazing ability to maintain morale."[42]

The strength of the NLF and the failure of halfhearted reform to consolidate the Diem regime revived the multilateral policy current. When revolutionary movements are strong some state managers argue that genuine reform is necessary and that the U.S. cannot afford to be associated with elites opposing needed social change. In this case the State Department, save for Secretary Rusk, and some CIA officials, became increasingly frustrated with Diem and broached the idea of a coup. Washington should make it clear, they argued, that more aid and greater military involvement was contingent on successful reform in the South. On the other hand, the containment current located in the Defense Department and the highest ranks of the CIA, advocated more military effort while going easy on Diem. His removal, they argued, carried the danger of a complete collapse of the Saigon regime, leaving only the NLF to fill the vacuum. The first set of officials, the multilateral current, included Roger Hilsman, Director of the State Department Bureau of Intelligence and Research, and Michael Forrestal, National Security Council staffer for Far Eastern Affairs. Their stress on reform was coupled with resistance to large-scale military operations, which they considered inappropriate for the nature of the struggle in Vietnam. This group also advocated *more* paramilitary forces, like the Special Forces. The multilateral current did *not* support withdrawal. The other set of officials pushed for more forces, but of a conventional order. In a pattern typical of decision-making in a crisis, Kennedy vacillated between the two sides, receiving contradictory intelligence assessments from each. In one instance, conflicting reports from a team visit by representatives of the State (multilateral) and Defense (containment) Departments led Kennedy to comment sarcastically: "You two visited the same country, didn't you?" While seemingly supportive of the quagmire focus on bureaucratically inspired confusion, these conflicts were primarily motivated by different choices for the most effective anticommunist course of action. The U.S. Embassy in Saigon began to encourage a cabal of generals led by Duong Van Minh (Big Minh), who assassinated Diem on November 1, 1963—twenty-one days before Kennedy's own life was ended in Dallas.[43] Minh's hints at neutralism were quickly ended by yet another coup led by General Kanh. A series of "mini-" and abortive coups gradually increased the power of the younger officers such as General Ky, who finally seized power in 1965.

In the meantime, covert operations against the North were expanded in late-1963. These were of three types, each provocative. Low-level reconnaissance flights with armed escorts were begun over Laos. OPLAN 34A included a variety of sabotage and psychological warfare measures carried out by CIA-trained commandoes; they spread propaganda leaflets and destroyed North Vietnamese facilities. The third measure was DESOTO patrols conducted within four nautical miles of the North Vietnamese coast to acquire visual, electronic and photographic intelligence.[44] In addition, the Seventh Fleet sporadically bombarded the North. Johnson and the leading state managers, all following the containment current, approved these operations in order to placate members of the rollback current. The containment current also wanted to signal Washington's commitment and to threaten the North with the possibility of even greater military force. The provocations of the DESOTO patrols led eventually to the Tonkin Gulf incident. On August 2, 1964, an American destroyer took one direct hit, later found to be a one-inch hole, from North Vietnamese torpedo boats who were operating within their territory. Two days later, the *USS Maddox* and the *USS Turner Joy* nearly shot each other up; in the confusion they called the incident another attack by North Vietnamese forces. Although this attack never occurred (Johnson later said that "For all I know, our Navy was shooting at whales out there"), the incident became a pretext for securing Congressional approval to expand the American role in Vietnam.[45] Washington had been planning to escalate the war for some time: drafts of a Congressional resolution had been prepared months in advance, but public opinion had remained an obstacle.[46] The U.S. had been pursuing an ever-intensifying covert war against the North. Now came the opportunity for additional overt commitment: a phony crisis staged for the benefit of Congress, the American people, and world opinion.[47]

Stage Five, 1964-1968: The Expensive War

From growing policy costs, especially the economic impact of the war, the Vietnamese resistance, and domestic opposition; and, among the state managers, from different perceptions of the proper role for the U.S. in the world arena, three distinct currents on the Vietnam war emerged: The rightwing or "win at any cost" current was rooted in rollback. The center or "stay the current course" current was rooted in containment. The left or "attempt to achieve a low-level stalemate" current was rooted in the multilateral position. These currents are called "right," "center," and "left" for editorial convenience—their shared assumptions and the structural location of the U.S. at the center of the world economy skewed the overall spectrum of these differences towards the Neanderthal. It is crucial to remember that these three policy currents evolve from the forces of opposition and the costs associated with Washington's efforts to control the future of Vietnam. The positions evolve out of specific conditions. They are not just made up by the state managers and debated in a vacuum.

The rest of this chapter details the three positions for the years leading up to the August 1967-March 1968 period that is analyzed in Chapters Seven and Eight. The reader may find it helpful to refer to Chart 3.1.

A. The Right

It is important to note a change of position among the right that occurred during the early-sixties. Declining U.S. power in the world arena had shifted the spectrum of debate among policy currents away from efforts to "liberate" Communist nations. A full rollback position was no longer possible, although a few diehards, like Curtis LeMay, continued to push it. Those formerly holding a rollback position continued to define their interests in Pacific terms; and the Vietnam War was especially crucial. What now distinguishes the right current from the containment or center position was greater willingness to use maximal military pressures against the North, even to the point of risking a confrontation with the Soviet Union and China. The rightwing current was also sustained by a commitment to a classic military definition of victory: forcing the other side to surrender. The right advocated a "systematic program of progressively heavy measures against North Vietnam, to be continued until current objectives were met. Negotiations were to be resisted...although to be entered ultimately, but they were [to be] carried on in conjunction with continued bombing attacks."[48] The goals of this program were to "bomb Hanoi to the conference table" through physical and human destruction, and to continue the bombing until the North capitulated.

The right, or "win at any cost" current, took as its rallying call the slogan "strike at the source of aggression." They thus implied that the Vietnam War could not be won within South Vietnam and that all sanctuaries—Cambodia, Laos, and areas of North Vietnam then off limits to American bombing—should be attacked. Members of the right thought that once Washington was committed, strong military actions should follow. The U.S. should escalate quickly, generally using air power, and destroy North Vietnam's economy and society, not merely its desire to wage war. The right, comparatively insensitive to international policy costs, was willing to risk confrontation with the Soviet Union and China, and argued that the sooner the war ended the lower the political and economic costs at home . Outside of the national security apparatus, the right included business enterprises that stood to profit from a strong U.S. military position in the Pacific, specific firms benefitting from the Vietnam War, and the vestiges of the China lobby.[49]

B. The Center

The containment current, or center, deserves close scrutiny because its logic dominated decision-making in Vietnam. The center placed the war in a global context. The U.S. was fighting to demonstrate that wars of national liberation could be defeated (whereas the right was fighting to defeat "international communism"). Those in the center current were anxious to contain China's influence and demonstrate a willingness to use force. The Cuban missile crisis left many state managers with the impression that a carefully controlled "graduated response," combined with threats of still greater damage, could force a weaker opponent to capitulate. The historical lesson, they argued, was the more Washington conveyed its willingness to use force, the less need there would be to actually use drastic measures in future confrontations. The U.S. had to commit itself in advance to the "defense of a country against communism." Failure to do so would cause allies to doubt American resolve, particularly in Asia where pro-American regimes were often based upon very fragile political foundations.

At the same time the center current feared that the drastic bombing program advocated by the right would invite Chinese intervention. The center did not want a direct clash with Peking, their slogan was "we seek no wider war." They rejected the "full squeeze" in favor of their own strategy of graduated escalation (the "slow squeeze"). And they conceived of bombing of the North in psychological rather than strategic terms. The Rostow thesis exemplified the center's justification for bombing the North:

> Military pressures against the external sources of an insurgency would bring the aggressor to an appreciation of the costs of his interference and he would reduce or eliminate his support for his insurgents. The exercise was primarily psy-

chological not necessarily strategic. The measures should greatly increase his uncertainty about the consequences of continued support of the insurgency.[50]

Here the *threatened* use of the full weight of American military power is supposed to cause an opponent to weigh their chances carefully. The "enemy," in this case Hanoi, chooses to withdraw rather than risk total destruction. The argument differs from both the right, who maintained that the U.S. would have to actually apply full military force, and from the left, who felt that focusing military pressures on the North, either directly, or in some scenario of graduated pressures, detracted from the concentration on political and economic reform needed in the South.

The importance that the center gave to "demonstrating their resolve" can be found in their version of the domino theory. Consider the following statement by William Bundy, Assistant Secretary of State for Far Eastern Affairs:

To me the Asian calculation was very much to the fore...It appeared to me that if we did not go in with ground troops you would see a maximum form of what has been described in short-hand as the domino consequence. That is China did loom very powerful at that period, in the eyes of people in the area...If we didn't act to hold this line, even though we might not be able to, there would be a rapidly unfolding effect that would be irreversible and it would embrace not only the mainland countries but Indonesia and indeed, the whole of...well roughly all...I wouldn't have said the Philippines myself and I certainly wouldn't have said Australia and I wouldn't have said back to Hawaii or some of the more extreme statements that I think General Taylor perhaps used on one or two occasions. But I would have said that mainland Southeast Asia, down to and including Indonesia, would be effectively incorporated in a loose bloc, not an absolutely rigidly controlled thing, but something that would be far more than a sphere of influence of China. It simply appeared as though China had a very strong position, as it were, behind the line that we were trying to defend and this was part of the overall picture. If we pulled out of South Vietnam and didn't do our damndest to see it through, then the shock of confidence to Southeast Asia would be so great that it would be a very dangerous thing indeed.[51]

In an address before the Research Institute of Japan in February 1965, Bundy argued that if the NLF was successful in Vietnam "in this key test of the new communist tactics of 'wars of national liberation,' then the Communists will use this technique with growing frequency elsewhere in Asia, Africa, and Latin America."[52] Here Bundy's scope is global: it was important for the U.S. to commit resources and "get bloodied," even if the effort turned out to be a losing one. The U.S. had made a direct commitment to maintain a non-Communist Vietnam in 1954, and again in 1961. That commitment had to be honored or the U.S. would appear as the "paper tiger" that the Chinese claimed it was. Washington's intervention would stabilize other nations, particularly Indonesia where the strength of the Communist Party was formidable.

In an important shift in strategic thinking from the fifties, Vietnam-as-a-domino is cast, for the center, in *symbolic* and *global* terms. The right current's version of the domino theory continued to be geographic: the "loss" of Vietnam would give "international Communism" a physical stepping stone to attack the rest of Southeast Asia, Indonesia and the Philippines. Each country would serve as a base to take over the next, leading to Communist control in the *region*. The left current did not believe in either version of the domino theory. Even a "successful" Communist movement could be stripped of its radicalism through a cooptive policy.

C. The Left
The left policy current was rooted in the multilateral postwar current; it tended to look first at Europe and the strength of the international economy, and only then at Vietnam. The NLF did not offer this group the same threat as it did the center and the right, for in their view the socialist content of the revolutionary program could always be altered by future trade arrangements. A contemporary example would be the policy favored by Senators Kennedy and McGovern of enticing Angola and the MPLA away from the Soviet Union through offers of government aid and foreign investment. The left current recognized that the Vietnamese could counter the U.S. military effort at any conceivable level of commitment. The more resources Washington committed, the greater the eventual defeat.

The left consciously attempted to lower the stakes in Vietnam. For example, Chester Cooper, at the time a middle level State Department official, carefully defined Washington's goals as "permitting the South Vietnamese to freely choose their own future" and an "organized and reliable peace."Cooper explicitly stated that the U.S. goal should *not* be "stopping Communist aggression once and for all in Southeast Asia" or "forcing North Vietnam to withdraw from South Vietnam," formulations favored by the two more militant currents.[53] In the left calculus, Vietnam was an annoying, destabilizing thorn, and not a place where a major U.S. commitment should be made. Once resources were committed, Washington should still explore "all avenues of diplomacy" (the left's slogan to find a solution unattainable by military means). The left was not more altruistic than the center or right. Not morality but a different conception of the proper global role for the U.S. motivated their decisions. The costs associated with the Vietnam intervention interfered with more important items on the agenda.

In practice the left current favored a minimal strategy which essentially "amounted to agreement to abide by the U.S. interpretation of the Geneva Accords."[54] The U.S. would make no large-scale military commitment and would accept neutralization and a coalition government. Washington would either "stand aside," thus dissociating itself from such a settlement, or "seek to cover a retreat by accepting negotiations."[55] This position was quickly rejected by the dominant center since the U.S. commitment was already high; withdrawal would "leave the considerable aftertaste of U.S. failure and ineptitude." As Johnson's commitment to greater intervention became apparent, the leading members of the left current, Averill Harriman, Roger Hilsman, Michael Forrestal and Paul Kattenburg, either resigned or were shunted aside where, in bureaucratic terms, they became "nonplayers."[56]

All of the state managers recognized that what they called the "European option," namely a passive Communist Party holding a subordinate position to a loyal center government, was impossible. But they differed among themselves over the relative importance of maintaining control over South Vietnam and the quantity of resources that should be committed to that goal. As those favoring paramilitary operations were pushed aside, the main battle came between those arguing for a program of rapidly escalating attacks against the North and those favoring a greater effort in the South. Should the U.S. try to "win" or "avoid losing?" The rightwing, led by the Joint Chiefs, said "go for a win." This would be possible, they added, only if ground troops were permitted to enter Cambodia and Laos. The center current would have none of this. When South Vietnamese General Nguyen Khanh beat his drums for a "march to the North," McNamara stiffly replied that the U.S. did "not intend to provide military support nor undertake the military objective of rolling back Communist control in North Vietnam."[57]

Strategic and Tactical Disputes

Between 1965, the date of the previous full-scale policy review, and 1968, the differences among the three policy currents remained embedded in strategic and tactical disputes. Each option reflected a broad orientation towards politics and the world economy. These disputes were a harbinger of the full-scale debate that would later emerge among different policy currents. Rapidly mounting policy costs, culminating in the March 1968 crisis, punctuated this bureaucratic protectionism. In the meantime the critical disputes were: (1) the clash over target selection for ROLLING THUNDER (the bombing campaign over North Vietnam); (2) differences over the use of ROLLING THUNDER as a "bargaining chip" in negotiations; (3) differences over the deployment of ground troops in the South; and (4) differences over the mobilization of the strategic reserve.

(1) Selection of Bombing Targets for ROLLING THUNDER.

The devastation that Washington unleashed on the Vietnamese makes it difficult to realize that the air war in the North was in fact conducted within limits. In the South, there were few such limits, and the crimes of the state managers in the "free-fire" zones will go down among the most infamous in history. The center current, however, managed to conduct the air war so as to convey to the Chinese and Russians an assurance that no direct attack would be made against them. Public speeches and diplomatic maneuvers frequently communicated "signals" to this effect. After the first year of ROLLING THUNDER the center bombed the North only to demonstrate resolve and to slow supply shipments moving south; there was little expectation that the bombing would have a specific strategic effect, such as forcing Hanoi to reconsider the costs of the war.

The rightwing current pushed for greater escalation over five kinds of targets: (a) bombing the rail lines leading to China; (b) bombing the buffer zone near the Chinese border; (c) bombing and mining the harbor in Haiphong; (d) bombing civilian centers such as Hanoi and Haiphong, and the dike system; and (e) bombing the POL (petroleum, oil and lubricants) depots, and military airfields in North Vietnam.

Chart 3.1
Policy Currents and the Vietnam War; Fall 1967
A. Differences in Orientation

	Left Policy Current	Center Policy Current	Right Policy Current
Definition of Winning	U.S. has already won, but is in danger of turning victory into defeat	Denying NLF victory, demonstrating credibility of U.S. to world allies	Imposing U.S. will after military defeat of the Vietnamese
Consequences of U.S. Defeat	Limited; Vietnam can be deradicalized by economic aid and private investment	Symbolic inspiration to other national liberation movements	Vietnam serves as a stepping-stone for Communists to conquer Southeast Asia (the domino theory)
Handling Domestic Dissent	An effective restraint limiting U.S. policy options	Deceive public through false promises of progress; maintain Great Society programs	Issue patriotic calls to national unity
Handling the Economy	Vietnam destroying domestic and international economy	U.S. can afford Vietnam war and Great Society without tax increase	Pass war-tax as part of national mobilization
Relations Among the Communist Countries	Moscow and Peking will not permit U.S. to achieve a military victory	Significant U.S. escalation will drive Moscow and Peking together	Tensions permit U.S. to adopt a more aggressive policy

B. Strategic Disputes

	Left Policy Current	Center Policy Current	Right Policy Current
Purpose of "ROLLING THUNDER"	Partial or total bombing halt	Interdict men & supplies moving from North to South; demonstrate resolve to Hanoi; boost morale of GVN	Strike Haiphong, Hanoi, dikes, airfields, China buffer zone, and mine the harbors
Negotiating Stance	Recognize NLF and achieve low-level stalemate	Enter only after a conciliatory move from the Vietnamese	Force capitulation on the battlefield
Deployment of Ground Troops	Enclave strategy around South Vietnamese cities	"Search and Destroy" missions in South Vietnam	Invade North Vietnam and "enemy sanctuaries" in Laos and Cambodia
Mobilization of Domestic Reserves	Avoid since move represents further commitment	Avoid due to high political and economic costs	Adopt to place U.S. on war-time footing and to demonstrate resolve

The first and second categories of targets symbolized hostile action towards China. The third category, the Haiphong docks, carried the danger of hitting Soviet freighters and other international shipping.[58] The systematic bombing of civilian centers and dikes would have signaled a shift away from restricted goals, such as forcing Hanoi to the conference table, to destruction of North Vietnam's population centers, and could have marked the beginning of an invasion from the South and the introduction of Chinese troops from the North.[59] Destruction of the POL depots and airfields could also have led to direct Chinese intervention, but for a different reason. Under an agreement between the two countries, China could service North Vietnam's MIGs if the latter's air bases were destroyed. Future air battles between American and North Vietnamese-piloted MIGs might then occur over Chinese air space and could cause a major incident between the two countries. A CIA assessment of possible Soviet and Chinese responses to various "bombing packages" noted that bombing

> north of the 20° without closing the ports would not bring
> on new or different Chinese or Soviet responses except for
> attacks on airfields. These might lead to greater Chinese
> involvement, especially if North Vietnam transferred air
> defense operations to China. If the ports were closed,
> however, there would be a direct challenge to the U.S.S.R.[60]

Admiral Sharp, then Commander of the Pacific Theater, summarized the rightwing position:

> The primary purpose of the air campaign against North
> Vietnam should have been to disrupt the enemy's economy
> and thus destroy his ability to wage war...Instead primary
> emphasis was put on seeking to cut down on the infiltration of
> men and material from North to South Vietnam. Now you can
> slow infiltration with air power...but you can never stop
> it... What my colleagues in the field and I [i.e., the rightwing
> policy current] wanted to do was bring the economy of North
> Vietnam to a halt. That is one of the major functions of air
> power in warfare... This would have deprived the enemy of his
> ability to support his forces in the South—and thus brought
> the war to a quick end.[61]

The center current was well aware of the dangers of an adventurous bombing program. The dominant group merely desired "containment," stopping the spread of socialism at the 17°. The "loss" of North Vietnam and China was recognized; the risk of including China in a general war in Southeast Asia was too high. Averill Harriman later commented on the rightwing point of view:

> The Soviet Union and China would not permit us to
> conquer North Vietnam without intervening and that's something the military don't seem to understand. The only ones
> who do understand it are people like [name deleted at
> Harriman's request] who are itching for a chance to drop
> nuclear bombs on China. He'd like to see us get overextended.[62]

William Bundy exemplified the center current's concern over the dangers of an adventurous bombing program:

> There continued to be fear that we might be bombing in a way that appeared to threaten China or the demise of the North Vietnamese regime and somehow cross an invisible line that would invoke Chinese intervention. This was a factor that continued even through the bombing programs of the spring and summer of 1967.[63]

McGeorge Bundy also argued that:

> The real choice is not between "doves and hawks." It is between those who would want to keep close and careful civilian control over a difficult and demanding contest and those who would use whatever force is thought necessary by any military leader in any service.[64]

The center current realized the policy implications of target selection and spent several hours each week, in a session called "Tuesday lunch," pouring over each potential target. Every one, right down to the smallest garage, was considered individually. In this manner control of the air war was assured.

By the middle of 1967, the left current saw little justification for bombing North Vietnam and privately supported a complete halt as a step towards achieving a lower cost stalemate. Within the national security apparatus, the need for bombing to support U.S. troops operating in the northern part of South Vietnam was strongly felt. As a result it was especially difficult to advocate an unconditional bombing halt explicitly; members of the left current generally pushed instead for a restriction of ROLLING THUNDER to the Ho Chi Minh Trail and the southern part of North Vietnam.

(2) ROLLING THUNDER and Negotiations

In addition to quarreling over target categories, the policy currents diverged over how to use ROLLING THUNDER in relation to negotiations. The rightwing current wanted to force Hanoi into total capitulation. If the full power of ROLLING THUNDER was unleashed, North Vietnam would surrender, and there would be little to negotiate. By mid-1967 neither the center nor the left position was particularly convinced of the likelihood of achieving ROLLING THUNDER's objective of interdicting men and supplies moving to the South. The two currents, however, were divided over a move signalling de-escalation from North Vietnam, *prior* to any form of bombing halt. Secretary of State Dean Rusk and Assistant Secretary of State for Far Eastern Affairs William Bundy maintained that North Vietnam should make the first move. Members of the left current in the Office of the Secretary of Defense—McNamara, Nitze, Warnke, and later, Clark Clifford—wanted Washington to take the first step.[65] Consider the following statement by William Bundy on the political and military aspects of ROLLING THUNDER:

> I was never one of those who thought that the bombing could be anything other than a mildly useful form of keeping down, to some extent, the flow of material from North to South. In other words in concrete military purpose I was always attracted to the idea that you laid off Hanoi and Haiphong and kept them, as it were, as hostages, which is a term actually used in some of the papers. We got into the extended bombing in April 1967 and on into August and continued thereafter to some extent to hit in that Hanoi and Haiphong area. This was something that I recommended against, not as a disaster, but as a mistake.[66]

Reluctance to bomb Hanoi and Haiphong systematically demonstrates rejection of the logic of the rightwing current. Next Bundy argues that in military terms, little was expected of the bombing. "As far as the military value," he later told an interviewer, "I was in common with almost all civilians except Walt Rostow that its [the bombing] basic utility was not all that important."[67] But, as Bundy also points out:

> By that time [the Summer of 1967] I'd always been worried about giving away—stopping the bombing—the bombing card (if you want to use the nasty technical jargon) for absolutely nothing but entering into talks that would have certain military disadvantages and would be the wrong way to start a negotiation. You traded one of your cards for very little...You wouldn't really have very much for it and that wasn't the way you could get a balanced negotiation underway.[68]

Johnson never entertained much hope for negotiations with the Vietnamese. He believed that the North Vietnamese would use talks and secret contacts to win concessions from the U.S. and to escape damage caused by the bombing. Johnson's thinking reflected the classic containment principle that negotiations only consolidated existing political and military conditions. In 1967 these were a stalemate and Johnson did not believe that the North Vietnamese would be willing to make terms. "If I were Ho Chi Minh," he repeatedly told his aides, "I would never negotiate."[69] And in fact Hanoi was not interested in negotiations that legitimized U.S. control on the South. At the same time world and U.S. opinion forced Johnson to make some public efforts towards reaching peace. U.S. dabbling with bombing pauses was designed to pacify the public, although the left current wanted to transform these partial and temporary bombing pauses into a genuine change in policy. The conflict between the left and center over the degree of negotiating leverage to be extracted from ROLLING THUNDER is reflected in the history of the "San Antonio formula."

In the summer of 1967 Henry Kissinger, serving at the time as a consultant to the Johnson Administration, and Herbert Marcovich, a French microbiologist, met in Paris at a meeting of the Pugwash Conference.[70] Marcovich mentioned that a good friend of his, Raymond Aubrac, was an old friend of Ho Chi Minh and suggested that the two Frenchmen might serve as a useful channel to the DRV. Kissinger met with Administration officials in Washington and was asked to convey the following message to Pham Van Dong through Aubrac and Marcovich:

> The United States is willing to stop the aerial and naval bombardment of North Vietnam if this will lead promptly to productive discussions between representatives of the United States and the DRV leading towards a resolution of the issues between them. We would assume that, while discussions proceed, either with public knowledge or secretly, the DRV would not take advantage of the bombing cessation or limitation. Any such move on their part would obviously be inconsistent with the movement towards a resolution of the issues between the United States and the DRV which the negotiations are intended to achieve.[71]

This later became known as the "San Antonio formula" and contained a key revision of the American position. The left current responsible for the new formulation included McNamara, who had shifted from the center to the left, Paul Nitze, Paul Warnke, and Nicholas deB. Katzenbach, Under Secretary of State. The formula, even in this private stage, had both "dovish" and "hawkish" interpretations. As communicated by Kissinger, "take advantage" was defined only by an *increase* in the movement of men and supplies into the South. A complete halt of men and supplies into the South was not required. When Marcovich mentioned the heavy bombing, then being intensified over North Vietnam, Kissinger replied that in the absence of negotiations the bombing would continue. Kissinger then added that effective August 24 there would be a noticeable change in the bombing pattern in the vicinity of Hanoi to guarantee the messengers' personal safety and as a token of Washington's good will. The restriction would hold for ten days. On August 21 and 22 heavy raids were carried out in the Hanoi area.[72] On August 25 Mai Van Bo, the North Vietnamese representative for Western Europe, rejected the visa applications of the Frenchmen saying that a visit to Hanoi "would be too dangerous."[73]

On August 31 the visa requests were again rejected. But on September 2 the Frenchmen were summoned and mysteriously told to make sure that nothing happened to Hanoi during the "next few days." They told Kissinger, who contacted William Bundy, and the bombing restrictions for Hanoi and vicinity were extended through September 7. On September 10 Bo told Marcovich that the American bombing of the DRV was illegal and must stop without conditions. The DRV representative pointed out that the American message, communicated along with escalation of attacks around Hanoi, constituted an ultimatum to the Vietnamese people; he asserted that the American propositions were "energetically rejected." Kissinger returned to Paris on September 13 with a proposal for direct contacts between Kissinger and a representative of the DRV. Bo, citing the continued threat of air attack, refused. Other exchanges between the Frenchmen and Bo continued but with no progress made. Kissinger returned to Paris for a final try in mid-October. Aubrac called Bo and told the North Vietnamese diplomat that he had something new to say. Bo told him that the "situation [was] worsening," that "the United States [was] continuing to escalate the war in an extremely grave manner," and that "under these conditions, words of peace are only trickery."

For the North Vietnamese these contacts occurred in the context of a protracted escalation extending from the Hanoi bombing of August 21 and 22 to strikes against the Phuc Yen airfield on October 25. Phuc Yen was the largest remaining unstruck MIG field and a center of much of North Vietnam's air defense control.[74]

On September 29, 1967, at the instigation of the left current in the Department of Defense, Johnson made the new formulation public. The President stated in San Antonio:

> As we have told Hanoi time and time again, the heart of the matter is this: The United States is willing immediately to stop all aerial and naval bombardment of North Vietnam when this leads to productive discussions. We would of course assume that while discussions proceed, North Vietnam would not take advantage of the bombing cessation or limitation.[75]

The formulation originated with Paul Warnke, Assistant Secretary of Defense for International Security Affairs, who would later argue that NVN had in fact met the conditions of the San Antonio formula and that the U.S. should stop ROLLING THUNDER and enter negotiations. Admiral U.S. Grant Sharp, a member of the rightwing current, later called Warnke, a corporation lawyer earning hundreds of thousands of dollars a year, "as close to being a Communist as one could be without actually becoming one."[76]

McNamara had introduced a final change in language. The original draft read "will lead to negotiations;" the soon-to-be-deposed Secretary of Defense changed the formulation to "will lead promptly to productive discussions." This recognized the DRV's distinction between "talks," or an exchange of views, and "negotiations" which would lead to a settlement but could only come after a complete bombing halt.[77] In the meantime, at least from McNamara's standpoint, the San Antonio formula removed the demand for military reciprocity on the part of the North Vietnamese.

The subtle distinctions between "negotiations" and "productive discussions" and between "cessation" and "not taking advantage" were not, however, publicly explained. The press assumed that "not taking advantage" meant absolute cessation of infiltration and that the San Antonio formula did not represent a change in policy. These impressions were confirmed by Dean Rusk's press conference of October 12; Rusk, a member of the center current, asserted that the San Antonio formula did not represent a change in American policy. Consider the ambiguity of the following exchange between Rusk and a reporter:

> Question: Mr. Secretary, you talked in your statement about the importance of precision and with that in mind, sir, I wonder if you could help us understand whether the United States now still requires a military sign of de-escalation from Hanoi in exchange for cessation of bombing, or will the President's statement about assuming Hanoi will not take advantage of a bombing halt represent a change.

> Answer: Now President Johnson in San Antonio stated an assumption. This is an assumption with respect to the condition imposed by Hanoi. The assumption would be that if we stopped the bombing there would not be military advantage taken by that cessation of the bombing by Hanoi.

> Now Hanoi knows what this means, and we have had not the slightest indication that Hanoi is prepared for those prompt and productive talks to which the President alluded in his San Antonio reference.

> Question: Mr. Secretary, I'm not clear yet on your expression of the President's statement in San Antonio. Is that intended to modify, reduce, or leave ambiguous our terms, our conditions for a bombing pause in North Vietnam?

> Answer: Well, I think we ought to just read the statement for what it says and reflect upon the act of reciprocity from Hanoi.

> Now you may wonder about the meaning of this expression that they will not take advantage of the bombing halt. There is no point, as I have said before in this conference—no point in my discussing the details of that with you because you can't stop the bombing. We are prepared to discuss the details of that with Hanoi. They know it—they know it.[78]

If Rusk was eager to start negotiations or even talks under the "dovish" interpretation of the San Antonio formula (i.e., that the rate of infiltration must not increase, but that it did not have to stop), then he would have made the position public. Rusk's "hawkish" interpretation reflected the conflict between State (center current) and Defense (left current) over the conditions for entering negotiations. By failing to clarify the deliberately ambiguous wording of the formula, Rusk sent contradictory signals to Hanoi. The American public certainly didn't realize the implied change in San Antonio. The *New York Times,* for example, did not even note the possibility of an alternative interpretation until it cited Henry Brandon's report to the *Sunday Times* of London, on January 31, 1968. Washington first admitted officially that San Antonio was a shift in policy when Clifford stated the "dovish" interpretation in his confirmation hearings on March 3, 1968. Even at this late date Walt Rostow was incensed by Clifford's revelation.[79] Even after its articulation, then, the San Antonio formula shows divided views over the relationship between ROLLING THUNDER and negotiations.

The quagmire, or traditional liberal interpretation, of secret contacts between North Vietnam and the U.S., such as those accompanying the San Antonio formula, stress the theme of missed opportunity. Had the overtures been handled with more diplomatic sophistication, it is argued, meaningful negotiations with the North Vietnamese would have developed. Negotiations did not occur because Johnson feared being duped by the Communists; or because of poor coordination between different agencies of the national security apparatus, the armed forces bombing while civilian officials offered the dove of peace. This interpretation assumes that a more fortuitous series of events would have brought Washington and Hanoi together and that serious talks leading to an agreement would have resulted. But this approach ignores the main objective of the center current: forcing Hanoi and the NLF to give up the revolution in South Vietnam. Johnson was not willing to enter serious negotiations until the Vietnamese capitulated. In the meantime the twists and turns marking Washington's positions are better understood as the outgrowth of the conflict between policy currrents than by bureaucratic or individual ineptitude.

(3) Deploying Ground Troops

The state managers were also divided over the deployment of U.S. ground troops. The left favored "enclaves;" the center "search-

and-destroy" missions; and the right the invasion of sanctuaries in Laos, Cambodia, and even North Vietnam itself.

During the 1965 policy discussions Chairman of the Joint Chiefs of Staff Earle Wheeler told Johnson that a victory in the sense of driving the NLF from South Vietnam would take between 700,000 and a million men and seven years.[80] McNamara recommended additional troop deployments to bring the total of U.S. personnel in Vietnam to 400,000 by the end of 1966, and possibly to add another 200,000 by the end of 1967; at the same time he warned that he "would not guarantee success" and that "even with the recommended deployments, we will be faced in early 1967 with a military standoff at a much higher level, with pacification still stalled, and with any prospect of military success marred by the chance of an active Chinese intervention."[81]

Despite this accurate pessimism Johnson went ahead, for the only two alternatives—pulling out or escalating to the brink of World War III—were both unacceptable to him. So he escalated, deepened the commitment, and deployed U.S. ground troops in an Asian land war, knowing that the chances of a quick victory were slight, but feeling that U.S. interests nonetheless dictated such a course of action.[82] Johnson sent Marines ashore at Danang, and later changed their deployment from passive defense of U.S. installations to active search-and-destroy missions.[83] Washington might not win, but neither would the NLF.

American ground troops were now engaged in direct combat and sustained heavy casualties. Yet there was no clear evidence that the military stalemate had been broken. Washington poured in more troops; the NLF and North Vietnamese countered easily. Domestic pressure against the expensive but inconclusive intervention began to mount. The state managers disagreed over the proper response, the best way of blunting public opposition at home while retaining the anticommunist commitment in Vietnam.

In the enclave strategy, favored by the left current, American troops would occupy coastal bases that afforded high levels of security, and would then patrol in the areas immediately surrounding the largest South Vietnamese cities. This would prevent the NLF from infiltrating heavily populated areas and would permit joint operations with the South Vietnamese Army for distances of up to fifty miles. The enclave strategy yielded tactical initiative to the "enemy," but to its proponents, tactical initiative was not a vital factor. Supporters of the enclave strategy expected the South Vietnamese to bear the brunt of the war while the U.S. provided tactical support in vital instances. As the war escalated and the number of American troops increased, the enclave theory attracted officials who were looking for a method of maintaining the American commitment at lower cost. The enclave strategy was thus the deployment favored by state managers seeking a low cost military stalemate.

Using the search-and-destroy strategy favored by the center current, American troops would sweep through NLF-controlled territory in the hope of discovering, engaging, and wiping out large units. The basic idea was to "take the war to the enemy," deny him "freedom of movement" and "take advantage of the superior fire power of the American forces." An attempt was made to defeat the NLF militarily, not merely deny victory. The key point is that domestic politics and the economics of the war prevented Washington from committing the necessary resources. The U.S. used troops in an aggressive strategy but never at a level that offered the slightest chance of defeating the Vietnamese revolution on the battlefield. The NLF and NVN forces demonstrated great capacity to counter additional American troops. Despite the added U.S. initiative, the NLF continued to control the timing and duration of military combat. As a result, search-and-destroy missions, originally an attempt to seek a win within existing political limits, became extremely expensive: costs grew both in terms of dollars, and, as more GI's died in well publicized weekly tallies, in terms of public opinion as well.[84]

The right felt that neither the enclave nor the more aggressive search-and-destroy deployments was adequate, and that victory would come only by eliminating the sanctuaries available to the NLF and NVN troops. Correspondent Drew Middleton used his experience to support the logic of the right current:

> [I was] accompanying an infantry batallion that had been driving a North Vietnamese unit westward in the area northwest of Saigon. The Americans had fought a series of small, furious, successful actions, and at the end of each engagement the enemy had fallen back, whipped on by our artillery. At nightfall on the third day, however, the operations

officer of the battalion, a hefty Hawaiian, turned to me, cursed briefly but strikingly, and said, "It's all over. The bastards have gone over into Cambodia—and just when we had them."

So the battalion set down to wait. A few days later it was sent elsewhere, and a few days after that the North Vietnamese recrossed the frontier into South Vietnam and resumed their war.[85]

Middleton articulates the views of the right when he contends that it was one of the most significant mistakes of the war to reject the Joint Chiefs of Staff's proposals to widen the conflict to Laos and Cambodia (and in some cases to North Vietnam itself).

(4) Mobilization of the Reserves

Neither the center nor the left policy current wanted to mobilize the reserves. Their reasons illustrate the close connection between foreign policy and the domestic economy, and a consequent desire to keep the war in as low a profile as possible. Mobilization of the reserves would undermine the center's argument that the war's costs were well within the capacity of the country. No extraordinary measures had to be taken. Secretary of Defense McNamara privately argued that "the call-up of the reserves presents extremely serious problems in many areas" especially when the country "is beginning to run near or at its capacity with the resulting probability of a shortage of certain skills and material. If this continues we may be facing wage and price controls, excess profit taxes etc., all of which will add fuel to the fire of those who say we cannot afford this. With all these conflicting pressures it is very difficult for the Administration to mobilize and maintain the required support in this country to carry on the war properly.[86] Presidential advisor Walt Rostow, a member of the right current, argued that a reserve call-up would "demonstrate our resolve to Hanoi" and serve as a unifying factor at home.[87] In response McNamara maintained that a call-up would increase domestic divisiveness and reveal to the North Vietnamese that the U.S. was having manpower problems. The issue festered within the national security apparatus, surfacing at critical policy junctures.[88] March 1968, as we shall see, was one such occasion.

By the end of 1967 each policy current on Vietnam had developed a different concept of winning. For the right a win was a classic military victory over the NLF. This goal, they argued, could be achieved only through extensive bombing of the North and invasion of the sanctuaries in Laos and Cambodia. "Don't worry," they counselled, "China and the Soviet Union will not respond in a major way." For the center a win meant not losing. Fight a war of attrition. Follow as aggressive a strategy as possible within existing limits. Live with and manage the high political and economic costs. Above all don't let the Saigon government fall. For the left a win entailed demonstrating that the U.S. had already made a genuine effort to help fight socialism in the underdeveloped world. Such U.S. intervention in these regions had definite limits, however, and in the case of Vietnam in 1967 these had already been reached. The left argued that the U.S. had already won—at least in their sense—and that other matters had far greater priority.

Conclusion

At this point the analytic narrative of the Vietnam War ends temporarily and we begin a closer examination of the rapidly increasing policy costs that gave rise to the policy currents outlined above. *Chapter Four* discusses aid from China and the Soviet Union to the Vietnamese and the response among U.S. decision-makers. In the final analysis, of course, only the Vietnamese could win their struggle. Aid from China and the Soviet Union was indispensable, but it was no substitute for the years of patient work by the NLF in the South. The peasantry were transformed into a politically conscious movement capable of stalemating the American military machine. Political development and revolutionary ideology took the place of advanced military technology. The Vietnamese are not a "super breed" of the human species. They suffered failures, made mistakes, lost battles as well as won them.[89] Wilfred Burchett describes the painstaking steps in forming an effective fighting force: initiation in the basic revolutionary texts and self-criticism led ultimately to military preparation, including full-scale mock-ups of battle sites.[90] The NLF took advantage of the narrow political base of the Saigon regime to form effective alliances with many non-communist sectors of the population. Its increasingly broad composition effectively thwarted Washington's long effort to control the future direction of Vietnam.

Another policy cost, another form of opposition against the state managers, was domestic opposition to the Vietnam War. *Chapter Five* analyzes the antiwar movement, which helped block further escalation and contributed to a sense of war-weariness among the majority of people.[91] The GI movement—newspapers, organizing, off-base coffee houses, etc.—began in this period, unleashing a process that would undermine the army as an "effective fighting force." Draft resistance also dramatized the unpopularity of the war among youth. The civil rights movement, the growing militancy of the black population, and the urban crisis helped deepen the sense of domestic upheaval. This chapter also discusses other forms of domestic opposition including the press, particularly the *New York Times,* which began to editorialize against any further escalation. In addition, the Democratic Party and the labor movement experienced internal divisions leading to the first serious questioning of the Cold War consensus among their mainstream constituents.

Chapter Six focuses on the economic impact of the Vietnam War. It makes the argument that in strictly economic terms the costs of the war were manageable, never reaching more than three or four percent of the GNP (compared with forty-five percent in World War II). But the expenditures in Vietnam came during relative prosperity and thus were not needed to stimulate the economy. Expenditures on World War II came in the midst of depression. In addition the Vietnam War's unpopularity prevented the adoption of monetary and fiscal controls. Johnson's political support depended on his Great Society programs; he wanted guns *and* butter *and* no tax increase. Many features of the current economic crisis stem from the 1965-1968 period. Johnson and McNamara lied about the costs of the war and increased the government deficit.[92] The drain of gold reserves and balance of payments problem accelerated. Inflation increased and the rate of increase of productivity declined. Economic competition from Europe and Japan mounted. Underlying these economic difficulties were the now huge expenditures on the air war and ground troops. Even the business community began to argue that the war was bad for the economy.

The next three chapters then, step back from the study of decision-making within the national security apparatus to examine the political and economic context which sustained the different policy currents. Once this is accomplished we will return to the detailed analysis of decision-making, tracing the three policy currents through the specific history of U.S. intervention in Vietnam between August 1967 and March 1968.

PART II: FORCES OF OPPOSITION

IV: PLAYING HARDBALL: SINO-SOVIET AID TO VIETNAM, THE SINO-SOVIET DISPUTE, VIETNAM AND NUCLEAR WEAPONS

We live in an increasingly chaotic world. The meaning and direction of international politics is more and more difficult to fathom. Internal conflicts among the socialist countries are becoming more acute, at times seeming more profound than the contradictions between the capitalist nations, or even than the division between capitalism and socialism itself. Ironically, the Vietnam War, once perceived as the key struggle between imperialism and wars of national liberation, has emerged in a more immediately significant role: that of intensifying the antagonism between China and the Soviet Union. The events are flabbergasting. Vietnamese troops enter Cambodia to overthrow a Communist government. China invades the Vietnamese border area in force in order "to teach Hanoi a lesson." Casualty figures are enormous. The independent left is virtually speechless.[1]

This chapter traces the background of the Sino-Soviet dispute as it affects Vietnam, and explores the reactions of U.S. policy-makers to the emerging Peking-Moscow-Hanoi triangle. In terms of the policy currents approach outlined in the preceding chapters, two themes are discussed: First, the Soviet Union and China, at least during the time when the U.S. was militarily involved in Indochina, did not permit their antagonism to weaken the Vietnamese to the point where effective resistance could not be conducted. Military and economic aid for the Vietnamese revolution became an oppositional force helping to create different policy currents among Washington decision-makers. Moscow's and Peking's reasons for supporting Hanoi may have been different, but the weapons, ammunition, fuel and food invariably came through. As one U.S. policy analyst ruefully put it: "the North Vietnamese and the combatants in the

South apparently never lacked food, munitions, fuel or such heavy material as tanks, rockets and artillery."[2] Of course that aid changed, both in quality and quantity. Shadings in diplomatic support given the Vietnamese by China and by the Soviet Union also existed, and were reflected in press treatments of the war in each of those countries. But the overall pattern was one of support. The Soviet Union organized many domestic demonstrations; demonstrators in Peking alone numbered in the millions on several occasions. Considering the treachery that followed the war of liberation it is remarkable that political and material assistance arrived in sufficient quantities.

Underlying the overall pattern of support lay an ever-intensifying conflict between the Soviet Union and China. This chapter examines both levels, that of support and that of tension between Vietnam's allies. Moscow and Peking had different ideas of how the Vietnamese should fight the U.S. Neither was reticent in trying to impose its views. The Soviet Union and China also fought over the method of transporting military supplies to Vietnam (creating a truly frightening situation that is outlined in this chapter). With the advantages of hindsight sharpened by the China-Vietnam War, it is now apparent that the tensions between Hanoi and Moscow, and especially between Hanoi and Peking, constituted virtually a second war for the Vietnamese.

The fact that the Soviet Union and China fought out their conflict, in the sixties, within the context of overall support, is due in no small part to the political skill of the Vietnamese. Their ability to maneuver among the Great Powers can be traced back to the end of World War II: at that time Ho Chi Minh accepted temporary French control in order to block the reimposition of Chinese warlords and the Kuomintang; soon after, he was countering the consolidation of French colonialism by an appeal to Washington. During the struggle against the U.S., Hanoi managed to play Moscow and Peking against each other, successfully avoiding any dependent relationship that would have terminated its leverage.[3] The fact that the Vietnamese were at war with an imperial power undoubtably helped, for neither socialist ally could afford, in the eyes of the rest of the world, to be saddled with the responsibility of defeat. Yet the Vietnamese had to be very sharp in their reactions with the "rear front."

The second theme of this chapter is the response of U.S.

decision-makers to Soviet and Chinese aid, responses that serve as the other source of policy currents. The state managers differed over their perceptions of the nature of the Vietnam conflict. The inherited ideology of the fifties maintained that wars of national liberation were actually extensions of either Moscow's or Peking's influence. In the sixties the rightwing continued to hold that view. The right also claimed that the U.S. could have used more military muscle, and that both Kennedy and Johnson overestimated Chinese and Soviet willingness to respond to U.S. escalation. Admiral U.S. Grant Sharp maintained:

> It may well be that our civilian leadership [i.e. the center current] believed that to use our military tools properly, to eliminate the enemy's ability to make war, would have been to risk a nuclear confrontation with the Soviet Union. Personally I believe that the risk was minimal; in any case, a nation which is not willing to take calculated risks to achieve its objectives should never go to war in the first place.[4]

Starting with the Kennedy Administration, the center current shifted its view, no longer seeing national liberation movements as the simple extension of China and the Soviet Union. But the center current also thought that these movements were themselves a threat and that direct military intervention against them should not be ruled out. Along with the right, the center felt that the turmoil of the Cultural Revolution had reduced the capacity and desire of the Chinese to respond to provocation. They welcomed this situation, and perceived the Cultural Revolution solely in terms of a factional power struggle. Unlike the right, however, the center argued that the threat of an American intervention would unify China and interrupt the process of disintegration. Thus for the right, the Cultural Revolution was an opportunity to apply greater military pressure; for the center, the U.S. had to avoid actions that could result in undesired unity among the Chinese.

The left current argued that Vietnam was a civil war between indigenous political groupings and that no direct U.S. interests were involved. The victors of this struggle, even if they claimed adherence to socialism or Marxist-Leninist ideology, could always be coopted by future economic arrangements. Averill Harriman, Roving Ambassador for the State Department, reflected this perspective in describing his shift from the center to the left policy current:

> I inherited the accepted point of view that we were fighting China in Southeast Asia. But in fact, Ho Chi Minh and his colleagues are fiercely nationalistic and they don't want to be too much under the influence of Moscow even though it is far away. They're not afraid of them, but they don't want to get involved in Moscow's and Peking's dispute. They want to be independent and they want to establish relations with us.[5]

Harriman felt that the North supported, but did not control, the NLF; that the NLF should participate in negotiations and that the Soviet Union desired a solution in Vietnam (since they found the situation advantageous to China).

The left was never really influential in determining the overall structure of policy. But it was a logical position to which the center current state managers were occasionally forced by crises such as that of March 1968.

In any case the Soviet Union and China continued to aid the Vietnamese. As far as the Johnson Administration was concerned little could be done about this state of affairs. Some decision-makers even argued that the U.S. bombing of the North was counter-productive — for every dollar of destruction caused by U.S. bombs, Hanoi successfully appealed to Moscow and Peking for two dollars worth of replacements. Some state managers were aware of dangers that the Sino-Soviet conflict held for the Vietnamese, but until Nixon and Kissinger, policy was not formulated around tensions within the socialist camp. (Of course Nixon and Kissinger eventually failed as well.) Thus, during the sixties, the U.S. faced both the stubborn resistance of the Vietnamese, and the varying — but still sufficient — aid supplied by Hanoi's two huge allies. The strength of the resistance and the amount of the aid contributed to the policy divisions among U.S. state managers.

At the same time some policy makers became frustrated with the negative impact of the Vietnam War on the nuclear balance with the Soviet Union. Money spent on conventional weaponry was sapping programs of missile development, production of nuclear warheads and deployment of an anti-ballistic missile system — all calculated to tilt the strategic equation in favor of the U.S. There followed a peculiar development: some of those most hostile to the Soviet Union, those forming a right policy current towards Moscow, joined forces with the left current on the Vietnam War. The right felt that inconclusive intervention in Vietnam was hurting more important defense programs—especially those aimed against the Soviet Union. As a result, the influence of the left current was temporarily improved by political forces not normally found in the same political camp. An analysis of this development is provided in this chapter as well.

There is no radical or Marxist theory that helps us understand relations among socialist countries. We require a much deeper understanding of the structure and politics of those states than is now available. We need a theory of nationalism as well. Radicals also tend to ignore the internal dynamics of the nuclear arms race; denouncing, rightfully, the human irrationality of the ever-increasing arsenal, but failing to examine the logic that state managers use to make decisions concerning their projected use. As a result of these problems, the analysis offered by this chapter is more "geopolitical" than "Marxist." One note of caution: If anything, both the Soviet Union and China conduct their foreign policy debates with even greater secrecy than the U.S. As a result, the evidence presented in this chapter is unavoidably fragmentary, and the arguments must be tentative.

Soviet Goals in Support of the Vietnamese Revolution

How best to support the Vietnamese revolution is a question that illustrates a general dilemma that has confronted Moscow since 1917: Should the most powerful socialist state use its influence to promote revolution and undermine the power of capitalism in the world arena, even though such actions may entail the sacrifice of immediate national interests and increase the possibility of nuclear war? Moscow's support of Vietnam legitimated the Soviet Union among underdeveloped countries and helped undermine the power of the U.S. Soviet assistance derived in part from ideology, reflecting some degree of genuine commitment to the struggle for socialism. Moscow also preferred to see the U.S. bogged down in an expensive but inconclusive war, and gave assistance to maintain this state of affairs. On the other hand, the Soviet Union did not want to create a direct confrontation with the U.S. over Vietnam for fear of curtailing the process of detente or producing a situation that could lead to nuclear war. In 1961 Khrushchev had expressed strong support for wars of national liberation. But by the mid-sixties Vietnam had become, in the terminology of the Soviet Union, a local war which carried the danger of expanding, through a series of mistakes and miscalculations, into a general war involving nuclear weapons. "The atomic bomb does not adhere to the class principle," read a CPSU statement, "it destroys everyone within the range of its devastating force."[6] Moscow's support for the revolution in Vietnam was tempered by the fear of a rapidly escalating conflict that might culminate in an atomic showdown with the U.S.

The Soviet Union also feared that its own foreign policy would be increasingly determined by a conflict which had transcended the definition of a war of national liberation. Instead of being free to pursue relations with the U.S., Western Europe and other nations, Moscow was close to being locked into a situation where the weaker country, Vietnam, was controlling the conditions affecting the diplomatic options of the stronger country, the Soviet Union. If Moscow intervened too strongly, the danger of confrontation with the U.S., threats to better relations with the West, and the loss of the economic and political advantages of detente, would all increase. But a policy of moderation carried the danger of severing the Vietnamese from vital material support and delegitimizing the Soviet Union in the eyes of the Third World. The result was vacillation in Soviet support for the Vietnamese between the end of World War II and 1965. From that date on, however, Soviet aid becomes more reliable, forming as good a record as we have of international solidarity between a socialist state and a revolutionary movement, given the realities of the world controlled by the West. A brief summary of that historical record follows.

Soviet Aid To Vietnam; 1945-1965

Between 1945 and 1965 Soviet support for Vietnamese revolutionaries was equivocal. At the end of World War II Moscow's diplomacy was Europe-centered, favoring French claims in Indochina over the Vietminh. This policy favored the French Communist

Party, who had warned that "premature adventures" in Indochina might "not be in line with Soviet perspectives."[7] After the PCF was removed from office in 1947, Moscow began to shift its support towards Vietnam, although diplomatic recognition to Ho Chi Minh was not granted until January 1950. Significant aid to the Vietminh did not flow until the U.S. intervened massively on behalf of the French efforts to reimpose colonial power.

Postwar Soviet-U.S.conflict over Indochina was played out in France. In each case big power interests operated against the Vietnamese. The U.S. had aided the French in Vietnam, in part to secure French support in re-establishing German influence and power within Europe. Washington's anti-colonial rhetoric was dropped in order to secure political and economic stability on the Continent. Moscow's turn to subordinate Vietnam to its European interests came in 1954. In January, U.S. Secretary of State John Foster Dulles announced the doctrine governing nuclear weapons of "massive retaliation." This gave good cause for alarm in Moscow, as did Dulles' efforts to secure united action among European countries, including the use of the atomic bomb, against the Vietminh. Moscow's response was a *de facto* understanding with Paris in which the U.S.S.R. coaxed the Vietminh to accept the Geneva settlement of 1954 in exchange for a French veto of the European defense community. A progressive government, led by Mendes-France, had come to power on promises to end the Indochina war within thirty days. Moscow and the new government were in a position to do each other a favor. French military involvement in Vietnam was ended. And Moscow at least temporarily succeeded in strengthening political forces arrayed against Germany. The tacit division of Vietnam undertaken at Geneva was recognized by the Soviet Union who proposed, in 1957, the admission of both Vietnams to the United Nations.[8] There is some evidence of Vietminh anger at these Soviet tactics, with some members leaving the movement in protest over the division, no matter how temporary, of their country.[9] Ho apparently used all of his influence to hold the Vietminh together. In the process some members of the Cambodian Communist Party became disgusted with what they took to be the imposition of *Vietnamese* national interests over their own. After all, the Vietminh gained part of their territory. After Geneva, the Cambodian Communists were forced to join, after years of fighting, the government of

Prince Sihanouk.[10] Hanoi endorsed Cambodian neutrality. Many Cambodian revolutionaries came to North Vietnam. Those who remained saw Geneva as a betrayal. The incident perpetrated a pattern of animosity *among* Indochinese revolutionaries which partially accounts for the recent Khmer-Vietnamese conflict.

Soviet-Vietnamese relations soured during the fifties. In 1961 Khrushchev appeared to give strong verbal support to wars of national liberation, but he moderated his stance a year later in the search for peaceful coexistence. The Soviet response to the Gulf of Tonkin attacks in 1964 were mild, certainly in comparison to the Chinese campaign of demonstrations and editorials attacking U.S. imperialism. During the early sixties, the Vietnamese appeared to lean towards the Chinese, criticizing, as did Peking, the test-ban treaty signed between Moscow and Washington in 1963. The Vietnamese theoretical journal *Hoc Tap* began to publish attacks on "revisionism." Khrushchev was angered by this tilt towards Peking, and threatened to remove the Soviet Union from co-chairmanship of the International Control Commission of the Geneva Accords.

As U.S. intervention escalated in 1964 and early 1965, the Vietnamese began to lean back towards their Soviet allies and the sophisticated weapons that were needed to counter the new military thrust.[11] Premier Alexei Kosygin visited Hanoi in February 1965 and signed a pact increasing military and economic aid to North Vietnam.[12] (The U.S. signalled its own determination to fight in Vietnam by bombing Hanoi proper in the middle of Kosygin's visit.) Diplomatically, Moscow gave strong support to the Vietnamese. In November 1964 the NLF established a permanent mission in Moscow. Immediately after Khrushchev's ouster the Soviet Union expressed confidence in the possibility that the '54 Accords might still serve as a legal basis for settlement; they later backed the formal positions of the NVN and NLF in South Vietnam. In early 1965 the Soviet Union informed Prime Minister Wilson—Britain was the other chair of the International Control Commission—that an international conference would have to wait until American aggression ceased. Soviet aid reached 550 million dollars in 1965 and would rise to more than one billion dollars in 1968.[13]

On his return from Hanoi, Kosygin stopped in Peking to discuss the possibility of greater unity of action between the Chinese and the Soviet Union in support of Vietnam. He proposed the establishment of air bases in Sinkiang and Yunan provinces located in the south of China. In addition Soviet freighters would have free access to a number of southern ports of China. Kosygin also asked for air rights to transport military supplies to North Vietnam. Moscow moderated its verbal attacks on Peking, proposing a temporary halt to the war of words as part of a campaign for "concrete measures" in support of North Vietnam. At roughly the same time the mayor of Peking, P'eng Chen, a close ally of Chinese President Liu Shao-chi, was visited by a delegation from the Japanese Communist Party who urged the Chinese to meet these Soviet proposals.[14] But Mao interpreted Kosygin's requests as an attempt to control China.[15] The Chinese leader later told a small number of Americans that the discussions with Kosygin were not very friendly.[16] He also told correspondent Edgar Snow that one of the reasons for the removal of Liu Shao-chi was the latter's desire to reactivate the Sino-Soviet alliance to counter the U.S. in Vietnam.

Chinese Interests During the War in Vietnam

The Chinese favored a protracted inconclusive conflict between the U.S. and the Vietnamese. This situation would: (a) embarrass the Soviet Union; (b) weaken U.S. power in Asia; (c) work against Soviet-U.S. detente; (d) avoid the dangers of a direct confrontation between the U.S. and China; and (e) prevent the emergence of another socialist center of influence in Asia implied by a Vietnamese victory. A more precise statement of purposes, even a more exact ordering of priorities, is difficult to formulate for it was precisely these issues that formed the foreign policy component of the debates of the Cultural Revolution. What was the best defense posture for China? In what manner should the Vietnamese Revolution be supported? Who was the main enemy to the world socialist movement—the U.S. or the Soviet Union? Conflict over these issues provided part of the internal political struggles of China in the mid- and late-sixties. And these struggles affected the course of events in Vietnam as well. In the midst of those disputes, one faction of the Chinese leadership, led by Mao, began to make solicitous overtures to Washington, signals which were ignored by the Johnson Administration, but not by Nixon and Kissinger. These signals carried one main message: at least some Chinese felt that a permanent U.S.

presence in South Vietnam, one that did not threaten China directly, would be welcome.

At first the Chinese position was straightforward. Together with the Soviet Union they supported the anti-French stage of the Vietnamese struggle. Vietminh troops trained in China, cadre received political training, and the Chinese served as advisors in Vietnam. China and the Soviet Union cooperated during this period. Both supported the Geneva Accords of 1954. Then relations among Hanoi's allies, and Hanoi's own choices, became much more difficult. In the early sixties, Hanoi feared that Soviet attempts to achieve nuclear security, such as the 1963 test-ban treaty, would come at the expense of support for national liberation movements. This was a militant period for the North Vietnamese (unlike the 1954-1959 years). Hanoi argued that constructing socialism in the north had to be combined with support of the resistance in the south. The Chinese press promptly published these statements—unlike later speeches made by North Vietnamese leaders which rejected Chinese advice.

During these years Hanoi qualified its tilt towards China to maintain some leverage with Moscow. By early 1965, and especially after Kosygin's visit, the number of attacks on "revisionism" in the North Vietnamese press began to decline, becoming rare by the middle of 1965. After 1966 the North Vietnamese became increasingly critical of China. Premier Pham Van Dong and General Vo Nguyen Giap published articles attacking the Chinese military posture. The doctrines of self-reliance and people's war, which gained such prominence during the Cultural Revolution, did not appear applicable to the intensified fighting in Vietnam[17]. The Vietnamese managed to avoid taking an explicit position on the political battles accompanying the Cultural Revolution although they did support the Soviet invasion of Czechoslovakia in 1968— which the Chinese denounced.

Despite their public rhetoric the Chinese did not want a direct clash with the U.S. In their view, the new intensity of the Vietnam War, fueled in part by modern Soviet weapons, carried the danger of spilling over into their own territory. Despite this legitimate fear there is some indication that Peking actually preferred a stable, low-level American presence in the south to a unified Vietnam. If true, the roots of the current Sino-Vietnamese hostilities can be traced back to the mid-sixties.[18] Most of the evidence to support this contention is admittedly sketchy. Information provided by Vietnamese sources after the China-Vietnam border war must be treated with reservation.

We do know that Peking approved of the Korean War negotiations which consolidated a long-term U.S. troop commitment. The Korean War may have convinced Mao that the U.S. could be stalemated militarily, as long as nuclear weapons were not deployed. Peking also disapproved of negotiations aimed at removing U.S. influence from South Vietnam. Mao may have also calculated that a comparatively stable U.S. military presence in Saigon would make it easier for an American President to argue that U.S. troops could be withdrawn from Taiwan without jeopardizing security interests in the Pacific. Peking feared that a unified Vietnam would compete for influence in Asia. Vietnam could possibly become an extension of Soviet interests. In the meantime, Chinese goals in Taiwan might be better achieved by maintaining a conciliatory posture towards the U.S. in Vietnam.

After 1965 Peking made it clear that it would not intervene directly in Vietnam unless China was attacked. In a January interview with Edgar Snow, Mao stated that Chinese armies would not go beyond their borders to fight in Vietnam.[19] Mao went on to list a number of possible outcomes in Vietnam. One possibility, "that U.S. troops might stay around Saigon, as in the case of South Korea," flew in the face of the stated position of the Vietnamese. Moreover the phrase, "around Saigon as in South Korea," hints that a divided Vietnam with U.S. troops in the South might be looked upon by the Chinese with some favor. Another possibility, Mao went on to inform Snow, was that "the fighting would go on perhaps for one or two more years. After that the U.S. troops would find it boring and might go home or somewhere else." The Chinese *People's Daily* provided some fatherly advice to the U.S.: "You are really over-exerting yourself," the paper editorialized, "choosing Indochina or Southeast Asia as the theater of war is extremely unfavorable to Washington." Even the standard warning issued to the U.S. was comparatively restrained: "If U.S. imperialism persists in spreading the flames of war and forces a war on us, then we shall have no other choice than to be resolved to take it on to the end."[20] The French emissary to Peking was told that the Americans, while enemies, could be respected. The Russians, though, were traitors who could never be forgiven.[21]

Between the spring of 1964 and the spring of 1966 the number of serious warnings issued by the Chinese against the U.S. declined— despite the fact that a major escalation of the war was taking place. In May 1966 Chou En-lai stated that "China will not take the initiative to provoke a war with the U.S.," although he went on to warn that "once in China the war will have no boundaries."[22] These statements were designed for two purposes. The first was to ward off rightwing forces in the U.S. who wanted to use the Vietnam War to provoke a clash with China. Peking wanted Washington to understand that any attempt to spread the conflict into Chinese territories would mean a protracted people's war. At the same time, the statements implied that China was not particularly concerned over the U.S. presence— as long as it was confined to South Vietnam. A delegation of visiting Japanese members of parliament were told by Chinese Foreign Minister Chen Yi on September 6, 1966:

> We shall not attack the United States. As a matter of fact, China is not strong enough to attack America. To tell the truth, America is afraid of China and China is somewhat afraid of America. I do not believe that the United States would invade present-day China. . . . I do not take a particularly pessimistic view of relations between the United States and China.[23]

Commenting on Minister Chen Yi's remarks the Polish party newspaper *Trybuna Ludu* pointed out:

> The calm, businesslike tone of this statement would arouse no objections were the PRC to pursue a policy of unity and cooperation with the Soviet Union and the entire socialist camp. However, in the light of the disruptive policy of the CPC, this statement acquires a somewhat different complexion.

> Commenting on Chen Yi's statement, *France-Presse* observed that it undoubtably confirms the opinion held by many observers that China is sharpening its conflict with the Soviet Union in order to prepare the ground for direct negotiations with the U.S. government.[24]

By the summer of 1966 the Mao-led faction had gained influence over the faction of the Chinese leadership more favorable to joint USSR-China action in the Vietnam War. Moscow, and its allies in Eastern Europe, feared that the Maoist leadership enjoyed a tacit understanding with the U.S. to avoid direct conflict over Vietnam.

Implications of the Cultural Revolution for China's Aid to Vietnam

Mao's tentative overtures to the U.S. did not come unopposed. In May 1965 Lo Jui-ch'ing, Army Chief of Staff, published an article in *Hung-ch'i* (Red Flag), the theoretical journal of the Chinese Communist Party, which drew a parallel between the American intervention in Southeast Asia and the Nazi blitzkrieg of Europe during World War II. Unlike Mao, who had maintained that U.S. troops did not constitute a major threat, Lo asserted that the American presence was a danger to both North Vietnam and China. The World War II analogy at least implicitly prepared the ground for joint USSR-Chinese action. Lo pointed out that the U.S. no longer had an atomic monopoly, and that nuclear weapons held by the socialist camp could deter imperialism, a sharp contrast to Mao's thesis of protracted guerilla war. Where Mao was reluctant to send any Chinese troops, Lo argued that China "was prepared to send out men to fight together with the people of Vietnam when they need us."[25] Lo expressed confidence in the ability of the Soviet people and army, and maintained that China and the Soviet Union "will be united on the basis of Marxist-Leninism and proletarian inter-nationalism and would fight shoulder to shoulder against U.S. imperialism." Imperialism could be frustrated "provided that we are good at uniting the socialist camp and the people's anti-imperialist forces in all countries as well as making use of the contradictions within the imperialist camp."

An editorial of the *People's Daily* responded to Lo, arguing that the U.S. "is in a much worse strategic position than was Hitler in his day," and that "it is much more difficult for the U.S. to unleash a world war." While Lo emphasized the nuclear deterrence offered by the Soviet Union, the *People's Daily* went on to maintain that "the struggle of the revolutionary peoples and the peace loving countries are the main deterrent forces." No reference was made to Moscow.

Lin Piao's famous thesis on people's war argued that wars of national liberation should use protracted guerilla tactics instead of conventional weaponry. While rhetorically siding with the Third World, Lin referred to the importance of self-reliance and thus, at least by implication, placed limits on the extent of China's support for other revolutionary movements. Where Lo had proposed an "active defense" against the U.S. in Vietnam, including regular infantry as in Korea, Lin was saying that people's war was preferable. Where Lo argued that the Chinese army would defeat U.S. imperialism, Lin maintained that Third World revolutionaries would do the job. Lo advocated a comparatively small mobile army, well-equipped and trained by the Soviet Union. Lin countered with claims that war with the West was improbable, the U.S. would not use nuclear weapons against national liberation movements, and reliance on the Soviet nuclear deterrence was therefore not necessary.[26] Finally, Lo and his supporters were more likely to press for reunification of South Vietnam than Mao and Lin Piao.

By August 1966 it had become clear that the Maoist forces had won the fight: China's aid to Vietnam would not include sophisticated weaponry. Lo was removed from his post as Army Chief of Staff. The last political act of Liu Shao-ch'i was a speech affirming an anti-Maoist form of support to the Vietnamese. "The Chinese people," the soon-to-be-deposed leader proclaimed, "would no longer be restricted and bound in any way in rendering support and aid to the Vietnamese people."[27] Peking now favored both in theory and in the type of aid that it provided, reliance on people's war rather than professional forces capable of using heavy weapons. This choice handicapped the Vietnamese in their struggle against the U.S.

The Sino-Soviet Dispute and Aid to Vietnam

The Sino-Soviet conflict became so intense that each side attempted, through the Vietnam War, to force its opponent into a confrontation with the U.S. The Vietnamese were in danger of becoming a pawn in a larger strategic triangle.[28] When Moscow suggested that fighter planes for the defense of North Vietnam be stationed in the south of China, Peking feared the possibility of intensified hostility between China and the U.S. Washington operated under the doctrine of "hot pursuit:" U.S. jets were permitted to pursue attacking aircraft back to their bases. If permission to base fighters in China was given, aerial dog fights between U.S. and NVN jets would occur over Chinese territory. Moreover, the rightwing current in the U.S., always looking for a chance to expand military pressures, would argue for protective reaction strikes against the Chinese mainland. In their shared hostility towards China, Moscow and the U.S. right may have been acting as silent partners: Moscow by suggesting an arrangement which could lead to future confrontation between the U.S. and China; the U.S. right by attempting to destroy all air bases *within* NVN capable of servicing MIGs, thus forcing Hanoi to station defensive aircraft in China.[29]

In addition to China's refusal to station fighters, Peking rejected Moscow's proposal to supply the Vietnamese by air over Chinese territory. China also refused to let its territory be used to train the Vietnamese in anti-aircraft weaponry.[30] In late-1965 the Soviet Union began charging China with removing certain weapons and delaying transit of rail shipments to Vietnam. (The Chinese claimed that they did not know if Vietnam "really wants this kind of military technique."[31] Apparently the Chinese were removing materials that did not conform to their idea of how the Vietnamese should be waging the battle against U.S. imperialism.) A Soviet radio broadcast maintained that the Chinese were "holding up freight trains and damaging military equipment" and that "the U.S. would not have risked bombing North Vietnam if Soviet anti-aircraft missiles were not being held at Chinese railroad stations."[32] The Soviet Union went on to claim that the Red Guards were replacing Soviet trademarks with Chinese characters during transit. From the Soviet standpoint, the failure of the Chinese to participate in unity of action hindered the Vietnamese effort against the U.S. "Had American imperialism encountered the joint rebuff of all socialist countries," Premier Kosygin argued in late 1966, "it is doubtless that a quick end would have been put to its outrage in Vietnam and aggression would have been cut short. China's position has become a serious obstacle in the struggle for this sacred cause."[33]

China never formally responded to the Soviet charges although some indication of their merit was indirectly provided by a *People's*

Daily editorial claiming that China never obstructed "the transshipment of all material supplies the Soviet side is willing to provide and the Vietnamese side is willing to accept."[34] A year later, in response to repeated Soviet accusations, the *People's Daily* offered the somewhat ambiguous formulation that "we have always transported in a responsible way every single bit of material in transit through China so long as the Vietnamese comrades wanted it."[35] The Vietnamese frequently issued statements denying "western news agencies' " reports of Chinese obstruction, but the Soviet Union persisted in its charges. Hanoi eventually found it necessary to meet Soviet shipments at the Soviet-Chinese border and provide an escort through Chinese territory.

What was behind the Chinese effort to obstruct the shipment of weapons? A strategy to produce greater tension between Moscow and Washington is one possible answer. The more these overland shipments were frustrated, the greater the pressure on the Soviet Union to supply the Vietnamese by freighter, especially through the port of Haiphong. The *Peking Review* maintained that Soviet Defense Minister "Malinovsky ought to know that besides ground and air communications, there are sea routes to link the various countries. . . . The Soviet Union has no common boundary with Cuba, yet it could ship rockets, nuclear weapons . . . it is not even that far from Vietnam; why can't it even ship conventional weapons there?"[36] Of course, if the Soviet Union did ship conventional weapons to Vietnam, the U.S. might have responded as it did in Cuba—which is exactly what Moscow feared.[37]

In 1966 the center current controlling U.S. policy in Vietnam declared the Haiphong port off-limits to U.S. military action. But its increased use by Soviet freighters, bringing military aid, would have added strength to the rightwing policy current. This bloc maintained that the U.S. should bomb the port, and perhaps even establish a naval blockade against all ships flying communist flags. If the scenario had been carried to its conclusion, the Chinese would have created mounting tension between the U.S. and the Soviet Union, possibly culminating in a major international confrontation like the Cuban crisis in 1962.

Like China, the Soviet Union wanted to avoid a confrontation with the U.S. When American planes did attack Soviet freighters in Haiphong, under circumstances which remain unclear, the Soviet press responded mildly, hoping to play down the significance of the event.[38] Also, the Soviet Union did not provide North Vietnam with weapons capable of striking the U.S. Seventh Fleet, then busy bombarding the North Vietnamese coast. Again Moscow may have reasoned that supplying ground-to-sea missiles for use against U.S. ships would have been risky. Rightwing currents within the U.S. would seize upon this pretext to urge invasion of North Vietnam or a confrontation with the Soviet Union elsewhere.

The summer of 1966 also marked the quiet emergence of the left wing policy current among Pentagon civilians (led by Secretary of Defense Robert McNamara).[39] Premier Kosygin's speech to the Supreme Soviet in August contained an appeal to these forces: "Today the aggressive military forces increasingly set the tone in American policy. . . . Aggressive moods obviously predominate in Washington at the present stage. But we also know that there are other, sounder tendencies there too. The strengthening of these tendencies will be received with due understanding on our part."[40] At the same time the Chinese-Soviet dispute over the shipment of weapons to Vietnam continued, encompassing such details as the cost and method of payment for the transport.[41]

The Soviet Union, meanwhile, supplied military experts to North Vietnam, trained pilots on its territory, and sent advanced MIG-21 jets to its socialist ally. Moscow loyally followed Hanoi's lead in outlining the conditions governing negotiated settlements. When Phan Van Dong told Harrison Salisbury of the *New York Times,* in January 1967, that the official Five-Points issued in 1965 were for discussion only, and not preconditions for opening peace talks, the Soviet Union underscored the announcement. This interview was widely regarded as a softening of the North Vietnamese position. It carried at least the possibility of new contacts between Hanoi and Washington. In an interview given by Foreign Minister Nguyen Duy Trinh to Wilfred Burchett, the North Vietnamese emphasized that talks would follow an unconditional halt of the bombing of the North—again a step back from previous demands that the U.S. withdraw entirely. This time the Chinese were the only communist country *not* to publish the change in position. After this interview, according to recent reports from Hanoi, the Chinese told the Vietnamese leaders that they were being paid to fight, not to waste money on delegations in Paris.[42] Chinese preference for a divided Vietnam can be detected in Mao's advice to the Provisional Government of South Vietnam: he urged them to forget their hopes of either overthrowing the Thieu regime, or of removing its President by peaceful means.[43] Peking did not endorse North Vietnam's decision to go for a victory in 1975—nor even Pol Pot's overthrow of Lon Nol in Cambodia. Even as the Vietnamese liberated the South, the Chinese were warning President Marcos of the Philippines not to permit Soviet influence to fill the vacuum left by the U.S. departure. Vice-Premier Deng Xiaoping told Marcos of the danger of "letting the tiger (the Soviet Union) in through the back door while repelling the wolf from the front gate."[44] Peking, in short, was interested in prolonging the war, not reaching terms acceptable to the Vietnamese.[45]

Summary

Washington decision-makers tried to respond to the strength of the Vietnamese resistance, a resistance that was aided in no small measure by economic and military assistance provided by the Soviet Union and China. Behind the support for the Vietnamese from its allies loomed the Sino-Soviet dispute. At times the tension between Moscow and Peking almost superceded the battle against the U.S. After the U.S. withdrew from Indochina, conflicts among Indochinese Communists continued to intensify. Cambodian Communists led by Pol Pot clashed with the Vietnamese, as did China and Vietnam in a costly border war. In the nineteen-sixties, however, the Johnson Administration could not break the basic pattern of assistance for the Vietnamese. Later, Nixon and Kissinger thought that they could use the Sino-Soviet dispute to defeat the Vietnamese through Moscow and Peking. They failed as well.

So far, this chapter has analyzed and attempted to strike a balance between the aid from Peking and Moscow and the tensions that existed among the Communist powers. The Sino-Soviet split was a silent factor of decision-making. The second half of this chapter examines another unobtrusive but critical element: the impact of the strategic (nuclear) balance with the Soviet Union on the Vietnam War. As Vietnam came to dominate U.S. foreign and defense policy some decision-makers, especially those hostile to the Soviet Union, felt that continuing in Vietnam was a less important commitment than making advances in nuclear weapons technology, advances that would permit strategic superiority. This current can be traced from early hardline views against the Soviet Union to those now arrayed against the passage of the SALT Treaty.[46] In the late nineteen-sixties, the rightwing strategic current joined with the leftwing Vietnam current, both hoping to scale down the intervention and achieve a low-cost stalemate. The center Vietnam current was forced to make concessions. Thus Vietnam decision-making is situated in two crucial contexts, each with international repercussions: the Sino-Soviet dispute, and the nuclear debate within the U.S.

The outline of the rest of the chapter follows: different currents on nuclear policy are outlined briefly. The logic that led members of the right current on nuclear policy towards the Soviet Union to become critical of the Vietnam War is then analyzed. Finally, an analysis of the ABM (antiballistic missile) decision reveals the rightwing pressures building against President Johnson and Secretary of Defense Robert McNamara.

Currents Concerning the Use of Nuclear Weapons

The concept of assured destruction served as the cornerstone of U.S. nuclear strategy in the nineteen-sixties. Assured destruction meant that the U.S. could inflict "unacceptable damage" on the Soviet Union or any other nation, even under conditions of a surprise attack or first-strike. Assured destruction was designed to deter a first-strike. In 1969 Secretary of Defense Clark Clifford defined this deterrance strategy:

> We must be prepared to maintain at all times strategic forces of such size and character, and exhibit so unquestionable a will to use them in retaliation if needed, that no nation could ever conceivably deem it to its advantage to launch a deliberate nuclear attack on the United States or its allies.[47]

Now the Soviet Union had also achieved assured destruction. No matter what the U.S. did, Moscow could inflict unacceptable damage on the U.S. Most nuclear strategists argued that the result was mutual assured destruction or MAD. Under the conditions of MAD neither side would initiate a first-strike, because such action would immediately result in the destruction of the attacking as well as the defending nation.

A few strategists did not accept MAD and pushed for a first-strike capacity. First-strike capacity assumes that the opening salvo of missiles from the attacking country is effective enough to eliminate the retaliatory second strike forces of the defending country. First-strike adherents want the United States to be able to launch a nuclear attack powerful enough to destroy the U.S.S.R.'s missile arsenal with only minimal damage to Americans. First-strike adherents push for counter-force targeting (aiming American missiles at Soviet missiles) rather than counter-city targeting (aiming missiles at Soviet population centers). Counter-city targeting sounds more ominous but its assumptions are actually those of MAD: it would inflict unacceptable losses to the civilian population. Counter-force targeting sounds more benign but it actually falls within first-strike logic—it poses the threat of a nuclear attack and escaping with minimal damage.

Among the MAD strategists three different positions could be noted: a minimal posture, parity, and superiority. The logic of the minimal posture can be expressed as follows: "If 2,000 bombs in the hands of either party is enough to entirely destroy the economy of the other, the fact that one side has 6,000 and the other 2,000 will be of relatively small significance." During a visit to the United Nations, Nikita Khrushchev expressed the minimal posture in succinct form: "You say that you have enough nuclear power to kill the population of the Soviet Union three times over. Well we only have enough to kill the population of the United States once—and that is enough."

Nuclear parity assumes rough equality between opposing nuclear arsenals. For example, the second round of SALT accepted parity as a starting point and tried to work out a system of balancing superiority in one field (for the United States, MIRV deployment) against superiority in another (for the U.S.S.R., total warhead tonnage). The Vladivostock Agreement pinned nuclear parity to an equal number of launchers (2,400 for each side).

The third possibility within MAD is nuclear superiority. U.S. advocates of superiority generally accept the capacity of the Soviet Union to inflict unacceptable damage, but maintain that it is still important for the United States to hold a lead in strategic development. The motives of the advocates of nuclear superiority are mixed.

Some hope that future technological innovation will translate superiority into a first-strike capability. Others, such as Paul Nitze, hold that superiority permits "negotiation from strength:" nuclear superiority becomes an advantage for bargaining in non-nuclear fields. During the Nixon Administration Nitze resigned as chief negotiator in SALT over the issue of superiority vs. parity.

The Vietnam War was fought under the umbrella of U.S.-Soviet antagonism and the stockpiling of huge amounts of nuclear overkill. From Washington's standpoint, one purpose of this stockpiling was to increase the plausibility of a U.S. first-strike. The more nuclear stockpiling, the greater the sense that the U.S. "will go first" during a confrontation with the Soviet Union. In theory, fear of a U.S. first-strike will make the Soviet Union more likely to avoid *non*-nuclear confrontations in situations that do not directly involve its interests. This is what Herman Kahn calls "Type II Deterrence," the accumulation of a nuclear arsenal that prevents Soviet retaliation to non-nuclear intervention by the United States. For example, the Soviet Union is not supposed to respond to the Bay of Pigs, U.S. intervention in the Dominican Republic, the introduction of U.S. troops in South Vietnam, or the continual bombing of North Vietnam, for fear of taking the first step in a scenario that would culminate in a U.S. first-strike. The threat of Washington going first makes Soviet response to U.S. counter-insurgency less likely.

In the meantime, the Soviet Union and China continued to supply North Vietnam with essential military aid, thus partially refuting the theory of "Type II deterrence." But the aid would not permit North Vietnam to carry the war to the U.S. in a manner that might bring in the Soviet Union directly. For example, North Vietnam never used ground-to-sea missiles or attacked with Soviet MIGs while the Navy's Seventh Fleet was in international waters. Thus the rules of the conflict betwen the North Vietnamese/NLF and Saigon/U.S. were determined in part by the strategic equation: the strategic balance was constantly in the background.

Washington also hoped that by refusing to ban explicitly the use of nuclear weapons in Indochina the North Vietnamese would be frightened and limit their aspirations. The possible use of nuclear weapons would cause Hanoi to succumb to the conventional bombing of ROLLING THUNDER. After the Soviet Union achieved guaranteed destruction in the early sixties, Washington became much more reluctant to entertain seriously the use of nuclear weapons. But the state managers still hoped to terrorize Hanoi into submission through the threat of their use.

The Shifting Nuclear Balance

During the Kennedy Administration the U.S. rapidly increased its inventory of ICBMs. The effort peaked at about the same time as the major escalation in Vietnam (late 1964-1965). Afterwards the number of missiles grew relatively slowly. In the meantime the Soviet Union embarked on a major missile program of its own. Moscow realized that a minimal posture *vis a vis* the U.S. was not sufficient to deter non-nuclear interventions. They built their arsenal to reduce the freedom of the U.S. to intervene with impunity. The advocates of nuclear supremacy in the U.S. then argued that the Soviet buildup had resulted in a loss of leverage for the U.S. in the world arena.

Chart 4.1, based on official Defense Department data, compares U.S. and Soviet ICBM strength. By 1966 the U.S. had more than one thousand ICBMs. The inventory remained fairly stable thereafter. The Soviet Union rapidly increased its ICBM strength from 250 missiles in mid-1966 to near parity by 1968. Washington, of course, was well aware of the Soviet push. Those policy makers wanting to maintain nuclear superiority were unhappy with budgetary restrictions that limited a U.S. response. As the total number of Soviet ICBMs threatened to catch up and finally pass the U.S. inventory, many members of the superiority camp viewed the Vietnam War with increasing disfavor, holding that disbursements in Southeast Asia were coming at the expense of the strategic arsenal. There was nothing wrong with killing Communists *per se*, even Vietnamese ones, went their argument, but not if it meant undermining the strategic balance. The "Soviet Union-as-prime-enemy" strategists pointed out that U.S. defense spending in 1968 totaled 75 billion dollars out of a GNP of 820 billion. Spending on strategic forces amounted to only 6.8 billion, or less than one percent of the GNP. In comparison, the U.S.S.R. spent somewhere between 55 and 70 billion for defense out of an estimated GNP of only 430 billion. Soviet spending on strategic forces was between 16 and 17.3

Chart 4.1
Comparative U.S./Soviet ICBM Strength

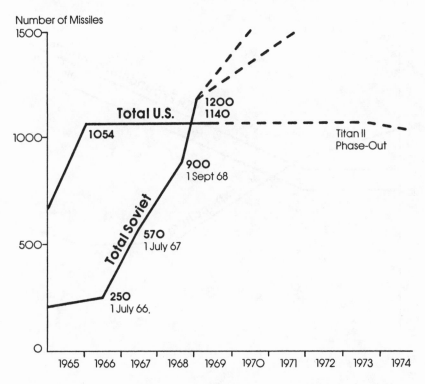

Number of Missiles

Source: Secretary Clifford's 15 Jan 69 Posture Statement and Previous Secretary of Defense Posture Statements.

billion or around four percent of the GNP.[48] In FY (Fiscal Year) 1964 the U.S. spent 5.8 billion dollars on missiles, or 23.8 percent of a total procurement of 24.4 billion. Spending on ammunition during the same year was 672 million dollars, or 2.8 percent of the total procurement budget. By FY 1967 spending on missiles had dropped to 4.5 billion, only 12.2 percent of a procurement budget that now stood at 37.4 billion. In the meantime the cost of ammunition, largely because it was being expended so rapidly in Vietnam, had risen to 3.6 billion and constituted 9.6 percent of the total program.[49]

Chart 4.2
Strategic Forces Expenditures
(in 1964 $)

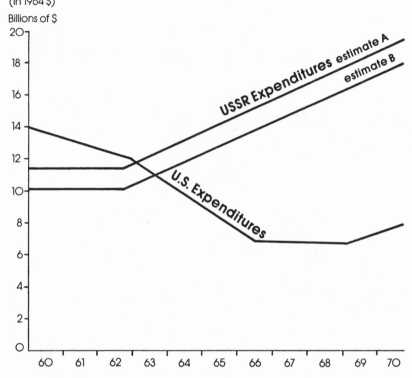

Billions of $

Sources: Department of Defense Releases, 15 Jan 69, 4 Feb 69, 18 Feb 69; Library of Congress Studies (SOSNOY); ASC Study, Changing Strategic Military Balance, USA/USSR.

These trends are further summarized in Chart 4.2 which compares the strategic force expenditures of the U.S. and the Soviet Union graphically, and in Table 4.1 which shows shifts in the defense budget away from general war (against the Soviet Union) and towards limited war (the category, in the terminology of the national security apparatus, in which the Vietnam War fell).

As Paul Nitze, then the Deputy Secretary of Defense and an advocate of nuclear superiority, later noted:

The Vietnam War was eroding the favorable position of the United States in the strategic field. The costs of the Vietnam War made it necessary to cut back on the basic capital expenditures necessary to maintain a favorable relationship in the area.[50]

Nitze had been a member of the rightwing policy current towards the Soviet Union since the late-forties, when he played a major role in drafting NSC-68; his current membership on the Committee for the Present Danger shows his consistency.[51] As part of the rightwing current towards the Soviet Union, he had become, however uneasily, allied with the leftwing policy current on Vietnam. This seemingly bizarre rationale for de-escalation—that the Vietnam War drained defense funds from the priority goal of strategic superiority over the Soviet Union—was in fact shared by some members of the capitalist class as well (see Chapter Six).

Table 4.1
Defense Obligations: General War Versus Limited War
(billions of dollars)

	Cold War (FY 1962)		Vietnam (FY 1966)	
	Amount	Percent	Amount	Percent
General War Capability				
Strategic Offensive Forces	8.9	29.8	5.1	13.1
Defense Forces	2.3	7.7	1.7	4.4
Subtotal	11.2	37.5	6.8	17.5
Limited War Capability				
General Purpose Forces	17.5	58.5	30.0	76.9
Airlift and Sealift	1.2	4.0	2.2	5.6
Subtotal	18.7	62.5	32.2	82.5
Total	29.9	100.0	39.0	100.0

Source: Murray L. Weidenbaum, "The Federal Budget and the Outlook for Defense Spending," Working Paper 6610, Washington University.

McNamara's Strategic Thinking and the ABM

Robert McNamara's private views of strategic policy were close to the minimal version of mutually assured destruction, but the political environment of the Pentagon demanded that the Secretary of Defense support at least the parity version of MAD. Above all, McNamara opposed the logic of nuclear superiority and first-strike. For McNamara neither the larger number of Soviet ICBMs, nor the larger size of their warheads, affected the chances for assured destruction on either side. McNamara was relatively comfortable with Soviet nuclear parity and hoped to reach some agreement for strategic arms limitation with the U.S.S.R.

Why did McNamara disagree with the nuclear superiority advocates? Why did he seek a limit to the arms race? On one level McNamara argued that a first-strike capability was technically impossible. On another he minimized the degree of political leverage that could be exerted from a position of superiority within MAD. But McNamara's world view was the most important reason. Initially McNamara desired to channel savings derived from strategic arms limitations to military expenditures on Vietnam; he reflected the center current's concern with underdeveloped nations and countering movements of national liberation. Roswell Gilpatric, McNamara's first deputy, summarized this thinking in a *Foreign Affairs* article. Gilpatric argued that nuclear parity with the Soviet Union implied a gradual reduction of tensions between the two largest nations.[52] But the Deputy Secretary of Defense also warned that this development did not imply a substantial reduction of the defense budget. Another threat, "wars of national liberation," had presented itself, compelling the United States to alter the composition of its military forces. McNamara put the Department of Defense through a fairly drastic overhaul. A test-ban treaty was signed with the Soviet Union. The relative strength of the Army was increased. Within the Army, "fire-brigade" and Special Forces units capable of fighting guerilla wars were developed. New weapon systems, such as the C-5A transport and the development of helicopter technology, also demonstrated the new emphasis on counter-insurgency.

During the mid-sixties, intelligence reports that the Soviet Union was building a defensive missile system (ABM) which would protect their own offensive missiles, were leaked to the press by rightwing currents on strategic policy.[53] The right argued that an effective Soviet shield would permit Moscow to attack with relative impunity. Retaliatory U.S. missiles could be shot down and the Soviet Union could escape with "acceptable damage." Even if Moscow did not strike first, the proponents of nuclear superiority feared that a fully developed ABM system would allow the U.S.S.R. greater influence in international affairs.

For McNamara, Soviet construction of an ABM system did not affect mutual assured destruction. Given the available and foreseeable state of technical knowledge, the construction of an impenetrable nuclear shield was impossible. Scientists likened the ABM to intercepting one bullet with another. (Actually, since missiles travel at over eighteen thousand miles an hour, even this analogy seems to understate the difficulties involved.) Furthermore, the Department of Defense developed during the sixties a series of penetration aids ("penaids") that increased the chances that any offensive weapon would reach its target. Incoming missile salvos would include dummy missiles, deflecting devices, and the like. The larger number of incoming and cheaper offensive missiles would overwhelm the smaller number of more expensive defensive weapons. And, of course, the Soviet Union enjoyed the same options: any marginal protection that the U.S. would acquire from ABM deployment would be quickly offset by more Soviet offensive missiles. For McNamara, a final argument against the ABM was its cost. By 1967 two-and-a-half billion dollars had been spent in research and development. In 1966 Congress appropriated 168 million dollars for production and deployment, but McNamara refused to spend it. In a period when Vietnam expenditures severely taxed the defense budget, the forty billion dollar cost (actually eighty billion since the actual cost, as McNamara knew, was normally twice that of the original estimate) required for full deployment would exacerbate the economic dangers already appearing on the horizon. The early sixties had been a period for expanding the defense budget; 1967 was not. These were the reasons behind McNamara's rejection of the ABM, but the task of actually defeating the right strategic current and the special interests behind the weapons system still remained.

Special interests pushed the ABM: the defense industries that stood to gain from contracts, and the "hawk" lobby in Congress, particularly on the Armed Services Committee. Senators Russell,

Jackson, and Thurmond all spoke out in favor of early deployment. The level of Congressional antagonism towards McNamara rose over the Secretary's decision to close several military bases and eliminate many reserve units (frequently staffed by Congressmen with reserve status). The rate of base closures increased as McNamara sought new sources of funds to secretly finance rapidly growing Vietnam expenditures. The Army also pushed the ABM since the weapon systems represented a chance to enter the nuclear arena. Within the Army, the departments supporting the project—air defense and missile defense—had to fight against the dominant ground combat divisions.[54] These special interests couched their arguments in strategic terms, contending that the United States needed the greatest protection that money could buy, and that ABM construction by the Soviet Union would tip the nuclear scales in their favor. Building one ABM shield, even if not perfect, would, they claimed, give the U.S. experience to build a better shield in the future.

McNamara's efforts to undercut arguments in favor of an ABM is an important example of politics within the national security apparatus. His earliest attempt to deflect deployment came in 1963-64, when he argued that civil defense should be procured before an ABM. McNamara was not really interested in civil defense; he met with the defense official in charge of the program only once or twice a year, and then only on budget matters.[55] McNamara knew that public opposition to a massive bomb and fall-out shelter program was quite strong. He counted on and got a stalemate, with Congress blocking his "request" for civil defense. McNamara could then claim that he had favored a defensive program without actually supporting ABM deployment. McNamara opposed the ABM because of its expense. Moscow could always counter-deploy offsetting offensive missiles. Yet the Secretary of Defense refused to sponsor Defense Department studies to see if this was in fact the Soviet intention.[56] McNamara also convened a meeting of Johnson, the Joint Chiefs and a number of scientists, including the past and current Special Assistant to the President for Science and Technology and Director of Defense Research and Engineering. This group agreed that an ABM system capable of defending the American people from Soviet attack was not feasible and should not be built.[57] But McNamara's main method of deflecting pressure for full ABM deployment was to improve offensive weapons; he MIRVed the Minutemen ICBMs in order to "guarantee penetration."[58]

Guaranteed penetration of any Soviet defensive system would continue the logic of mutually assured destruction and undermine the rationale of an American ABM system. McNamara made public the development of the Polaris missile through its several stages, until the submarine-based ICBM emerged as the Poseidon. He described the evolution of the Minuteman ICBM through several generations, and discussed the introduction of MIRV technology. In his public statements McNamara took great pains to point out that the number of warheads, not the number of missiles or the total tonnage of nuclear warheads, was the most salient factor in assessing nuclear superiority. Using this measure, McNamara leaked the information that the United States enjoyed a superiority ratio of 3 or 4 to one over the Soviet Union. The Secretary of Defense even made a rare public admission of error while arguing that nuclear superiority was useless, with or without ABM deployment:

> One point should be made quite clear however: our current numerical superiority over the Soviet Union in reliable, accurate, and effective warheads is both greater than we had originally planned and more than we require. In the larger equation of security our superiority is of limited significance, for even with our current superiority, or indeed with any numerical superiority realistically attainable, the blunt, inescapable fact remains that the Soviet Union, with its present forces, could still effectively destroy the United States, even after absorbing the full weight of an American first strike.[59]

The strategy of improving offensive missiles as a method of deflecting pressure for a full deployment was only partially successful. To delay a decision, McNamara would occasionally trickle research and development funds into various supporting projects. At the level of inter-service rivalries, the Army complained most about the slow progress and the Air Force least. General J.P. McConnell, Air Force Chief of Staff, testified to an Armed Forces Committee in February 1967 against full deployment of an ABM system:

My opinion was, and still is, that we should commence deployment of about a $3.5 to $4.0 billion anti-ballistic missile defense capability. In my opinion that will do everything that we can expect a reasonable missile defense to do. We cannot possibly defend against a full scale ballistic attack with anti-ballistic missiles, even as they can't defend against us.[60]

The Air Force was particularly happy with the alternative, MIRV development. They hoped that MIRVing the Minuteman would restore first-strike capability.[61]

In 1967 the tide turned in favor of ABM deployment by two entirely extrinsic issues: presidential politics and the air war over North Vietnam. Johnson realized that a decision to forgo deployment would become critical during the campaign. He and the Democrats would invite charges of being "soft on Communism." Indeed, Michigan Governor George Romney, then the leading Republican candidate, had already hinted at an "ABM gap." The Republican National Committee issued a fifty-five page pamphlet called "Is LBJ Right?" which analyzed the security implications of Johnson's reluctance to deploy an ABM.

On September 18, 1967, at a meeting of the United Press International Editors and Publishers in San Francisco, Secretary of Defense Robert McNamara announced the deployment of a limited antiballistic missile system. McNamara informed his audience that the Army had been directed to proceed with the construction of a five billion dollar system to be deployed against the threat of a nuclear attack *from China* during the mid-seventies. According to Phil Goulding, the Assistant Secretary of Defense for Public Affairs, "no subject was more important to McNamara than nuclear strategy" and "the Secretary exerted more personal effort to explain this speech to the press (and thus to the people) than any other he made in office."[62] Three-quarters of the speech was devoted to an exposition of nuclear strategy and to the merits of substituting MIRVed offensive weapons for full anti-Soviet ABM deployment. McNamara was so concerned that the press interpret the decision his way that two days before the speech he took the extraordinary step of individually briefing the most prestigious members of the Washington press corps.[63] McNamara showed each of the newspapermen a section of the Posture Statement that he had submitted to Congress the previous January. In the statement he argued that a *Chinese* threat to the United States could materialize in the mid-seventies and that an "austere" ABM defense "might" offer a high degree of protection from attack by that country through that decade. Goulding argues that McNamara and Cy Vance, then his deputy, inserted the section of the Posture Statement to provide a ready rationale for limited deployment, in case their efforts to ward off a thick ABM failed.

McNamara took extraordinary steps to assure the public that the five billion "thin" defense against China would not expand into a forty billion "thick" defense against the Soviet Union. A special question and answer essay for the Washington press corps was prepared. McNamara even changed names (from Nike-X to Sentinel) to help distinguish the two systems. A different general, Lieutenant General Alfred D. Starbird, was placed in charge of the Sentinel program. Lieutenant General Austin W. Betts remained responsible for the Nike-X.

The Chinese rationale for ABM construction was clearly a fabrication. If offensive weapons served as credible deterrence against the Soviet Union, would they not serve the same function against China? The United States possessed an equal capacity for destroying China's military forces and society. Would not that deter an attack? Even McNamara pointed out that China, despite its rhetoric, had shown caution whenever a potential nuclear encounter loomed. In his words, "despite raucous propaganda to the effect that the 'atomic bomb is a paper tiger,' there is ample evidence that China well appreciates the destructive power of nuclear weapons. She has been cautious to avoid any action that might end in nuclear clash with the United States, however wild their words, and understandably so.[64]" The Secretary of Defense was, therefore, on shaky ground when he argued later that China might miscalculate and attempt an insane suicidal attack upon the United States. In 1967 China, still in the midst of the Cultural Revolution, evidenced little desire to attack anyone. Actually her entire foreign policy during the Cultural Revolution was extremely circumspect, as already noted. McNamara also argued (at a Congressional Hearing in March) that the lead time for developing an ABM defense against China was *less* than the lead time that China would require to build an offensive capacity.

Consequently, there was no need to begin ABM construction until the Chinese began building their system. True, the Chinese detonated a hydrogen bomb in 1967, but this event was political and aimed at the Soviet Union. As there was no indication of a long-range ICBM program, there was extremely little merit in McNamara's proposal of a Chinese oriented ABM. In the words of one defense analyst, "Bob had been whipped on the ABM. But he was determined to give it the least possible chance for expansion. He deliberately chose the worst credible rationale for its deployment."[65] McNamara's private disgust with the China rationale emerges in *Essence of Security*, a collection of his speeches. McNamara ordered Henry Trewhitt, the compiler, to separate the defense of the "thin" ABM from the body of the San Francisco speech. Trewhitt "banished" the section to an appendix.[66]

The timing of the ABM decision suggests an additional rationale: the need to compromise with rightwing forces pushing for an escalation of the Vietnam War. By late 1966 and into 1967 the U.S. had become stalemated militarily and the initial response, especially from the right, was frustration. Policy discussions concerning the ABM occurred in the immediate context of an expanded air war over North Vietnam. Vietnam and the ABM were the two main agenda items at meetings at LBJ's Texas ranch on November 3 and November 10, 1966.[67] Both the ABM and pressure to bomb additional targets in the North came up again on December 6th. At that time McNamara, Vance, Johnson and Rostow heard the Joint Chiefs give their argument for "Posture A," or coverage against a Chinese attack. The Joint Chiefs also made it clear that they expected Posture A to evolve into "Posture B" or full defense against a Soviet attack.[68] The Chiefs threatened to resign if the ABM was not deployed.[69] On the very same day, U.S. Navy jets were bombing Hanoi, interrupting expected U.S.-North Vietnam contacts in Warsaw.[70] Thus Johnson was under the simultaneous pressures of escalation in Vietnam, resuming the arms race with the Soviet Union through a massive ABM program, and covering his right flank for the upcoming presidential race. Johnson gave McNamara a last chance to reach an arms agreement with the Soviet Union. But McNamara's efforts at the Glassboro summit meeting in June failed. Johnson had to compromise somewhere. Escalation of the war could bring the U.S. dangerously close to direct confrontation with the Soviet Union and China. LBJ wanted another four years. That left the ABM. Johnson directed McNamara to proceed with deployment. The option was not whether or not to build; the only choice was big or small. In effect the message to McNamara was "spend five billion dollars, call it an ABM, come up with a credible rationale." McNamara, playing the game which does not permit revealing the domestic pressures that contribute to decision-making in foreign policy, chose the rationale of China. As part of the bargain, the Joint Chiefs were free to call the "thin" anti-Chinese system a first step to full anti-Soviet deployment.

The U.S. constructed a minimal ABM to assure Johnson and McNamara control over the Vietnam War and to maximize Johnson's chances of retaining the Presidency. The ABM was essentially a compromise with certain specific interests and the right strategic policy current, made in order to retain control over more important issues. The decision contained no intrinsic rationale; it could not be justified in terms of strategic policy alone.

Radicals are usually uncomfortable with bureaucratic explanations such as these, for they emphasize the irrationality of the decision-making process over that of class interests. Except for a small number of defense contractors, there were no economic benefits to be gained from constructing an ABM system. Not only would the five billion dollars (actually ten billion, allowing for the "normal" cost overruns) be wasteful in human terms, but the expenditure, considering the already swollen defense budget, would further undermine economic stability. In political and strategic terms, the ABM directly contradicted McNamara's stated policy. Neither windfall profits for defense contractors, nor a shortcoming in the American strategic arsenal explains the ABM decision. The ABM was an unwelcome albatross forced upon Johnson and McNamara.

Yet it is still possible to develop a radical explanation of the ABM decision — and on far more specific grounds than the broad historical context of the arms race and its overall consequences. Such an explanation requires that the fluidity of state politics be taken seriously, that the dominant need of maintaining control over the Vietnam War be recognized, and that the process as well as the outcomes of decision-making be fully appreciated. The bureaucratic maneuvers surrounding the ABM do "make sense" from a radical standpoint, once situated in the conflict among different policy currents. The ABM constitutes a retreat forced upon the center Vietnam current by the right strategic current.

This chapter has focused on one type of opposition confronting the U.S.: that emanating from the Vietnamese and their allies. This opposition, in combination with the state managers own dispositions and perceptions of the Vietnam conflict, contributed to the formation of distinct policy currents. The next chapter examines another constraint on U.S. intervention, that of domestic opposition.

V: DOMESTIC OPPOSITION

In late 1966, when restrictions on the bombing of Hanoi and Haiphong were still in effect, a group of military officers visited Lyndon Johnson to press for a new bombing program, one which would attack the industrial capacity of those cities and block the vital Haiphong harbor. The military men employed an analogy. Using an atomic bomb at the end of World War II, they argued, had saved 750,000 lives. Concentrated attacks on North Vietnamese urban centers would also save American lives and shorten the war.

Johnson appeared fascinated with the projection and its implications. He asked to see the staffers who had developed the methodology for the study. This group was brought into the Oval Office. Johnson pretended to be interested in the details of their work, and the recommendation to bomb Hanoi and Haiphong as a way to save American lives, but suddenly he announced, "I have one more problem for your computer — will you feed into it how long it will take five hundred thousand angry Americans to climb that White House wall out there and lynch their President if he does something like that?"[1]

The episode illustrates how the antiwar movement, and the President's perception of the antiwar movement, can influence policy, in this case restricting the available escalatory options by making their potential domestic costs too high. Thus Admiral Thomas Moorer, then Chief of Naval Operations and later Chairman of the Joint Chiefs of Staff, testified before Congress: *"If domestic restraints were relaxed,* the U.S. would have the option of bombing Haiphong harbor in North Vietnam and launching amphibious assaults behind North Vietnamese lines."[2]

This chapter examines domestic opposition to the Vietnam War and analyzes its political character. Demonstrating the actual impact of domestic opposition within the decision-making process itself is a task reserved for the detailed history of August 1967 to March 1968 that is presented in Chapters Seven and Eight.

Policy Currents and Domestic Opposition

Policy currents emerge from forces of opposition. The previous chapter analyzed those of international character: the strength of the Vietnamese Revolution, and material and diplomatic assistance from the Soviet Union and China. This chapter focuses on the constraints on Vietnam decision-making imposed by domestic opposition. That task is greatly complicated by the variety of political tendencies generally lumped together under the term "domestic opposition." Does domestic opposition refer only to the antiwar movement? What is the relationship between the antiwar movement and the broader, but less cohesive, opposition offered by public opinion that has turned against the war? Does domestic opposition include "elite" opinions? Are only conscious efforts to oppose the war, such as participating in demonstrations, counted as antiwar activity? How does one situate theoretically the impact of indirect forms of opposition, such as declining presidential popularity, that restrict the range of options available to decision-makers?

The problem posed by these different forms of domestic opposition is partially resolved by decomposing that concept into distinct categories. The first component is the antiwar movement, those people consciously opposed to the war and taking action to stop it. While politically diverse, participants in the antiwar movement shared a common experience of explicit opposition and activity based on that opposition. Some demonstrated, some wrote letters to Washington, others organized local protests such as placing advertisements in newspapers. As the size of the antiwar movement grew, the state managers became increasingly aware that the consequences of escalation in Vietnam would be more vocal and hostile opposition in the streets. But the extent and influence of domestic opposition was far broader than the antiwar movement itself. The second component of domestic opposition is the more diffuse but still important constraint exercised by public opinion. While more nebulous than the antiwar movement, public opinion against the war contributed to a general atmosphere of war weariness, dissent and dissatisfaction. Like the antiwar movement itself, public opinion formed an obstacle to escalation that greatly limited the range of options available to Vietnam decision-makers. As public dissatisfaction mounted, Johnson's personal popularity declined. Public opinion contributed to the economic costs of the war as well. As Secretary of Treasury Walter Heller later put it, there was "an unwillingness to loose the flood of debate on Vietnam for which a tax increase. proposal would provide the tempting occasion."[3] As a result, the fiscal and monetary controls normally associated with a war economy were not adopted. Thus public opinion, together with the antiwar movement, indirectly increased inflationary pressures within the economy and catalyzed resentment within the capitalist class over Vietnam. As a pressure on the state managers, the antiwar movement was comparatively firm. There was little that the government could do to reduce the size of the antiwar movement — short of withdrawing from Vietnam itself. Public opinion, while also powerful, carried a more diffuse quality, leaving it partially subject to government manipulation through the press or through promises of progress.

The third component of domestic opposition, elite opinion, consists of the views of the press, capitalist class, and private study groups. Elite opinion reproduces the policy divisions found within the state. Different editorial positions in major newspapers, for example, largely parallel the differences found among the state managers. Each position serves as an ideological bridge linking state managers with other defenders of the capitalist order. This chapter will illustrate the concept of ideological bridges in two ways: by focusing on the political differences within the press, and by analyzing reports from private study groups. In each case, differences among elite views outside of the state largely duplicate the differences among the state managers themselves. These differences are best understood within the context of policy currents.

Policy currents emerge from forces of opposition and from the responses of decision-makers. In this particular case, the left, right, and center currents disagreed over the best way to grapple with domestic dissent. The left current worried about the extent of that opposition, especially the antiwar movement, finding a connection with the civil rights and black power movements, and with urban decay. For the left policy current, the antiwar movement, and even hostile public opinion, were symptomatic of a deeper social malaise. A new commitment to social expenditures had to be made. The expense of the Vietnam War delayed the funding of cooptive measures against movements that in their eyes threatened the established order. For the left, the growth of the antiwar movement and the other insurgencies of the sixties made the domestic front more important than military victory in Vietnam.

Domestic dissent was also a constraint for the right policy current. Like the left, individuals holding this position thought that the U.S. effort in Vietnam was severely weakened by the lack of support at home. Unlike the left, they felt that domestic opposition, especially public opinion, could be swung back behind the war effort by patriotic appeals, mobilization of the reserves, and new military measures that promised early success. (The left thought that mobilization of the reserves would only fuel further dissent.) The right felt that participants in the antiwar movement were traitors to their country, but that dissent in the form of public opinion "turned-off to the war" was soft, and that renewed military efforts to end the war quickly would gain support.

The center was stuck with a high cost, high profile war. They did not want to escalate, as the right desired, for fear of provoking Moscow and Peking. Nor did this group choose the low-cost stalemate favored by the left which would have recognized some territorial and political rights for the NLF. In the meantime, the rapidly mounting body count, the lack of progress, and the economic cost of the war all deepened dissent. As a response, the center current promised early success, despite *knowing* that the U.S. was not following measures that would win the war. The center chose to lie to the American public. On many occasions, Johnson was told by his key advisors that the Vietnamese resistance would not crumble. National Security Advisor McGeorge Bundy advised Johnson on February 8, 1965: "At its very best the struggle in Vietnam will be long. It seems important to us that this fundamental fact be made clear and our understanding of it be made clear to our own people... there is no shortcut to success in South Vietnam."[4] In fact the American people were never told of intelligence assessments maintaining that a million ground troops and a seven to ten year commitment were needed to win.[5] Johnson and the rest of the center current feared the public debate that such information would have produced. The center was trapped; they had to systematically deceive the American public, promise early success. Johnson essentially lied from 1965 to 1968.[6] He knew that the war was not being won, but he did not — or could not — do anything different. The strategy eventually rebounded. Gradually the deception became more apparent, leading to the famous "credibility gap." Ironically, Johnson's method of defusing public opposition eventually led to further intensification of domestic pressure against the state managers.

Domestic opposition had three components: the antiwar movement, public opinion, and elite opinion. The antiwar movement and public opinion served as constraints on decision-making, and contributed to the forces of opposition that produce policy currents. Elite opinion fell within the realm of policy currents. Let us examine the composition and political character of domestic opposition a little more closely.

The Antiwar Movement

The antiwar movement served both to check further escalation and to pressure for de-escalation. Estimates of its size vary. Cautious judges place the number of participants in antiwar demonstrations involving one thousand or more at 300,000 in 1968 (up from 53,000 in 1965).[7] If we expand the concept of antiwar activity to include participation in smaller demonstrations, signing newspaper advertisements against the war, and sending letters and telegrams to Congress and the President, the numbers increase from one million in 1965 to two to three million by early 1968.[8] A spring 1967 study estimated the number of active demonstrators at just under two million.[9] The October 21, 1967 March on Washington attracted 250,000, with over 50,000 marching on to the Pentagon itself. International demonstrations were organized by more than one hundred organizations and were centered in Stockholm, London, Vienna, Brussels and Bologna. Over the first two weeks of July 1967, a series of major confrontations occurred in Stockholm, in front of the American Embassy.[10] Despite its growth, however, the antiwar movement's composition remained quite narrow. Significant labor participation in public demonstrations did not emerge until 1970.

Draft resistance was one focal point of the movement and intensified dramatically during the year before Johnson's March 31, 1968 address. Public draft card burning on a large scale started in Central Park, New York in April 1967. October 16 marked the first national draft card turn-in; December 4, the second. The third national draft card turn-in was April 3, 1968 only four days after Johnson announced that he would not seek another presidential term. The Oakland, October 16-21 Stop the Draft Week featured a variety of tactics, each representing a different tendency, but all aimed at interfering directly with the induction process. The Oakland demonstrations culminated in a street battle with police, the news of which quickly spread through the rest of the country. For some antiwar activists, Oakland represented a new step, the beginning of urban guerilla warfare that would eventually link up with the increased intensity of racial rebellions.[11] At the University of Wisconsin and the Whitehall Induction Center in New York, efforts to interfere with normal procedures were also carried out. In early January, Dr. Benjamin Spock, Reverend William Sloan Coffin, Michael Ferber, Mitchell Goodman, and Marcus Raskin were indicted for counseling violation of the Selective Service Act. Widespread distrust of the draft system was shown when a poll found that only 43 percent thought that draft boards were "fair" (in comparison to 60 percent during the Korean War and 79 percent for World War II).[12]

Resistance to the Vietnam War within the armed forces developed somewhat later. After 1969 the U.S. Army virtually ceased effective operation in Vietnam; desertions, "fragging" of officers, and outright refusal to enter combat reached unprecedented proportions.[13] "Search and destroy" missions turned into "search and avoid" missions. Table 5-1, a compilation of the number of fragging incidents in the U.S. Army in Vietnam, and Table 5-2, which compares AWOL (Absent Without Leave) and desertion rates for the Army and Marine Corps for World War II, Korea and Vietnam, give some indication of this trend. Between 1969 and 1971 the number of fragging incidents went up almost three hundred percent. The AWOL and desertion rates in Vietnam show a steady increase from 1965, when U.S. troops began to fight on a sustained basis.

Table 5.1
Fragging Incidents, U.S. Army Vietnam, 1969-71

	1969	1970	1971
Total incidents	126	271	333
Actual assaults[1]	96	209	222
Possible assaults[2]	30	62	111
Total incidents per 1,000 strength at midyear	0.35	0.91	1.75
Deaths	37	34	12
Intended victim			
Officer/NCO	70	154	158
Enlisted man	17	40	43
Vietnamese	7	20	28
Unknown	32	57	104

Sources: U.S. House, Committee on Appropriations, Subcommittee on Department of Defense, *DOD Appropriations for 1972*, Hearings, 92nd Congress, 1st sess., part 9, 17 May-23 September 1971, p. 585 (updated later), OASD (Comptroller), *Selected Manpower Statistics*, May 1975, p. 63. Adopted from Guenter Lowy, *America in Vietnam*, New York, Oxford University Press, 1978, p. 156.

[1]Actual assaults: Intent to kill, do bodily harm or intimidate is the determined motive.

[2]Possible assaults: Intent to kill, do bodily harm or intimidate is a possible motive.

These developments were rooted in the illegitimacy and the inconclusive character of the policies followed by the Johnson Administration.[14]

The first major public act of Army resistance came in June 1966 when three privates from Fort Hood, Texas refused orders to ship out to Vietnam. The three were followed by Ronald Lockman, "I follow the Fort Hood Three, who will follow me?" Lockman was in fact followed by other individual acts of resistance. Captain Howard Levy refused to teach medicine to Green Berets, and Captain Dale Noyd refused to instruct new bombing pilots. In April 1967 five GIs staged a pray-in for peace. Two refused an order to stop praying and were court-martialed. Individual acts of resistance were now supported by newspapers and off-base coffeehouses, thus providing an on-going organization to GI resistance. Some members of the armed

Table 5.2

Worldwide AWOL and Desertion Rates
World War II, Korea and Vietnam
(Per 1,000 Average Enlisted Monthly Strength)

| | Army | | Marine Corps | |
	AWOL	Desertion	AWOL	Desertion
World War II				
CY 1943	•	•	•	FY 8.8
CY 1944	•	63.0	•	FY 6.9
CY 1945	•	45.2	•	FY 5.4
Korean War				
FY 1951	•	CY 14.3	•	10.1
FY 1952	181.0	22.0	•	19.7
FY 1953	158.0	22.3	•	29.6
Vietnam War				
FY 1965	60.1	15.7	•	18.8
FY 1966	57.2	14.7	•	16.1
FY 1967	78.0	21.4	•	26.8
FY 1968	89.7	29.1	•	30.7
FY 1969	112.3	42.4	•	40.2
FY 1970	132.5	52.3	174.3	59.6
FY 1971	176.9	73.5	166.6	56.2
FY 1972	166.4	62.0	170.0	65.3
FY 1973	159.0	52.0	234.3	63.2

* Data not available.

Source: Data provided by OASD (Manpower and Reserve Affairs). Adopted from Guenter Levy, *America in Vietnam*, New York, Oxford University Press, 1978. p. 157.

---

forces voted with their feet. The desertion rate in 1966 was 14.7 per thousand and rose to 26.2 per thousand in 1968 and 52.3 per thousand in 1970.[15] The American Serviceman's Union attempted to develop a list of GI rights. And on university and college campuses ROTC programs came under attack. In some cases these training centers for junior officers were closed down.

The armed forces movements had a different class character than the civilian movement. That fact, in addition to the specific conditions of each type of opposition and the different form of leadership, makes it difficult to speak of a single unified antiwar movement. Indeed, the antiwar movement was composed of groups and individuals from different social backgrounds, forming diverse political tendencies and favoring alternative sets of tactics and goals. What the participants in the antiwar movement shared was a conscious opposition to the Vietnam War and a willingness to take action in an attempt to stop it.

This was a time of flux and confusion — both ideologically and strategically. To many antiwar activists, liberalism appeared severely compromised, even bankrupt. Liberal heroes such as Hubert Humphrey, Abe Fortas, and Arthur Goldberg lost credibility time and again by defending U.S. intervention in Vietnam. The Americans for Democratic Action, that quintessential liberal organization, was completely divided on the war issue. Campus teach-ins also contributed to the delegitimation of liberalism. Faculty participation often catalyzed student rejection of the war. Political philosophies favoring participation through established channels, channels which reinforced passivity and ineffectiveness, were put to a severe test by those demanding genuine influence over their country's national policies and control over their own institutions. But the attacks on liberalism were not accompanied by the emergence of a coherent opposition ideology. The antiwar movement missed many opportunities to move beyond single issue politics. Some observers saw the April 1967 National Conference of New Politics as one chance to develop a coherent radical opposition by articulating a socialist alternative. But the conference collapsed in sectarian bickering and racial antagonism. Even the choice of tactics produced extensive disagreement within the antiwar movement. The Students for a Democratic Society decided that demonstrations were no longer radical enough — just when their strength and influence were beginning to mushroom. In June, 1967, the SDS Convention passed a resolution regretting "the decision of the National Mobilization Committee to call for a March on Washington in October [because] these large demonstrations . . . can have no significant effect on American policy in Vietnam. Further they delude many participants into thinking that the 'democratic process' in America functions in a meaningful way."[16] Many activists identified radical politics either with particular moral positions or with particular tactics.

At the same time the impact of antiwar activity on the state managers was often visible and dramatic. At one point during the

October 1967 March on the Pentagon, Secretary of Defense Robert McNamara could be seen gazing out of his window at the tens of thousands assembled below. For many state managers, public speaking became an adventure. In an interview, Assistant Secretary of State William Bundy communicated his sense of growing antiwar opposition to his speaking efforts:

> Just to give a personal reaction and feeling of the opposition, because one watched this very closely, I spoke at the National Student Association in August [1967]. There was predictable opposition but they did hear me out. By October, when I spoke at Stanford, it was touch and go whether you could be heard out. I was heard out but you could sense that things were much worse than before.[17]

Johnson was virtually restricted to army bases and conservative assemblies. One of the most violent demonstrations occurred on November 14th when Secretary of State Dean Rusk spoke before the Foreign Policy Association at the New York Hilton. The Fifth Avenue Peace Parade Committee had organized a demonstration to protest but had been denied, until the last minute, a parade permit by the New York Police Department. Two or three thousand demonstrators edged towards violence when the crowd was ordered from areas it had been permitted to occupy. About two hundred members of the SDS chapter at Columbia University were determined to follow the example of the Oakland draft protest and take up street action. The police surrounded those attempting to stop limousines and Cadillacs and began to attack the crowd with clubs. Some protesters broke away, started to move towards Fifth Avenue, but were deflected south to Times Square where they broke windows at the Armed Forces Recruiting Station. One of the most dramatic moments was provided by Eartha Kitt who, displaying a noble sense of courage and timing, denounced the war before a January White House gathering.[18] The incident, and Lady Bird Johnson's horrified reaction, was widely reported in the press. Efforts to bring the war home and against broader targets would intensify over the next year. Internal memoranda reprinted in the Pentagon Papers indicate that the state managers feared that a consequence of continued escalation would be a stronger antiwar movement.[19]

The fear inspired by the antiwar movement shows up in post-

Watergate revelations of domestic spying by the FBI, Army Intelligence, and CIA. Then Director of Central Intelligence Richard Helms has testified that, in violation of the original charter prohibiting domestic surveillance, that he was ordered by Johnson to investigate Vietnam War protesters.[20] Helms complied, establishing the beginnings of the domestic intelligence apparatus that eventually backfired in Watergate. It became a classic case of the chickens coming home to roost. Watergate, the political crisis that weakened the executive branch to the point where the anti-communist commitment in Vietnam could not be followed, was rooted in the success and influence of the antiwar movement and the efforts of the Johnson and Nixon Administrations to repress it.

The antiwar movement did not end the Vietnam War but it limited the freedom of action available to decision-makers in several distinct ways: the ability of the government to mobilize domestic support for the war was greatly reduced, with a major escalation including the possible use of nuclear weapons and an invasion of North Vietnam ruled out; the capacity of the military to fight was weakened, in part due to rapidly widening dissent in the ranks; the tenor of the domestic political climate was changed with aspects of liberalism and the Cold War view of a bipolar world severely shaken; and, importantly, a broader, more diffuse, but nonetheless effective form of opposition, that of public dissatisfaction with the war, was stimulated. The antiwar movement was composed of those opposed to the war and taking conscious action to stop it. While not offering the same kind of opposition, public dissatisfaction with the Vietnam War also constrained decision-makers. It is to an analysis of that second form of domestic opposition that we now turn.

Public Opinion and War Weariness

Public opinion polling assumes that society is composed of an aggregation of disparate individuals. It tells us little if anything about the degree of commitment each respondent feels towards his or her answer. We do not know whether an individual represents or speaks for an important group or class. Each individual is assumed to have equal influence in the determination of political outcomes. Each individual is supposed to play an active role in formulating his or her opinion. The direct management of public opinion and other, less obvious, determining influences, such as political culture, tend to be ignored.[21] An image of a pluralist society emerges from the detailed description and analysis of cross-cutting cleavages; the creation of such an image is one of the more subtle functions of public opinion polling. Polling also operates, through the exclusion and legitimation of different alternatives, as a choice restricting mechanism.[22]

As a result of these considerations, radicals generally distrust public opinion polls, preferring to concentrate on the impact of social movements. Yet policy-makers are highly aware of public opinion polls. Until he became unpopular, Johnson used to carry copies of the latest polls in his coat pocket. Visitors to the White House who hinted that the country was not entirely behind the war effort would quickly be accosted with the latest figures. After late 1967, when the polls finally showed less than fifty percent approval of his Presidency, Johnson dropped his habit of carrying the results with him.

Thus, despite the reservations outlined above, public opinion polls do demonstrate some of the pressures operating on policy makers. The influence of the antiwar movement, while direct and overt, did not exhaust the extent of domestic opposition. In addition to direct participation in the movement itself, millions of Americans, most of whom did not appreciate "the protesters and peace-niks," began to develop a diffuse and somewhat inchoate sense of war weariness. As the war dragged on and on, the U.S. people became more impatient. The majority were not opposed in principle to the Vietnam War, but were certainly frustrated with the lack of progress. Some of this sentiment, admittedly, came from opinion further to the right than the Administration's. These objectors were weary of the war and urged a big push to get it over with. Many others were to the left. Unfortunately for the center policy current, both hawkish and dovish impatience pushed Vietnam policy towards the left current. The option of significant escalation favored by the right position was ruled out (although not without a battle) by the strength of the Vietnamese, by the willingness of Moscow and Peking to defend North Vietnam and the NLF, and by potential public unrest in the United States. Public disapproval of the Vietnam War also prevented the passage of taxes which could have reduced the adverse economic impact of the war outlined in the next chapter. Taken together, these diverse forms of public hostility towards the Vietnam

War produced a significant break in the anticommunist imperatives that had dominated American foreign policy since World War II.

The actual influence of public opinion is quite complicated and variable. In March 1968 public opinion focused on the narrow issue of the war; its intensity helped force a change in policy. Unlike the antiwar movement, the influence of public opinion was *both* large and subject to manipulation. After his election in 1968, Richard Nixon had to respond in some manner; public hostility towards the way in which Johnson pursued the war *forced* Nixon to do something different. Yet the new President was able to circumvent this pressure, leaving the impression that steps to reduce the costs of the war were actually a prelude to negotiated settlement. He thus coped, temporarily, with that sector of domestic opposition which was simply "weary." Both the antiwar movement and public opinion were exerting pressure to change policy. But Nixon's promise of a "secret peace plan" and his request for a moratorium on criticism successfully divided the passive yet effective opposition from the more active current. The antiwar movement went on — but so did the war.

A summary of the swing in public opinion against the Vietnam War follows. Table 5.3 reports the results of polls of President Johnson's performance rating, as well as his handling of Vietnam, between June 1967 and March 1968. In August 1967 the rating performance becomes negative for the first time during his Presidency. Johnson's popularity bounces back somewhat, declines again after the TET Offensive, and sinks to its lowest point (thirty-six percent expressing approval) in late March 1968. Johnson's performance rating on Vietnam follows a similar pattern, hitting its low point in late March (twenty-six percent expressing approval).

The public was not always fooled by the many propaganda efforts engineered by the Johnson Administration. Many remained unconvinced that the South Vietnamese elections, held September 3, 1967, would produce political stability: "Of the seventy-three percent who have followed the election campaign," a poll of Americans found, "more say the South Vietnamese will not be able to establish a stable government than say they will be able to do so. The public is divided as to whether a civilian or military man should head the government, and opinion is closely divided as to whether the campaign has been fairly conducted."[23] There were signs of public rejection. On October 25, 1967, forty-six percent said that it had

Table 5.3
President Johnson's Popularity and Handling of the Vietnam War, June 1967-March 1968

Johnson's Popularity
Question: "Do you approve or disapprove of the way Johnson is handling his job as President?"

Date	Approve	Disapprove	No Opinion
June 1967 (early)	44	40	16
June 1967 (late)	52	35	13
August 1967	39	47	14
September 1967	39	47	13
October 1967	38	50	12
November 1967	41	49	10
December 1967	46	41	13
January 1968	48	39	13
February 1968	41	47	12
March 1968 (early)	41	48	11
March 1968 (late)	36	52	12

Johnson's Handling of Vietnam
Question: "Do you approve or disapprove of the way President Johnson is handling the situation in Vietnam?"

Date			
June 1967 (early)	43	42	15
June 1967 (late)	43	43	14
July 1967	33	52	15
August 1967	33	54	13
November 1967	35	52	13
December 1967	40	48	12
January 1968	39	47	14
February 1968	35	54	11
March 1968 (early)	32	57	11
March 1968 (late)	26	63	11

Source: *Gallup Opinion Index*

---

been a mistake to become involved in Vietnam, almost twice as many as had held that view in August 1965 (twenty-four percent).[24] The TET Offensive was particularly critical in the shift of U.S. public opinion. Respondents classifying themselves as "doves" rose from forty percent in January 1968 to sixty percent by the end of March.[25]

Another important measure of public opinion was its reaction to a bombing cessation. In April, in response to the question "Do you approve of President Johnson's decision to stop (sic) the bombing of North Vietnam?'', sixty-four percent gave their approval and only twenty-six percent disapproved. Ten percent had no opinion.[26]

The growing dissent of the American people also appears by comparing attitudes towards earlier wars. Chart 5.1 utilizes three different indices to contrast the popularity of World War II, the Korean War, and the Vietnam War. Dissent during the three wars, part one of the table, is measured by public disapproval of the original decision to commit U.S. military men to combat. During World War II dissent declined twenty-six points. During the Korean War dissent increased sixteen or thirty points (depending on the survey). At the beginning of 1970, dissent during the Vietnam War had increased thirty-three points. Even by early 1968 the percentage dissenting had increased dramatically.

Part two of the table compares public disapproval of the President during the same three years. Disapproval of Roosevelt started from a low twenty-three percent in 1942 and declined further to nineteen percent by 1944. Disapproval of Truman increased from a substantial forty-four percent in mid-1950 to fifty-six percent three years later. Disapproval of Johnson rose from a remarkably low eight percent in mid-1965 to forty-five percent in mid-1968. On the more limited issue of LBJ's handling of Vietnam, the percentage disapproving rose from twenty-eight in mid-1965 to over fifty by March 1968.

Evasiveness during the three wars is compared in part three by examining the number of appeals per thousand filed by those receiving 1-A classification (the most eligible group) by the selective service. During World War II evasiveness declined twenty-three percent. During the Korean War the number of appeals increased remarkably (rising from one in mid-1950 to forty-seven in mid-1953). The pattern is even stronger for Vietnam. The number of appeals increased from four per thousand in July 1965 to seventy-nine in July 1968.

International opposition to the U.S. intervention also grew, particularly over the issue of bombing North Vietnam. U.S. Ambassador William Heath left Sweden after Olaf Palme, Minister of Education, marched at the head of a "pro-Viet Cong" demonstration in Stockholm. In West Germany, the Vietnam issue led to a split within the governing coalition. Willy Brandt, then Foreign Minister

Chart 5.1
Dissent During World War II, the Korean War, and the War in Vietnam

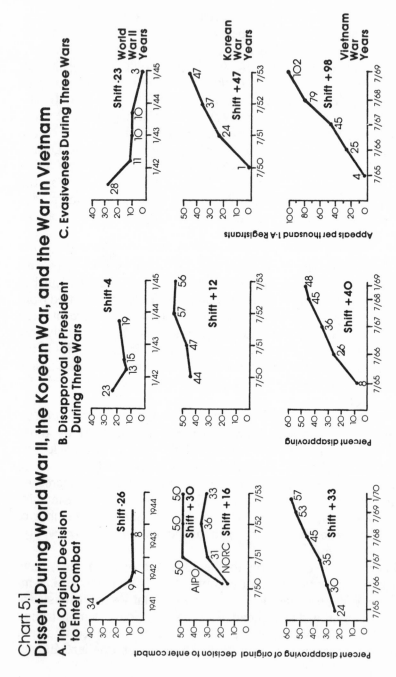

A. The Original Decision to Enter Combat

B. Disapproval of President During Three Wars

C. Evasiveness During Three Wars

Source: Robert Smith, "Disaffection, Delegitimation and Consequences: Aggregate Trends for World War II, Korea and Vietnam," Charles Moskos (ed.), *Public Opinion and the Military Establishment*, Beverly Hills, Sage Publications, 1971.

and chairman of the executive committee of the Social Democratic Party called for an immediate halt to the bombing of North Vietnam and endorsed the peace proposals of United Nations Secretary General U Thant. Chancellor Kiesinger of the Christian Democrats supported American policy. General Charles De Gaulle, of course, savored every moment of U.S. intervention since it aided his efforts to chart an independent course for France in Europe. In Britain, the Labor Party's Harold Wilson gave vocal support to U.S. policy, but denied any direct aid. He came under severe pressure from his own party to be more critical of U.S. efforts in Vietnam. The March 1968 issue of *Interplay* contained an extensive review of European opinion in London, Bonn, Rome, Paris, and Moscow, the majority in each case opposing U.S. policy. An international Gallup Poll conducted in twelve non-socialist countries in late-1967 found widespread disapproval of U.S. intervention in Vietnam. Participants in Finland, Sweden, Brazil, France, India, Uruguay, Argentina and West Germany voted overwhelmingly for U.S. withdrawal. In England and Canada a slimmer majority thought that the U.S. should withdraw. Majority support for U.S. policy could be found only in the U.S. and Australia.[27]

As discussed so far, public opinion reflects the views of the country as a whole. What about particular groups and classes? Are there any significant differences from the national pattern?

One common assumption is that the vast majority of blue-collar workers, construction workers and other constituents of the so-called "silent majority" suppported the Vietnam War and urged their President to even greater levels of escalation. In Seymour Martin Lipsit's theory of "working-class authoritarianism," low education, little reading, low levels of political interest and fewer organizational affiliations explain a presumed relationship between lower social class and authoritarian attitudes and political behavior — in this case favoring extreme military pressures to end the war as quickly as possible.[28] But the relationship between lower status and support for escalation is not supported by the available evidence. Several public opinion studies note that individuals with higher status were *more* likely to support escalation and were *more* opposed to withdrawal from Vietnam.[29] A 1968 study found fifty-nine percent of those with low social position, forty percent with intermediate, and thirty-one percent with high social position favoring withdrawal of American troops.[30] A series of local referendums on the Vietnam War held in Detroit, Cambridge and Lincoln, Massachusetts, Dearborn, Michigan, San Francisco, and Madison, Wisconsin tell the same story.[31] In each case districts containing people with low incomes, little schooling, and "low-status" occupations were more hostile to the war. These findings have been confirmed by Richard Hamilton who found during both the Korean and Vietnam Wars more support for intensification of the war — the so-called "tough" alternative — among high status occupations and high incomes.[32] Thus, instead of "blue-collar authoritarianism," we are faced with "upper middle-class authoritarianism."[33] The only exception to this trend appears to be the case of professionals holding two or more degrees, although the studies show mixed findings even in this category. A study of university professors, for example, in the Greater Boston area, confirmed the commonly-held view that the highly educated were the most opposed to the war, although the differences from the rest of the population were not as large as expected by the authors of the study.[34]

Other significant differences from the national averages can be found among Jews, blacks, and, to a lesser extent, women, each group being disposed towards dovish responses.[35] Interestingly, youth did not appear more critical of the Vietnam War than other age groups. The so-called generation gap is largely limited to college youth and their parents. On the whole younger respondents (those under thirty) were not inclined towards dovish responses. Data collected in late 1968 indicate that college-educated whites in their twenties were more likely to justify the war and support escalation than elderly people of grade school education.[36]

Table 5.4 summarizes these findings, showing greater sympathy for pulling out of Vietnam or initiating a ceasefire among nonwhites, females, those over thirty-five, individuals in working-class occupations and those with lower levels of education and income in both 1964 and 1968. Over those four years, in all categories, responses were less likely to favor intensification of the war effort.

One can exaggerate and romanticize the increasing opposition to Johnson's Vietnam policy shown by public opinion polls. Demonstrations at community colleges and rebellions in the army had a working-class character, but the majority of blue-collar workers did little to consciously fight the war, even as they disagreed with

Table 5.4
Policy Alternatives in the Vietnam War By Different Social Groups, 1964 and 1968¹

Social Groups	1964				1968			
	Pull Out	Ceasefire	Escalate	N	Pull Out	Ceasefire	Escalate	N
Race								
Non-white	25%	50%	25%	(65)	29%	51%	20%	(153)
White	15%	36%	49%	(894)	21%	40%	40%	(1239)
Sex								
Female	16%	45%	40%	(469)	25%	44%	31%	(779)
Male	11%	31%	58%	(456)	18%	37%	45%	(617)
Age								
Old (60-plus)	22%	38%	40%	(172)	31%	39%	30%	(314)
Middle (35-59)	14%	38%	49%	(459)	19%	43%	38%	(690)
Young (18-34)	9%	38%	53%	(300)	19%	39%	42%	(392)
Occupation								
Working	14%	41%	45%	(37)	19%	40%	41%	(560)
Lower Middle	9%	40%	51%	(106)	21%	41%	37%	(155)
Upper Middle	9%	35%	55%	(258)	19%	43%	38%	(427)
Education								
Less than high school	18%	44%	38%	(330)	25%	39%	35%	(542)
High school, H.S.-plus	11%	35%	54%	(469)	19%	40%	41%	(663)
College graduate	10%	33%	58%	(135)	19%	48%	33%	(187)
Income								
5,000	21%	42%	37%	(285)	30%	40%	30%	(376)
5-10,000	9%	39%	52%	(392)	19%	37%	44%	(539)
10,000-plus	12%	32%	56%	(220)	18%	46%	36%	(441)
Total	13%	38%	49%	(926)	22%	41%	37%	(1396)

¹Those without opinion omitted from table

Source: James Wright, "The Working Class, Authoritarianism, and the War in Vietnam," *Social Problems,* Fall, 1972

Johnson's policy. It should also be recognized that some opponents of the war opted for *greater* escalation. By 1968 sixty percent of the public saw the original decision to go to war as a mistake, yet the number of those who wanted to end the war through escalation continued to outweigh those favoring withdrawal.[37] Responses such as these gave sustenance to the rightwing policy current, which held that support for the war could be mobilized by adopting new offensive measures. Even *among* those who viewed the war as a mistake, almost as many favored escalation as withdrawal.[38]

Approximately half of those voting for McCarthy in the New Hampshire primary considered themselves hawks. Their vote for the Minnesota Senator was based only on their opposition to Johnson's policies. One poll found that "Of those who favored McCarthy before the Democratic Convention but who switched to some other candidate by November, a plurality had switched to Wallace."[39] Opposition to strikes, demonstrations and other forms of visible protest against the war also ran high. Even among those favoring complete withdrawal from Vietnam, fifty-three percent put public protesters on the negative side of a "feeling scale."[40] Yet, although the opposition came from widely different positions, the net result was to increase the public's sense of war weariness, especially when asked to provide increased revenues to pay for the war. More and more, Johnson was the focus of public antagonism. In this way, both kinds of opposition, hawks and doves, contributed to the change in policy.

A further important development during this period was the emerging split within the labor movement over the Vietnam War. The leaders of the AFL-CIO continued to be strong supporters of Johnson's Vietnam policy. A statement passed by the AFL-CIO Executive Council in Chicago in August 1966 was typical. It read in part "those who would deny our military forces unstinting support are, in effect, aiding the Communist enemy of our country — at the very moment when it is bearing the heaviest burdens in the defense of world peace and freedom."[41] Johnson would frequently speak before labor conventions when in need of a friendly audience.

By 1967 the labor monolith had begun to change. On the 11th and 12th of November the Labor Leadership Assembly for Peace met in Chicago. While only four national leaders of the AFL-CIO were in attendance, the meeting represented a significant break in labor's unstinting support of the Cold War. Individual unions taking stands on the war included Local 1199, the Negro American Labor Council, the Missouri Teamsters, District 65 of the Retail, Wholesale and Department Store Workers, the Amalgamated Clothing Workers and the Trade Union Division of SANE. On November 27, 1967 Dr. Martin Luther King spoke before a labor audience that included 523 leaders from 50 international unions in 38 states, and from hundreds of local unions throughout the country.[42] The widespread feeling that the war was responsible for the decline in real wages was one motive behind the large turn-out.

These activities were still minor when measured against the majority of the leadership of organized labor. But labor opposition contributed powerfully to the gradual dissolution of the governing coalition within the Democratic Party. Another sign of the Party's growing fragmentation included Johnson's declining prospects for re-election. Breakaway movements such as Allard Lowenstein's "Dump Johnson" campaign became more common. Relations between labor, reform groups, and ethnic political machines became shaky. Important party officials began to oppose Johnson.

Thus far two kinds of domestic opposition have been outlined: one emanating from the antiwar movement; the other from the more amorphous level of public opinion. As an oppositional force on the state managers, the antiwar movement was comparatively firm, and growing in intensity. The impact of public opinion was more diverse, leading to different responses among the state managers. The left current accepted the inevitability of growing opposition and argued that the U.S. should lower the political costs of the Vietnam War. The right thought that public opinion could be rallied around a new military drive and patriotic appeals. For the center current, domestic opposition contained one clear message: "do something different." For Johnson the message was "do something different or you won't get elected again." Since Johnson and the center current felt that they could not move towards the right for fear of provoking the Chinese and the Soviet Union, and adding to international rage, domestic dissent, and the economic cost of the war, the net effect of the amorphous call for something different was effective pressure on the center current to move towards the left current.

Now we turn towards opinion among representatives of the capitalist class. In the theoretical chapter outlining the concept of policy currents it was argued that similar political positions could be identified among state managers, members of the economic elite, and other defenders of the capitalist order including the press, private study groups, and prestigious committees.[43] Roughly similar political positions constitute an "ideological bridge" linking different agents of influence and power together in a consistent policy current. A number of different bridges exist since more than one policy position can be identified within the state. The remainder of this chapter illustrates the notion of an ideological bridge by tracing the left, center, and right policy currents on Vietnam found among the state managers, within the press and private study groups. The next chapter, examining the economic impact of the war, looks at policy currents within the economic elite itself.

Policy Currents in the Press and Private Study Groups

Interviews with some of the state managers in the Johnson Administration have confirmed already strong evidence that the leaders of the national security apparatus are avid readers of the nation's most influential press. Johnson placed the United Press International and Associated Press teletype services in a room close to his office. Several respondents told of meetings in which aides would rush into the Oval Office carrying the latest clippings off the newswire. Johnson was rarely more than ten minutes behind the latest developments (and the latest editorial positions). Both William Bundy and Dean Rusk were dismayed by the general erosion of press support for the Administration. Rusk felt that the "loss" of the most influential representatives of the press and media — the *New York Times*, the *Washington Post*, the *Wall Street Journal*, the networks, and the newsweeklies — produced an important problem for the Administration.[44] Bundy noted a stream of editors and former enthusiasts for the war telling him "we can't support any increase now . . . you've just got to be finding a way to wind this down and get out of it in some limited time."[45]

A survey by the *Boston Globe* in February 1968 (Table 5.5) showed the editorial position of 39 major newspapers with a total circulation of twenty-two million.[46] Four (the *Chicago Tribune*, the *Cincinnati Enquirer*, the *New York Daily News*, and the *St. Louis*

Table 5.5
Positions of Major U.S. Newspapers, February, 1968

Right Policy Current
Call for an all-out win policy

Chicago Tribune
Cincinnati Enquirer
New York Daily News
St. Louis Globe-Democrat

Center Policy Current
Support the Administration's
Vietnam policies with
no major reservations

Atlanta Constitution
Boston Herald-Traveler
Dallas Times-Herald
Denver Post
Detroit News
Hartford Courant
Houston Chronicle
Nashville Tennessean
New Orleans Times-Picayune
Newsday
Philadelphia Inquirer
Portland Oregonian
Providence Journal
Richmond Times-Dispatch
Washington Star

Left Policy Current
Support the U.S. commitment,
but oppose further escalation,
favor de-escalation, halt or
limitation of bombing, and
increased peace efforts

Boston Globe
Charlotte Observer
Chicago Daily News
Chicago Sun-Times
Christian Science Monitor
Cleveland Plain Dealer
Des Moines Register and Tribune
Detroit Free Press
Kansas City Star
Los Angeles Times
Louisville Courier-Journal
Miami Herald
Milwaukee Journal
Minneapolis Star-Tribune
New York Post
New York Times
Sacramento Bee
San Francisco Chronicle
St. Louis Post-Dispatch
Washington Post

Call for an immediate
pull-out

None

Source Min S Yee, *Boston Sunday Globe*, February 18, 1968, page A-2.

Globe-Democrat) called for an all-out win policy (and support of the rightwing policy current). Of the remaining thirty-five papers, twenty supported the U.S. commitment with reservations. They either opposed further escalation, or they favored de-escalation through halting or limiting the bombing while increasing the peace effort (the left policy current). The remaining fifteen supported the Administration's Vietnam policies with no major reservations (the center current). The survey also reported that during 1967, seven papers (the *Charlotte Observer*, the *Cleveland Plain Dealer*, the *Detroit Free Press*, the *Kansas City Star*, the *Los Angeles Times*, the *Minneapolis Star Tribune*, and the *Richmond Times Dispatch*) had shifted towards a more critical and dovish position (from center to left). The four papers calling for an all-out win policy also broke with the Administration during 1967 (and moved from center to right). No paper called for immediate withdrawal, a position falling outside of the three policy currents.

This interpretation, locating editorial differences within the framework of competing policy currents, differs both from those who maintain that the press is a loyal servant of government, and from those who argue that the press serves as an independent voice, effectively checking illegitimate government actions. The press did not speak with one voice. Examples of syncophantic support for U.S. intervention can be located, as can damning criticisms of the war. These criticisms were generally pragmatic, based on comparisons of government claims for success with the actual difficulties encountered in trying to defeat the NLF. In the sense that these limited objections contributed to general war weariness they were nonetheless influential.[47] Fall 1967 marked the emergence of a "credibility gap," a widely felt difference between the administration's public optimism and the the slow progress revealed by the press. A Gallup Poll taken during the fall reported a three-to-one majority maintaining that a credibility gap did indeed exist.

No paper expressed fundamental disagreements with the Administration's goals in Vietnam. None, for example, called for an immediate pull-out. None developed a criticism of the interventionist thrust of American foreign policy. In this sense the press remained within the limits of loyal criticism. That section of the press which was critical focused on much narrower, but still decisive grounds; they attacked the inflated optimism of those officials trying to sell the war to the American public. Thus, although the press did not really question goals, it did help undermine the legitimacy of the Administration.[48] Press criticisms of the Vietnam effort reverberated among the public, thus contributing to the level of domestic opposition, and limiting the options available to the state managers.

Press coverage of the Vietnam War presents two histories: one of abetting attempts by the state managers to deceive the public; the other, one of limited independence. The tension between the two perspectives, the press as state servant and ideological partner and the press as government critic (at least on the narrow grounds outlined above), serves as the starting-point for an analysis of the press that recognizes its ideological function without situating the actual reporting within a deterministic framework.[49]

In December 1967, while ROLLING THUNDER, the bombing program against North Vietnam, intensified, two private study groups published assessments of the Vietnam situation. The Carnegie Endowment for International Peace produced a short position paper, corresponding to the left policy current, known as the "Bermuda Statement."[50] The group did not repudiate the U.S. commitment in Vietnam, but they did urge that Washington: (1) make every effort to reduce violence in the South, and especially concentrate on providing "protection for the people of South Vietnam" rather than on the "military destruction of communist forces;" (2) stop unconditionally the bombing of North Vietnam; (3) pressure the government of South Vietnam to assume greater responsibility for political and military programs; and (4) recognize the NLF as "an organized factor in the political life of South Vietnam." In these respects the Bermuda Statement went further than it was possible for left policy current members within the state to argue in internal deliberations. The actual exercise of power tends to diminish the differences among policy currents as expressed within the state itself. Yet the basic logic of the Statement, favoring political reform in South Vietnam over still greater military measures, duplicates the private thoughts, in late 1967, of Secretary of Defense Robert McNamara and key members of his civilian staff.

On December 20, fourteen Asian scholars issued a position paper paralleling that of the center current. Unlike the Bermuda Statement, the report backed Administration policy; William Bundy later cited it as supportive.[51] The scope of the paper was regional;

U.S. presence in Southeast Asia had been of crucial importance in preventing the fall of "weaker" nations to Communism. The case of Indonesia was cited in particular. U.S. withdrawal from South Vietnam under "conditions of Communist victory" would be "disastrous for free people everywhere." The report went on to suggest that the South Vietnam government carry more of the war's burden, and strongly urged that the U.S. not escalate the war in a manner that suggested "totalistic policies."[52]

The Bermuda Statement and the Asian scholars paper serve as examples of study groups whose positions dovetail with those of conflicting policy currents within the state. During a period in which both the costs and the pressures for escalation in Vietnam were rapidly mounting, the two groups specifically rejected, in their criticism of any significant step-up in ROLLING THUNDER, the right policy current.[53] This is not to suggest that rightwing study groups did not exist.[54] Indeed, a systematic compilation of foreign policy meetings and associations would produce the full spectrum of positions found among the state managers.

Ideological bridges, or common positions among different defenders of the capitalist order, help us situate political debate; in this case the different positions are responses to pressures exerted by the Vietnamese, domestic dissent and the economic costs of the Vietnam War. Individuals may move from positions of prominence — key policy-forming groups or even the economic elite itself — to the key command posts of the state. They move, in other words, from one "part" of a policy current to another. On a descriptive level this pattern corresponds to theories of political power that emphasize the direct influence of the capitalist class. Such theories, however, fail to capture the influence of popular forces on the decision-making process. The positions powerful individuals express reflect the strength of oppositional forces and policy costs which effectively constrain the freedom of action available to state managers and, indeed, to the capitalist class itself.

This chapter has described one kind of oppositional force, that of domestic dissent among the public, and outlined the responses favored by different state managers. Domestic opposition was divided into three categories: the antiwar movement, comparatively resistant to attempts at manipulation; a more fluid form, public opinion, both powerful and more subject to manipulation; and two examples of "elite opinion," that of the press and private study groups, which were located within the framework of policy currents, and which could be cited by different state managers as support for their own position. The next chapter describes still another policy cost, that of the economic impact of the Vietnam War, and examines the reaction within the capitalist class and state managers.

VI: THE VIETNAM WAR, THE ECONOMY AND THE CAPITALIST CLASS

The direct cost of the Vietnam War is conservatively estimated at one hundred and fifty billion dollars. That money could have helped balance the federal budget, funded a comprehensive national health care system, provided financial relief for urban areas in crisis, covered the cost of retooling the U.S. industry so that antipollution standards could be met, subsidized research and development of a solar energy program, or initiated a program to substantially reduce racial inequality. Indirect costs were even greater. Estimates of the productive labor resources lost on the war run in the tens of billions. Wassily Leontif's cost-benefit analysis of the Vietnam War's economic impact concludes that the standard of living of the average American was lowered two percent.[1] In one year, social expenditures were cut by twelve billion dollars in order to pay for the war. Interest rates started their upward climb. Had funds allocated to the national security apparatus for Vietnam's destruction been directed towards boosting productive capacity, all of us would have received a two-week paid vacation for each of six years, all without lowering output.[2] Of course U.S. citizens paid for the war in non-economic forms as well, death to over fifty thousand and anguish to their families being the most important.

This chapter, analyzing the economic impact of the Vietnam War, is divided into two parts. The first outlines the actual performance of the economy during the escalation of the Vietnam effort between 1965 and 1968. The second outlines the response of the capitalist class, particularly its increasing tendency to voice doubts about the immediate economic future. The capitalist class became more critical of the Administration's Vietnam policy, especially its economic consequences, and argued that the costs

181

associated with that effort should be reduced. But its message, while more and more insistent, did not take the form of a clear-cut alternative. The responsibility of charting policy, of responding to the diffuse signal "to change," remained that of the state managers. The state managers differed among themselves about what to do. But it became increasingly clear that they had to do something. The economy and the views of the capitalist class became, in other words, a political constraint, an obstacle, that contributed to the formation of specific policy currents around the Vietnam War. The explanatory sequence runs from (a) the "objective" state of the economy; to (b) the declining confidence of the capitalist class in the quality of the economic management offered by the Administration; to (c) a debate within the state over the best way to reduce the economic impact of the Vietnam War; to (d) a crisis atmosphere, culminating in March 1968, when the economic situation and the dissatisfaction of the capitalist class penetrate and inform the state's crucial decisions. This chapter covers the first two parts of the sequence. The third and fourth steps are included in the analysis of the August 1967 to March 1968 period found in Chapters Seven and Eight.

A. The War and the Economy

To study the impact of the Vietnam War the economy's performance is compared over three different periods. Period I is the pre-Vietnam build-up extending from 1961 to the end of 1964; Period II is the build-up's first phase, and runs from January 1965 to June 1966; Period III, the second phase of the Vietnam build-up, starts in July 1966 and ends in March 1968. Two distinct economic tendencies appear. Defense spending during Period II, between 1965 and the middle of 1966, stimulated the economy; the major economic indicators show significant increases over the 1961-1964 period. After mid-1966, however, because of abrupt increases in defense spending without fiscal and monetary controls, economic danger signs develop. Johnson wanted guns (the Vietnam War) *and* butter (the Great Society) *and* freedom from economic controls — and this was impossible.

To measure the economy's performance over the three periods, ten economic indicators were selected. A summary of the trends for each follows. Those readers preferring more detail are urged to consult the Economic Appendix. In the meantime, Table 6.1 captures the basic pattern. For each indicator a comparison is made of the average annual increase within each of the three periods under study. In some instances the indicator actually declines (here a minus sign is used). The annual rate of increase, or rate of decline, within each period is provided as well. In most cases Period II shows an improvement over Period I and Period III shows a decline in performance compared with Period II — thus providing support for the hypothesis that expenditures for the Vietnam War gave an initial boost to the economy, but then became an economic liability.

The *Business Week* Index

The *Business Week* index (1957-1959 = 100) is itself a composite of various indicators of economic performance (including raw steel production, automobile production, electric power, crude oil refinery runs, paperboard production, carloadings, intercity truck tonnage, machinery production, transportation equipment, and construction). Between 1961 and 1964 the *Business Week* index increased from 109 to 133, averaging six points a year (or an average annual rate of increase of 5.5 percent). Between 1965 and mid-1966 the index increased from 133 to 156, averaging 15.3 points (or a rate of increase of 11.5 percent per year). But, between mid-1966 and March 1968, the index rose only from 156 to 161. This represents an average annual increase of 2.9 points, or an average annual rate of increase of only 1.9 percent.[3]

Balance of Trade

The second indicator is the balance of trade or the surplus of exports over imports. A strong economy produces competitively priced goods that are attractive in foreign markets. Businessmen have traditionally regarded these exports as a crucial outlet for domestic markets that often appeared saturated.[4] Over 1963 and 1964 exports rose at an annual rate of 14.9 percent.[5] Import increases averaged 13.8 percent. The result was a healthy increase in the trade balance from 4,832 to 7,141 million dollars (or an average annual rate of increase of thirty-seven percent). During Period II exports increased 5.8 percent annually, but import increases averaged 10.5 percent. The result was a slippage in the trade surplus (to 5,263 million in the second quarter of 1966). This represents an annual rate of decrease in the balance of trade of 17.8 percent. In Period III the rate of decrease in the balance of trade accelerated rapidly. Exports continued to increase slowly (at an average annual rate of 6.5 percent), but imports surged (up 13.5 percent a year). The trade surplus was virtually wiped out, falling to only 1,304 million during the first quarter of 1968, or an average annual rate of decrease of forty-two percent. (The trend would continue, with the trade surplus completely eliminated in 1971.)[6]

Reserve Assets

Reserve assets are held by the federal government and are a measure of the strength of a nation's currency in international markets. Between 1961 and 1964 these holdings fell at a relatively slow 785 million a year (or an average rate of decline of 4.6 percent). During Period II the rate of depreciation increased to 7.4 percent; in Period III the rate of depreciation rose to 11.5 percent. Between mid-1966 and March 1968, U.S. reserve assets fell at an annual rate of over one-and-a-half billion dollars. Particularly noteworthy is the loss of over 900 million in the month of December 1967 and 1.2 billion in March 1968! The rapid depletion of reserve assets during these two months contributed a sense of urgency and crisis to Vietnam decision-making.

Other signs of the relative decline of the U.S. in the world economy exist.[7] Between 1966 and 1968 U.S. financial transfers abroad increased, as did the military's share in the balance of payments deficit. Southeast Asia expenditures accounted for three-quarters of the increase in the total adverse balance of payments from 2.1 billion in 1966 to 3.3 billion in 1968.[8] The share of world trade captured by the American economy also suffered a slow decline during the Vietnam War period. In 1961 the U.S. accounted for 17.7 percent of world exports, Industrial Europe for 34.4 percent, and Japan for 3.6 percent. By 1968 the United States accounted for 16.3 percent, with Industrial Europe and Japan increasing their shares to 37.5 percent and 6.1 percent respectively.[9]

Table 6.1
Economic Indicators, Average Annual Increase, and Average Annual Rate of Increase, for Selected Periods

Economic Indicator	Period I 1961-1964	Period II 1965-mid 1966	Period III mid '66-March '68
Business Week Index	6.0 (5.5%)	15.3 (11.5%)	2.9 (1.9%)
Balance of Trade[1,3]	1,789 (37.0%)	-1,270 (-17.8%)	-2,247 (-42.9%)
Reserve Assets[1]	-785 (-4.6%)	-1,119 (-7.4%)	-1,549 (-11.5%)
Gross National Product[2]	41.2 (7.9%)	53.1 (8.0%)	44.5 (5.9%)
Gross National Product[2] (constant 1958 $)	29.9 (6.0%)	30.0 (5.0%)	19.9 (3.0%)
Corporate Profits[2]	6.5 (12.8%)	6.8 (9.3%)	-0.2 (-0.3%)
Index of Industrial Production	8.4 (7.7%)	11.8 (8.5%)	2.7 (1.7%)
Index of Productivity	5.2 (4.8%)	1.5 (1.2%)	2.5 (2.3%)
Consumer Price Index[3]	1.7 (1.7%)	3.0 (2.9%)	2.9 (2.7%)
Federal Government Budget Surplus[2]	1.3	1.2	-8.2

[1]Millions of dollars

[2]Billions of dollars

[3]Average computed over the 1963-1964 period

Sources *Business Week; Economic Report of the President,* selected years, *Survey of Current Business,* selected years; *Monthly Labor Review,* October, 1967, October, 1968.

Gross National Product

The basic pattern of increased economic performance in Period II over Period I, followed by a dramatic decline in Period III, is repeated for the domestic economy. Between 1961 and 1964 the Gross National Product increased at an annual rate of 7.9 percent (averaging 41.2 billion a year). Between 1965 and mid-1966 the GNP continued to increase at eight percent a year (or 53.1 billion dollars). But between mid-1966 and March 1968 the rate of increase in the GNP dropped to five percent (44.5 billion) a year. This pattern becomes stronger when we examine the rate of increase of the GNP in constant 1958 dollars. The average annual rate of increase during Period I is six percent (19.9 billion). During Period II the GNP continues to show a healthy real gain of five percent (30 billion a year). But between mid-1966 and March 1968 the average rate of increase in the GNP falls to three percent (and the average annual increase in the GNP down to 19.9 billion).

Corporate Profits

Corporate profits before taxes for all industries increased at the healthy rates of 12.8 percent for Period I and 9.3 percent for Period II. But over Period III corporate profits actually fell from 84.2 billion during the third quarter of 1966 to 83.8 billion in the first quarter of 1968. One might expect that this indicator would be particularly unsettling to the business community. Indeed, Louis Lundborg, Chairman of the Board of the Bank of America, complained in congressional testimony that after rising seventy-one percent in the four years prior to escalation in Vietnam, corporate profits only rose 9.2 percent between 1966 and 1968.[10]

Index of Industrial Production

The rate of annual increase in the index of industrial production was 7.7 percent in Period I and 8.5 percent in Period II. During Period III the average annual rate of increase in this important indicator fell to 1.7 percent. After climbing from 78.5 percent in 1961 to 90.5 percent in 1966, the rate of capacity utilization, another indicator of the strength of an economy, fell to 84.4 percent in 1968.[11]

Index of Productivity

The labor productivity index is a particularly critical measure of economic performance. Through higher productivity, increases in unit labor costs can be held below increases in wages. An owner of a firm does not have to worry about paying higher wages if increases in productivity result in lower labor costs per unit. Productivity increases are thus a hedge against labor demands for more money. During Period I the index of productivity, in this case measured as private nonfarm output per man-hour, averaged an annual increase of 4.8 percent. The rate of increase fell to 1.2 percent between 1965 and mid-1966 (Period II) and 2.3 percent between mid-1966 and March 1968 (Period III). This lower rate of improvement in productivity was a source of great concern for the economic elite. A report on the economic consequences of the Vietnam War, prepared by the Committee for Economic Development, found that unit labor costs only rose one-half of one percent between 1961 and 1964.[12] In manufacturing, unit labor costs actually declined one percent. In other words, increases in productivity enabled manufacturers to lower their per unit labor costs, despite paying higher wages. But between 1965 and 1966 unit labor costs increased at an overall 3.7 percent rate, and at a 2.7 percent rate in manufacturing. By the 1966-67 period the rate of increase in unit labor costs had risen to 4.5 percent. In the manufacturing sector the increase was 5.1 percent. The resulting pressure to pass on these costs to consumers contributed to inflation.

Inflation

The Consumer Price Index rose very slowly (1.7 percent) during the first half of the nineteen-sixties but increased to 2.9 percent in Period II and 2.7 percent in Period III. Of particular importance is a four percent increase between the first quarter of 1967 and the first quarter of 1968. While the four percent rate pales along the current level, the figure does represent the highest rate of inflation since the Korean War and provoked both anxiety and higher interest rates within financial circles. Between 1966 and 1968 interest rates for high-grade municipal bonds increased from 3.82 percent to 4.51 percent, for short-term bank loans to businesses from 6.00 percent to 6.68 percent, and for new home mortgages from 6.29 percent to 7.13 percent. The discount rate for the Federal Reserve Bank went from 4.50 percent to 5.17 percent.[13]

The increase in consumer prices also offset wage gains obtained by labor unions in negotiated settlements. From 1960 to 1964 spendable earnings in real terms increased by eleven percent; from 1965 to 1970 they decreased by 1.5 percent.[14] The American public suffered in other ways as well. Between 1962 and 1964 the share of GNP taken by defense spending dropped from 9.2 percent to 7.3 percent with personal consumption expenditures holding stable at 63.4 percent. The share taken by defense rose to 8.1 percent in 1966, and then to 9.2 percent in 1967, while personal consumption fell first to 62.2 percent, and then to 62.0 percent.[15]

One source of the current high inflation is the emergence of a huge deficit in federal government financing. In Period I, government receipts averaged an annual increase of 6.7 percent.[16] Increases in government expenditures averaged only 5.2 percent. The result was an erasure of most of the annual federal deficit, which stood at 3.8 billion in 1961 (a surplus of 1.4 billion was achieved in 1965). During Period II federal receipts increased at an average rate of 9.5 percent (11.7 billion) and federal expenditures at 10.5 percent (12.5 billion). During Period III the federal deficit increased enormously. Receipts continued to increase 9.3 percent annually, but expenditures increased at a 15.4 percent rate. The surplus of the federal government, which had been averaging 1.3 billion in Period I, and 1.2 billion in Period II, was ended. Over Period III the annual federal *deficit* was 8.2 billion dollars.

By early 1966 the economy was booming. Unemployment was down from a high of 6.7 percent in 1961 to four percent (thus meeting the Administration's definition of full employment). Industrial plants were operating at ninety percent of capacity. Consumer and wholesale price increases were very low (averaging only 1.3 percent per year since 1958). The Administration's economic policy, including an investment tax credit in 1964 and a slow increase in money supply, combined with a low federal discount rate, appeared successful. In its early stages, the Vietnam build-up was commonly viewed as helping the economy. The Federal Reserve Bank of New York pointed out that "while the share of the GNP directly attributable to defense requirements was a relatively modest 8.5 percent, enlarged defense outlays for goods and services accounted for nearly twenty-five percent of the increase in GNP in 1966."[17] The Bank also noted that "the military build-up and the demand pressures associated with it affected nearly every sector of economic activity." Normally the federal government would have taken fiscal and monetary steps to slow the economy at this point. The Johnson Administration did not and could not. And the capitalist class began to express its displeasure.

B. The Capitalist Class and the Vietnam War

The danger signs appearing in the economy constitute the first stage of the analysis of the relationship between the economy and Vietnam decision-making; the corporate critique of the war's economic impact forms the second.

Taken in its entirety, business opinion tends to be politically diffuse, but enormously influential. In reaction to the economy, declining business confidence became a policy cost contributing to disagreements among the state managers. Some members of the capitalist class did attempt to balance the negative economic impact of the Vietnam War with the necessity of retaining the anti-communist commitment. These examples of politically astute business opinion, which *did* engage the dilemmas of Vietnam policy, fall within the framework of policy currents in the following manner. Specific policy recommendations regarding U.S. intervention in Vietnam are made. But the consensus in the business community breaks down. Some would significantly escalate the war; others would reduce the U.S. commitment. In fact the resulting political disagreements within the capitalist class substantially reproduce policy conflicts among the state managers. The links between similar political positions in the capitalist class and among the state managers form, as in the case of elite opinion outlined in the previous chapter, ideological bridges. Policy conflicts within the state are mirrored by disagreement within the capitalist class, at least in instances where representatives of that class formulate explicit policy recommendations. More commonly, business asserts its unhappiness with the Administration's economic management. Business loses confidence in the state. And the state must do something to get it back.

As long as overall confidence in the economy is retained the state managers are comparatively free to formulate policy. In this respect the views of the capitalist class are more like a political barometer than a firm directive. By the Fall of 1967 the capitalist class agreed that the Vietnam War was bad for the economy. Declining economic performance resulted in lower business confidence in the management offered by the Administration. The state managers had to try to improve the economic climate. This much concerns the influence of the capitalist class as a whole, one that is both powerful but not articulated at the level of specific policy. The business community was primarily concerned with the proper management of the war's economic impact and a reduction of war-related costs; there is little evidence of pressures for unilateral withdrawal. Most reports and individuals specifically avoided a political stance on the Vietnam War itself. The goals of intervention were still important. Wall Street did not become altruistic. Top business leaders were squeezed between their anticommunist political commitments and the higher economic costs of securing that commitment. More and more began to vote with their pocketbooks. Business wanted the destabilizing effects of the war to be reduced through "effective and responsible federal action." Its message is no more specific than that.

The opinions reconstructed below are drawn from a variety of sources: official position statements by assorted business organizations, editorial opinion in business journals, speeches and public statements of influential individuals from the business community, statistics showing stock market reaction to war-related events, and lower confidence in the economy as mirrored in declining investment levels.[18]

Business was not always worried about the Vietnam War. At first strong support was given to U.S. intervention and the goal of defeating the Vietnamese revolution. An advertisement in the *New York Times* on September 9, 1965, placed by the Committee for an Effective and Durable Peace in Asia, explained and supported U.S. action in Vietnam. Among the forty-seven signatories were members of Johnson's economic planning staff, directors of the Council of Foreign Relations, planners for the Committee for Economic Development, civilians formerly associated with various Central Intelligence Activities, and important members of the Senior Advisory Group on Vietnam (a select group of leading businessmen and ex-government officials).[19]

While most business support came on political grounds, in recognition that defeating the National Liberation Front was of real and symbolic importance, some also predicted future economic gain. A *Fortune* editorial noted that

> Even now as the fighting rages, the U.S. is building in Vietnam and neighboring Thailand the 'infrastructure' of future economic development. Once the drain of the war has ended, these harbors, bridges, roads, power stations, and other facilities will pay enormous dividends. Unless we glimpse the opportunity behind the agony in Vietnam, recognizing the strategy and economic imperative of our commitment in Asia, we won't really understand what the war is about.[20]

Representatives of business opinion noted the stimulating effect played by higher defense spending during the first year of the Vietnam build-up. At the time there was some fear that the defense cut-backs of 1963 and 1964 might have an adverse economic effect, especially on industries and localities heavily dependent on defense contracts and military installations. The Vietnam build-up alleviated most of this fear. The Dow Jones average rose from 861 in late July 1965 to a then historical high of 999.15 on February 9, 1966. *Wall Street Journal* analysts noted that increased military outlays were responsible, spurring an economy threatening to go sluggish. But Vietnam-related expenditures quickly changed from a brief and limited stimulant to an economic albatross. And influential members of the business community began to complain.

Individuals, Organizations, and the Business Press

Ralph Lazarus, President of the Federated Department Stores and a member of the Business Council, held a press conference in May 1967 to denounce Johnson's "war budget." Lazarus estimated that the actual costs of the war for FY 1968 would hit twenty-seven billion dollars or five billion more than the official estimate. Johnson confidante Abe Fortas phoned Lazarus and told him to tone down his estimates, as they were inaccurate and unsettling to the President. Yet the actual costs turned out to be even higher than Lazarus had estimated.[21]

Lazarus was not alone. Louis Lundborg, Chairman of the Board of the Bank of America, told the Senate Foreign Relations Committee: "The escalation of the war in Vietnam has seriously distorted the American economy, has inflamed inflationary pressures, has drained resources that are desperately needed to overcome serious domestic problems confronting our country, and has dampened the rate of growth in profits on both a before and after-tax base."[22]

Lundborg was followed by Thomas Watson, Chairman of the Board of IBM, who argued before the same Committee:

> The war in Vietnam is the major factor which has turned our healthy economy into an unhealthy one... During...the first two years of escalation in Vietnam (1965-66), we were in a period of rising prosperity. Sales and profits were strong, and the country was reaching full employment. The war and a very strong consumer market base at home combined to overcommit us economically. This overcommitment fueled inflationary pressures and distortions began to appear.[23]

In a widely reported speech before the Commonwealth Club of San Francisco, Marriner Eccles, Chairman of the Board of Utah Construction and Mining and former Chairman of the Federal Reserve Board under Roosevelt and Truman, went so far as to argue for immediate withdrawal.[24] The next day the *San Francisco Examiner* noted editorially that the most surprising aspect of the event was the warm reception given Eccles' views by attending businessmen. Eccles noted the economic dislocations associated with the war. But even more interesting was his suggestion of a withdrawal that would proceed so fast that negotiations with North Vietnam and the NLF would not even be necessary. Eccles argued that "Russia is glad to see us bogged down in Vietnam, diverting multi-billions of our reserves and millions of our manpower, while it is rapidly growing in the nuclear arms race. While the United States lags in its nuclear defense the Soviet Union is rushing ahead. There are some that believe today's nuclear balance has already shifted to Russia."[25] Eccles even suggested that a "Communist Vietnam" would be desirable, a useful buffer against the expansion of Chinese power. Eccles' emphasis on the U.S. strategic balance with the Soviet Union provides an example of an "ideological bridge" to the state, for his views correspond with the rationale of de-escalation elucidated by Deputy Secretary of Defense Paul Nitze (although Nitze did not advocate complete withdrawal).[26]

The analysis offered by the Committee for Economic Development, a business-dominated study group, focused more typically on the impact of the Vietnam War on the general economic climate.[27] For the CED, the "inflationary psychology" born in World War II and the postwar period had exhausted itself between 1958 and 1964. By the mid-sixties, reduced government spending helped to lower the growth of aggregate demand, producing both slower growth and higher unemployment. In terms of price stability, however, the policy was extremely successful. By early 1965 the CED expected that higher levels of employment and a higher growth rate could be achieved without drastic price increases. But Vietnam-expenditures destroyed this corporate utopia. Inflationary pressures were singled out as particular villains since they cut into the CED's sacred god: the growth of exports.

The Committee's proposed remedy also reflected majority business sentiment. Its focus of attack was domestic inflation. Another CED report concluded that "the origins of the present inflation can be directly traced to the sudden and excessive expansion of aggregate demand that accompanied the build-up of the military conflict in Vietnam after mid-1965, and the failure to adopt prompt and adequate fiscal measures to counteract this expansion."[28] The CED study of the impact of Vietnam spending recommended a number of measures: a cut in the money supply; an increase in taxes; a slower rate of growth in government expenditures, especially *non*defense spending; lower outlays for the space program; and a "stretch-out" of federal highway, harbor, and bridge construction. The proposed tax surcharge was viewed as a necessary evil.[29] On the critical issue of cuts in defense spending the Committee stated that the United States should spend "whatever necessary" but that "the figures are not sacrosanct." The report also hinted at defense theories "that are not necessarily validated" and suggested that further cuts might be made in out-dated programs.

Fortune magazine published a number of articles critical of the management of Vietnam and defense expenditures.[30] An editorial in the February 1968 issue blamed Vietnam for the country's financial difficulties. It noted that the Federal Reserve Board's index of industrial production had dropped half a point during the previous year, that inventory levels rose more than eight percent since "consumers were not indulging themselves,' that housing starts were down, and that net exports had slipped. The editorial concluded with a veiled demand that Johnson not seek re-nomination: "We think that the combination of inflation at home, a consequent worsening of our balance of payments abroad, and the imposition of what amounts to exchange controls over external dollar transactions, adds up to clouds much bigger than the President's hand."[31] Finally, *Fortune* called for the removal of the "weary, harried, and often irascible" Henry Fowler as Secretary of the Treasury. The April issue pointed out that the war was a military stalemate.

The position of *Business Week* was even more straightforward. An editorial of March 30, 1968, just one day before Johnson's abdication speech, stated:

> Somehow the United States is going to have to bring its international commitments into line with its resources— military, economic and political. Of these, the political resource—in other words the price the people of the United States are willing to pay to keep order in the world—may be the most crucial. The forging of that new policy must begin in Vietnam. Immediately that means the U.S. must try to de-escalate the war and enter into negotiations with the Vietcong and North Vietnam.[32]

Business Week coupled its support for de-escalation with a call for fiscal restraint, noting four areas of economic instability: the gold crisis, balance of payments, inflation, and the tax surcharge.

A series of articles published in the *Wall Street Journal* during March exemplified business concern with the economic ramifications of the war. An editorial argued that "the Administration is duty bound to recognize that no battle and no war is worth any price, no matter how ruinous, and that in the case of Vietnam it may be failing for the simple reason that the whole place and the cause is collapsing from within."[33]

In 1969 *Fortune* reported the results of a poll conducted among three hundred chief executives from among the five hundred largest corporations and fifty largest banks.[34] According to this poll, businessmen felt that "the Vietnam War is *the* most critical and pressing issue facing the country, and one of the most serious threats to the economy at the present time (a threat even greater than inflation)." Almost two-thirds of the sample thought that defense expenditures were unduly high. Eighty-one percent of the heads of banks and insurance companies felt that defense programs were wasteful and inefficient. Among those chief executives with large (over ten percent) sales to defense, however, only forty-two percent complained of this problem. There was widespread support (by a margin of almost ten-to-one) for a continuation of the ten percent surtax.

More than a quarter of the executives reported that they had converted from hawks to doves on the Vietnam War in the past year (which, allowing for a period to conduct and compile the survey, extends back into the immediate post-TET period). There were some differences of opinion. At one extreme a California industrialist was "willing to lose face to disengage as rapidly as possible" since the war was "destroying the feeling in youth of loyalty for the U.S.A." A Pennsylvania industrialist whose company did an exceptional amount of defense business lay at the other end of the spectrum. "It's the military versus the State Department," he noted, and "I feel that we should let the military get in there and clean up the job."[35]

The *Fortune* poll was of businessmen from the largest corporations. The membership of Business Executives for Peace (BEP), the most dovish business group, was predominantly middle-level executives from middle-sized corporations. A BEP spokesman acknowledged that one of the major difficulties of the organization was attracting "name executives" from major corporations. BEP was organized in 1967 by Henry Niles, a Baltimore executive. While most of the group's antiwar activity occurred during the 1969-1970 period, earlier efforts included an advertisement in the May 28, 1967 edition of the *New York Times* and a letter to Johnson in September of the same year. But BEP's advocacy of immediate withdrawal and its organizational activity was an exception and far too radical for most businessmen. At its peak BEP claimed only two thousand members.

Political Limits to Economic Controls

Could the deleterious influence of Vietnam on the economy have been avoided? By and large the capitalist class thought that it could, but that a key condition—proper economic management—was missing. Business-sponsored studies comparing the economic impact of the Vietnam and Korean Wars indicated that the former was at least theoretically affordable. In each war Department of Defense expenditures rose thirty billion dollars (from twelve billion in Fiscal Year (FY) 1950 to forty-four billion in FY 1954, and from forty-six billion in FY 1965 to seventy-six billion in FY 1968).[36] Yet military expenditures as a percentage of the GNP rose from five to twelve percent during the Korean War and only from seven to ten percent during Vietnam. The number of men in the armed services rose from 1.5 million to 3.6 million in the Korean War compared to an increase from 2.7 to 3.4 million in the Vietnam War.[37] The effect of the Korean War on unemployment rates was also more dramatic. During the Korean War the rate fell from 5.4 percent in 1949 to 2.9 percent in 1953. During the Vietnam War the rate fell from 4.8 percent in 1964 to 3.2 percent by early 1968.[38] Despite the relatively greater impact of the Korean War on an economy roughly half the size of that during the mid-sixties, the economic difficulties associated with the Korean War were generally smaller. Consumer prices rose only two percent between 1951 and 1952. The economy expanded at a 5.2 percent real growth rate, yet interest rates remained low (around three percent).[39] Part of the reason for the better record during the Korean War was the different starting point. Increased defense expenditures came during the post-war recession largely produced by drastic cuts in federal spending following World War II. By contrast the Vietnam expansion came on an economy generally operating near normal, though showing some sluggish tendencies. But the main difference between Korea and Vietnam was the domestic political conditions prevailing during each war. Quiescence generally dominated the early fifties; social activism marked the mid- and late-sixties. Curtailing government spending on social needs was possible during Korea, impossible in the case of Vietnam.[40]

In its official statements, the Johnson Administration claimed that the economic impact of the Vietnam War was minimal. Secretary of Defense Robert McNamara testified to this effect before Congress in February 1966:

> The defense program should not be a major factor contributing to inflationary pressures. I say this even though you are

now considering a $12.3 billion supplemental to the fiscal year 1966 defense budget...defense expenditure will, in effect, be no more of an inflationary element in fiscal years 1966 and 1967 by virtue of their relative demand on the economy than they were in the period from 1960 to 1964, and therefore by themselves are not sufficient cause for predicting inflation.[41]

A year later, in response to a question from Senator Stuart Symington, McNamara replied "...there are many things, many prices, that we pay for the war in South Vietnam, some very heavy prices indeed, but in my opinion one of them is not a strain on our economy."[42] The 1966 *Economic Report of the President* downplayed the impact of the war and President Johnson promised that the nation could handle a war in Vietnam and a war on poverty simultaneously. The Council of Economic Advisors began to take a more cautious approach and the 1967 edition of the President's economic report acknowledged that the war posed some economic problems. Yet the report concluded that "excessive demand is not now a serious threat" and that "1967 will witness progress toward greater price stability."[43]

The business community began to distrust official economic predictions and criticized the quality of economic management offered by the Administration. Most business leaders felt that the 1964 tax cut should have been revoked the following year. Instead its stimulating effect was piled on top of the military build-up. Much greater restraint should have been exercised in non-military federal expenditures. The liberal monetary policy, which included large increases in the money supply, should have been reversed. As late as December 1965 several Administration spokesmen complained of the restraints imposed by the Federal Reserve System. But the increase in the federal discount rate was too little and came too late. The needed tax increase was not forthcoming. The Administration favored the risks of inflation over the risks of unemployment. Many noted that the increases in the GNP and reduction in unemployment were artificial reflections of large Vietnam outlays. By mid-1967 federal spending accounted for twenty-three percent of the Gross National Product. Official Department of Labor data about the effects of Vietnam expenditures on employment were questioned by an Ad Hoc Committee of the Chamber of Commerce studying the effects of Vietnam spending. The Committee argued that the official figure of one million Vietnam-created jobs grossly underestimated the extent to which low unemployment rates depended on the conflict in Southeast Asia.[44]

Inflation was another major problem that representatives of the capitalist class thought that Administration policy in Vietnam was exacerbating. As Arthur Burns, later Chairman of the Federal Reserve Board, put it in 1969:

> If the government had foreseen how rapidly the cost of the Vietnam War would mount and if it had taken promptly the restraining measures needed to keep the aggregate demand for goods and services from outrunning the nation's capacity to produce, the new round of inflation that we have experienced since 1964 could have been prevented.[45]

Between 1965 and 1967 defense spending increased fifty percent, rising from seven percent to 9.5 percent of the Gross National Product. But each Administration budget after FY 1965 underestimated the cost of the Vietnam War by half. The Administration compounded this error with overly optimistic estimates of an early end to hostilities. As a result the accompanying fiscal and monetary measures were inadequate. Senator William Proxmire, Chairman of the Joint Economic Committee, reflected this viewpoint in his opening statement during hearings on the economic impact of the war:

> In 1966 our Government made a serious economic policy blunder. Our fiscal policy was established early in 1966...on the assumption that the Vietnam War would cost $10 billion. It is clear to me that we would have reduced spending and/or increased taxes—possibly both—if we had better and more accurate information.[46]

More specific examples of Administration miscalculations included a failure to understand the distinctions among Congressional obligations, Congressional appropriations, and actual expenditures. According to economist Murray Weidenbaum, a specialist on defense spending:

The policy implication of this is that the official budget and economic reports were very slow to pick up the expansionary impact of the Vietnam buildup, but very quick to take account of the deflationary impact of the expansion in revenues. The net result is that the Federal Government, though apparently following a non-inflationary economic policy in 1966, was actually a major source of inflationary pressure in the American economy during that time.[47]

Nor was the different impact of defense expenditures on the private sector and public sector fully understood.[48] Federal authorities did not properly allow for lead times in approving, spending and actually receiving deliveries of various items in the defense budget (the lead time ranges from six months in the case of uniforms to fifteen months for tanks and over two years for aircraft). On the most particular level, the Administration failed to issue the traditional mid-year review of the Federal budget in 1966. The June and July issues of the Department of Defense "Monthly Report on the Status of Funds," the most detailed source of defense-spending information, simply never appeared. The September issue arrived in mid-December, too late for those making forecasts for the upcoming year.

These examples of poor management did little to ease mounting fears that Johnson's Vietnam policy would undercut economic stability. McNamara and Johnson knew full well that Vietnam was costing far more than their estimates to Congress revealed. Privately, they justified their misrepresentations on the grounds that a fully informed Congress would vote whatever Johnson wanted on the war, but cut back on social programs.[49] So on the actual economic cost of the war and on promises of early success, Johnson and McNamara lied to Congress, to the American people, and to the capitalist class.

Business reports blamed the Administration for not using fiscal and monetary levers such as a tax increase, or a cut in domestic spending. The failure of government to reduce its own spending during the early build-up period produced an economic situation which could result in direct controls. And the business community was almost unanimous in its opposition to direct controls on wages and prices or on foreign investment. But business did not say why government spending was not reduced. Business remained comparatively unaware of the pressures on Johnson emanating from the urban crisis and from movements of blacks and the poor, pressures that dictated an expansion of social programs. In combination with the antiwar movement, these political developments threatened the structure of stability. But the capitalist class tended to focus more narrowly on measures which would lead more immediately to economic normalcy. If adopted, however, these fiscally conservative measures would have exacerbated the social crisis of the sixties. It was up to the state to respond to movements from below even if doing so involved a clash with business. By eliminating the possibility of lower domestic spending and the controls normally deployed during wartime, these social movements increased the economic impact of the Vietnam War.[50]

Leading members of the capitalist class recognized that it was the political climate, not the absence or misuse of technical knowledge, that prevented the Administration from adopting the usual countervailing fiscal and monetary tools. In testimony before the Senate Foreign Relations Committee, Charles Schultze discussed the economic problems of the period, and especially the growth of inflation:

> Our earlier inflation is in part due to the fact that we wouldn't cover the financial cost of the war in taxes and finally in turn, one of the reasons we wouldn't cover the financial costs of the war in taxes was because it was basically an unpopular war... The inflation that we are trying to stop originated from a combination of the Vietnam War on the one hand and our political inability to finance it on the other.[51]

Herbert Stein, later Nixon's Chairman of the Council of Economic Advisors, argued in a similar vein:

> In the early days of this inflation, in 1965 and 1968, it was considered that the American people would not stand for a tax increase, even though we were increasing government expenditures. So the government then in power, responding to what it thought the American people wanted from them, deferred action to raise taxes, which might have slowed down inflation, for three years. Now this doesn't mean that the American people were voting explicitly for inflation, but being so reluctant to have a tax increase, they created the conditions.[52]

Stein is wrong, of course, to blame the American people for not eagerly agreeing to a tax increase so that Vietnamese could be killed without causing inflation, but his assertion that domestic dissent prevented normal economic management is accurate nonetheless.

The Stock-Market, Investment Levels, and Business Confidence

Some of the loss of business confidence that has been outlined above can be traced within the stock-market, although any effort to measure investor attitudes through correlations between war news and the Dow-Jones average faces severe difficulties. A hypothetical relationship may be obscured by unrelated events acting in an opposite direction. There is the issue of the relevant time frame. Investors may have anticipated a major announcement, with the index rising or falling before the event itself. Or investors may be uncertain, with the index reacting a week or more later. The question of small versus large-scale investors also arises. Despite these difficulties one study did attempt to demonstrate a statistical relationship between "hawkish" and "dovish" news and the Dow-Jones average. Three alternative theories of how the financial community views the economic consequences of military intervention were tested:

a. the simple Marxist—since the war is always "bullish" for the economy, investors will react positively to news of escalation;
b. the simple inverse Marxist—since the war hurts the economy in a variety of ways including inflation, balance of payments, higher interest rates etc., the market will respond favorably to news of de-escalation;
c. the modified Marxist—spending on a small war increases aggregate demand and fuels the economy. Investors react favorably as long as there is no risk of a confrontation or major war with another power. After the 'small' war becomes a 'large' war investors respond negatively.[53]

While the study failed to distinguish adequately between a "small" war and "large" war, the "modified Marxist approach" comes closest to the hypothesis presented earlier, namely that

Vietnam expenditures first stimulated, and later hindered, the economy. The results of the study provided greater support for the modified Marxist hypothesis than either of the others. By the beginning of 1967 investor attitudes turned against the war, producing as the only statistically significant finding a positive relationship between conciliatory acts and higher Dow-Jones averages. The major escalation of the air war in September-October 1967 parallels a fall in stock prices. The announcement of a partial bombing halt, the opening of "talks" with the North Vietnamese, and a complete bombing halt, parallel a bullish market for the rest of 1968.

An examination of the behavior of the stock market during the Korean War provides an interesting point of comparison. Immediately prior to the Korean War the economy was recessionary. One would expect that the increased level of aggregate demand produced by Korean expenditures would also lead to more favorable attitudes among investors. This turns out to be the case. During the early stages of the Korean War investors greeted escalatory news with higher stock prices. By the end of the Korean War investors were lukewarm towards the prospect of continued fighting (but still far from the level of hostility generated by possible Vietnam expansion). The strong positive correlation between de-escalatory events and stock prices increases during the Vietnam War, and the absence of any such relationship for the Korean War, suggests that business attitudes were accurately responding to the deleterious effects of Vietnam spending.

A letter to his fellow businessmen in the securities industry, written by Wheelock Whitney, a first vice-president of the Investment Bankers Association and a governor of the Association of Stock Exchange, condemned U.S. intervention in strong terms. "The true villain is the war," Whitney wrote, which "imperils our customers and our industry...perhaps our whole way of life in America...Public confidence will not likely be restored until the war is ended."[54] The stock market continued to respond to war developments, the Dow-Jones index dropping from a peak of 943.08 on September 25, 1967 to 825.13 on March 21, one week before Johnson's speech (See Chart 6.1). Early January peace rumors brought a brief rally but during the first two weeks of the TET Offensive the index plummeted thirty-four points. On the first day of trading after Johnson's speech the market leapt twenty points. By

Chart 6.1
Dow-Jones Industrial Stock Index
August 1, 1967-April 15, 1968

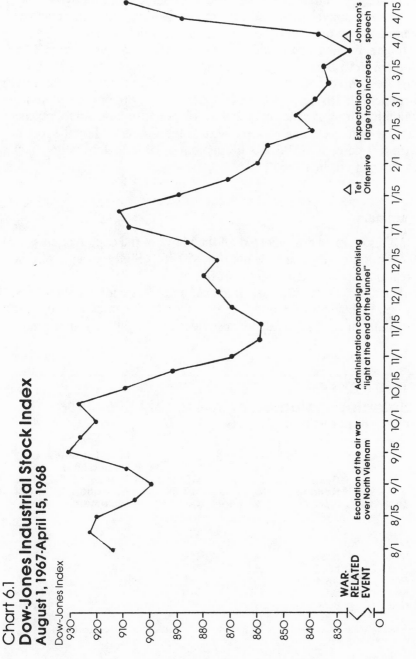

Source *Business Week*

April 15 the market was back above the nine hundred mark.

Selected investment indicators also demonstrated that business confidence in the economy was beginning to erode (See Table 6.2). After increasing one percent between 1962 and 1965 (from 14.8 percent to 15.8 percent) and climbing to 16.2 percent in 1966, gross private domestic investment as a proportion of the Gross National Product fell 1.6 percent (to 14.6 percent) over the next two years. Manufacturing expenditures for new plant and equipment followed a similar pattern, rising as a percent of the Gross National Product from 2.7 percent in 1962 to 3.8 percent in 1966, before falling back to 3.3 percent in 1968.

Summary

This chapter has reported on the views of the capitalist class as they stood during the first quarter of 1968. Study groups, official position papers, and influential business circles all spoke out strongly against the de-stabilizing effect of high Vietnam expenditures. A poll of business opinion, the behavior of the stock market, and declining business confidence as evidenced by different investment

Table 6.2
Selected Indicators of Investment, 1962-1968
(billions of dollars)

Year	Gross National Product	Gross Private Domestic Investment	GDI as a % of GNP	Manufacturer's Expenditures for New Plant and Equipment	ME as a % of GNP
1962	560.9	83.0	14.8	15.1	2.7
1963	592.5	87.1	14.7	16.2	2.8
1964	630.9	94.0	14.9	19.3	3.1
1965	684.2	108.1	15.8	23.4	3.4
1966	749.4	121.4	16.2	28.2	3.8
1967	798.6	116.6	14.6	28.5	3.6
1968	863.0	126.0	14.6	28.4	3.3

Source: Adapted from the Economic Report of the President, 1973; Rudell, "Economic Impact of the Vietnamese War", p. 282.

indicators conform to the overall pattern of growing criticism of the Administration's course of action. But the capitalist class *did not* attack the principle behind U.S. intervention in Vietnam. Differences over the relative importance of Vietnam and the proper method of managing its economic costs existed within the capitalist class and, as we shall see, paralleled to a large extent divisions among the state managers. These intraclass differences, as well as the comparatively imprecise message to "do something now," meant that it was the responsibility of the state to create a policy alternative that would mitigate the economic cost of the war, while simultaneously establishing the anticommunist commitment on a more solid political and economic footing.

While recognizing the critical impact of the capitalist class on policy, this interpretation differs from the perspective stressing the direct control of the capitalist class in two ways. First, taken from the level of the capitalist class as a whole, the state managers receive general messages concerning the economic climate. These messages carry influence but are not elaborated in the form of specific policy recommendations. The signals are strong enough that the state managers have to pay attention, but still so diffuse that the state managers continue to disagree about how to respond. Second, *some* representatives of the capitalist class *do* have clear ideas on the policy level which are conveyed to the state managers. But this communication reflects a particular political position within the business community. No vehicle for expressing *general class interests* at the level of *specific policy* exists. Precisely at the point where the *form* of the relationship between a representative of the capitalist class and the state managers appears to be one of direct influence, the *content* of the relationship is most likely to reflect a particular policy current. Where a member of the capitalist class communicates an explicit policy to the state, the political position is usually subscribed to by only part of that class and by only some state managers. The detailed history of Vietnam decision-making that follows in the next two chapters illustrates both levels: the general impact of an unstable economy and a particularly powerful example of influence by members of the capitalist class on state decisions. But this influence is captured better at the level of contending policy currents than at the level of the control of the entire capitalist class over state policy.

PART III: U.S. POLICY IN DETAIL

VII: THE COLLAPSE OF THE CENTER: AUGUST 1967 TO THE TET OFFENSIVE

The TET Offensive, launched on January 31, 1968, by the National Liberation Front, spoke convincingly of the abject failure of the American effort. Coordinated assaults developed along the entire length of the country. Five of the six largest cities were attacked, as were thirty-six of the forty-four provincial capitals.[1] NLF sappers infiltrated the American embassy compound. Elsewhere in Saigon, several thousand occupied strategic areas. Heavy fighting continued in My Tho, Can Tho, Soc Trang, Vinh Long and Rack Gia of the Mekong Delta; in large sections of the central highlands; and in Ben Tre, where an American major announced to the assembled press that "it was necessary to destroy the city in order to save it." Hue was the scene of particularly heavy house-to-house fighting and high American casualties. Over eighty percent of the inner city was destroyed and some parts of the city, once taken by the NLF, were not recaptured for more than a month. Military bases at Dalat, Da Nang, and Phu Bai came under heavy attack. In Quang Ngai, the NLF stormed through the city, freeing all prisoners from the local jail.

A second round began on February 28. The Ton Son Nhut airport near Saigon was shelled and the provincial capital of Phan Tiet seized. During the third week of the offensive the U.S. Command announced record casualty figures: 543 killed and 2,500 wounded in one week. ARVN, the South Vietnamese army, continued its remarkable record of tactical ineptitude, poor morale, high desertion levels and corruption.

The TET Offensive shattered an illusory calm that had prevailed over much of South Vietnam during the Fall of 1967. Administration spokesmen redoubled their public relations efforts, claiming in speech after speech that "the tide had turned," and that "the light at

209

the end of the tunnel" could now be seen. In fact, as the Vietnamese had so rudely demonstrated, U.S. intervention in Vietnam had been stalemated and the strategy followed by the center policy current — search-and-destroy missions, bombing North Vietnam to demonstrate resolve and to interdict men and supplies moving south, and manipulative management of the economy and public opinion at home — was bankrupt. For much of the Fall, members of the right-wing current expressed their displeasure with the strategy favored by the center and pushed for more severe measures against the North. The right attempted to use the alarm that followed TET to their own advantage. The first of the two chapters that follow analyzes the escalatory pressures building over those months and in the two weeks immediately following TET. Its purpose is to show how the center policy current became untenable between August 1967 and February 1968. A shift towards the left or the right was inevitable. The second chapter describes the successful effort of the left current to finally push their program on the reluctant Johnson. This chapter offers a detailed analysis of how an alternative policy current is chosen. It provides a case study of how state managers respond to an unstable political environment and to changed signals from the capitalist class. In sections of both chapters theoretical critiques will be offered of both the "quagmire" and "policy by direct control of the capitalist class" interpretations of the Vietnam War.

Before proceeding with the detailed analysis of decision-making the main theoretical argument will be briefly summarized. From World War II the United States followed a deliberate policy of attempting to defeat the Vietnamese revolutionary movement. This commitment was far from accidental. Washington merely applied in Vietnam general principles that governed foreign policy elsewhere: guaranteeing the access of U.S. based multinational corporations to the economies of other countries, preventing the spread of socialism, and attempting to defeat, militarily if necessary, revolutionary movements seeking greater control over their nation's future. In doing so the U.S. gradually turned its back on the hopes for meaningful reform with which it had been identified by many of the world's citizens for much of the century. Within these general principles moved distinct policy currents or disagreements within the capitalist class, its representatives, and especially among the state

managers. These policy currents had two sources: forces of
opposition to the U.S., and different lessons arising from the history
of administering foreign policy. Forces of opposition restrict U.S.
power but also display characteristics that encourage state managers
to believe that a strategy to limit their influence can be devised. In the
case of the Vietnam War the impact of three different forces of
opposition were discussed.

The first was the resistance of the Vietnamese, aided by ①
diplomatic support and materiel assistance from the Soviet Union
and China. All efforts on the part of Washington to reduce the
dedication of the Vietnamese to fight for their independence met with
failure. The state managers disagreed over possible responses. Their
battles were fueled by the Sino-Soviet dispute which carried extreme
dangers for the Vietnamese. Some state managers argued that the
conflict between Vietnam's allies made it possible for the U.S. to
take more provocative measures in Vietnam without fear of retaliation or counter-escalation from Moscow or Peking. Others maintained that drastic steps on the part of the U.S. would only unify
China and the Soviet Union. At any rate, the basic conflict between
the Vietnamese and the U.S. was supplemented by splits between
Vietnam and its allies and by policy debates within Washington
itself. This analysis of international forces also traced the post-
liberation tensions among Vietnam, Cambodia and China to the
Sino-Soviet dispute and the early history of the triangular relationship among Peking, Moscow and Washington.

The second oppositional force was domestic. The comparatively ②
firm antiwar movement combined with the more fluid public opinion
and general war weariness to limit the escalatory options available to
the state managers. Some government officials argued that the U.S.
could not escalate for fear of inflaming the war at home. Others,
however, maintained that a program of determined military attacks
was just what was needed to swing domestic opinion back in favor of
the war effort. A third form of opinion, that of elite views, was
situated within the framework of policy currents. Arguments voiced
by the mainstream press and private study groups substantially
reproduced debates within the state itself.

The third form of opposition, that offered by the capitalist class, ③
arose from the deteriorating business climate. After the U.S. build-
up in 1965 the economy received an immediate boost, but then

gradually deteriorated so that by 1967 complaints from the capitalist class regarding the impact of the Vietnam War began to be heard. Most of the capitalist class focused on the economy itself, and on the quality of economic management offered by the Administration. Business confidence was lowered. The resulting signal to the state managers was strong, but also diffuse. It was left to the state to develop specific policy on Vietnam. Political opinions on the Vietnam War itself could be detected among the capitalist class. As with elite opinion, however, these perspectives generally fell within the framework of policy currents.

The absorption of these forces of opposition into policy delibera-tions occurs through ideological filters, or lessons from the history of conducting foreign policy. The historical lesson of the left current was "never use force until all avenues of diplomacy have been exhausted." The current can be traced to the multilateral perspec-tive, operating at the end of World War II, which focused on the expansion of world trade and reform of precapitalist social structures to secure a "Pax Americana." Limited economic development in the Third World would provide a market for U.S. exports. Economic ties were the most effective response to militant revolutionary regimes. Socialism might win in name, but foreign aid and private investment could always coopt radical programs. The left current resisted the militarization of U.S. intervention in Vietnam, but never the anticommunist commitment itself.

The historical lesson of the center current was that the U.S. must be "prepared and willing to use force to demonstrate that we are the world's strongest nation." Yet the level, direction, and intensity of this force must be carefully watched for a nuclear confrontation with the Soviet Union must be avoided. The center current can be traced to the containment principles that have generally governed U.S. foreign policy since World War II. In Vietnam the center was willing, even eager, to commit the U.S. to direct military involve-ment, but watched the response of the Soviet Union and China carefully.

The right had no such qualms. Under its historical lesson, "there is no substitute for victory," the U.S. would have further intensified the bombing of the North, committed yet more ground troops to the South, and invaded Laos, Cambodia and even North Vietnam itself. This perspective was rooted in the rollback orientation generally operating in the Pacific until the early nineteen-sixties, which refused to recognize the "loss" of mainland China, North Korea and North Vietnam.

The left, center and right policy currents on the Vietnam War differed on a number of important issues: the choice of bombing targets over North Vietnam, the deployment of ground troops in the South, whether the strategic reserves should be mobilized at home, the importance of conducting negotiations with Hanoi, how to handle public opinion, whether the domino theory could be applied to Southeast Asia, how to manage the economy, whether the U.S. was winning in Vietnam, and, indeed, what constituted winning in the first place. (The reader wishing to refresh their memory on these disputes can refer to Chart 3.1 on pp. 100-01.)

Until 1967 the center current controlled Vietnam policy. But the intensification of each force of opposition, and the inability to respond effectively, left that strategy bankrupt. The analysis of Vietnam decision-making that follows, focusing on the search for an alternative strategy, is based on the conflict among the three policy currents. In the Fall of 1967 it looked as though the right might get its way.

Pressures for Escalation

By mid-summer of 1967 pressures for escalation had reached a new peak. Under the slogan, "there is no substitute for victory," the right called for a reduction of the costs of the Vietnam War through a rapid escalation of the air war over the North: they argued that this action would substitute for a costly ground war and bring the conflict to a quick end. In the discussion of bombing policy then taking place in Washington the Joint Chiefs defended "Alternative A":

[The U.S. must make] an intensified attack on the Hanoi-Haiphong logistic base. Under this Alternative we would continue attack on enemy installations and industry and would conduct an intensified, concurrent and sustained effort against all elements of land, sea and air lines of communication in North Vietnam — especially those entering and departing the Hanoi-Haiphong area. Foreign shipping would be 'shouldered out' of Haiphong by a series of air attacks on the center of the port complex. The harbor and approaches would be mined, forcing foreign shipping out into the nearby estuaries for offloading by lighterage. Intensive and systematic armed reconnaissance would be carried out against the roads and railroads from China (especially the northeast railroad), against the coastal shipping and coastal trans-shipment locations, and against all other land lines of communications. The eight major operational airfields would be systematically attacked, and the deep-water ports of Cam Pha and Hon Gai would be struck or mined as required.[2]

None of these proposals were new. The Joint Chiefs had pushed for these targets from the start of the war. Only the development of a political environment where these proposals might be adopted was unique. The plan carried all of the danger signs of a major escalation (attacks on Hanoi-Haiphong, foreign shipping, the airfields, the railroads, and the Chinese buffer zones). The rightwing advocated the removal of the ten-mile limit imposed around Hanoi, along with attacks on Hanoi's thermal power plant and the Phuc Yen airfield, the only major airbase remaining in North Vietnam. Among the arguments offered by the military were weather (September and October being the last months of clear skies), and "pilot morale." Admiral Sharp argued that "the morale of our air crews understandably rose when briefed to strike the Phuc Yen airfield and its MIGs — a target which has continually jeopardized their well-being."[3] "Pilot morale" had little to do with the rationale for the Phuc Yen attack. Sharp was primarily interested in forcing North Vietnamese MIGs to operate out of China. The Joint Chiefs coupled their request for more ground troops with a call-up of the military reserves: each action generating additional momentum towards escalation.[4]

A memorandum written by General Earle Wheeler, Chairman of the Joint Chiefs of Staff, and sent to Secretary of Defense Robert McNamara, was another maneuver designed to further the right's program for escalation:

MEMORANDUM FOR THE SECRETARY OF
DEFENSE
JCSM-555-67 Oct. 17, 1967
Subject: Increased Pressures on North Vietnam

1. Reference is made to:
   a. NSAM 288, dated 17 March 1964,
      subject: "Implementation of
      South Vietnam program."
      . . . .
      . . . .
4. Military objectives in Southeast
   Asia have been conducted within a
   framework of policy guidelines established to achieve US objectives
   without expanding the conflict.
   Principal among these policy guidelines are:
   a. we seek to avoid widening the war
      into a conflict with Communist
      China or the USSR.
   b. we have no *present* intention of
      invading North Vietnam.
   c. we do not seek the overthrow of
      the Government of NVN
   d. we are guided by the principles
      set forth in the Geneva Accords
      of 1954 and 1962. [emphasis in
      the original].[5]

Wheeler, responding to a formal request from the President, realized that his memorandum to the Secretary of Defense would be part of the historical record. The Chairman of the Joint Chiefs of Staff carefully endorsed the existing policy guidelines. But a close reading of the memorandum reveals a difference between Wheeler's goals and those of the center policy current.

Wheeler refers to NSAM 288 (National Security Action Memorandum) of March 17, 1964, which contained one of the most comprehensive statements of U.S. policy objectives in Vietnam. NSAM 288 said in part:

Unless we can achieve this objective [defeat of the NLF] in South Vietnam, almost all of Southeast Asia will probably fall under Communist dominance (all of Vietnam, Laos, and Cambodia), accommodate to Communism so as to remove

effective U.S. and anti-Communist influence (Burma), or fall
under the domination of forces not now explicitly Communist
but likely then to become so (Indonesia taking over Malaysia). Thailand might hold for a period without help, but would
be under grave pressure. Even the Philippines would become
shaky, and the threat to India on the West, Australia and New
Zealand to the South, and Taiwan, Korea, and Japan to the
North and East would be greatly increased.

All of the consequences would probably have been true
even if the U.S. had not since 1954, and especially since
1961, become so heavily engaged in South Vietnam. However that fact accentuates the impact of a Communist South
Vietnam, not only in Asia, but in the rest of the world, where
the South Vietnam conflict is regarded as a test case of U.S.
capacity to help a nation to meet the Communist 'war of
liberation.'

Thus purely in terms of foreign policy the stakes are high.[6]

Paragraph four of Wheeler's memorandum faithfully repeats
official civilian policy. Yet there is one danger sign: the italicization of
"present" in point 4b ("we have no *present* intention of invading North
Vietnam") raises the possibility that the right was preparing the ground
work for a change of strategy. As we shall see they almost succeeded.

Wheeler's memorandum included an appendix which advocated
several specific actions:

- eliminating Hanoi and Haiphong prohibited areas
- reducing CPR Buffer Zone to 10 miles
- conducting unrestricted attacks against LOC, rail lines,
roads up to five miles from CPR border
- authorizing CINCPAC strikes and restrike prerogatives
for all targets outside of redefined restricted areas
- permitting JCS to authorize strikes against targets in the
redefined restricted areas on a case-by-case basis (to include
the Haiphong port)
- mining NVN deep water ports.[7]

Striking any of these new targets would increase the chances of a
confrontation between the United States and the Soviet Union or
China.

By the end of 1967 some members of the center policy current, led by a different logic, also entertained escalation. The center thought it was fighting a limited war. McGeorge Bundy called the bombing of the North "the most accurate and restrained in history."[8] The center current did not desire complete destruction of North Vietnam. Total capitulation or unconditional surrender was not necessary — only that the North stop fighting in the South. But the gradual progression and escalation of the war had produced the following dilemma: the members of the center current had devised and implemented a bombing program that reflected their "limited" goal, but the scenario of "gradual pressures" had been exhausted with no sign of bending from the North Vietnamese. All roads lay in the same direction: the right desired escalation, hoping to destroy North Vietnam, possibly to create a situation of direct confrontation with China; the military desired escalation because of their training and attitude towards warfare; and members of the center leant towards escalation, hoping to "turn the screw" the magic notch that would produce negotiations on their own terms.

Congressional hawks, especially on the Armed Services Committee, were especially vocal in their demands for fewer restrictions on ROLLING THUNDER. From the perspective of the Presidency and the forthcoming elections, the increasingly unpopular war had to be ended in a hurry. Public opinion polls, then showing a slight majority in favor of escalation, may have tempted Johnson to consider further military steps. General Westmoreland and Ambassador Bunker were brought home for speaking tours as part of an attempt to drum up additional public support for the Administration. Richard Nixon, in a *Christian Science Monitor* interview, called for "massive pressure short of nuclear weapons to shorten the war." In the context of these pressures for escalation even the critics among the state managers felt constrained to back military measures. Their efforts to secure a policy with lower costs were hopeless in this political climate.

The Stennis Hearings: Right and Left Clash Over the Bombing of North Vietnam

The Hearings held by the Stennis Subcommittee of the Senate Armed Services Committee during August 1967 provide a public glimpse into the disputes among different policy currents. From the point of view of the Committee, most of whom sided with the right, the specific purpose of the Hearings was to force the approval of an additional fifty-seven bombing targets in North Vietnam on a reluctant Administration, and to obtain a greater voice for the military in the selection of targets. Behind their formal approval of the stated objectives of ROLLING THUNDER, representatives of first the right and then the left policy currents voiced their objections. The immediate outcome of the Hearings was a moderate escalation of the air war over North Vietnam, but the left current centered among the civilian staff at the Pentagon was bolstered by the testimony of Secretary of Defense Robert McNamara.

Until August, target selection was the exclusive concern of Rusk, McNamara, Rostow, and Johnson — all civilians — and occasional invited guests at the weekly meeting known as the "Tuesday Cabinet."[9] Before the start of the Hearings and in anticipation of the findings of such confirmed hawks as Senators Stennis, Symington, Jackson, Cannon, Smith, Thurmond, Byrd, and Miller, President Johnson authorized the bombardment of an additional sixteen targets and an expansion of armed reconnaissance. Six of the new targets were within the ten-mile inner circle of Hanoi. Nine of the targets were located along the northeast rail line in the China buffer zone. The closest target was only eight miles from the border.[10]

The Subcommittee heard testimony from the military leaders responsible for the conduct of ROLLING THUNDER. The parade included Admiral U.S. Grant Sharp, Commander-in-Chief of the Pacific; the Chairman of the Joint Chiefs of Staff; and the commander and deputy commander of the 7th Air Force in Saigon. Many of the right privately favored a qualitative shift, signifying an alternative Vietnam strategy, in the bombing of the North, but chose, in this public forum, to defend ROLLING THUNDER as successful *within* the objectives defined by the center. All echoed a common theme: the air war was a vital element of overall United States strategy in Vietnam. The bombing held down casualties, inflicted extensive disruption on North Vietnam, severely checked and raised the cost of infiltrating men and supplies into the South, and reduced the ability of the "enemy" to mount sustained combat operations. Without the bombing North Vietnam could double the number of troops in the South and free as many as half a million people now at work repairing damage from ROLLING THUNDER. To stay even, the United States would be forced to counter with as many as 800,000 additional troops at a cost of 75 billion dollars.[11] In support of his testimony Admiral Sharp quoted from *Hoc Tap*, the theoretical journal of the North Vietnamese Communist Party: "The war is creating very great manpower demands. We must extol the labor duty of each citizen to the fatherland and mobilize everyone to participate in production and combat and serving in the fighting."[12] "North Vietnam was hurting" ran the general consensus among the military.

As expected, the Stennis Committee responded favorably to the military. Their final report noted that "civilian authority consistently overruled the unanimous recommendations of military commanders and the Joint Chiefs of Staff for a systematic, timely, and hard-hitting integrated air campaign against the vital North Vietnamese targets."[13] Our "air might" had been "fragmented" by "overly restrictive controls" and the doctrine of "gradualism." The full potential of American air power had been "shackled" and civilian policy had "permitted the build-up of what had become the world's most formidable anti-aircraft defenses." The Committee noted in its conclusion that "in view of the unsatisfactory progress of the war, logic and prudence requires that the decision be with the unanimous weight of professional military judgment."[14]

As a result of the pressure exerted by the Committee, Johnson removed most of the 57 targets on the restricted list. One of these, Cam Pha, North Vietnam's largest port, which had been specifically rejected as a target twice earlier, was struck for the first time on September 10. On formal grounds at least, the inclusion of General Wheeler as a regular member of the Tuesday Cabinet raised the influence of the military (and the right current) in the decision-making hierarchy. The military, now authorized to strike near the Chinese border and near the center of Hanoi, took the opportunity to engage in even more provocative action. Two "mistakes" were reported during the course of the Hearings. On August 21 two Grumman A-6A Intruder Navy jets were downed in Chinese territory. One crewman was captured, three were killed. The next day Agence France-Presse reported extensive bombing damage in downtown Hanoi.[15] A medical clinic, civilian homes, and the National Education Authority were destroyed. A Pentagon spokesman later declared that the intended target was the Canal des Rapides railroad and highway bridge five miles to the northeast of Hanoi. The attacks, however, were not isolated, and consisted of a series of waves focused on the same point. The two provocations and the Hearings occurred simultaneously: a coincidence, or designed to force an escalation? The evidence does not permit a final judgment, but it seems likely that the right current was taking advantage of the relatively sanguine political atmosphere provided by the Hearings to force a greater escalation than formally authorized by the President.

The Subcommittee also heard from another witness, Secretary of Defense Robert McNamara, who attempted to block any further escalation of the bombing. For the first time he publicly revealed his deep skepticism toward the efficiency of ROLLING THUNGER. In the process McNamara gave part of the left policy current perspective.[16] To block escalation effectively, McNamara felt that a defense of the existing program was necessary. If McNamara became totally critical of ROLLING THUNDER, he would compromise severely his position as overseer of the military. A Secretary of Defense with a reputation as a "dove" would be completely ineffective within the Pentagon. So McNamara defended ROLLING THUNDER's three objectives in order to prevent additional escalation. The three objectives were: (1) reducing the flow and raising the cost of infiltrating men and supplies to the South; (2) raising the morale of the South Vietnamese; and (3) demonstrating American resolve to the leaders of North Vietnam. Measured against these objectives ROLLING THUNDER was a success: "I would like to restate my view," McNamara testified, "that the present objectives of our bombing in the South were soundly conceived and are being effectively pursued. They are consistent with our overall purpose in Vietnam and with our effort to confine the conflict."[17] "Under unfavorable circumstances," he added, "our military forces have done a superb job in making continued infiltration more difficult and expensive."[18] McNamara ran down one of his usual lists: 173,000 sorties had been flown; 4,100 vehicles, 7,400 watercraft, 1,400 railroad rolling stock, 57 significant bridges, and 50 major rail yards had been destroyed. McNamara pointed out that the Air Force and the Navy now had 359 total targets on their lists, and that a total of 1900 targets had been struck since the air war began. Without the bombing Saigon would lose faith; with the bombing North Vietnam knew that Washington was committed.

But McNamara's main intention was to block further escalation, and here his argument closely paralleled the critique of the air war developing outside of the Administration. The bombing of North Vietnam, no matter how thorough, could never win the war by itself; ROLLING THUNDER could not substitute for counter-insurgency in the South. Moreover, an expanded bombing program entailed risks with China. No bombing could achieve complete interdiction. "Enemy requirements" in the South were estimated at only fifteen tons a day. A few trucks could do the job even if the actual amount were five times this estimate. The capacity of North Vietnam's "highly diversified transportation system," consisting of motor vehicles, bicycles, sampans, rail, and foot power, was very large compared to the small volume of requirements in the South. The military had argued that closing North Vietnam's harbors could weaken Hanoi's war-making capacity. McNamara pointed out that while North Vietnam's current imports ran to 5,800 tons a day, the actual capacity was even greater (14,000 tons). Assuming the military could close the harbor, North Vietnam could still import over 8,400 tons a day via the railways and by road from China. Furthermore, the assumption that closing Haiphong and the other ports would completely end all sea-borne traffic was itself erroneous. North Vietnam could still use "over-the-beach" operations to acquire needed materiel.

In answer to the right current argument that ROLLING THUNDER could break the will of the North Vietnamese, McNamara pointed out that bombing industrial plants put little pressure on a largely agrarian economy. The Pepco plant in Alexandria, Virginia alone produced five times the power of all North Vietnam before the bombing began. All war-related activities and essential services could be provided by 2,000 diesel-driven generating sets hidden in the hills.[19] Knocking out small power plants in heavily defended areas with high risks to civilians could bring no measurable return except additional international hostility and a higher rate of pilot loss. The North Vietnamese people were used to hardship, discipline, and remained committed to the revolutionary leadership: in McNamara's jargon, the people "continued to respond to the political direction of the Hanoi regime." The North Vietnamese leaders had given no indication that they could be forced to negotiate under the pressure of bombing.[20] Finally, McNamara pointed out that the military had failed to establish a hard connection between the bombing in the North and United States casualties in the South. The Secretary of Defense concluded that ROLLING THUNDER, with its limited objectives, could play a useful role, but that a "less discriminating bombing program" could do no more and "would involve risks which at present I regard as too high to accept."[21] The implications of McNamara's testimony were far-reaching. Bombing at any level would not force Hanoi to the conference table. The "defeat of communism" must be sought in the South not in the North. Even though McNamara did not so state explicitly, the logic of his argument showed that the center strategy of bombing the North to reach a political settlement in the South was completely bankrupt.

The Stennis Hearings helped to polarize political positions among the state managers. The rightwing current managed to secure a moderate increase in the intensity of ROLLING THUNDER. In this sense the coalition of military officials and hawk Congressmen was successful. On the other hand the center contained the pressure for escalation, prevented it from assuming major proportions, and firmly prohibited strikes of major targets such as Haiphong. Moreover, McNamara's testimony fueled internal dissent within the Pentagon. Members of the left policy current, Paul Nitze, Deputy Secretary of Defense; Paul Warnke, Assistant Secretary of Defense for International Security Affairs; and Townsend Hoopes, Under Secretary of the Air Force, had already communicated their doubts to Secretary McNamara.[22] McNamara's public analysis of the inability of ROLLING THUNDER to win the Vietnam War, no matter which targets were selected, immediately sparked additional criticism of the war effort. Johnson, a President demanding complete loyalty and privately furious with McNamara, was sufficiently disturbed by his Secretary's testimony to call a news conference and deny the existence of any differences among his advisors. Off the record, Johnson was later heard to remark bitterly to a Senator that "McNamara has gone dovish on me." But McNamara's criticisms stiffened and eventually resulted in a memorandum to Johnson that called for a total bombing halt. McNamara was fired later in the year.

The Limits of ROLLING THUNDER: The Left Critique

Members of the left policy current did not believe that bombing North Vietnam could win the political battle in the South. They wanted to stop the bombing, and enter negotiations with the Vietnamese. Three internal studies of ROLLING THUNDER, authorized by McNamara shortly after the Stennis Hearings, illustrate the left critique. The first, "A Study of the Political-Military Implications of the Cessation of Aerial Bombardment and the Initiation of Negotiations" (SEACABIN), was the first attempt to pull together a comprehensive position on the question of the bombing halt. The conclusion, drafted by the pro-bombing Joint Chiefs, was a carefully worded compromise among the different agencies represented on the study group. "On balance," the report concluded, "the greatest risk to the United States military is an ambiguous response (by the North Vietnamese following a unilateral bombing halt) in which the DRV [Democratic Republic of Vietnam] would appear to engage in productive talks in order to gain time to concurrently regenerate support facilities in North Vietnam and gradually build up personnel strength and support bases in Laos, Cambodia and South Vietnam."[23] While this conclusion did not in itself threaten the logic of the center current, many of the particular arguments demonstrated the inadequacy of the bombing program, particularly its inability to obtain stated objectives. The Joint Chiefs were especially dissatisfied with the detailed critique of the bombing's effectiveness. They dispatched a dissenting memorandum to the Secretary of Defense, reiterating their view that the bombing program was effective.

Given this attitude, the Joint Chiefs must have been even more alarmed by the JASON study commissioned by McNamara on August 25, 1967, (the date of the Stennis Hearings), but not completed until after his departure as Secretary of Defense.[24] The report was extremely pessimistic. Not only had ROLLING THUNDER failed to limit Hanoi's ability to mount and support military operations in the South, but the analysts could not even theoretically devise a program that would produce such a result. The study noted that the morale of the South Vietnamese rose after the bombing program was initiated. But soon afterwards morale flagged again and only increasing degrees of escalation could maintain its "buoyancy." Thus the effect of the bombing was transient —

effective as a morale booster at first, but quickly fading away as the particular escalating incident established itself as the expected pattern. On the capacity of ROLLING THUNDER to weaken Hanoi's desire to wage war, the report concluded that "the bombing campaign against North Vietnam has not discernibly weakened the determination of the North Vietnamese leaders to continue to direct and support the insurgency in the South."[25]

The third study undertaken by the national security apparatus concerned the economic effects of the bombing and was undertaken by the Systems Analysis Office of the Defense Department. The paper examined the impact of the bombing upon the GNP of North Vietnam and the labor supply utilization. The report was pessimistic considering in its conclusion even the possibility that the bombing was, in economic terms, completely counter-productive. Alain Enthoven, the Assistant Secretary of Defense (Systems Analysis) stated in a cover memorandum to McNamara:

> The bombing has not been very successful in imposing economic losses on the North. Losses in domestic production have been more than replaced by imports and the availability of manpower, particularly because of the natural growth in the labor force has been adequate to meet wartime needs. It is likely that North Vietnam will continue to be able to meet extra manpower and economic requirements caused by the bombing short of attacks on population centers or the cities.[26]

Criticism of ROLLING THUNDER's effectiveness did not invariably lead towards the left policy current. The CIA's analysis of the 1966 bombing of North Vietnam, for example, was quite pessimistic, as a summary prepared for the *Pentagon Papers* demonstrates:

> The program had also become expensive. 318 ROLL-ING THUNDER aircraft were lost during 1966, as compared with 171 in 1965 (though the loss rate dropped from .66% of attack sorties in 1965 to .39% in 1966). CIA estimated that the direct operational cost of the program came to $1,247 million in 1966 as compared with $460 million in 1965.
> Economic damage to NVN went up from $36 million in 1965 to $94 million in 1966 and military damage from $34

million to $36 million. As CIA computed it, however, it cost the U.S. $9.6 to inflict $1 worth of damage in 1966, as compared with $6.6 in 1965.[27]

For reports such as these the CIA acquired a reputation for honesty and independence, aided, ironically, by the publication of the *Pentagon Papers*. But this accurate pessimism did not lead the Agency to support de-escalation. During the early period of ROLL-ING THUNDER, the CIA recommended a bombing program of *greater intensity* to be redirected against the "will of the regime as a target system."[28] The "will of the regime" is a euphemism for civilian targets.

In addition, members of the left current pointed out, ROLLING THUNDER was hampered by weather conditions and poor bombing performance.[29] From late September to May, most of North Vietnam was covered with heavy fog, punctuated by periods of rainfall ranging from moderate to monsoon. Visual bombing attacks were possible only five days a month. Frequently, two or three weeks would pass without the minimum standard for visual bombing (a ten thousand foot ceiling and five-mile horizontal visibility).[30] According to official estimates, in clear weather conditions a diving aircraft could expect to place fifty percent of its bombs within a 400 foot circle. In bad weather the size of the circle increased to 1,500 to 1,800 feet. At this level of accuracy, given the small size of most targets in North Vietnam, a larger number of separate attacks were often required to achieve destruction. The Vietnamese proved to be remarkably resilient, especially near Hanoi and Haiphong where anti-aircraft guns were particularly thick.

Bombing accuracy, however, depended not only on the extrinsic elements of weather and opposition defense, but could be severely limited by political conditions within the national security apparatus itself. The history of conflict among policy currents helps to explain the poor performance of U.S. jets in bombing Vietnam. During the nineteen-fifties, the center current had relied on "massive retaliation," a strategic principle stressing the use of missiles and bombers in an anticipated show-down with the Soviet Union. The development of tactical aircraft capable of pin-point bombing was not stressed. Dramatic increases in precision and performance depended on developing a new generation of aircraft. Now, the lead time for aircraft development is unusually long — five to six years.

Shortly after assuming office Secretary of Defense McNamara, under the new doctrine of "flexible response," began to develop the F-111, a jet that was supposed to fly close to the ground at supersonic speeds, or slowly if need be, to operate in total darkness or inclement weather, to take off from rough and short airfields, and to deliver bombs with greater accuracy than could be achieved visually. All of these characteristics were necessary to improve the level of bombing performance. Later, the dramatic failure of the F-111 coincided with and contributed to the crisis atmosphere which produced a shift in Vietnam policy. In the meantime, the legacy of the fifties' doctrine of massive retaliation, a legacy measured by the absence of modern jets, continued to hamper U.S. efforts over North Vietnam.

Interservice rivalries also contributed to the ineffectiveness of ROLLING THUNDER. The sortie rate (the number of raids flown by each plane over a given period of time) was used to measure the performance of each squadron and of each service. The higher the sortie rate, the greater the efficiency of the squadron, and hence the greater the percentage of future budget allotments and the greater the likelihood that promotion would follow. To maximize the sortie rate, pilots would often fly twice a day. To get back to the base in time to refuel and fly another mission, pilots would either fly the shortest route over areas jammed with anti-aircraft guns and SAM missiles, or avoid the target area altogether and drop their bombs in the ocean. They would then return to base, refuel, reload, and fly to the Ho Chi Minh trail. Aided by peasants with radios stationed around these bases, Hanoi would time the planes' activities and alert the infiltration corridors. Fifteen minutes before the planes' arrival, trucks would move off the trail, wait for the bombing of the now empty road to finish, and then continue on to the South. The result, in the words of a military officer writing from the perspective of the left current, was an "extremely high sortie rate, a waste of ordnance, an appallingly high percentage of planes shot down, and few targets hit with any degree of accuracy."[31] In this example, interservice rivalry, a classic bureaucratic influence, does not explain *why* or *what* the planes were bombing, but does partially explain why they missed so much.[32]

McNamara's War?

Secretary of Defense McNamara is often identified with the program budgeting techniques that he introduced to the Pentagon. Often he is criticized for relying too heavily on these techniques especially by advocates of the quagmire interpretation who stress distortions in the decision-making process. No system, no decision-making technique, runs the critique, could capture all of the subtlety of history, the contradictions and dilemmas of politics, or the value of a superior weapon on the battlefield. The methodology of cost-effectiveness not only measured and compared alternative goals, but it dictated the choice of goals. Dedicated to improving rationality, McNamara was hopelessly naive and politically blind. Vietnam, for example, became a desperate quagmire because McNamara insisted on quantifying everything. Body counts, kill ratios, loss of weapons, winning the hearts and minds of the Vietnamese — everything that had to do with the war was reduced to a sterile number. McNamara's assessments excluded the country's unique history and its powerful commitment to the struggle for independence. McNamara did not understand Vietnam. David Halberstam, for example, concludes his long portrait of the Secretary of Defense with this comment:

> He attached his name and reputation to the possibility and hope for victory, caught himself more deeply in the tarbaby of Vietnam, and limited himself greatly in his future actions. It is not a particularly happy chapter in his life; he did not serve himself or his country well; he was, there is no kinder or gentler word for it, a fool.[33]

In fact McNamara was a competent state manager. Far from being a self-deceiving fool, McNamara understood the political climate of the national security apparatus. Program budgeting was supposed to serve as a technical aid to planning, but it also aided centralization of control in the Office of the Secretary of Defense. As Charles Hitch, one of the original advocates of program budgeting, testified before Congress, "program decisions are decisions of the sort which can only be made by the Secretary, and therefore the role of the Secretary and of the Secretary's advisors will be greater."[34]

McNamara later wrote that "the direction of the Department of Defense demands, not only strong civilian control, but a Secretary's role that consists of active, imaginative, and decisive leadership of the establishment at large, and not the passive action of simply refereeing the disputes of traditional and partisan factions."[35] In other words, McNamara not only aided the shift in control over defense policy from Congress to the executive branch (a process pretty much completed by the early-sixties) but he changed the *style* of decision-making. Instead of a passive, legislative role like that of referee choosing among competing interests of roughly equal power he played an active executive role which included the formation of policy.[36] McNamara saw his "position here as being that of a leader, not a judge. I'm here to originate and stimulate new ideas and programs, not just referee arguments and harmonize interests. Using deliberate analysis to force alternative programs to the surface, and then making fundamental choices among them is fundamental."[37] The military hated McNamara: his administrative policies threatened the structure of specific interests which they had arbitrated among themselves for so long.

Under McNamara civilian control over specific programs was far greater than in the Eisenhower Administration. Program budgeting permitted the Secretary's staff to examine both the level of appropriations to each service *and* the content of the service programs as well. The interservice rivalries, bureaucratic battles, clashes between civilians and military, and lobbying of specific interests that normally mark the daily routine of the Defense Department did not disappear under McNamara's reign. As a matter of fact they became more acute. The Cuban Missile Crisis, the issue of a new manned bomber, the censure of speeches to be delivered by high military officials, the question of a propulsion system for new aircraft carriers, the test-ban treaty, the F-111, and the cost-effectiveness decision-making technique itself, were all sources of particularly intense battles. McNamara won each of these fights. Indeed, McNamara could win any battle that he chose to fight. But the politics of the specific interests dictated that he not fight every battle. McNamara understood, as must any successful politician, that the realm of possibilities at any particular moment is limited, and that compromises are often necessary. In exchange for their support for the test-ban treaty, the Army received the go-ahead on the development of chemical and biological weapons. Large increases in the defense budget also helped to mollify the Joint Chiefs. (One is tempted to posit an inverse relationship between a low defense budget and the degree of civilian control over specific programs.) To blunt the thrust for the ABM, McNamara gave the Air Force permission to develop MIRVed missiles. In making these decisions, McNamara sometimes ignored the results of his own cost-effectiveness studies. His critics feel that these cases illuminate the irrationality of the decision-making technique. For McNamara, however, program budgeting crystallized the policy implications of his choices *and* increased his power. Program budgeting was *both* a contribution to rationality *and* a weapon in McNamara's political battles. The cases in which McNamara ignored his own studies stand as mute testimony to the continued influence of specific parochial interests and to the continued significance of policy disputes within capitalism's governing apparatus, but not to McNamara's individual incompetence or his lack of power.

McNamara's decisions on the Vietnam War cannot be understood apart from this larger arena of Pentagon politics. McNamara was fighting many different battles simultaneously. The imposition of target limits by civilians at the Tuesday lunch, McNamara's criticism of the effectiveness of ROLLING THUNDER, and his use of systems analysis studies to back up his arguments, were to the military all indications of how short their leash had become. Some major compromises emerged, one being the precise number of ground troops. McNamara felt that the costs of fifty or a hundred thousand more ground troops were less damaging than the policy choices and international risks contained in ROLLING THUNDER. More troops just cost more money; mining the Haiphong harbor could mean a confrontation with the Soviet Union. So McNamara would fly out to Honolulu or Saigon and bargain with Westmoreland over the precise number of troops.[38] In the meantime the Secretary of Defense retained control over bombing targets.

President Johnson's ultimate control over policy required all state managers to formally subscribe to the center position. But McNamara attempted to take actions that implicitly followed the left current. His experimentation, ultimately unsuccessful, with an electronic barrier, to be constructed across the DMZ separating North from South Vietnam, is an example. The proposal, which would later become a point of public ridicule, was originally intended to provide an effective argument, within the national security apparatus, for bringing ROLLING THUNDER to a halt. Bombing men and supplies as they moved south wasn't working. Under the barrier scheme the U.S. would attempt to dam up the flow at one particular point. The political liabilities of bombing the North could be jettisoned while continuing the anticommunist commitment in the South. A premise of the barrier was that the existing bombing program was not "breaking Hanoi's will," and that political conditions in the South should be the focus of strategy.[39] This was precisely the thinking of the left current.

At any rate, in 1967 McNamara and his civilian staff in the Pentagon came to the conclusion that the war had reached a military stalemate. Townsend Hoopes, then Under Secretary of the Air Force, represents this position perfectly in his analysis of "unpalatable facts":

(1) available North Vietnamese manpower for practical purposes inexhaustible; (2) Russian and Chinese supply of weapons, equipment, and food had made good the material losses caused by both the bombing in the North and the fighting in the South; (3) such supply was contributing to a measurable strengthening of North Vietnamese military power; (4) Russia and China could maintain the present level of material support, and Russia could provide even more sophisticated weapons; (5) the bombing had neither stopped nor slowed down the rate of infiltration; (6) in the circumstances, the rate of inflation seemed to be a matter within Hanoi's control within broad limits, i.e., the spigot could be opened up by North Vietnam; (7) the important constraints on infiltration were not factors in the North (e.g., limits on manpower, supplies, trucks), but rather factors in the South, especially the limited capacity of the VC infrastructure to accept, distribute, and manage additional troops and supplies.[40]

McNamara developed an even more pessimistic indictment shortly before leaving office. At the Tuesday lunch meeting of October 31, 1967 he told Johnson that the current course of action in Southeast Asia was "dangerous, costly, and unsatisfactory."[41] At Johnson's suggestion McNamara set down his thoughts in a memorandum entitled "Outlook if Present Course is Continued" (November 1, 1967). In the report, the Secretary of Defense repeated his critique of the effectiveness of the air war over North Vietnam, but he extended his analysis to other areas as well. To McNamara, a military victory in Vietnam was impossible. He recommended publicly announcing a ceiling for the number of U.S. troops, a stabilization of air operations, and a full bombing halt before the end of 1967. Johnson circulated McNamara's recommendations among other officials. Their response shows continued strong support for the center current. McGeorge Bundy, Walt Rostow, Maxwell Taylor, Abe Fortas, Clark Clifford, William Westmoreland, Ellsworth Bunker, and Dean Rusk disagreed with major portions of McNamara's recommendations. (Although by November, McNamara seems to have won his point on the limited effectiveness of the bombing of North Vietnam.)

South Vietnam: Political Conditions

In the meantime the Saigon government had failed to establish any legitimacy. In the Spring of 1966 Buddhist demonstrations started in Saigon and spread quickly to other cities. Military force was used to end Buddhist seizure of power in both Danang and Hue. Public criticism in the U.S. and throughout the world forced Thieu and Ky to announce the setting up of a constituent assembly and eventual transition to civilian rule. The ensuing elections, held on September 11, 1966, were boycotted by the NLF, by the United Buddhist Church, and by representatives of the Roman Catholic, Cao Dai, Hoa Hao, and Protestant communities. The new Assembly, heavily stacked in favor of Thieu and Ky, debated the merits of parliamentary versus presidential rule and surprised no one with their eventual vote for the latter. In the next elections, held on September 5, 1967, Thieu received only 34.8 percent of the ballots cast, despite dispensing more than fifty million piasters in bribes. The areas controlled by the NLF — approximately forty percent of the country — did not participate in the elections.[42] Troung Dinh Dzu, the peace candidate advocating talks with the NLF and an unconditional end to the bombing, campaigned under the symbol of the dove and received a surprising seventeen percent of the total vote. Thieu's opponent claimed that his supporters had been refused paper ballots on the pretext that the supply had been exhausted. Other candidates made the same charge. While Johnson and the American press hailed the election as "a new step in Asian democracy," the elections committee of the assembly found in it "a series of irregularities." They decided by sixteen votes to two, with one abstention, to recommend invalidation of the entire election. *Le Monde*, after a close analysis of the election returns, noted that in the countryside, where the opposition to Saigon was strong, Thieu and Ky fared better than in the larger towns. The explanation of the paradox, it was hinted, was that the absence of observers in the countryside had enabled Thieu and Ky to manipulate the results in their favor.[43] Relative calm followed the September elections and lasted until the New Year, encouraging U.S. optimism. The calm could not have been more misleading: the NLF was planning for the TET Offensive.[44]

Reactions to TET

However one assesses its military aspects, the political impact of the TET Offensive on the American public was profound. Johnson told reporters that the TET attacks had been "anticipated, prepared for and met" and that the enemy had suffered a "complete failure."[45] Yet its political and psychological victory cannot be denied. By 1968 television coverage of the war had reached massive proportions. Each night, fifty million Americans were treated, visually and viscerally, to the drama of the TET battles. A number of seemingly minor incidents fueled additional public resentment. Brigadier General Nguyen Ngoc Loan, Chief of the South Vietnamese National Police, killed a NLF suspect in the middle of a busy Saigon street. Pictures of the murder were splashed over the front pages of major newspapers. A Japanese camera team also managed to capture the scene and the execution was then re-run over national television. The havoc dominating the evening news and dinner helped convince many that Johnson had misled the public, and that the U.S. effort would never succeed. Bunker and Westmoreland's confident assertions of early victory were no longer remotely credible. Indeed their optimistic predictions became an additional source of sarcastic gibes to be hurled at the Administration. A typical instance is the opening of one of Art Buchwald's columns in the *Washington Post*:

LITTLE BIG HORN, Dakota, June 27, 1876 — Gen. George Armstrong Custer said today in an exclusive interview with this correspondent that the battle of Little Big Horn had just turned the corner and he could now see the light at the end of the tunnel.

"We have the Sioux on the run," Gen. Custer told me, "Of course, we still have some cleaning up to do, but the Redskins are hurting badly and it will only be a matter of time before they give in."[46]

TET's shattering impact also enabled many correspondents harboring private doubts over the conduct of the war to voice their criticisms publicly. Frank McGee of NBC; Walter Cronkite of CBS; *Time; Life;* and *Newsweek*, all former supporters of the Administration, became strong critics.

There were other battlefield tensions as well. Khe Sanh, a remote military base just South of the DMZ, was surrounded under conditions reminiscent in many ways of Dien Bien Phu.[47] After publicly committing himself to the defense of the Khe Sanh, Johnson became concerned that he might have to make a choice between using nuclear weapons or withdrawing in humiliating defeat. Johnson made the Joint Chiefs sign a statement that Khe Sanh could be held with conventional weaponry. The Air Force dropped an incredible amount of bombs on the surrounding hills. In Khe Sanh itself, permission was given to use special artillery ammunition with new antipersonnel capabilities. Nonetheless General William Westmoreland, U.S. Field Commander in Vietnam, initiated a secret staff study of the possible use of tactical nuclear bombs. Westmoreland later noted:

> If Washington officials were so intent on "sending a message" [a premise of the center current] to Hanoi, surely small tactical nuclear weapons would be a way to tell Hanoi something, just as two atomic bombs had spoken convincingly to Japanese officials during World War II and the threat of atomic bombs induced the North Koreans to accept meaningful negotiations during the Korean War. It could be that use of a few small tactical nuclear weapons in Vietnam — or even the threat of them — might have quickly brought the war there to an end. No one could say so with certainty, of course, but

surely a detailed consideration of the possibility was warranted. Although I established a small secret group to study the subject, Washington so feared that some word of it might reach the press that I was told to desist. I felt at that time and even more so now that to fail to consider this alternative was a mistake.[48]

The Vietnamese still had uncommitted divisions in the North and the military command feared that these troops would make a massive attack across the DMZ. In such circumstances, Westmoreland cabled Washington, "I visualize that either tactical nuclear weapons or chemical agents would be active candidates for employment."[49] When the Vietnamese withdrew, the right current claimed a victory for massive and concentrated air power. The left current claimed that the Vietnamese were making a conciliatory signal in an effort to start negotiations.[50]

Elsewhere, on January 23, North Korea seized an intelligence ship, the *USS Pueblo*, after it entered its territorial waters, ordering it into the harbor of Wonsan. Precise details of the *Pueblo*'s movements, including the number of times it entered North Korean waters, and the orders and motivations of the Pacific Fleet commanders monitoring the mission are still obscure.[51] Peter Scott has argued that the *Pueblo* incident was deliberately staged by rightwing forces in order to increase the pressure for escalation in Vietnam. Seoul's initial response was to tell Washington that it would move its two and a half divisions (46,000 troops), then stationed in South Vietnam, back to South Korea to protect the "homeland". Since Johnson strove to portray the war effort as one of "allies," this withdrawal would be disastrous. Moreover, if South Korean troops departed, there would be added pressure on the center policy current either to supply more U.S. troops, or to permit significant escalation of the air war. The nuclear powered aircraft carrier *Enterprise* was diverted from its route towards Vietnam to the Sea of Japan. Cy Vance was dispatched to promise continued American assistance and prevail upon the South Koreans the necessity of their troops' remaining in South Vietnam. On January 25, Johnson made a concession to the right and mobilized 14,000 reserves.

During the same week, in Laos, the village of Nam Nga, only thirty-five miles north of the royal capital of Luang Prabang, was captured. The *Economist* complained that the North Vietnamese

316th Division had also crossed from Dien Bien Phu into Nan Bac valley only sixty miles from the city.[52] The military significance of these events was limited, but they did provide additional evidence for rightwing arguments that the "Communist world" was launching a coordinated world-wide attack.[53]

Walt Rostow, stoking the fires on the right, asked Westmoreland if he thought there "was a relationship between the activities in South Vietnam (the TET Offensive) and those in Korea." Westmoreland and Bunker caught the signal and, playing the bureaucratic game, cabled back, "It would seem to us that there is a relationship."[54] Westmoreland was also asked by Wheeler if the situation after the *Pueblo* incident would calm down or get worse. The answer: it would get worse.[55]

The Origins of the "(Johnson) — Westmoreland Troop Request"

In his memoirs, and during a 1970 televised interview, Johnson maintained that he and Secretary of State Dean Rusk initiated decisions that blocked a military request, coming after the TET Offensive, for over two hundred thousand troops.[56] Johnson asserted in the CBS interview that he and Rusk were responsible for the partial bombing halt over North Vietnam that was announced at the end of March:

> Secretary Rusk came back and said . . . "Now I think the time's come when we can stop the bombing." Some of them suggested — I think Secretary Clifford suggested, and we and some of the others joined him — that we stop the bombing on the condition that the North Vietnamese do something. And Secretary Rusk said, "That won't work; it's reciprocity and won't work. We ought to just stop the bombing." I said, "Get on your horses and get me a plan!"[57]

Johnson, in other words, states that he *willingly* moved towards a partial bombing halt (towards the left current). His claim is inaccurate: Johnson's "deviations" during February and March were towards the right current. The President inspired the "Westmoreland troop request;" hence the subtitle of this section: "The (Johnson) — Westmoreland Troop Request."

Johnson's initial reaction to TET was to defend the logic of his own center strategy. The U.S. was winning the war of attrition. TET was only an act of desperation. During the Offensive Johnson instructed Westmoreland to display public confidence. "The President desires," read a cable from the Chairman of the Joint Chiefs of Staff, "that you make a brief personal comment to the press at least once each day during the current period of mounting VC/NVA activity. The purpose of such statements should be to convey to the American public your confidence in our capability to blunt these enemy moves and to reassure the public here that you have the situation under control."[58]

Westmoreland, a member of the right current, but a loyal soldier, complied. His initial post-TET assessments were optimistic: "I don't believe that the enemy has any great capacity to assume any general offensive in the near future. He has been hurt and hurt badly. He is tired."[59] During the early days of the TET Offensive, the Joint Chiefs asked for closer bombing of Hanoi and Haiphong, but not for more troops. The right current wanted more troops only if these were to be used in new missions in Laos, Cambodia and North Vietnam. A February 8 "in-depth requirement study" cabled from Westmoreland to Wheeler placed first priority on the improvement of South Vietnamese forces. Additional U.S. ground forces was third in priority.[60] In Westmoreland's first post-TET assessment, additional troops were not necessary *as long as the ground war was confined to South Vietnam.* A February 4 report was optimistic except for the northern-most I Corps. The Commander of U.S. forces in South Vietnam even moved elements of the 101st Airborne away from protection of the cities to the beseiged area. Three days after a February 9 inquiry from McNamara, the Joint Chiefs replied that while needs in South Vietnam were pressing, any further reduction in the U.S. strategic reserve would be intolerable and would seriously compromise the U.S. worldwide force posture. The Joint Chiefs of Staff concluded that "a decision to deploy reinforcements to Vietnam [should] be deferred at this time."[61]

The domestic reaction to TET was enormous. Johnson's own political position was in great jeopardy. He toyed with escalation, but a suitable public rationale had to be created. So after TET Johnson encouraged Wheeler to reverse Westmoreland's claim that no significant troop increase was necessary; he thus undercut his own previous instructions to Westmoreland. Why assert that the U.S. had successfully countered the TET Offensive and, simultaneously, claim that the U.S. needed more ground troops? There is only one possible answer. Johnson wanted finally to "nail the coonskin to the wall." Besides escalating within the strategy of the center, Johnson was now considering moving troops into Laos to cut off the Ho Chi Minh Trail, raiding NLF sanctuaries in Cambodia, and launching an amphibious invasion of the North, either just above the DMZ or near Vinh. Johnson evoked the "(Johnson) — Westmoreland troop request" by employing one of the most sophisticated techniques of bureaucratic warfare: encouraging, and hiding behind, an organizational interest that could be counted on to push for a secretly favored policy. By not identifying himself with the troop request, even within the national security apparatus, Johnson gained additional flexibility. Johnson knew the military wanted to "take the wraps off the war." In the immediate aftermath of TET, he used Westmoreland to test the response to escalation. Johnson was well aware of the political and economic pressures opposing a large troop increase. He cleverly protected himself from the consequences of possible defeat by making Wheeler and Westmoreland serve as intermediaries. If the ploy failed, they would take the heat.

Johnson's willingness to entertain measures consistent with the right can be documented in several ways. A cable from Wheeler to Westmoreland is one:

(February 3, 1968) Wheeler to Westmoreland: THE PRESIDENT ASKS ME IS THERE ANY REINFORCEMENT OR HELP THAT WE CAN GIVE YOU.

(February 8, 1968) Wheeler to Westmoreland: DO YOU NEED REINFORCEMENTS? OUR CAPABILITIES ARE LIMITED. WE CAN PROVIDE THE 82ND AIRBORNE DIVISION AND ABOUT ONE HALF A MARINE CORPS DIVISION, BOTH LOADED WITH VIETNAM VETERANS. HOWEVER, IF YOU SHOULD CONSIDER REINFORCEMENT IMPERATIVE, YOU SHOULD NOT BE BOUND BY EARLIER AGREEMENTS . . . UNITED STATES GOVERNMENT IS NOT PREPARED TO ACCEPT DEFEAT IN VIET-

NAM. IN SUMMARY IF YOU NEED MORE TROOPS
ASK FOR THEM.[62]

It is difficult for any general to resist this sort of urging.
Westmoreland was hesitant at first. As he later told an interviewer,
"It seemed to me that for political reasons or otherwise, the president
and the Joint Chiefs of Staff were anxious to send me reinforcements.
We did a little sparring back and forth. My first thought was not to
ask for any, but the signals from Washington got stronger."[63]
Wheeler found Westmoreland's initial requests "not direct enough."
Westmoreland's return cable of February 12 called for the 82nd
Airborne and half of the Marine division (a total of 10,500 men).
Westmoreland wanted to see if a shift in strategy was in the cards as
well. He asked Johnson to authorize an amphibious invasion of the
North, an action long favored by the right policy current, noting that
"surf conditions would permit the operation to start in April."[64]
Wheeler reported back the same day with approval of the troop
request and news that the new men would start arriving February 26.

A few days later, Wheeler went to Saigon with what seemed to be
a Presidential sanction for a large troop request and further hints of a
change in strategy. Before leaving Washington, Wheeler and the rest
of the Joint Chiefs worked out a preliminary version of what later
became known as the "Westmoreland troop request."[65] In Saigon,
Wheeler reported a "conversation with a 'senior authority' during
which he was directed to ask Westmoreland 'if there is any help we
can give you.'"[66] Westmoreland felt "that the president and his
advisors were receptive to proposals concerning a new strategy.
There were signals from both Washington and the United States
Pacific Command (CINCPAC) in Hawaii indicating that a reappraisal of national policy might result in lifting the previously
imposed troop ceiling."[67] Wheeler and Westmoreland shared an
understanding that the large troop request would only be approved if
new strategic objectives were accepted.[68] Westmoreland later
remembered:

> Wheeler came over to me and we talked about this (the
> plan to "go for broke" in pursuit of victory in Vietnam) very
> frankly. We both agreed that this was a benchmark in the
> history of the war; that it was only logical for the Administra-
> tion to reassess their strategy and determine if they were going

to make a change in policy and strategy. Wheeler faced me with a proposition: Assuming that there is a change in strategy that will inevitably involve a call-up of reserves, and the (new) strategy is one towards putting more pressure on the enemy to end this thing once and for all, to include a step-up of bombing and put maximum pressure throughout the whole structure with a possibility of lifting some of the political constraints, geographical-style (I don't have to spell this out further); you develop a plan, a reinforcement plan under those assumptions.[69]

Coming up with a plausible public rationale for the troops presented some difficulty. The actual reason, to provide manpower for an invasion of the North could not be stated in official cables, which would eventually become part of the historical record. Westmoreland's initial post-TET reports had been optimistic, so the need for emergency reinforcements could not be used either. The justification in Westmoreland's February 12 cable asking for a small augmentation was murky: the troops are needed, he argued, "not because I fear defeat if I am not reinforced but because I do not feel I can fully grasp the initiative from the recently reinforced enemy without them."[70] Walt Rostow, another member of the right current, tried to help in the search for a suitable official rationale. On February 23, the same day that Wheeler arrived in Saigon for his four-day visit, the Presidential advisor cabled that "there is a suggestion in intelligence that additional North Vietnamese regulars are being brought South — perhaps two additional divisions. It well may be that the enemy is about to make a virtually total effort with the capital he has at hand. He may then try to lock us into negotiations at his peak position before we can counter attack."[71]

Wheeler and Westmoreland eventually decided to base "their" request on a revised estimate of the size of the "enemy forces" in South Vietnam. If the U.S. defense during TET had been as successful as Westmoreland first claimed, then the NLF and North Vietnamese must be down to one-third of their original attack force. MACV (Military Advisory Command, Vietnam) intelligence proceeded to revise the estimate of the original size of the enemy forces committed to the TET Offensive (from 67,000 up to 84,000).[72] Wheeler and Westmoreland then proceeded to revise the optimism of Westmoreland's initial reports. The new line argued that the "enemy" was hurt, but also that "he" had taken over the countryside and was recruiting rapidly. In the new assessment, there remained a chance that the NLF would mount another wave of attacks. Enemy determination remained strong. The South Vietnamese troops were still cloistered in the cities. ARVN's effectiveness had been sorely tested. While their performance was not without value, a continued role for U.S. ground troops was seen for the foreseeable future.[73]

These remarkable revisions in intelligence assessments pose most sharply a problem stressed in the quagmire perspective. Do bureaucratically-derived political pressures distort information so much that decision-making reflects parochial interests within the state instead of objective conditions on the battlefield? Was U.S. policy in Vietnam determined by an overriding anticommunist imperative — or by disputes among different state agencies? On the surface, the existence of shifting intelligence estimates within and between various agencies appears to support the quagmire position.[74] Policy can hardly be rational with organizational warfare raging within the national security apparatus. To provide a rationale for more U.S. troops the initial estimate of the number of NLF soldiers was revised upwards, even while the military clung tenaciously to the argument that TET was a military defeat for the Vietnamese. Bureaucratic forces, in this case located in the military, seem to dominate policy. Certainly the orthodox radical framework, stressing administrative rationality in the interests of the capitalist class, appears hopelessly out of place. Through the policy currents perspective, however, one can appreciate the significance of these internal differences, but need not fall back upon a bureaucratic explanation of their origin.

The U.S. estimated that 45,000 NLF troops were killed or seriously disabled during TET. The figure, while probably exaggerated, remained fixed in intelligence assessments. A low estimate of the number of NLF troops committed to fight in TET results in a high proportion killed in battle. Given the original estimate of 67,000 troops, the U.S. would have killed two-thirds of the TET attack force. This assessment supported the argument that the U.S. was both effective on the battlefield and about to win the war; it also bolstered the center policy current. Then the signals emanating from Washington appeared supportive of a strategy shift. The problem for the right was how to sustain that direction without explicitly advocating a change or looking bad by claiming now that TET was a military defeat for the U.S. Increasing the estimate of the number of NLF troops to 84,000 left the Vietnamese still capable of mounting an attack without undermining the military's assertion that they operated effectively — after all, even with the new estimate, half of the attack force was still killed. But now the U.S. military command had created a suitable justification for more troops, and had not said that they would be used to invade North Vietnam.

Intelligence assessments certainly shifted, the issue is the source: organizational self-interest (the quagmire approach), or changed political conditions that appeared to support a change in strategy (the policy currents approach). After TET, the problem facing Johnson was to create a rationale to support the right current for which he would not be publicly responsible. The signal was communicated through the Chairman of the Joint Chiefs of Staff and pressures to revise the NLF "order of battle" ensued.[75] Widespread perception in the U.S. that Johnson's (center current) strategy was not working led to experimentation with the right, which led in turn to messages to revise intelligence estimates. But the resulting bureaucratic behavior, manipulation of the "facts", was determined by the interplay among policy currents. This explanation is precisely the opposite from that predicted by the quagmire approach and its focus on the influence of competing organizational interests on decision-making.

The Right is Stalemated

Johnson sought support for his program of escalation. On February 2, he met for one-and-a-half hours with General Matt Ridgway, seeking his opinion of an invasion of North Vietnam and a large increase of American combat force in Southeast Asia.[76] Ridgway advised against both.[77] Later in the month Johnson consulted former Secretary of State Dean Acheson. The President respected Acheson's experience and unblemished reputation. In a similar role during the Cuban Missile Crisis, Acheson had recommended air strikes against Soviet missile placements to be followed up by a ground invasion.[78] In this case, however, the move backfired. Acheson insisted that he be given time to speak with whomever he pleased in the national security apparatus. Philip Habib, Deputy

Assistant Secretary of State; George Carver of the C.I.A.; and General De Puy of the staff of the Joint Chiefs were among those questioned. After two weeks Acheson reported back that unless Johnson was willing to commit full resources for over five years the war could not be won. Acheson also informed the President that "the Joint Chiefs of Staff don't know what they are talking about," that no one believed Johnson's speeches, and that public opinion in the country had turned against the war.

In the meantime Wheeler finished his negotiations with Westmoreland. He cabled a report to Washington which managed to provide a rationale for more troops without explicitly arguing for a new strategy — and without admitting that the military had been caught unaware by the TET Offensive. The Chairman of the Joint Chiefs carefully straddled the line between optimism (which would have undermined the rationale for more troops) and pessimism (which would have undermined the sense that the military were doing a good job). He maintained that the "current situation in Vietnam is still developing and fraught with opportunities as well as dangers" and that "the enemy failed to achieve his initial objective but is continuing his effort. Although many of his units were badly hurt, the judgment is that he has the will and capacity to continue."[79] Wheeler broke down the request for 206,756 troops as follows: approximately 108,000 men over the following two months, another 42,000 by September, and the final group of 56,000 by the end of 1968. Wheeler gave no official support, at this time, to expanding the war into Laos, Cambodia and North Vietnam. He later explained that the prevailing atmosphere in the Pentagon (the left current) and State Department (the center current) would kill the chances for a large troop increase if it came accompanied by such expansionary proposals.[80] After the troop increase was secured, Wheeler planned to propose the strategy change formally. But all camps in Washington were already aware of the full implications of the troop request. They realized that its approval would signal adoption of the right current and a major expansion of the war.[81]

On the morning of February 28 the state managers met over breakfast to hear Wheeler's somber oral report and to discuss the troop request.[82] Wheeler stressed that "the enemy" retained the capacity to launch a second wave of attacks.

During these preliminary discussions several points were underscored. To meet the request, argued McNamara, who by now fully endorsed the left policy current, Washington would have to call up 280,000 reserves for all services. The length of service in Vietnam would have to be increased: men would be recalled for second and even third tours of duty. The draft call would be raised. The request would encounter substantial difficulties with Congressional hawks, who tied any mobilization program to the removal of restraints on ROLLING THUNDER. The dollar cost was high, estimated at an additional ten billion for FY 1969 and fifteen billion for FY 1970. Other points of discussion included the role and strength of the South Vietnamese forces and the capacity of the NLF and the North Vietnamese to respond to any major increase in the number of U.S. troops. General Wheeler recommended that the three-phased increase be implemented. Wheeler said that he would like to meet in Honolulu with the Joint Chiefs; Westmoreland and his staff; and the Secretaries of the Navy, Army and Air Force to work out the details. McNamara argued against this proposal, favoring instead a small emergency increase of 15,000 men.

In his memoirs Johnson maintains that he was not prepared to make any judgment at that time. Instead he ordered Clark Clifford, who would replace McNamara as Secretary of Defense on March 1, to explore the "demanding problems" associated with the troop request. Johnson's version of the directive to Clifford follows:

> As I indicated at breakfast this morning, I wish you to develop by Monday morning, March 4th, recommendations in response to the situation presented us by General Wheeler and his preliminary proposals.
>
> I wish alternatives to be examined and, if possible, agreed recommendations to emerge which reconcile the military, diplomatic, economic, Congressional and public opinion problems involved.[83]

The key words are Johnson's request for "alternatives" and for different "recommendations," implying that the decision was yet to be made. Johnson maintains that he stayed neutral on the subject of the troop increase: "I told my advisors that I was not prepared to make any judgment at that time."[84] He states that "as February ended an intensive review of our entire position was taking place inside the government. We were at one of those critical junctures where several possible trails lay before us, and I would have to choose which one to follow. I wanted all the expertise, opinions, ideas, and judgment I could possibly get before I made that decision."[85]

Significantly Clark Clifford recalls Johnson's February 28 directive differently: "[I] was directed as my first assignment, to chair a task force named by the president to determine how this new requirement (the 206,000 troops) could be met. We were not instructed to assess the need for substantial increases in men and materiel; we were to devise the means by which they could be provided."[86]

Clifford's version of the directive supports the argument that Johnson continued to entertain a possible shift to the right policy current.[87] But Johnson was brought short by McNamara and Clifford, who chose not to circulate the full text of his directive within the bureaucracy.[88] At the first meeting of the task force Clifford broadened the scope of inquiry. He opened the door to a general policy review by asking questions about the ability of the 206,000 troops to bring the U.S. closer to its objectives. The resulting "A to Z Policy Review" provided a full study of the costs and benefits of U.S. intervention in Vietnam as seen by the left policy current. During the rest of March the struggle to *implement* the left policy of lower costs raged furiously.

VIII: THE CRISIS: FEBRUARY-MARCH 1968

By March 1968 the costs associated with the Administration's Vietnam policy had become overwhelming. Johnson had to prepare the groundwork for a policy with lower costs and was forced to withdraw from the presidential race. Under the Nixon Administration, this policy would be known as Vietnamization. Several events contributed to the crisis atmosphere of March, of which the most dramatic was the TET Offensive. At the same time, the international monetary system came literally to the point of collapse. The Kerner Commission Report on racial disorders laid bare the deepening social and racial crisis in the United States, while Johnson's defeat in the New Hampshire primary attested convincingly to the extent of the President's unpopularity. All of the state managers felt they were operating in a unique, pressure-packed situation — an atmosphere of almost desperate crisis.

Policy currents arise from forces of opposition, each of which intensified over the month. The Vietnamese were firm on the battlefield. Domestic dissent intensified. And a gold crisis vividly illustrated the weakness of the economy. Johnson also had to consider his own interests. Should he protect his chances for another Presidential term? Or recognize his growing unpopularity and remove himself from the race? Defeat on the battlefield, economic pressure, public opinion, and presidential politics were like clamps on a vice, clamps which had been closing for some time but whose squeeze had now become inexorably tight. The state managers caught in its grip disagreed among themselves on the best way to alleviate the pressure, but there was unanimous recognition that something had to be done. As the clamps tightened, disagreement grew more violent. At the level of policy currents, the center position

245

became extremely tenuous. The high cost policy (thirty billion dollars a year, a restricted airwar over the North, and high U.S. casualties) was clearly bankrupt and had to be changed. Washington could either escalate the war, hoping to achieve a quick victory (favored by the right); or retrench in order to cut losses (favored by the left). Representatives of the three policy currents fought over two main issues: (1) should the U.S. introduce an additional 206,000 ground troops as a prelude for expanding the ground war into Cambodia, Laos, and even North Vietnam? and (2) should the U.S. institute a partial bombing halt over North Vietnam in an effort to initiate negotiations? These issues were discussed in a comprehensive policy review carried out under the new Secretary of Defense Clark Clifford, a review that enabled members of the left policy current located in the Pentagon to state fully their case.

The "A to Z Review": The Logic of the Left Policy Current

On the afternoon of February 28 the "A to Z Review" task group, formed by Johnson to discuss the introduction of two hundred thousand additional troops, held its first meeting. Clifford and McNamara shifted the discussion from the issue of how best to meet the "(Johnson) — Westmoreland troop request" to a general review of Vietnam policy. Those present were drawn from each policy current. Attending besides Clifford and McNamara, were Secretary of State Dean Rusk, who attended only this meeting; Treasury Secretary Henry Fowler; Under Secretary of State Katzenbach; Philip Habib, representing William Bundy, the Assistant Secretary of State for Far Eastern Affairs; Deputy Secretary of Defense Paul Nitze; Assistant Secretary of Defense Paul Warnke; Richard Helms of the Central Intelligence Agency; Walt Rostow, Presidential Advisor on National Security; and General Maxwell Taylor, Johnson's military advisor.

Discussion was divided into a number of subject areas, reflecting the broad range of issues involved in the request for more troops. The task force considered possible courses of action open to the United States and the "enemy." They reviewed implications of the troop request in military, diplomatic, economic, and Congressional contexts. They explored its potential effect on public opinion, both domestic and international. They tried to gauge its political ramifications in the broadest sense, including those affecting Vietnam internally. And they attempted to generate negotiating alternatives. Here are some of the conclusions from the perspective of the left policy current.

(1) The Ground War in the South was Stalemated:

The center current believed that the U.S. was winning the war of attrition and that the Vietnamese were running out of manpower. But a CIA paper argued that the war had reached a military stalemate, with or without a sizeable U.S. troop increase:

> Question: What is the likely course of events in South Vietnam over the next 10 months assuming no change in U.S. policy or force levels?
>
> Answer: In the assumed circumstances a total military victory by the Allies or the Communists is highly unlikely in the next 10 months. It is manifestly impossible for the Communists to drive U.S. forces out of the country. It is equally out of the question for US/GVN forces to clear South Vietnam of Communist forces. . .
>
> Question: What is the likely NVA/VC strategy over the next ten months if U.S. forces are increased by 50,000, by 100,000, or by 200,000?
>
> Answer: We would expect the Communists to continue the war. They still have resources available in North Vietnam and within South Vietnam to increase their troop strength. Their strong logistical effort and their ability to organize and exploit the people under their control in the South enable them to counter U.S. increases by smaller increases of their own. . .[1]

A Systems Analysis paper, prepared in the Pentagon, echoed the same theme:

> We know that despite a massive influx of 500,000 troops, 1.2 million tons of bombs a year, 400,000 attack sorties per year, 200,000 enemy KIA in three years, 20,000 US KIA, etc., our control of the countryside and the defense of the urban areas is now essentially at pre-August 1965 levels. We have achieved stalemate at a high commitment. A new strategy must be sought.[2]

A new strategy was offered by International Security Affairs (ISA), under the direction of Paul Warnke, who recommended an end to search-and-destroy missions and closer attention to the defense of populated areas.[3] From Warnke's left current perspective the altered troop deployment was a chance to cut costs.[4] Military representatives to the "A to Z Review" protested that abandoning the initiative to "the enemy" would leave allied forces and South Vietnamese cities more, not less, vulnerable.[5]

(2) The Vietnamese Thought They Were Winning:

Undermining the will to resist was a crucial element of the center current strategy. Despite massive U.S. intervention the Vietnamese showed no signs of crumbling. The CIA circulated a captured document indicating that Hanoi believed it was operating from a position of strength after the TET Offensive.[6] Another Agency paper argued that North Vietnam's manpower resources and will to resist were both high.

(3) The Soviet Union and China Would Respond to U.S. Escalation

Those in the center current who entertained a shift in strategy towards the right did not want to bring the U.S. and China into the war. The "A to Z Review" considered the possible reactions of the Soviet Union and China to increased pressure on North Vietnam. CIA analysts, William Bundy, and Ambassador Thompson, via cable from Moscow, considered the possible reactions of the Soviet Union to mining the harbor of Haiphong; a general intensification of ROLLING THUNDER, including direct attacks on Hanoi and Haiphong population centers; and an Inchon-type landing along the North Vietnamese coast. There was general agreement that both the Soviet Union and China would respond to serious escalation. Bundy noted that China would send "volunteers" if the U.S. invaded North Vietnam. Thompson mentioned that the Soviet Union would not want to appear to do less than China.[7] Having been recently frustrated at the Budapest Conference (where Rumania successfully sought greater independence from the Soviet bloc), the Soviet Union would be especially likely to demonstrate support for national liberation movements. Thompson cited increased Soviet commitment and contact with the North Vietnamese and with the NLF as evidence of this attitude. All agreed as well that the Soviet Union and

China could easily reestablish a military stalemate.

At this point the Sino-Soviet split seemed to be operating against escalation. By mining Haiphong and throwing the burden of supplying North Vietnam onto the rail lines, the U.S. would increase Chinese leverage in Hanoi. Despite evidence that the Red Guards had been halting trains carrying Soviet supplies through China, some argued that "China would by all means make sure that the flow of both Soviet and Chinese materiel for North Vietnam — by land and sea — would continue uninterrupted."[8] This would not be in U.S. interests, for China would "welcome the additional influence it would gain as the remaining link on North Vietnam's life line." The Soviet Union and China would work out cooperative arrangements for the enlarged transit. One paper argued that "we do not believe this would truly drive the Soviets and Chinese together, but it would force them to take a wider range of common positions that would certainly not be favorable to our basic interests."[9]

(4) Intensification of ROLLING THUNDER Would Not Work:

Predictably the Joint Chiefs of Staff weighed in with a program for escalation. They recommended the mining of Haiphong, and the reduction of restricted areas in Hanoi, Haiphong, and the Northeast coastal areas. They urged destruction of war supporting facilities, as well as those producing items vital to the economy. The U.S. must attack enemy defenses in order to protect its strike forces, destroy enemy gun crews and weapons, and force enemy expenditure of ammunition. In addition, pilots would conduct air attacks throughout as large an area and as continuously as possible. They would destroy lines of communication, targets and associated facilities. Their goal would be to disperse material and supplies, and to suppress normal activities through the threat of bombardment.[10] This program implied turning North Vietnam into a vast "free fire zone," and spreading fear throughout the civilian population by creating a huge number of casualties.

The Office of the Secretary of Defense under the direction of Paul Warnke prepared a second paper on the effectiveness of the bombing. The paper followed the left current, arguing "that it has become abundantly clear that no level of bombing can prevent the North Vietnamese from supplying the necessary forces and materiel to maintain their military operations in the South."[11] On the issue of Haiphong, the Warnke paper argued that the port was not a point of entry for most military supplies, which came predominantly via the rail routes from China. High airplane and pilot losses with minimal benefits could be expected from shrinking the areas of control around Hanoi and Haiphong. The Warnke paper also argued that the systematic and daily bombing of the two large cities might serve as some kind of "flash-point" beyond which the British Government and other "key third nations" might withdraw their support.[12]

The importance of the dispute about bombing cannot be over-estimated. In the midst of a program whose intensity roughly matched the combined Allied effort against Germany, a significant number of officials were arguing that the bombing was not working and could not be made to work. And the Secretary of Defense agreed with them. True, their opposition was pragmatic, not moral. But the limited nature of their critique does not alter in any way the fact that the Administration could not justify bombing North Vietnam — even on its own terms.

(5) Domestic Factors Militated Against Meeting the Troop Request:

Economic factors and public opinion were also discussed. Secretary of Treasury Fowler analyzed pessimistically the economic implications of larger troop commitments. Domestic programs would be cut, as would other defense expenditures and foreign aid. The defense budget would grow by ten billion dollars. Only formal war mobilization including a large tax increase, wage and price controls, and credit restrictions, could prevent devaluation of the dollar.[13] Assistant Secretary of Defense (Public Affairs) Phil Goulding argued that there "had been no preparation of public opinion" for a large-scale mobilization. The Administration had repeatedly argued that the Vietnam commitment could be met without undue strain and that we had been the victor in the TET battles. Now the public would be asked to support 200,000 more men in Vietnam, the call-up of another 280,000 reserves, and the drafting of an additional 200,000. A new wave of antiwar demonstrations and draft resistance efforts could be expected. Meeting the large troop request, in the words of the Assistant Secretary of Defense, would involve the "gravest domestic risks."[14]

Another ISA paper, prepared under the direction of Paul

Warnke, reflected the importance of economic instability and domestic criticism on Vietnam decision-making:

> We will have to mobilize reserves, increase our budget by billions, and see U.S. casualties climb to 1,300-1,400 per month. Our balance of payments will be worsened considerably, and we will need a larger tax increase — justified as a war tax, or wage and price controls. . .
>
> It will be difficult to convince the critics that we are not simply destroying South Vietnam in order to 'save' it and that we genuinely want peace talks. This growing disaffection accompanied, as it certainly will be, by increased defiance of the draft and growing unrest in the cities because of the belief that we are neglecting domestic problems, runs great risks of provoking a domestic crisis of unprecedented proportions.[15]

Thus the left current was aware and accepted the constraints imposed by two kinds of obstacles: the economy and domestic dissent. In addition, its representatives could not devise a program to undermine Vietnamese resistance, nor limit the support given by the Soviet Union or China to their ally. For them, a change in strategy was the only possible answer.

A Period of Flux

On Monday, March 4, the new Secretary of Defense Clark Clifford transmitted the recommendations of the task force to Johnson without expressing his steadily growing private doubts. Given the varied political composition of the entire "A to Z Review" group, these formal conclusions could not be exclusively those of the left current. The task force recommended: (a) a modest increase in ground troops (23,000); (b) a larger role for the South Vietnamese in the war effort; (c) an in-depth study of possible alternative strategies; (d) a reserve call-up of unstated proportions; and (e) no new negotiation initiative on the scale of San Antonio. The left current did not yet control, or even influence, final decisions. William Bundy, a member of the center current, argued in an Appendix that the San Antonio formula was "rock bottom."[16] While the Clifford group had discussed a partial bombing halt, no mention of it appeared in the final report. Disagreement on the effectiveness of bombing was acknowledged by the inclusion of separate Joint Chiefs of Staff and Defense staff papers. The group reserved decision on the additional 183,000 troops until new requirements could be assessed on a "week-by-week" basis.[17]

Although Rostow, Fowler, Taylor, Wheeler and Rusk appeared to favor a continued high commitment along the lines of the center current, Johnson later noted that he "detected among a few advisors a sense of pessimism far deeper than I myself felt."[18] During the previous week Westmoreland had delivered several optimistic reports from Saigon. Johnson said that he was encouraged by them. Westmoreland and Sharp also filed separate recommendations for broadening the war. Given the signalling of Johnson's disposition, each was confident that the "wraps would finally be taken off." On March 2 Westmoreland pushed for the implementation of OPERATION EL PASO, which would have moved several divisions through Khe Sanh into Laos as soon as troops were available. Two days later Sharp recommended OPERATION DURANGO, an amphibious landing on the southern part of North Vietnam.[19] As the March 4 meeting ended Johnson asked Wheeler if he had informed Westmoreland that 23,000 troops would be arriving by June. Wheeler replied that he had not (expecting that Johnson would approve the full 206,000). Wheeler was still hopeful that Johnson would finally accept the recommendations of the right.

On the night of March 31, President Johnson gave a nationwide television address in which he announced a partial bombing halt over the North. Johnson did not refer to the possibility of sending two hundred thousand more ground troops to Vietnam. The speech was thus in the direction favored by the left current. Johnson also announced that he would not seek another term as President. Did Johnson take these decision on his own or were they forced upon him? The answer is crucial for judging the validity of the policy current perspective.

According to Johnson, the March 4 discussion produced the first direct proposal to limit the bombing to the North Vietnam panhandle. Rusk suggested that the U.S. could stop most of the bombing during the rainy season (which permitted bombing on an average of only four days a month) without too much military risk. On the next day Rusk drafted, for Presidential address, a paragraph containing the partial bombing halt. The bombing would be suspended except for the "area associated with the fighting zone." Rusk called for a "de facto halt in the Southern panhandle" with Washington waiting to see "if we get a de facto response from Hanoi." The suggested dividing line was the nineteenth parallel, with everything below that point, including Vinh, subject to attack. Johnson would have us believe that he was deeply impressed by the proposal, that he wondered privately about the effect if he announced simultaneously that he would not run for the Presidency in 1968. He tells us that he instructed his staff not to enter a stand-in candidate to run against Senator McCarthy in the Massachusetts primary. Rusk was about to send the proposal to Bunker for discussion of how best to sell the idea to Thieu, but Johnson, citing the possibility of adverse and premature publicity, intervened. Johnson reports that "we were about to make a change in strategy."[20]

Johnson was a member of the center policy current. After TET he considered a shift in strategy towards the right. The Vietnam War would only end when the North Vietnamese withdrew from the South, not before. Washington would not unilaterally de-escalate. Yet Johnson would have us believe that his announcement of a partial bombing halt and his *de facto* ceiling on the number of ground troops in the South were made voluntarily, and that these decisions were made during the first week of March. In fact Johnson was dragged, kicking and screaming, to the left policy current content of the March 31 speech. And the decisions were made in the last days of the month. Afterwards Johnson struggled to reconsolidate the center. He did not expect the North Vietnamese to respond favorably to the speech, thus clearing the way to return to the old strategy.

Johnson's actions cannot be explained by such individual factors as an erratic personality, as much as his demeanor tempts us to entertain this possibility. In shifting between the right, center and left positions Johnson was only conforming to a standard typical of Presidents under crisis. State managers are generally identified with a particular policy current. Presidents usually favor a particular policy, but their leadership position and personal interests makes consistency next-to-impossible. At heart Johnson was a member of the center current. During the TET/March crisis he dabbled with the right, and eventually was forced to make decisions that opened the door to the left. Johnson would have us believe that the partial bombing halt and the rejected troop request were his decisions. In fact, Johnson *had* to make those decisions. He had no choice.

Specifically, Johnson's effort to convince us that his change in policy came during the first week of March can be countered on three grounds: First, the origin of the partial bombing halt can be traced earlier. McNamara first formally proposed the idea to Johnson on May 20, 1967.[21] Rusk and Katzenbach suggested consideration of a partial bombing halt in November, 1967, in response to McNamara's final memorandum calling for a total bombing halt. A partial bombing halt was also discussed during the Clifford task force deliberations. Second, neither Rusk nor Johnson expected North Vietnam to respond favorably to a partial bombing halt. Rusk still tied a complete cessation of the bombing to some act of reciprocity from the North Vietnamese. The Secretary of State knew that Hanoi demanded "an unconditional halt" before negotiations could start; North Vietnam's "failure to respond" to a partial bombing halt could thus clear the way for future escalation.[22] Third, after March 4, Johnson reverted back to his "natural position" at the center, opposing the partial bombing halt (favored by the left current) until it was forced upon him later in the month. Johnson then seized the opportunity to relieve political pressure for a change in strategy by adopting that change as his own. Rusk, who had the strongest influence with Johnson, saw the pressure building for a partial bombing halt. Recognizing the affinity between himself and Rusk, Johnson covered his options by permitting Rusk to develop his proposal. Thus both the left and the center currents, for separate reasons, began to support a partial bombing halt. Rusk's March 4 proposal was an effort to reduce the political costs of the current strategy. Clifford, on the other hand, was firmly convinced by the "A to Z Review" for the need for a genuine shift. His support for a partial bombing halt came from his membership in the left current. Rusk and Johnson wanted a partial bombing halt only to reduce the clamor for a change in strategy. They did not expect that Hanoi would respond, and thus prepared the grounds for "safely" continuing the earlier strategy. The center could then bomb the North and claim that the Administration had done all it could to encourage negotiations. For Clifford, of course, a partial bombing halt was only the first step in a permanent change in strategy designed to reduce the war's economic and political costs along the grounds favored by the left.

Clark Clifford: The Center Shifts to the Left

Secretary of Defense Clark Clifford entered the Pentagon with a well-deserved reputation as a hawk — which is exactly what Johnson wanted. His passage from a strong defender of existing policy to the left current illustrates how untenable the center position had become. Johnson passed over Paul Nitze, McNamara's logical replacement, because he was suspected for his opposition to the bombing of the North.[23] At first Nitze, Warnke, Goulding and other civilians in the Pentagon who opposed Johnson's policy, were disappointed with the news of Clifford's nomination.[24] The international press also thought of Clifford as a hard-liner on Vietnam, some even contrasting the views of the new Secretary of Defense with McNamara's criticism of the bombing.

Clifford had served as special advisor to Truman and contributed to postwar defense reorganization legislation. To him, the original involvement in Vietnam was "based on sound and unassailable principles, thoroughly consistent with our self-interest and responsibilities."[25] Clifford did entertain some doubts about Vietnam. In 1965 he did not see how the introduction of U.S. ground troops could bring decisive results, and he feared that the commitment might become open-ended.[26] Yet Johnson counted the new Secretary of Defense as one of his most reliable supporters, later commenting that Clifford and Fortas had been consulted on every major decision of his Presidency. Clifford also served as chairman of the Foreign Intelligence Advisory Board and as an envoy on several diplomatic missions. He opposed the 37-day bombing halt over the Christmas 1965-New Year 1966 period, arguing that the halt would be construed by Hanoi as a sign of weakness.[27] Clifford's response to NcNamara's November proposal for an unconditional bombing halt over North Vietnam was among the most negative.[28] Even Rostow regarded Clifford as an ally, suggesting him to Johnson as the chair for the "A to Z Review."[29] When Clifford became designate Secretary of Defense, the Joint Chiefs probably took the announcement as a sign of Johnson's commitment to escalation in Vietnam. Clifford told one visitor in early February "we have been suckers and we are going to quit being suckers. There is no point in this kind of negotiation. The next time, they come to us, and they had better mean it! San Antonio is the final formula — the furthest we can go."[30]

As one of his tasks, Johnson asked Clifford to recruit Vietnam military commitments from our "allies" along the Pacific Rim. Clifford later noted that an early source of his skepticism was the failure of the Philippines, Thailand, Australia, and New Zealand to mount anything near their effort of World War II. He returned from the disappointing trip "puzzled, troubled and confused," thinking perhaps that the U.S. was exaggerating the danger of Vietnam to the stability of the rest of Southeast Asia and Western Pacific.[31]

The precise interpretation of the San Antonio formula provides an opportunity to illustrate both Clifford's deepening doubts and the conflict between policy currents. Under the San Antonio formula the Vietnamese could not take advantage of a bombing halt. At issue was the definition of "not take advantage." The left favored a "soft" version in which normal resupply levels would be permitted during a bombing halt. The center favored a "hard" version in which no resupply efforts could be conducted. The left was attempting to establish the conditions for negotiations leading to a low-level stalemate; the center was trying to find out if the Vietnamese would capitulate. The right didn't even want to play the game, preferring an intensified bombing program without these useless overtures. San Antonio presented a formal (yet ambiguous) position which members of different policy currents attempted to use on the basis of their particular interpretations.

Clifford's testimony at his January 25 confirmation hearing supported the left current interpretation. A week earlier journalists had been told in a background session that no infiltration or resupply of North Vietnamese troops would be permitted after a U.S. bombing halt.[32] But when Senator Strom Thurmond asked if the North Vietnamese would be required to stop their military activities in exchange for a cessation of the bombing under the San Antonio formula, Clifford replied "No, that is not what I said. I do not expect them to stop their military activities. I would expect them to follow the language of the President (and not take advantage of the bombing halt)."

> Thurmond: What do you mean by taking advantage if they continue in their military activities?
> Clifford: Their military activity will continue in South Vietnam I assume until there is a cease-fire agreed upon. I assume

that they will continue to transport the normal amount of goods, munitions and men to South Vietnam.[33]

Rusk, Rostow and Johnson were incensed by Clifford's testimony (feeling that the still-to-be-confirmed Secretary of Defense was already making policy). Clifford received a polite dressing down from Johnson. But three days later the State Department formally confirmed Clifford's interpretation of the San Antonio formula as the official position of the U.S.[34]

In the final analysis, Clifford's doubts stemmed from the costs of the Vietnam stalemate. These hardened when the Joint Chiefs of Staff failed to give an adequate explanation of the benefits to be derived from an additional two hundred thousand troops. Clifford received no assurance that the additional troops would do the job; nor was he told how many more might be needed. Members of the left policy current in the Pentagon told Clifford that the "enemy" could meet the build-up with an increase of their own. After four years of direct involvement no one could see any diminution in the will of the Vietnamese. Bombing could inflict heavy casualties, but by itself never stop the war. Stepping up the bombing would not decrease American casualties. Decreasing the bombing would not significantly increase them. The South Vietnamese were not ready to replace our troops and no one knew when they would be. Despite the outflow of public statements, no one could offer an estimate of when "the light at the end of the tunnel" would be reached.[35]

The other considerations for Clifford were political and economic. He asked for and received an estimate of the high cost of the additional troops from Fowler. The impact on the economy was so great that credit restrictions, a tax increase, and wage and price controls could be expected. Fowler also noted that the balance of payments problems were worsening by at least half a billion dollars a year. Clifford thought that the dollar was already in trouble and that another twelve billion added to Vietnam spending would lead to even more controls on foreign investment. Clifford became more aware of domestic dissent. He later complained that "draft card burnings, marches in the streets, problems on school campuses, bitterness and divisiveness were rampant."[36] Significantly Clifford concluded that "even accepting the validity of our objective in Vietnam, that objective had to be viewed in the context of our overall national interest, and could not be sensibly pursued at a price so high as to impair our ability to achieve other, and perhaps even more important, foreign policy objectives."[37] This was the logic of the most important member of the left policy current.

Congress and the Politics of Reserve Units

The call-up of additional reserves was an extremely sensitive issue. Favored by the right as a way to catalyze patriotic support, the center and left feared that mobilization would exacerbate domestic dissent and further undermine business confidence in the economy. After the *Pueblo* incident fourteen thousand reservists were mobilized. The "(Johnson) — Westmoreland troop request" would require an additional quarter of a million reservists. Mobilization would entail economic controls and the consent of Congress (in effect placing the nation on wartime footing). On the other hand, a successful battle to send additional reserves to Vietnam, under the rhetoric of national commitment and resolve, offered certain advantages. As part of his experimentation with the right, Johnson explored this possibility with Congress.

After Wheeler returned from Vietnam with the "(Johnson) — Westmoreland troop request," Johnson ordered Wheeler and Clifford to quietly consult Richard Russell, John Stennis, and other influential Congressmen on the right. In the meantime the decibel level from Congressional doves rose steadily after TET. Many members of the center and former supporters of Johnson's Vietnam policy, including Thurston Morton, Paul Findley, Claude Pepper, Al Ullman, Morris Udall and Tip O'Neill, shifted their positions. The Hill demanded that Congress be consulted before any additional troops be sent to Vietnam. On March 7 a group of prominent senators made a formal announcement to this effect. On March 18 nearly one third of the House of Representatives, 98 Republicans and 41 Democrats, joined in a resolution calling for an immediate Congressional review of U.S. policy in Southeast Asia. As Congress polarized, members of both the left and right currents attacked Johnson. Rightwing Senator Karl Mundt warned Rusk during the latter's Congressional testimony "that the shift of opinion in this country is in the wrong direction." Even stalwarts like Richard

Russell were telling Johnson that they could no longer support "piecemeal escalation" of the war; additional ground troops or mobilization of the reserves would not receive their support unless the "wraps" were taken off the bombing of the North. "If we are not willing to take this calculated risk" (using air power to the fullest), Russell told a Veterans of Foreign Wars dinner, "we should not still be increasing the half a million men in Vietnam who are exposed to danger from weapons that might have been kept from the hand of the enemy."[38]

Wilbur Mills reflected still another current of opposition, that of fiscal conservatism. Mills did not oppose a troop increase and the reserve package as such. Johnson had requested a much needed tax increase or tax surcharge on August 3, 1967. Mills tied this legislation to a reduction in federal spending of about ten billion dollars, half of which was to come from domestic programs. With the Great Society programs threatened, another source of Johnson's political support would ebb away. For example, a Johnson-sponsored health care plan was warmly greeted in Congress. But many members pointed out that the costs of the war prevented full implementation of the one hundred billion dollar program.

Racial turmoil served as an important background to the reserve issue. With only two-thirds of a combat-ready division left in the country, many politicians wondered if "adequate protection" would be available during anticipated racial rebellions. State governors resisted the mobilization of the national guard, arguing that the troops were necessary to protect the cities for the up-coming "hot summer." One Department of Defense paper warned that any announced Vietnam build-up must also "prove that the nation still has the resources left for the ghetto fight."[39]

Presidential Politics

Johnson would have us believe that his decision to withdraw from the Presidential race was made well before March. There is some supporting evidence. He mentioned the possibility of withdrawing to Westmoreland during the latter's November trip to Washington. At one time or another Johnson discussed the possibility with almost every member of his staff. Johnson tells us that he almost included an announcement of his withdrawal in his 1968 State of the Union address.[40] Rusk also knew that Johnson entertained doubts about another term. But it was the decisive events of March, including the entry of Robert Kennedy into the Presidential race, which forced him out of office.

Johnson continued to meet with his political advisors during March. James Rowe agreed to be co-chairman of Citizens for Johnson in 1968. Marvin Watson, a close political aide, continued his efforts to line up Democrats behind Johnson. In mid-March Johnson personally asked Terry Sanford, governor of North Carolina, to be campaign manager. When queried about Johnson's plans, Clark Clifford replied that he did not expect to be a caretaker Secretary of Defense. Johnson recalled George Reedy to his White House staff and assigned him to resurrect the Democratic National Committee. Many members of Johnson's staff, including Reedy, had heard him muse over the possibility of leaving politics before; few really believed him.[41]

On the eve of the New Hampshire primary Johnson still looked like a sure winner. His campaign took a hard-line with some pamphlets claiming that a vote for dove candidate Eugene McCarthy was a vote for surrender. Governor John King predicted that McCarthy would receive twenty-five percent of the vote. Other observers, with less interest in over-estimating McCarthy's prospects, expected the Minnesota Senator to receive only twelve to eighteen percent of the vote. In fact, McCarthy, aided by the publication of a *New York Times* article on the possibility of 206,000 additional troops for Vietnam, received over forty-two percent of the vote. When Republican cross-over and out-of-state absentee ballots were counted, McCarthy emerged as the narrow victor over the President of the United States.

A few days later Kennedy announced that he was reconsidering his earlier decision not to run for the Presidency. On March 16 Kennedy announced that he would run and immediately spoke before huge and enthusiastic crowds at Kansas State University and the University of Kansas. Kennedy's behind the scenes maneuverings included a proposal, relayed to Johnson through Clifford, that the President submit his Vietnam policy to a special study committee in exchange for Kennedy's promise not to run. The committee would largely include members of the left policy current: Generals Norstad and Ridgway, Edwin Reischauer, Roswell Gilpatric, Kingman Brewster, Carl Kaysen, Mike Mansfield, John Sherman Cooper, and George Aiken.[42] Johnson rejected the offer citing: (1) his opposition to any deal linking policy to Presidential politics, (2) the impact of public doubt on his Vietnam policy, (3) the group's usurpation of Presidential power, (4) the risk of hardening Hanoi's resolve, and (5) the non-objective composition of the group. The move did not work. Kennedy probably never expected that it would; he merely used the study committee as a ploy to clear the way for his own candidacy.

Not every sign was bad. Johnson was still the leading contender — at least in mid-March. A special poll taken by the *New York Times* found sixty-five percent of the delegates expecting to back Johnson. (Johnson was thought to have 1725, with 970 for both Kennedy and McCarthy.) Ladbroke's, one of London's leading book makers, gave 6 to 4 odds that Johnson would take the nomination, and 2 to 1 that the Democrats would win the election. Eight thousand pounds were taken in on the first day of betting. Johnson had two other reasons to be optimistic. The threatened third party never appeared. And with Romney and Rockefeller out of the running by mid-March, no Republican would emerge to Johnson's left on the war issue. Nixon's "secret peace plan" made for effective propaganda, but the public and the press were clamoring for details. Johnson could feel relatively secure that Nixon, once he revealed his plan, would not appear as a Vietnam dove.[43]

Johnson had not yet lost complete control over the Democratic Party; but the divisiveness and bitterness within its ranks spoke of a long drawn out battle.[44] Internal dissent grew during the month. The Democratic coalition was beginning to unravel. Professional politicians who ran the urban machines were being undermined by reform movements and an influx of young Democrats. One cornerstone of the Democratic coalition was continual expansion of the federal pie satisfying the special interests among the ranks. In exchange, the President was normally left free to conduct an independent foreign policy. The drain of the Vietnam War now began to shrink the pie, and the ranks began to attack the foreign policy. Had Johnson decided to carry through his fight, the Democratic party would have been left in shambles.

The March public opinion polls placed Johnson in an increasingly unfavorable light. His popularity hit a new low, with fifty-two percent disapproving of his handling of the presidency. Only thirty-six percent approved. His record was even worse on the Vietnam issue (sixty-three percent to twenty-six percent). A Gallup test run of the November election found Nixon with forty-one percent of the vote, Johnson with thirty-nine percent, and fourteen percent for Wallace.

Perhaps the most telling development came in Wisconsin. Johnson mobilized his cabinet under O'Brien to work hard on his behalf. (For security reasons Johnson himself could not campaign.) The Wisconsin campaign suffered from a lack of volunteers and from general apathy. On March 29, a phone call from Larry O'Brien warned Johnson to expect a low vote in the primary, probably below thirty percent. At that point Johnson realized that the battle had been lost. Yet Johnson's ambivalence carried right through to the final twenty-four hours. He showed Humphrey a copy of his withdrawal statement immediately prior to the Vice-President's departures for Mexico on the 30th, but warned him that he had still not decided for sure whether he was going to read it. Johnson's decision came in the final hours, not during the first week of March as he states in his memoirs.

The Gold Crisis

During March, business confidence in the quality of economic management offered by the Administration continued to plummet. A remarkable number of signs pointing towards economic crisis appeared, each contributing to the rising clamor within the economic elite for a reconsideration of Vietnam policy. Many of these danger signals developed in the international arena. In November 1967 Britain devalued the pound. On December 10, Frederick Deming of the U.S. Treasury Department flew to Basel for a meeting of the Bank of International Settlements. The Trip's purpose was to encourage other members of the Group of Ten (the United States, Canada, Britain, Italy, Japan, Belgium, Sweden, the Netherlands, Germany and France) to step up their schedule of gold deposits within the Bank of England and thus dampen gold speculation. But

Deming's trip also heightened speculation and tension in bullion markets, encouraging the impression that the U.S. no longer trusted its European partners. That month, U.S. Federal reserve assets dropped nine hundred million dollars.

While European bankers were in no position to dictate terms to Washington, many complained of the inflationary impact of the war on the Continent. In particular, the economic instability associated with Vietnam aided French attempts to chart an independent course from the U.S. French Finance Minister Michel Debre leaked false information which exaggerated the U.S. balance of payments deficit to the financial editor of *Le Monde*. The subsequent columns fueled speculation and promoted distrust among the Group of Ten. In early March, *Le Monde* carried a story that the U.S. balance of payments deficit for the first quarter would be around two billion dollars (a rate of over eight billion for the entire year). The news led to still more speculation and pressure on the dollar.[45]

Several European correspondents also noted that dollars spent by U.S. forces in Vietnam would find their way into the hands of the NLF. Peasants, merchants, prostitutes, street vendors and others would funnel some of their money to Vietnamese revolutionaries, who then sent these dollars to the Bank of France, where the desired effect of maintaining financial pressure on the U.S. would be assured.[46] The U.S. racial situation was still another source of worry for the Europeans. News of racial strife was featured in their press. European bankers feared that a new wave of social programs made necessary by the crisis would bring more inflation and instability.[47]

In March, pressure on the dollar began to mount once again. By the end of the first week gold purchases reached a new peak. Washington drew two hundred million from its reserves. On March 9 London announced plans to withdraw all British troops east of the Suez by the end of 1971. The move would place an added burden on United States military forces and add pressure on the dollar. On the following day William McChesney Martin, chairman of the Federal Reserve System, visited Basel to secure a renewed commitment by all participating nations to maintain the price of gold at thirty-five dollars an ounce. France wanted to double the price of gold. On March 14 the U.S. lost 372 million dollars in gold trading. Losses for the next day of trading of at least one billion were feared.[48] At Washington's request the London gold market was closed. Congress also lifted the twenty-five percent gold cover for the dollar, but by a much more narrow margin than the White House had expected. The close vote (39 to 37) reflected an effort to tie the legislation to an Administration promise to reduce federal spending. Bankers called a Federal Reserve Board decision to raise the discount rate from 4½ to 5½% "too little, too late." Gold coin selling was halted. European bankers refused to accept American travelers checks.

On the weekend of March 16 and 17 and against the news that the price of gold on the Paris market had reached forty-four dollars an ounce, the chiefs of the central banks of the seven Gold Pool nations met in Washington.[49] The Group announced the establishment of a two-tier system for trading gold with an official price governing transactions among the seven, and a free market price established by private trading. An additional four billion in credits was extended to the United States. On the next day of trading the New York Stock Market was up briefly on the news, but by afternoon it had returned to its sluggish pattern.

On March 19 England announced an "iron budget" and austerity program. The tax increases — all indirect — were twice as high as expected. The budget raised the spectre of the difficult postwar period. In a move widely regarded as a retaliation against France, the U.S. Senate voted March 28 to refuse to sell gold to any nation more than ninety days in arrears on its debt.

Over March 27-30 a meeting of the Group of Ten in Stockholm announced agreement on the creation of Special Drawing Rights or "paper gold." SDRs would bring a substantial additional liquidity into the international monetary system (and subsidize the U.S. dollar outflow for an extended period).

A March 26 *New York Times* editorial reported that the CIA, State, and Treasury Departments were opposed to a troop increase, at least partially in response to criticism from Europe. European bankers feared another run on the dollar if the reserves were activated. While the precise content of their meetings remain unknown, Johnson did meet, in mid-March, with Andre Meyer and at least one group of influential bankers.[50] At a meeting in the Cabinet Room on March 15, Rusk said his greatest concern was the effect that a troop increase might have on the monetary system.[51] Without passage of a tax bill, adding two hundred thousand troops could set off a new panic in Europe.

Johnson Tries to Hold the Center

The left and center state managers at the Pentagon, CIA, State, and Treasury were firmly set against such major shifts in ground strategy as an expansion of the war into Laos, Cambodia and North Vietnam. But Johnson still expected to deploy more troops. And he was not convinced that a partial bombing halt was necessary in order to reduce political costs. On March 13 Johnson approved an additional thirty thousand troops, an eight thousand man increase over the Clifford task force recommendations.[52] A reserve call of fifty thousand was planned for March.[53] The Secretary of the Army urged that Westmoreland also receive 13,500 support troops.[54] The original "(Johnson) — Westmoreland" recommendations for 260,000 more reserves were scaled down, but would still cost an estimated two billion in 1968 and five billion in 1969.

Johnson's hawkish tendencies during the middle of March were not restricted to adding ground troops. On March 15, U.N. Ambassador Goldberg presented a detailed memorandum to the President calling for an unconditional halt to the bombing of North Vietnam.[55] Johnson's reaction to the Goldberg proposal has been published in several accounts: "Let's get one thing clear," Johnson said angrily, "I'm not going to stop the bombing. I have heard every argument on the subject, and I am not interested in further discussion. I have made up my mind. I am not going to stop it."[56]

In the meantime Johnson waged an unsuccessful fight to obtain greater public support for his policy. The two-day testimony of Secretary of State Rusk before the largely hostile Senate Foreign Relations Committee ended in stalemate. The *New York Times* and *Washington Post* used the stand-off as additional ammunition in their fight for a change in policy.[57] Clifford was due to testify after Rusk but demurred because of his own developing doubts. The official reason was the unfamiliarity of the Secretary of Defense with his new position. Johnson and Clifford decided that instead Nitze should testify. Nitze drafted both a letter to Johnson outlining his own doubts and a short note recognizing that Johnson might "prefer that he not continue" as Deputy Secretary of Defense. When Nitze showed him the note, Clifford prevailed upon Nitze to remove any reference to resignation. Nitze did so, forwarding only the critique of current Vietnam policy to Johnson. Clifford was greatly impressed by the depth of Nitze's conviction ("I had no idea you felt so strongly," he told his assistant.). Nitze later felt that this was another factor that helped Clifford to resolve his own doubts.[58] Nitze's memorandum received an angry response from Johnson, and he was no longer welcome at the meetings of the Tuesday cabinet.[59]

Warnke was the next choice and willing to testify, but Fulbright insisted upon Clifford. At this point Clifford contacted Fulbright, telling the Senator of his own growing doubts, and of the extent of policy reappraisal in the executive branch. Fulbright dropped the matter.

Nitze's near resignation captured the mood of several leading Pentagon officials. Both Under Secretary of the Air Force Townsend Hoopes and Warnke contemplated resignation. McNamara's forced retirement was portrayed by the press as a resignation. Secretary John Gardner of Health, Education and Welfare had recently resigned over the war. Johnson rejected Goldberg's offer to resign (coming along with his bombing halt proposal) citing "the bunching of Cabinet resignations."

On March 18 Johnson hit the road, trying to drum up some support with public speeches. At meetings of the National Farmers Union and the National Alliance of Businessmen Johnson called for national unity and support ("The time has come when we ought to stand up and be counted, when we ought to support our leaders, our government, our men, and our allies until aggression is stopped, whenever it has occurred.") He implied that there would be no change in policy ("Those of you who think that you can save lives by moving the battlefield in from the mountains to the cities where the people live, have another think coming.").

In private Johnson dismissed as eurocentric the arguments of left current representatives such as George Ball and George Kennan. Johnson could even claim that those focusing on the world economy and the interests of multinational corporations were racist, willing to take action for countries inhabited by white people but not willing to stand by commitments made to yellow people.[60]

Johnson continued to straddle the bombing issue until late in the month. At a long evening meeting with Senate Majority Leader Mike Mansfield on March 27, Johnson read portions of his planned speech and claims to have told the Senator of his intentions "to end all bombing north of the 20th Parallel."[61] Mansfield, however, doesn't remember the meeting the same way: "When he finished reading the speech, I told him that I thought it would be a mistake to make the speech because it offered no hope to the people and it only indicated further involvement. He did not mention the possibility of ending the bombing north of the 20th Parallel."[62] Warnke, Nitze, and even Clifford feared that their battle was lost.

Meanwhile, in South Vietnam, the military and the Saigon government picked up Johnson's clues. March 21 marked the biggest strike at the North in a month. U.S. jets bombed and strafed inside the city limits of Haiphong, and came within four miles of the center of Hanoi.[63] The bombing thus ignored the ten mile limit which had been imposed by the Secretary of Defense and the President around North Vietnam's capital. U.S. jets also struck rail lines within eighteen miles of the Chinese border. An unmanned reconnaissance plane was shot down over Chinese territory. Vice-President Ky called for "volunteers" for a "march to the North."

The Senior Advisory Group on Vietnam

The Senior Advisory Group on Vietnam, composed of leading businessmen and former state managers, had met several times to approve the general goals and conduct of the war. In 1965 these "Wise Men," as they were sometimes called, endorsed the war's escalation, including sustained bombing of North Vietnam and the introduction of American ground troops into the South. On November 2, 1967, following a series of official briefings, they gave their general approbation to the war (with only George Ball dissenting). A single major suggestion came out of the November meeting: it concerned the need for better public relations.[64]

At the Tuesday lunch of March 19, Clifford, facing an impasse in his efforts to change the direction of Vietnam strategy, suggested to Johnson that the "Wise Men" be convened once more. Clifford had been in touch with some of the Group's members and knew that Bundy and Dillon had changed their affiliations (from the center to the left policy current). Maxwell Taylor later suspected that "the Pentagon doves . . . had got to some of the visitors and had impregnated them with their doubts."[65] Johnson, facing resistance to his own plan for escalation and confident of the past record of the Group, agreed to the meeting.

The Group met on March 25, read some background papers, and dined with Rusk, Clifford, Fowler, Harriman, W. Bundy, Helms, Katzenbach, Nitze, and John McConnell of the Air Force representing the Joint Chiefs. After dinner the officials left and the Group received briefings from Philip Habib, deputy to William Bundy at the State Department; Major General William DuPuy from the Joint Chiefs of Staff; and George Carver from the Central Intelligence Agency. Habib told the Group that the Saigon government was weaker than generally believed before TET. The pacification program had been set back; the refugee problem was serious. DePuy and Carver touched on some of the same themes, although their disagreement over estimates of the strength of the "enemy" forces perpetuated the intelligence battle mentioned earlier. DePuy's lower estimate of the strength of the Vietnamese, reflecting known military units, was optimistic. Carver's higher estimate, including all paramilitary and guerilla forces, was pessimistic. The disparity was as great as three hundred thousand men.

Arthur Goldberg undermined much of the argument for additional troops during the following exchange:

> The briefing began with the military officer saying that the other side had suffered 45,000 deaths during the TET offensive.
>
> Goldberg then asked what our own wounded-to-killed ratios were.
>
> "Seven to one," the officer answered, "because we saved a lot of men with helicopters."
>
> "What," asked Goldberg, "was the enemy strength as of February 1, when TET started?"
>
> "Between 160,000 and 175,000," the briefer answered.
>
> "What is their wounded-to-killed ratio?" Goldberg asked.
>
> "We use a figure of three and a half to one," the officer said.
>
> "Well, if that's true, then they have no effective forces left in the field," Goldberg said. What followed was a very long and devastating silence.[66]

Both the partial bombing halt and the request for the 206,000 additional troops were discussed during the meeting. The forces of opposition arrayed against the U.S. were clearly reflected in the deliberations. Cyrus Vance later told a reporter that "we were weighing not only what was happening in Vietnam, but the social and political effect in the United States, the impact on the U.S. economy, and the attitude of other nations. The divisiveness in the country was growing with such acuteness that it threatened to tear the United States apart."[67]

Among the Group only Ball had strong previous misgivings about the course of the war. Yet after deliberations that night and the next morning, only Taylor, Fortas and Murphy defended current strategy. Taylor's views were essentially those expressed at the Clifford task force meetings and communicated to Johnson independently in his March 4 analysis. He strongly urged a call-up of reserves which was not only "justified by military considerations, but would have a useful political value in demonstrating to our friends and enemies alike that we meant business and did not consider turning back. Particularly it would remind our citizens that, though technically not at war, we were in a situation of emergency which placed on them duties and responsibilities analogous to those of a state of declared war."[68] Robert Murphy thought it would be a good idea if the CIA would assassinate Ho Chi Minh.[69]

The rest of the "Wise Men" sought means to cut back the economic and political costs of the war. Ball, Acheson, Bundy, Dillon, Vance, Goldberg and Ridgway thought a significant change in policy was necessary. The main thrust of their remarks was towards unilateral de-escalation. McCloy, Lodge, Dean and Bradley attempted to stake out a middle course between the left and center currents. Lodge later read a prepared statement before Johnson opting for a shift away from "search-and-destroy" missions. The basic emphasis should be "territorial, constabulary and counter-terroristic."[70] But Lodge also recommended against a new policy on the bombing of the North.[71]

At lunch the next day they communicated their views to Johnson and defended their position when questioned individually. Significantly the Group did not call for withdrawal. Nor did the Group call for Johnson to step down. When Johnson reported that he felt the majority favored disengagement, McGeorge Bundy corrected this to "de-escalation." Bundy urged that the U.S. should maintain its commitment, but shift more of the burden to the South Vietnamese. Ridgway also stressed the need to ask more of the South Vietnamese, including the rapid development of leadership, weapons and training. He also advocated the imposition of a two-year time limit in order to prod the GVN into action. He was opposed to further troop increases.[72] Acheson and Wheeler, who along with Abrams attended the luncheon, clashed over the former's description of the U.S. policy as seeking a military victory. Acheson, Bundy (an architect of the 1965 escalation), and Vance (a presidential favorite), were probably the most influential in the Group. Once Bundy had viewed the bombing as a bargaining chip; now its domestic costs were too high.

Acheson's rationale was similar to that of Nitze. Vietnam was less important than the deteriorating strategic balance *vis a vis* the Soviet Union. At a dinner at his home in late-March, Acheson handed Harry McPherson, Johnson's speech writer, a newspaper editorial from the *Winston-Salem Sunday Journal and Sentinel*:

> The war has made all of us — all of us — lose sight of our national purposes. We need to stand back and get our priorities right. Enemy No. One is Russia. Enemy No. Two is China. The vital strategic areas in their proper order are Western Europe (particularly Germany), Japan, the Middle East, Latin America — and only then Southeast Asia. The most crucial priority of all of course is the home front.[73]

Acheson gave the editorial to McPherson with the words "This represents my view precisely. I could have written it myself." On the next day McPherson sent the editorial to the President.

How are we to interpret the influence of the Senior Advisory Group? As representatives of the capitalist class? As former state managers? Or as a bureaucratic ploy cleverly devised by Clark Clifford to obtain a change in policy? Each angle contains an element of truth.

Most radical interpretations view the Group as a vehicle for transmitting the opinions of the capitalist class directly to the state managers.[74] The argument carries a great deal of plausibility. Chart 8.1 gives the economic and political affiliations of each member and

Chart 8.1
Political Positions & Institutional Affiliations of the Senior Advisory Group on Vietnam

Name	Occupation Affiliation	Former State Position	Policy Current Nov. '67	Policy Current Mar. '68
Dean Acheson	Corporate lawyer; member CFR[1]	Secretary of State, Truman Administration	Center	Left
George Ball	Corporate lawyer; investment banker; member CFR	Undersecretary of State, Johnson Administration	Left	Left
General Omar Bradley	Chairman of Board, Bulova Watch Company	Chairman, Joint Chiefs of Staff	Center	Center[2]
McGeorge Bundy	President, Ford Foundation; CFR	Special Assistant to President for National Security, Kennedy and Johnson Administrations	Center	Left
Arthur Dean	Corporate lawyer; member CFR	Korean War negotiator	Center	Center[2]
C. Douglas Dillon	Investment banker; member CFR	Secretary of Treasury, Johnson Administration	Center	Left
Abe Fortas	Corporate lawyer; Director, Federated Department Stores	Associate Justice, U.S. Supreme Court	Center	Center
Arthur Goldberg	Labor lawyer; member CFR	Ambassador to United Nations	Not Present	Left
Henry Cabot Lodge	General counsel, *Time, Life, Fortune*; member CFR	Ambassador to South Vietnam	Center	Center[2]
John McCloy	Corporate lawyer; banker; member CFR	Assistant Secretary of War, World War II	Center	Center[2]
Robert Murphy	Chairman, Corning Glass; Director, Morgan Guaranty; member CFR	Under Secretary of State, Eisenhower Administration	Center	Center
General Matt Ridgway	Director, Apollo Industries, Colt Industries; member CFR	Commander U.S. troops, Korean War	Center	Left
Maxwell Taylor	Chairman of Board, Mexican Light and Power Co; member CFR	Chairman, Joint Chiefs of Staff; U.S. Ambassador to South Vietnam	Center	Right
Cyrus Vance	Corporate lawyer; member CFR	Deputy Secretary of Defense, Johnson Admin.	Center	Left

[1]Council on Foreign Relations   [2]Combined elements of Center and Left

it is immediately apparent that nearly all wielded considerable corporate power. Ball, Bundy, Dillon, Vance, Dean, McCloy, Murphy, and Lodge were members of the economic elite, and the heads of some of the leading corporations, law firms, investment banks, and foundations. All but two of the Group were members of the Council of Foreign Relations, a body held by many radicals to be responsible for formulating a consensus in the corporate general interest. But it is important to speculate a little more closely on the criteria for membership and the political dynamics of such a select group. None save for Abe Fortas, present as Johnson's informant, were directly involved in decision-making on the war. All of the participants enjoyed extensive experience as former members of the national security apparatus. In fact, it is possible to argue that membership was contingent on prior careers in the state. There were no representatives from the economic elite *qua* economic elite. David Rockefeller or his equivalent was not present. Dillon's participation, for example, derived more from his previous position as Secretary of Treasury than from his current position at Dillon, Read, a leading corporate law firm. Moreover the members of the Council of Foreign Relations disagreed with each other; no corporate consensus could be detected among them. There is a unifying theme which runs between the different theoretical foci (the Group as representatives of the capitalist class, as former state officials, or as a bureaucratic maneuver). It links the shift in views of November 1967 and March 1968, and accounts for the type of policy review that was conducted (situating Vietnam within a broad economic and political context). That theme is the inability to sustain the center current strategy and an unwillingness to adopt the course of action favored by the right. Only Ball (and perhaps Goldberg) were legitimate members of the left policy current. The others were forced, as Johnson soon would be, by a shifting calculus of costs, towards the left current. They resisted this movement, as Johnson would, and in the process conceived the embryo of what the Nixon Administration eventually called Vietnamization. In the meantime, the Group's new opinion had a profound impact on Johnson. As Clifford later recalled:

> The president could hardly believe his ears. I knew by his attitude. He dismissed Rusk, Rostow, and myself after their first reaction, so that they wouldn't be affected or inhibited by

our judgment or that of other members of the administration. By the time he had finished, he said that 'somebody had poisoned the well.' He tried to find out who had done so. He called back George Carver and General DePuy. He was so shocked by the change in attitude of the Wise Men that he wanted to hear the briefings they had received. The meeting with the Wise Men served the purpose that I hoped it would. It really shook the president.[75]

The March 31 Speech

Soon after TET, Johnson decided to deliver a major Vietnam address. The various drafts of the speech — over fifteen in all — reflect the thinking of the President at each point during the month. The earliest, written in early March, are hawkish. The drafts become progressively dovish, but only after New Hampshire, the gold crisis, and the meeting of the Wise Men.

Harry McPherson, Johnson's speech writer, completed an early version on March 10. It promised 206,000 troops, a reserve call-up, and a ten percent tax surcharge. There was a call for unity in a period of crisis, and an invocation of Colonel Travis and the spirit of the Alamo. The draft of March 22 was also hawkish. It called for continued resolve and a tax surcharge; it reasserted the importance of Vietnam. Thirty thousand troops would be sent to Vietnam and a draft call of fifty thousand would be announced for March. There was no mention of a partial bombing halt.

McPherson remembers March 28 as the date of reversal. At Rusk's office, McPherson, Clifford, Rostow and William Bundy met to polish the final draft of the speech. Johnson's opening lines were still "Tonight I want to speak to you about the war in Southeast Asia." In the ensuing substitution of a "peace" draft, Clifford was the key figure. His most persuasive argument stressed the extent of public opposition, both in business and in the antiwar movement. McPherson's recollection of the main thrust of Clifford's remarks provide a remarkable testimony to the impact of the capitalist class when it deserts Presidential policy:

> Now I make it a practice to keep in touch with friends in business and the law across the land. I ask them their views about various matters. Until a few months ago, they were

generally supportive of the war. They were a little disturbed about the overheating of the economy and the flight of gold, but they assumed that these things would be brought under control; and in any event they thought it was important to stop the Communists in Vietnam.

Now all that has changed. There has been a tremendous erosion of support for the war among these men. . . The idea of going deeper into the bog strikes them as mad. They want to see us get out of it.

These are leaders of opinion in their communities. What they believe is sooner or later believed by many other people. It would be very difficult — I believe it would be impossible — for the president to maintain public support for the war without the support of these men.[76]

Clifford continued talking for several hours, concluding with an argument for a partial bombing halt north of the 20th Parallel. (On the same day Clifford sent a draft of a partial bombing halt announcement directly to Johnson.) Significantly, Rusk offered no opposition to the idea. McPherson was directed to prepare a new draft of Johnson's speech. Much discussion ensued over how to inform Washington's Pacific "allies" and the military chain of command of this policy alteration. In these final days the military had very little impact. Indicative of the degree to which CINCPAC (Admiral Sharp) was frozen out of the March deliberations is his late notification of the partial bombing halt: on March 30 at a SEATO meeting in New Zealand.[77]

In his television address to the nation, Johnson gave no indication of the previous month's political turmoil within the national security apparatus. The speech neither acknowledged nor rejected the 206,000 troops, only that 13,500 support troops would supplement the original 10,500 sent in mid-February. The speech did not include a formal troop ceiling (as urged by Warnke). Johnson announced a partial bombing halt but did not specify a boundary for U.S. attacks over North Vietnam.[78] Roughly a quarter of the address was devoted to economic matters. Johnson estimated the additional expenditures associated with the support troops and equipment for the South Vietnamese at 2.5 billion in FY 1969 and 2.6 billion in FY 1970. He raised the spectre of a twenty billion dollar budget deficit unless Congress passed a tax bill or drastically reduced expenditures.[79]

Most analysts of the March 1968 decision maintain that Secretary of Defense Clark Clifford was primarily responsible for the change in strategy. Johnson insists that he and Rusk were responsible for the partial bombing halt. Both interpretations are correct. Johnson's speech straddled the center and left positions. The center wanted to ease domestic criticisms of existing strategy, thus continuing its attempts at manipulating public opinion. No change in strategy was contemplated. The left wanted to use the momentum created by the speech to push further for a new course of action. Thus the intense conflict between policy currents never abated, continuing right through the rest of the Democratic Administration. Both center and left struggled to define the political aftermath of March 31. Clifford never really changed Johnson's mind. In April, that is *after* his withdrawal speech, Johnson, after hearing Clifford analyze the Vietnam situation, replied "Old friend, I don't agree with a word that you have said."[80]

For the center, bombing pauses had always been used to manipulate U.S. public opinion, not to increase the chances for negotiations. Rusk's cable to Ambassador Lodge, sent in connection with a 37-day pause between December 25, 1965 and January 31, 1966, argued that "the prospect of large-scale reinforcement in men and defense budget increases of some twenty billion for the next eighteen month period requires solid preparation of the American public. A crucial element will be clear demonstration that we have explored fully every alternative but that the aggressor has left no choice."[81]

Similarly, Johnson and Rusk intended to use this bombing halt to relieve political pressure rather than as an entry to meaningful negotiations. Johnson did not expect that Hanoi would respond. He could then argue that he had tried and that it was now time to turn on the juice. If Hanoi did in fact respond, talks might follow and Johnson would appear to the public as a man seriously interested in peace. If suitable terms could be reached before mid-summer a draft from the Democratic Party was still a possibility. Alternatively, if (as expected) Hanoi did not respond, the road to escalation would be open once again. The State Department cable instructing U.S. Ambassadors on how to brief the heads of friendly Asian governments supports the interpretation that Rusk and Johnson had little intention of negotiating, and may have been preparing the ground for escalation. It states in part, "you should call attention to force increases that would be announced at the same time and would make clear our continued resolve."[82] The cable then assesses the chances of a favorable response from Hanoi:

(b)You should make clear that Hanoi is most likely to denounce the project and thus free our hand after a short period. Nonetheless we might wish to continue the limitation even after a formal denunciation in order to reinforce its sincerity and put the monkey firmly on Hanoi's back for whatever follows. Of course any major military change could compel full scale resumption at any time.

(c)With or without denunciation, Hanoi might well feel limited in conducting any major offensives at least in the northern areas. If they did so, this could ease the pressure where it is most potentially serious. If they did not, then this would give us a clear field for whatever actions were then required.[83]

The cable goes on to cite the weather rationale for restricting the bombing north of the 20th Parallel, concluding "hence we are not giving up anything really serious in this time frame." It adds that "air power now used north of the 20th Parallel can probably be used in Laos (where no policy change is planned) and in South Vietnam." Any assessment of Rusk and Johnson's intentions must confront their demand for reciprocity before instituting a complete bombing halt. Here is the last section of the cable:

Insofar as our announcement foreshadows any possibility of a complete bombing stoppage, in the event Hanoi really exercises reciprocal restraints, we regard this as unlikely. But in any case, the period of demonstrated restraint would probably have to continue for a *period of several weeks* and we would have time to appraise the situation and consult carefully with them before we undertook any such action.[84]

By this time Wheeler had also recognized that some type of bombing pause was needed in order to regain public support for the war effort. A week earlier, a meeting including Clifford, Humphrey, Rusk, Rostow, Wheeler and McPherson, killed the possibility of any major troop increase. On the following day, Wheeler flew, at Johnson's direction, to Clark Field in the Philippines to meet

Westmoreland. The Commander of U.S. troops in Vietnam later recalled:

> [Wheeler] told me that a significant change in our military strategy for the Vietnam war was extremely remote, and that the administration had decided against a large call-up of reserves. Consequently, since we could not execute the strategic options that General Wheeler and I had discussed in February, the question of deploying major additional forces to South Vietnam became a moot issue.[85]

Now Wheeler cabled back to Westmoreland, informing him of the partial bombing halt but saying nothing of possible negotiations. Wheeler stressed the necessity of blunting domestic opposition:

> (a) Since the TET offensive, support of the American public and the Congress for the war in Southeast Asia has decreased at an accelerating rate. Many of the strongest proponents of forceful action in Vietnam have reversed their position, have moved to neutral ground or are wavering. If this trend continues unchecked, public support of our objectives in Southeast Asia will be too frail to sustain the effort.
>
> (b) Weather over the northern portion of North Vietnam will continue unsuitable for air operations during the next 30 days; therefore if a cessation of air operations is to be undertaken, now is the best time from the military standpoint.[86]

For Clifford and the rest of the left current centered at the Pentagon the partial bombing halt represented an entirely different kind of opportunity. Their interest was to continue the policy shift in the direction of a low-level stalemate. Clifford was well aware of the motivations of Johnson, Rusk and Wheeler for a bombing pause. Clifford later commented on this:

> I was never conscious during this period that Secretary Rusk deviated from policy. His idea concerning a bombing pause was based upon the fact that bad weather would allow us to cut back the bombing as a gesture, that such a gesture wouldn't cost much. Then when the other side did nothing, we could bear down on them. His bombing-pause proposal seemed to me to be designed to provide the basis for greater

pressure in the future... But it was anticipated that it would be rejected, and this would be the basis of launching a more effective and far-reaching attack against North Vietnam. I did not get the impression at the time that there was a similarity in approach between Rusk and me.[87]

With both left and center supporting a partial bombing halt — although for different reasons — the precise formulation of the announcement became an important battleground. The 20th Parallel had been chosen as the dividing line. A paragraph in the March 29 draft, representing the formulation preferred by the center, read:

> Beginning immediately, and without waiting for any signal from Hanoi, we will confine our air and naval attacks in North Vietnam to the military targets south of the 20th Parallel. That parallel runs about 75 miles south of the cities of Hanoi and Haiphong. North Vietnam's military reaction to this change in our bombing programs will determine both our willingness to confine it — and the reasonableness of our assumption that they would not take advantage of a complete bombing halt during the course of negotiations.[88]

On March 30 Acting Secretary of State Katzenbach, a member of the left policy current, replaced the paragraph:

> Tonight I have ordered our aircraft to make no attacks on North Vietnam, except in the area north of the demilitarized zone where the continuing enemy build-up directly threatens allied forward positions and where the movement of their troops and supplies are clearly related to this threat.[89]

Katzenbach felt the new formulation had a better chance of producing a favorable response from North Vietnam. Clifford went over the speech for hours, changing belligerent references to softer formulations, each designed to increase the chances for talks, a series of mutually de-escalatory steps, and finally negotiations. By this time Rusk had left for a meeting in New Zealand and there was little argument over Clifford's political editing. The center and right currents understood the need for a temporary pause — which they preferred to call a "stopping" — as a prelude to an intensified effort.

In its details the partial bombing halt contained concessions to members of the right current. For the center current these concessions increased the possibility that Hanoi would reject the proposal, thus preparing the grounds for later, politically safe, escalation. Two versions of the bombing halt, one at the 19th Parallel, the other at the 20th, were discussed during March. The 20th Parallel limit, decided upon at the insistence of Rostow and Wheeler, included two targets of significance: Thanh Hoa, a railway switching point 210 miles north of the DMZ, and Route 7 as it entered Laos.[90] Rusk had continued to point out during the deliberations that bad weather over North Vietnam would restrict operations anyway. Only five percent of the sorties at that time were above the 20th Parallel.

Johnson's speech did not articulate a boundary line in order to influence public opinion in the U.S. His wording leaves the impression that only the area immediately north of the DMZ would be subject to attack. In fact the 20th Parallel is more than 250 miles north. If the American public retained the impression that attacks occurred only near the DMZ, the subsequent expected rejection by the North Vietnamese would appear especially unreasonable.[91] But an unspecified limit would have enabled members of the right policy current to bomb far to the north and destroy any chances for a response from Hanoi. It is thus significant that all communication, save the public address itself, referred specifically to the 20th Parallel.[92]

On the day after the speech, U.S. jets struck right up to the limit. MACV (the Command in Vietnam) made sure that the U.S. press knew of the raids (thereby minimizing the sense of de-escalation of the bombing). The number of bombing attacks on North Vietnam actually *increased* after the partial bombing halt.[93] Fulbright denounced the raids near the 20th Parallel as a deception of the American public — for which Clifford and Goulding were extremely angry. In their eyes Fulbright was playing into the hands of the right by minimizing the shift in policy.[94] In the meantime, the military was authorized to continue air reconnaissance operations over *all* of North Vietnam.[95]

During a series of post-March press conferences Clifford attempted to establish the *de facto* troop ceiling that had been omitted in Johnson's speech. By referring to the 549,000 troops in Vietnam as the "ceiling at this time" the Secretary of Defense hoped to direct the press toward the word "ceiling." The inclusion of "at this time" covered him with Johnson. The more the press referred to troop "ceilings," the more difficult it became for Johnson to introduce more troops into Vietnam. As long as Johnson did not contradict Clifford or order him privately to drop references to a troop ceiling, an implicit policy change was being sustained.[96]

In the meantime, the reconnaissance flights over North Vietnam continued. In an effort to start negotiations, Hanoi moderated its demand that peace talks could not begin until all acts of war against North Vietnam were ended; such acts included the reconnaissance flights. They were now willing to talk when all acts of force, which did not include these flights, were terminated. Hanoi, of course, reserved the right to shoot at these planes which were violating its air space. North Vietnam's defensive measures provided a pretext for the center current to order "protective reaction" raids against air defense sites. In practice, "protective reaction" was used as a cover for preplanned strikes against a variety of targets.[97] A president operating from the left policy current would have seen Hanoi's shift in language as a step towards negotiations and would have responded, perhaps by ordering an end to the flights. One operating from the center, such as Johnson, and later Nixon, could use the military engagements sparked by reconnaissance flights to open the return route to center current principles.

The Significance of March 31

What then was the significance of March 1968? At first the Paris talks, initiated after the partial bombing halt, were unfruitful. But just before the November elections it appeared as though a settlement might be worked out. If so, the agreement would have swung the closely contested Presidential race in favor of Hubert Humphrey. The bombing halt was made total. In Saigon, U.S. Ambassador Ellsworth Bunker asked President Thieu for his reaction to the proposed settlement. Thieu balked, hoping to obtain a better deal from Nixon.[98] No dramatic shift in American foreign policy occurred. After Nixon's election the commitment to secure a win as defined by the center — using force to prevent the Vietnamese revolution from seizing power in the south — remained as strong as ever. Under the policy of a man who had run as a peace candidate, four million tons of bombs were dropped, millions of Vietnamese were killed, millions of refugees were "generated," and thousands of Americans lost their lives. As a Republican, Nixon retained greater confidence from the business community, even though the long-run trend of the economy continued downhill. The capitalist class did not complain about Nixon's low-cost counter-revolutionary policy in Vietnam. Nixon also managed to convince most Americans and the press that he was slowly withdrawing from Southeast Asia. Public opposition was "soft": it figured in decision-making, yet was subject to manipulation. Thus Nixon was able to protect himself better from the constraints of the forces of opposition: the Vietnamese, aided by the Chinese and the Soviet Union; the complaints voiced by the capitalist class over the state of the economy; and domestic dissent. He enjoyed an element of freedom in Vietnam decision-making that would have been unavailable to a Democratic President. Humphrey would have been forced to follow left current principles and, had he been elected in 1968, the U.S. and the Vietnamese would have signed a Peace Treaty, along the lines of the 1973 Paris Accords, in early 1969.

Why would Humphrey have followed the essential outlines of the left policy current? As argued above, that current gained more influence during the last months of the Johnson Presidency, first by blocking rightwing requests for more troops and an expanded mission in Vietnam (invading Cambodia, Laos, and North Vietnam itself), and later by initiating a partial bombing halt and then a total bombing halt over North Vietnam. A *de facto* troop ceiling was established as well. Over the summer of 1968 negotiations with the Vietnamese were started in Paris and there were favorable signs of progress. Had Humphrey been elected this momentum would have continued. The state managers holding the key positions in the national security apparatus, especially those in the Pentagon, believed that this was the proper course of action. True, they were only responding to pressures exercised by the Vietnamese and domestic opposition. But they translated these pressures into a policy of reconciliation. They recognized that the U.S. had limited power in Vietnam.

But Nixon was elected, a President who reestablished the center policy in new form.[99] Nixon and Kissinger accepted the necessity of lowering the economic and political costs of the war. They initiated a program of gradual withdrawal of U.S. troops (in the process blunting hostile public opinion and pressures from the press). But the new Administration renewed the anticommunist commitment in

Vietnam with an innovative strategy. Like Johnson, Nixon had to respond to oppositional forces. But Nixon translated these constraints differently, coming up with a new policy in the process. Nixon and Kissinger began to explore the constraints imposed by the Soviet Union and China, constraints that the Johnson Administration regarded as fixed. Their version of detente attempted to link technical aid, expanded commerce, and improved bilateral relations between Washington and Moscow and Washington and Peking to reduced support from the Soviet Union and China for the Vietnamese. Although this policy ultimately failed, it did permit the U.S. to bomb targets in the North, and to sponsor invasions of Cambodia and Laos, without producing a direct confrontation with North Vietnam's allies. To mine the Haiphong harbor would have been a dangerous measure in 1967. By 1972 such an action no longer carried the likelihood of a showdown between the U.S. and the U.S.S.R. With intensified bombing, threatened escalation, and attempts to play-off the socialist countries against each other, Nixon and Kissinger borrowed some pages from the right. Like the left, Nixon and Kissinger understood that bombing the North could not interdict men and supplies moving south. But this was not their purpose. Their selection of bombing targets in the North was deliberately erratic. They bombed dikes and civilian centers in an effort to spread terror among the North Vietnamese and to force eventual capitulation. But these measures, especially the bombing of Cambodia and the air strikes in North Vietnam under the rhetoric of "protective action," required extreme secrecy.[100] Eventually Nixon suffered his own TET — the 1972 Spring Offensive. Defeat on the battlefield, in combination with the 1972 presidential elections, resulted in the Peace Treaty of 1973. Nixon was able to manipulate public opinion, to convince many Americans that the Vietnam War was finally over. But there was no diminution of the anticommunist commitment, only new and secret means to secure it. Nixon and Kissinger had no intention of permitting the Saigon government to be overthrown or voted out of office. Should circumstances demand it, Nixon promised Thieu, the U.S. would intervene massively. When exposed, the measures taken to maintain secrecy — wiretaps, domestic surveillance of war protesters, security squads directed against Nixon opponents within the state itself — backfired, producing a domestic crisis known as Watergate. While Nixon and

Kissinger were temporarily able to deceive many Americans, their fear of domestic dissent became their ultimate downfall. Public and Congressional ire was aroused, the executive branch temporarily weakened. One outcome, the War Powers Act, denied state managers the use of military force in Indochina. Without the ability to bomb, Nixon and Kissinger could not maintain their strategy. In the final analysis, the Vietnamese and the American people blocked the efforts of the national security apparatus to defeat the Vietnamese Revolution. And the Vietnamese Revolution finally assumed power in April 1975.

The infamous record of Nixon and Kissinger obscures the fact that March 1968 was the highwater mark of U.S. intervention in Vietnam. Johnson's speech embodies a crucial failure: Washington's vast effort to retain a client regime in Saigon and to secure a symbolic defeat of a national liberation movement had been unsuccessful. Limits were placed on the level of U.S. ground troops. The United States had been checked. Nixon enjoyed fewer options. These were both dangerous and deployed cleverly, but his reliance on covert means was ultimately unsuccessful. The United States had been defeated.

PART IV: CONCLUSION

IX: THE PERMANENCE OF POLICY
POLICY CURRENTS: U.S. POLICY TOWARD
POST-LIBERATION VIETNAM

Finally, in 1975, Washington was forced to withdraw from Vietnam. The United States had failed—after more than thirty years of trying. And the costs of that effort were enormous. For a brief time, Americans, both policy elites and the public at large, attempted to learn from the experience. Some decision-makers concluded that the U.S. should not rely upon military intervention to exercise power. In their view, the world was a complicated place badly in need of reform. Unless social change was encouraged other Vietnams, and their attendant problems for the U.S., would mushroom. The proper response, the best way to blunt these revolutionary threats, was not armed force but modification of the economic and political inequalities that existed between the developed and undeveloped nations. These policy elites argued that the U.S. should not identify itself with repressive regimes in the Third World. They called for lower defense budgets and greater foreign aid. A few even maintained that the U.S. should lead the way in establishing worldwide economic reform and joined leaders from the undeveloped countries in calling for a New International Economic Order. In addition, direct military intervention was ruled out by domestic political considerations. A poll taken in May 1976 by Potomac Associates clearly showed American attitudes arrayed against the use of U.S. troops in anything other than the most extreme circumstances.[1] When confronted with a list of seven lessons from the Vietnam experience, more agreed (forty-seven percent) with the statement "We should not have gotten directly involved in a land war in Asia in the first place" than with any of the other possibilities. More agreed with the statement, "There was no real national security interest of the United States at stake, so we shouldn't have gone into Vietnam to begin with," than with the statement, "We should have used more military force to win the war." In part, Jimmy Carter was elected President because he seemed to represent these views more than any other candidate. Carter's initial appointments to key positions also reflected this reluctance to solve foreign policy problems with armed force. Washington appeared to recognize that it could not possibly control every political development in the world. American power was limited.

At the same time, other policy-makers were disturbed by this acceptance of a diminution in American power and by what they took to be a timorous response. This second group, including members of the Committee on the Present Danger, the Coalition for a Democratic Majority, the Heritage Foundation, the American Security Council, and other representatives of the newly emergent right, argued that Soviet military strength was steadily growing, that in real dollars the U.S. defense budget was declining, and that Washington's inability to "project power" in the world arena created a "power vacuum" into which Moscow was now stepping. U.S. acquiescence in this state of affairs was derisively labeled the "Vietnam syndrome." Over the course of the late-seventies, this second group increased its influence, both outside of government and within the Carter Administration itself. While most press, media and academic commentary focused on U.S.-U.S.S.R. relations, particularly the declining fortunes of SALT II, as the critical policy issue in this shift, U.S.-Vietnamese relations also reflected and contributed further momentum to this general slide to the right in foreign and defense policy.

Now, advisors and members of the new Reagan Administration talk about the possibility of fighting and winning nuclear war and taking "direct action" against movements for national liberation. These movements are, in turn, seen as mere proxies for Soviet influence. Huge increases in the defense budget are also in the offering. This ominous situation returns us to the set of questions raised at the beginning of this book: describing and analyzing disagreements among the policy elite, understanding the origin of these divisions, and creating alternative policies that do not serve the narrow set of interests contained in the existing spectrum of policy currents. Accordingly this concluding chapter has three parts: an *historical* analysis of contending policy currents among U.S. decision-makers after the "loss" of Vietnam, a *theoretical* recapitulation of the policy currents perspective, and a *political* argument focusing on the influence of popular forces on foreign policy.

Policy Currents After 1975

The history of U.S. intervention in Vietnam has been marked by the interplay among three different policy currents. Key decision-makers of the Carter Presidency were divided over crucial issues such as the provision of postwar reconstruction, the pace of normalizing relations between Vietnam and the United States, and whether U.S. policy towards Vietnam should be viewed bilaterally or in the context of the triangular relationship among Washington, Moscow and Peking. In turn, these particular issues reflected long-standing debates over the relative importance of Vietnam to American control over the world's economic resources and political structure. A brief analysis of that debate follows.

Over the years, representatives of the left current in Vietnam followed the principles of multilateralism, particularly in the emphasis on diplomacy and economic relationships as means to dilute revolutionary fervor. Members of the left current never ruled out military force entirely, but thought that such a course of action should not define American policy. Indeed, the main criticism offered by members of the left current was that Vietnam was defined by the center and the right as a military battle rather than a political battle that contained military aspects. After 1975 advocates of the left approach argued that U.S. interests would be served best by normalizing relations with Vietnam and by developing commercial ties that would woo that country away from either the Soviet Union or China.[2] Specifically, the U.S. should meet Nixon's pledge to contribute to Vietnam's postwar reconstruction and lift the trade embargo imposed by President Ford immediately after the liberation of the south. The left current now feels that there are potential business interests to consider as well: Vietnam has substantial, high-grade coal deposits, oil reserves of unknown quantity, and a large market of fifty million people. The left also argues that Vietnam, together with the ASEAN nations (Indonesia, Malaysia, the Philippines, Singapore, and Thailand), can play a major role in promoting economic development in the region. Thus enticed, Vietnam would contribute to stability and mutual prosperity. Vietnam might continue to be governed by a communist party, but its influence would not be revolutionary.

Taking as its principle that the U.S. is not the strongest nation in the world unless it acts like it, members of the center current have always emphasized the symbolic and global importance of Vietnam: first as a test case of the ability of the U.S. to defeat wars of national liberation, later as evidence of U.S. determination and resolve, and finally as an example of Washington's willingness to stand by its allies. Representatives of the center continue to argue that the U.S. cannot permit Vietnam to serve as an inspirational example to the rest of the underdeveloped world. Washington should not normalize relations, provide economic aid or funds for reconstruction, or lift the trade embargo. Not content with the havoc wreaked by years of direct military intervention, the center current has followed a deliberate policy of destabilizing already fragile economic and political conditions by encouraging tensions among Vietnam, China, and Cambodia. Vietnam must be punished.

The right has always seen Vietnam in regional rather than global terms. During the Vietnam War its members took a straightforward approach: once committed the U.S. should follow through with all the resources at its disposal. There is no substitute for victory. During the Vietnam War the difference distinguishing the right from the center largely revolved around the application of military force. With that option ruled out in Southeast Asia, at least in the shortrun, the right no longer offers a policy alternative to the center's determination to punish Vietnam. As a result, the political spectrum containing three policy currents, generally characterizing the U.S. intervention from World War II to 1975, has become transformed. Now there are only two policy camps. The right, of course, has strongly supported the destabilization strategy, especially playing the "China card," and has been active in other policy areas, especially in the push for higher military spending and the fight against the ratification of SALT II. Let us now examine the interplay among these currents in the specifics of post-1975 U.S. policy.

In the spring of 1975, the Vietnamese armed forces liberated the Central Highlands, Danang and Hue and began a powerful southern sweep. The U.S., while no longer directly engaged from the military standpoint, nonetheless maintained a huge embassy complex, an advisory command to the South Vietnamese army, and a substantial intelligence operation. Washington also supported thousands of U.S. civilians, many of whom were former members of the armed forces who had served tours of duty in Vietnam. This "army" serviced and maintained sophisticated military equipment used against the Vietnamese revolutionaries.

Just before reaching Saigon, the victorious troops paused to give the U.S. time to carry out an orderly retreat. But President Ford and Secretary of State Kissinger, members of the center current, did not take advantage of this opportunity, feeling that such a withdrawal would lead to doubts in governments around the world concerning the commitment of the U.S. to stand by its allies. So the American leaders delayed, eventually succeeding in making the evacuation from Saigon as chaotic as possible. They thus created the image of an immanent "bloodbath" and contributed to confusion and apprehension within Vietnam.

The right current had always thought that Kissinger "had been taken in Paris" and, once it became apparent that the U.S. would have to withdraw, that the evacuation should be carried out as swiftly and completely as possible.[3] The right had no patience for psychological power plays, such as attempting to project strength in the midst of defeat. Vietnam was lost. Washington's dithering caused the loss of more than two billion dollars of military equipment. During the rapid withdrawal the U.S. Embassy also failed to meet its promise of protection to agents that had provided intelligence on the revolutionary forces, and had failed to leave other agents "in place" so that information could be gathered on the new regime. This would be the last disagreement between center and right on Vietnam.

After the Vietnamese seized power, the U.S. declared a trade embargo which not only denied access to vitally needed replacement parts, but cut off the possibility of the new government building economic relationships independent of Moscow and Peking. In the United Nations, the U.S. refused to recognize the new revolutionary government. In 1973 Nixon had secretly pledged $3-4 billion of aid to the Vietnamese "without any political conditions."[4] But now Washington declared the Paris Agreements "null and void," thus declining to honor its commitment to the postwar reconstruction of Indochina until Vietnam complied with the impossible demand of making a "full and complete" accounting of all Americans missing in action (MIA). There was no progress towards the normalization of relations.

Such was the state of affairs when Jimmy Carter was elected President of the United States in 1976. During his campaign Carter promised a number of new directions in foreign policy: a commitment to a world without nuclear weapons, a renewed policy of detente with the Soviet Union, a more realistic approach towards "Eurocommunism," a promise that food would never be used as a political weapon, and a human rights policy that would be applied against rightwing dictatorships as well as communist states. Carter combined a number of diverse tendencies in his key foreign policy appointments. His selection of Andrew Young to represent the U.S. at the United Nations was both a concession to left current critiques of the previous Administration and a payoff to black leaders who had been instrumental in helping Carter gain the presidency.[5]

"It is in the U.S. interest to have a strong Vietnam," Young declared during his Senate confirmation hearings. He went on to add that "Vietnam as an independent entity in Southeast Asia with some strength is one of the things that curtails the expansion of the People's Republic of China." In outlining these views Young articulated several assumptions of the left current: that the consequences of a "victory" by a socialist movement can be contained, that there is no automatic "domino effect" in which revolution automatically spreads to neighboring countries, and that economic radicalism can be dampened through commercial ties. Young and his counterparts at the State Department wanted to normalize relations with Vietnam and China simultaneously. Other members of the Carter Administration were more hostile to the Soviet Union and attempted to manipulate other policy areas in order to undermine detente. These state officials advocated closer relations to China and a hard line towards Vietnam. While they were also critical of Young's comments it appeared that Washington would improve its relations with its former antagonist in Indochina.

Shortly after the Carter Administration entered office, the Vietnamese began to call U.S. promises for postwar economic assistance a "moral" rather than a "legal" obligation. In turn Carter softened the U.S. position to seek a "satisfactory" rather than a "full and complete" accounting of American MIAs. In March 1977 a high-level U.S. delegation headed by Leonard Woodcock visited

Hanoi. Within the U.S. it was widely noted that the new Vietnamese regime not only refused to supply captured American weapons to guerillas in Malaysia, the Philippines, and Thailand, but rejected purchase offers from Libya, North Korea, Peru, Pakistan, and Turkey.[6] The U.S. dropped its opposition to Vietnam's entry to the United Nations and in September that country was admitted to full membership.

But these hopeful signs soon ended. Congress voted to extend the trade embargo and prohibited U.S. negotiators from even discussing economic assistance with the Vietnamese. The probable turning point between left and center was the stalemated U.S.-Vietnamese talks conducted in December 1977. Two months later the U.S. expelled Vietnam's U.N. Ambassador for alleged involvement in spying. Zbigniew Brzezinski's visit to China in May marked the end of the always incomplete influence of the left current. In Peking, Carter's Assistant for National Security Affairs joined his hosts in a toast condemning "regional hegemony," the Chinese code word for Vietnam. The reference also linked Vietnam with the Soviet camp, a position that Hanoi resisted for as long as possible.

The previous December Phnom Penh had broken relations with Vietnam and, following a visit to Peking by Pol Pot, the border conflict between Vietnam and Cambodia began to take on larger proportions. For Vietnam the stabilization of the agriculturally important border area was a necessary prelude to economic normalcy. China withdrew its technicians from Vietnam, closed some key consulates, and terminated all assistance projects. Immediately after Brzezinski's visit, Peking began to refer to the "persecution" of the Hoa (ethinc Chinese) in Vietnam. The combination of these radio broadcasts and efforts to end their traditional control over the Vietnamese economy contributed to a massive exodus of Hoa, who accounted for seventy-five percent of the "boat people" leaving Vietnam in the fall of 1978. In June of that year, following the failure of Washington to end the trade embargo, Vietnam joined COMECON, the Soviet-led trade bloc. During meetings held at the U.N. between U.S. and Vietnamese officials in September and October, the Vietnamese dropped all references to postwar reconstruction as a condition for normalization of relations. But the U.S. response was not favorable.

The Vietnamese must have decided that Washington's policy was irrevocably belligerent. There was little left to concede, little left to lose. On November 3, Hanoi signed a Treaty of Friendship and Cooperation with the Soviet Union which included a mutual consultation pact should either nation be threatened by war. A month later 100,000 Vietnamese, together with 20,000 Cambodians who had fled the terror of the Pol Pot government, invaded Cambodia, installing Heng Samrin of the Kampuchean National Union for National Salvation in power. It is entirely possible that a more sympathetic policy from Washington would have produced a more temperate response from Hanoi.

The center current now played the China card. On December 15, amid great fanfare, Washington recognized the Peking government. In February 1979, China, following a visit of Chinese Vice Premier Deng Xiao-ping to the U.S., invaded Vietnam in order "to teach some necessary lessons." Peking was kind enough to give Washington 24-hour notice.[7] Despite presenting its approach in the conflicts as "evenhanded," the U.S. took a definite stand in favor of the Chinese. Washington's formal statements called on Vietnam to withdraw its troops from Cambodia (labeled an "invasion") and on China to withdraw its troops from Vietnam (labeled a "border penetration").[8] Complying with Washington would have been of no great expense to China, but would have probably resulted in the return of Pol Pot to Phnom Penh. Washington continued to refuse to recognize Vietnam but did not permit China's actions to interfere with developing economic relations and perhaps military assistance as well. The U.S. condemned Vietnam for violating human rights yet voted to seat the infamous Pol Pot in the United Nations as the legitimate representative of Cambodia.

But the worst was yet to come. Not content with clever diplomatic means of exacerbating long-standing tensions among the Communist governments in the region, Washington turned to food as a political weapon. In both Cambodia and Vietnam agricultural production had dropped precipitously. The reasons were severe flooding, managerial limitations, the havoc left by American ecocide, the policies of the new governments, and the difficulty and danger of clearing unexploded U.S. ordnance. In Vietnam the authorities feared that the Hoa would serve as "fifth column" agents for China, and encouraged a massive emigration. The Cambodian population, terrorized first by American bombs and later by Pol Pot, was completely uprooted. After the fall of Pol Pot many fled towards the Thai border only to serve as a propaganda for Western news reports portraying the Vietnamese as the new despots. Some of these unfortunate refugees became unwilling buffers between the remnants of the Pol Pot military forces and the Vietnamese.

During 1979, Washington first ignored, and then highlighted the plight of Cambodian refugees, depending on the political situation prevailing at the moment. In March the American Embassy in Bangkok reported both low levels of food supplies in Cambodia and dismal future prospects. Only ten percent of the land was under cultivation. Assume, for the moment, that the Carter Administration stood by its promise to feed people no matter the political outcome. Then a political consequence of acting on the Embassy report would have been to strengthen the Vietnamese-supported government in Phnom Penh. The general implication would have been *de facto* recognition that the U.S. had been defeated and that normalized relations would follow. This would be the policy favored by the left current. But Carter did not stand by his promises. Appearances to the contrary, the U.S. did not lead the world in relief efforts. According to a state official who attended several policy meetings, "In July, the CIA and some members of State were still talking about famine as if it were a propaganda tool of Hanoi to get the United States to feed and recognize the Hang Samrin government."[9] A firm U.S. commitment to provide $69 million in famine relief was not made until October 24, long after international relief agencies and other countries, both West and East, became active. Washington began to play up the famine only after it became possible to pin the Vietnamese and the new Cambodian government, rather than Pol Pot, with responsibility for the desperate situation. Thus the center current's use of aid was frequently cynical. After the U.S. started to send supplies, the State Department claimed that the authorities in Phnom Penh were stockpiling food to prevent it from reaching those who were hungry. But some members of international relief agencies claimed that it was the U.S. which was playing cold-war politics with relief. "Since the United States got religion on the Cambodia famine," said one coordinator attempting to distribute food without regard to politics, "the Americans have been telling us what to do."[10] On the Thai border, food and other forms of relief were distributed in proportion to the opposition a group offered to the Vietnamese-backed Cambodia government. For their part, the Vietnamese maintain that the situation in Cambodia has improved. Cu Dinh Ba, counselor for the Vietnamese at the United Nations, calls "this so-called famine a trap, a Chinese plot. The only problem facing Kampuchea is the return of Pol Pot...the West is playing up [the famine] to supply food and ammunition to the Pol Pot forces."[11]

The U.S. has at least temporarily succeeded in fulfilling two principles of the center current: that the world is polarized into two camps, East and West, with every other country choosing sides, and that the U.S. has to act like the world's strongest nation. In fulfillment of the first, Washington has forced the realignment of the Southeast Asia region so that China and Khmer Rouge leader Pol Pot are firmly aligned with the West. Peking encourages Thailand and the Philippines to maintain their military ties with the U.S. And Vietnam, despite its efforts to establish relations with the U.S. and Europe, is now identified by many countries, along with the Heng Samrin government in Cambodia, as satellites of the Soviet Union. The multi-alignment approach of cultivating cross-cutting ties and obligations among the countries of Southeast Asia, advocated by the left current as the best way to secure American interests, is not permitted. To fulfill the second principle, Washington has succeeded in punishing Vietnam and Cambodia. The refugee crisis has been used to further destabilize those countries. Aid originally destined for Vietnam's economy has been diverted. Vietnam's already overtaxed economy has suffered further from the strain of attempting to feed as many Cambodians as possible. Other Western nations have cut off aid as a sign of disapproval.

So Washington retained the counter-revolutionary commitment. There has been no change since 1975—indeed since 1945. Only the method of exercising that commitment has changed. The U.S. is no longer able to use military force directly. Yet, in a very real sense, the Vietnam War continues. The United States is still trying to punish Vietnam.

Policy Currents: A Recapitulation

The tenacity of the counter-revolutionary commitment displayed by the U.S. in Vietnam, together with new examples of hostility towards radical movements in Chile, Nicaragua, Timor, Iran, El Salvador, and other countries serve as a reminder that, despite their differences, policy-makers belonging to different policy currents share a broad set of goals: maintaining the power of the U.S. in the world arena, undermining the influence of socialism, and preserving the "right" of U.S. based multinational corporations to participate in the economies of other nations. Whose interests are served by these general goals? This book has assumed that the answer offered by radicals, that there is a strong correlation between these goals and the interests of the dominant economic class, is essentially correct. But it is necessary to ask another series of questions. More specifically, how is it possible to argue that U.S. intervention in Vietnam reflected dominant economic interests, and to argue as well that the capitalist class *did not* make the key decisions affecting the course of that intervention? The answer is that the key decisions were made by the state managers who believed in the same set of principles and goals. These state managers enjoyed a great amount of power. But were they free to set out any strategy that they wanted? No, the state managers were constrained by different forces of opposition, namely the Vietnamese aided by the Soviet Union and China, and by domestic opposition to the Vietnam War. In addition, the capitalist class vetoed any strategy that undermined the economy. The state managers had to retain the confidence of the business community. In responding to these varied pressures the state managers disagreed with each other. These disagreements were sustained by tendencies to draw different lessons from the history of foreign policy. Analytically, the result is a theoretical tension between seeing the Vietnam War as serving specific class interests and recognizing that significant political differences exist among that class and its key representatives, the state managers. The concept of policy currents addresses that theoretical tension. Policy currents are alternative conceptions, found among the capitalist class, state managers, and other defenders of the capitalist order, for exercising U.S. power within the limits imposed by different kinds of oppositional forces.

These policy divisions evolve from different "readings" or interpretations of the world situation. Differences among policy currents are sustained by specific institutional interests, be they economic (within the capitalist class) or organizational (within the state itself). But these divisions are primarily based on opposing political forces and on historical lessons. Thus, the main explanation for the slide to the right in Vietnam policy during the Carter Administration is the shifting constellation of these forces of opposition. During the Vietnam War the most important of these oppositional forces was the Vietnamese themselves, aided in no small measure by the Soviet Union and China. The Sino-Soviet split emerged and deepened over the course of the Vietnam War. But U.S. policy did not then exploit that rift. And, despite some close calls, the Vietnamese were able to use tensions between their allies to their own advantage. Ironically, it has been in peace rather than war that the U.S. has been most successful in manipulating the Sino-Soviet split to its own advantage. Rightwing political forces have been increasingly successful in using China against the Vietnamese.

Over the first eighteen months of the Carter Administration, while the left current exercised some influence, Peking's relations with Hanoi were comparatively good. Within China, one immediate consequence of the ouster of the radical Gang of Four leadership was a new—but temporary—direction in foreign policy. Economic assistance projects with Vietnam were started. But an anticipated rapprochement with the Soviet Union was never culminated. Despite conservative changes in domestic policy, China began to once again follow a militant anti-Soviet foreign policy. The U.S. was able to exploit this decision, along with the historical enmity between Vietnam and Cambodia, to its own advantage. Long-standing tensions between Moscow and Peking, and Hanoi and Phnom Penh, intensified. No longer faced with the military threat of the U.S., the armies of China and Vietnam and Cambodia and Vietnam clashed in direct conflict. Support from Vietnam's allies proved to be weaker during peace than during war.

A second change in the forces of opposition has been in the political climate within the United States. Carter inherited the presidency during a period where U.S. political institutions were widely distrusted. Many Americans felt that the Vietnam War had been wrong and that the U.S. should not commit itself to intervention against revolutionary movements. Public opinion polls found two-thirds of the country in favor of food and medical assistance to

Vietnam, and a majority willing to contribute industrial and farm equipment.[12] Over the late-seventies, however, public opinion on foreign policy was no longer stimulated by an antiwar movement and became much more amorphous. One result was greater freedom for the state managers to follow a more belligerent strategy.

The third change involves Vietnam's relationship to the U.S. economy. In 1968, the capitalist class, which never thought much of Vietnam in economic terms, began to criticize the war. Secretary of Defense Clark Clifford, while trying to shift Vietnam strategy during that time, reminded the other state managers that "it would be difficult—I believe it would be impossible—for the President to maintain public support for the war without the support of [my] friends in business and law across the land." On face value Clifford's statement implies that a President can find it difficult to follow a policy that undermines the confidence of the business community. In fact, in 1968, business vetoed Johnson's Vietnam policy and an alternative had to be found. The capitalist class did not *dictate policy,* but contributed to overwhelming pressures for a *change in policy* then operating against the state managers. Johnson had to respond in some way.

Vietnam now plays a far different economic role. The interests of the capitalist class lead in a different direction. In April 1977 Hanoi published a remarkably liberal foreign investment code aimed at encouraging foreign participation in three areas: oil, export industries, and manufacturing. Foreign investors were permitted to hold up to 47 percent in joint ventures for domestic markets and maintain sole ownership and management of companies producing for export. While the tax rate was relatively high, and the non-nationalization guarantee comparatively short (10-15 years), Hanoi also indicated a willingness to negotiate further liberalization measures on a case-by-case basis.[13] Nonetheless U.S. based multi-national corporations were not that interested in doing business with Vietnam for fear of upsetting possible deals with China. In May 1979 U.S. banks and oil companies passed up a chance to visit Vietnam for fear that their tentative arrangements with China would be jeopardized.[14] The same behavior can be traced in British and Japanese firms. Thus the main pattern of signals emanating from the capitalist class to the state managers continues to be a comparatively diffuse business confidence, rather than policy recommendations in the literal sense. The capitalist class now identifies China's vast potential market as offering greater possibilities to alleviate contemporary economic problems than that of Vietnam. As is usual the multinational corporations vote with their pocketbook. In this case such messages do not favor Vietnam and the state managers are more free to tilt towards Peking.

Thus, the differences among policy currents lie in the opposition to U.S. efforts to impose hegemony. The Vietnamese and domestic opposition frustrated these efforts, leading in turn to disagreements among the policymakers themselves. In no sense are these political divisions based on morality. There is nothing about their own code of ethics that prevents the state managers from abusing the population of the Third World. During the Vietnam War, representatives of the left, center and right policy currents disagreed with one another, but never over the "right" of the U.S. to intervene to protect what the state managers defined as legitimate national security interests. A leading member of the left current, Clark Clifford, continued to regard the original decision to intervene to be based on "unassailable principles"—even while he became more critical of Johnson's Vietnam policy. Nor did different policy currents disagree over the use of military force to kill Vietnamese who opposed American designs in Indochina. Disagreement did develop, but it was over the balance of military force versus the introduction of necessary political and social reforms. The argument was not over the use of force *per se* but over the type and intensity of force to be applied. Therefore, policy currents are not based on different ethical stands among the state managers but upon the forces arrayed against them.

At the same time, divisions among state managers are sustained by a tendency to draw different historical lessons. For the left current the appropriate lesson was the success of diplomacy and economic ties in diluting the radicalism of revolutionary governments. "Human nature is capitalist," ran their reasoning, "and this is no less true for Communist-led societies than for private enterprise systems." For the center current the appropriate historical lesson was the importance of combatting aggression with force. Vietnam was another Munich. "Unless we actively intervene to hold the line against this new form of aggression," ran their argument, "communism will spread and our allies will be discouraged." The stakes in Vietnam were thus global. The entire set of economic and political arrangements that secured the world system were at question. For the right current the appropriate historical lesson to be applied in Vietnam was "once committed to the use of military force there is no substitute for victory." Indecisive wars only inflame opposition at home. Wars fought against movements for national liberation should strike "at the source of aggression." No sanctuaries should be permitted.

These lessons were drawn from the history of foreign policy. The current danger is that, under conditions where the forces of opposition operating against the state managers are not strong, the rightwing lesson has been more fully sustained by the Vietnam experience than any of the others. U.S. intervention in Indochina has become only one further example of the difficulties of fighting a limited conventional war. For policy-makers drawn to the right, the specific lesson of the Vietnam War is that U.S. intervention against a national liberation movement will not provoke domestic opposition if that intervention appears to be decisive. Decision-makers have a breathing space before public reaction begins to build. And the U.S. should not restrict itself to attacking the revolutionary movement itself. "No sanctuaries." "Strike at the source of aggression." The implication, if we use Africa and Central America as recent examples, is that the U.S. should use force against Cuba and possibly punish even the Soviet Union as well.

What can change the situation? Only renewed opposition at home. Only a resurgence of antiwar sentiment within the United States.

Opposition at Home

The long duration of U.S. intervention in Vietnam and the level of resources wasted in that effort, both human and material, can be understood in only one way. Washington was attempting to defend world capitalism. U.S. intervention was only one example of a global commitment to counter-revolution, Vietnam was only one country on a long list. Iran, Laos, Italy, Chile, the Dominican Republic, Angola, Cuba, Cambodia, Lebanon, and, most recently, El Salvador are among the countries where the U.S. has intervened with military force or covert means with the goal of securing compliant regimes. With that general purpose in mind, the state managers consistently enjoyed the support of the capitalist class and elite opinion.

The U.S. fought in Vietnam to preserve the rules of the game, to enforce the general principles governing U.S. foreign policy. But was Vietnam a success? Judged against the current definition of American interests the answer would have to be "Yes, Vietnam was a limited success." Of course the U.S. "lost" Vietnam. Neither the left, nor the right, nor the center offered a strategy that could defeat the Vietnamese Revolution. Popular support for that revolution, in combination with opposition in the U.S., ultimately limited Washington's attempt to impose its control—no matter the form of that effort. The center strategy, that followed for the most part by Washington, was bankrupt by 1968. The high-cost stalemate provoked too much opposition at home and was too expensive in terms of American lives and dollars. Even the capitalist class didn't think too much of the strategy and told the decisionmakers so in no uncertain terms. The center strategy was one of attrition. Yet it was the Vietnamese who proved that they had more resources. The most important of these resources was political, the depth of support for the NLF. The left strategy—gradual U.S. military withdrawal, political recognition of the NLF, and eventual elections—would have resulted in the "loss" of Vietnam as well. That is because the Vietnamese, under the leadership of the Communist Party, would have won those elections. Any measure that would have permitted an authentic political role for the NLF would have simultaneously undermined the power of the Saigon government. That is why, since 1954, Washington refused to permit free elections as a means to determine the political future of Vietnam. Members of the left current argued that a political movement that came to power by free elections would have had an entirely different attitude towards the U.S. than a movement that came to power by military force. That movement would, for example, be less dependent on the Soviet Union. But it would have been an oppositional government nonetheless. The right policy current advocated greater use of military force, invading "sanctuaries" in Cambodia and Laos, and taking sterner measures against the North itself, including a ground invasion and sustained bombing of civilian targets.[15] This strategy would have also led to failure. The geographical dimensions of the war would have widened. And the U.S. would have been involved in a fight within North

Vietnamese territory. The Vietnamese never showed signs that an invasion would diminish their will to fight. Indeed, an American invasion would have provoked responses from China and the Soviet Union and led to still greater domestic opposition. By expanding the war the U.S. might have killed more Vietnamese, but it would not have come closer to winning. It would be hard to label heightened tensions with Moscow and Peking and political unrest at home a "success."

Therefore, of the three strategies, *none* led to success in the sense of holding on to Vietnam. Yet, on another level, U.S. intervention in Vietnam has been a success—when measured against the interests of the capitalist class. While losing Vietnam, Washington has succeeded in demonstrating that efforts on the part of Third World countries to chart an independent economic and political course will meet reprisals. Washington punished, severely punished, the Vietnamese for winning. The threat of "another Vietnam" has remained a central component of American foreign policy. This intimidation has not enjoyed absolute success. Revolutionary movements have come to power in other countries besides Vietnam. But these movements have also measured the brutality of U.S. actions in Vietnam. And avoiding that punishment has become part of the political calculations made by the leaders of these movements. The U.S. continues to rely on military threats to exercise global influence. Vietnam was a dramatic object lesson.

As discussed in most of this book, success has been measured against the interests of the prevailing class. For the American people, however, the Vietnam War was an unqualified disaster. A disaster not only in terms of the huge expense, lives lost, and still other lives wasted by emotional and physical wounds, but also by the failure of the U.S. to alter its conception of national security interests. Policy elites and most Americans continue to define national security interests in military terms. Yet, after unprecedented military expenditures over the last thirty years, genuine security remains as elusive as ever. The Defense Department has spent more. But we feel less safe. In terms of popular attitudes the Vietnam experience was an opportunity to change that definition of national security and to seek genuine peace by encouraging fundamental change in the social structure of undeveloped countries.

It was also a lost opportunity—at least in the short-run. Americans continue to oppose direct U.S. military intervention in situations similar to Vietnam. But no strong movement capable of reorienting foreign and defense policy on a fundamental basis exists. In the meantime, in the absence of genuine change in the Third World, other Vietnams are recreated continually. And with Washington consistently siding with repressive elites against popular movements, the spectre of American military might being deployed against forces for change reappears again and again. It might be charged that these insurgencies are only puppets of Moscow. Yet the Soviet Union as a social model enjoys little appeal. In fact, it is American intransigence in the face of needed change that drives revolutionary movements towards Moscow. Most leaders of these movements would prefer normal relations with the U.S., including access to our technology and economic assistance. But Washington's failure to side with movements for change continually places the U.S. in confrontational situations that jeopardize our security. National liberation movements are much less of a threat to the interests of the American people than the actions taken by the state managers to defeat those movements. From this standpoint, the "lesson" of Vietnam is that our own peace and prosperity depends upon promoting political and economic changes that lead to greater social justice in the international arena. It is unlikely that the state managers or capitalist class will, on their own, take this course. A fundamental shift in orientation, a change in our very definition of national interest and security, can only come through popular pressure, in the creation of an alternative movement.

At this point we are returned to a theoretical tension raised first in the introduction, but embedded as well in virtually every page of this book. And that is the difference between viewing policy as emanating ultimately from the global interests of the capitalist class and recognizing that there are significant differences between different members of that class and their representatives in the state. Policy currents help bridge the gap between these different kinds of analyses. On the one hand, the fundamental orientation of each policy current is to defend the existing order. The differences are pragmatic, over the best way to preserve U.S. international control. Morality and justice for the world's people do not come into play. The supporters of each current argue that their approach will, in the long-run, best stabilize world capitalism and the position of the U.S. within it.

On the other hand, a range of possibilities exists within capitalism. Which policy is followed makes a difference. Some alternatives improve the chances for peace and increase the freedom of movement for oppositional movements of various sorts in the Third World. If followed systematically, a foreign policy based on a left current in policy areas such as nuclear arms, southern Africa, Southeast Asia, a new international economic order, and Latin America would substantially improve political and economic freedoms in the world, and add to the safety of those living in it—even though that world would still be dominated by capitalism.

For socialists the dilemma becomes one of presenting policies that can ultimately transform the structure of international relations while simultaneously attempting to influence contemporary debates and decisions. The Vietnamese and the antiwar movement demonstrated that people do make history. The difficulty is to trace the impact of popular forces on elite politics without becoming trapped in overly narrow campaigns that merely attempt to affect the balance among different policy currents. There are times to stake out new political ground and there are times, particularly where world peace is an issue, where one has to be content with reform. There can be no rigid formula that guides these choices. To make these decisions wisely, to learn how to balance the advantages and dangers of each turn, we need to enter and learn a language and structure of politics that is not only unfamiliar, but based on principles that are antithetical to our own. We need, in other words, to know the logic, as well as exposing the dangers, of capitalism. We need to understand, intimately understand, a political arena that is oriented against us. We must learn to make decisions that take into account the range of possibilities within capitalism without losing sight of the need to transform capitalism as a whole. That project is undeniably hard. But, as the Vietnamese so vividly demonstrated, that project is also very possible.

ECONOMIC APPENDIX

Chart I
Business Week Index,[1] 1961-1968,
with Average Annual Increases for Selected Periods

(1957-1959=100)

6.0 %
Period I

15.3%
Period II

2.9%
Period III

July 1961 · July 1962 · July 1963 · July 1964 · July 1965 · July 1966 · July 1967 · July 1968

[1]The *Business Week* index is a composite of various indicators of economic performance including raw steel production, automobile production, electric power, crude oil refinery runs, paperboard production, carloadings, intercity truck tonnage, machinery production, transportation equipment, and construction.

Source: *Business Week* (selected issues)

Table I

United States Exports, Imports and Balance of Trade, 1963-1968

With Average Annual Increases Over Selected Periods, Quarterly Figures at Seasonally Adjusted Annual Rates[1]
(millions of dollars)

Year	Exports	Imports	Balance of Trade	
1963	30,140	25,308	4,832	
1964	37,098	28,688	8,409	Period I
1965	39,176	32,275	7,141	
1966 I	42,112	36,080	6,032	
II	42,580	37,344	5,236	Period II
III	43,648	39,112	4,536	
IV	44,236	39,716	4,520	
1967 I	45,484	40,312	5,172	
II	45,508	40,432	5,076	
III	46,052	40,616	5,436	
IV	45,984	42,592	3,392	
1968 I	47,440	46,136	1,304	Period III

Average Annual Increases and Average Annual Percentage Changes Over Selected Periods

Period I	4,518	(14.9%)	3,484	(13.8%)	1,789	(37.0%)
Period II	2,269	(5.8%)	3,379	(10.5%)	-1,270	(-17.8%)
Period III	2,777	(6.5%)	5,024	(13.5%)	-2,247	(-42.9%)

[1] A minus sign indicates a decrease.

Source: *Economic Report of the President to Congress*, Selected Years.

309

Table II
United States Reserve Assets, 1961-1968
With Average Annual Decreases Over Selected Periods
(millions of dollars)

Year		Reserve Assets	Average Annual Decrease	Average Annual Percent Decrease	
1961		16,947			
1962		16,057			**Period I:**
1963		15,596			
1964		15,471	785	4.6%	**1961-1964**
1965	January	(15,208)			
1966	January	(13,811)			
	February	(13,811)			
	March	(13,738)			
	April	(13,668)			
	May	(13,582)			**Period II:**
	June	(13,529)	1,119	7.4%	**1965-mid 1966**
	July	(13,413)			
	August	(13,319)			
	September	(13,356)			
	October	(13,311)			
	November	(13,262)			
	December	(13,235)			
1967	January	(13,202)			
	February	(13,161)			
	March	(13,184)			
	April	(13,234)			
	May	(13,214)			
	June	(13,169)			
	July	(13,136)			
	August	(13,075)			
	September	(13,077)			
	October	(13,039)			
	November	(12,965)			
	December	(12,065)			
1968	January	(12,003)			**Period III:**
	February	(11,900)			**mid 1966-**
	March	(10,703)	1,549	11.5%	**March 1968**

Source: *Economic Report of the President to Congress,* Selected Years.

Table III
United States Financial Transfers Abroad, 1961-1968[1]

(millions of dollars)

Year	Total Amount	
1961	11,688	
1962	11,434	
1963	13,216	
1964	15,370	4.9% increase per annum
1965	12,864	
1966	14,565	_____
1967	17,624	
1968	17,734	10.9% increase per annum

[1]U.S. financial transfers include U.S. private capital (net), U.S. government grants and loans (net), foreign earnings of capital in the U.S., military expenditures abroad, and remittances and pensions.
Source: Raymond Mikesell, *The U.S. Balance of Payments and the International Role of the Dollar*, pp. 126-7.

Table IV
United States Military Balance of Payments, 1961-1968

(billions of dollars)

Fiscal Year	Net Adverse Balance Excluding South East Asia	Net Adverse Balance South East Asia	Total Adverse Balance
1961	2.8	–	2.8
1962	2.1	–	2.1
1963	1.6	.1	1.7
1964	1.6	.1	1.7
1965	1.2	.2	1.4
1966	1.4	.7	2.1
1967	1.1	1.3	2.4
1968	1.7	1.6	3.3

Sources: "Defense Budget Highlights," *Industry Defense Bulletin*, February 1967; and Clark Clifford, Secretary of Defense, The 1970 Budget and Defense Program for Fiscal Years 1970-1974. Reprinted in special issue of *Journal of Radical Political Economists*, "The War and Its Impact on the Economy," August 1970.

311

Table V
United States, Industrial Europe, Japanese Exports, 1961-1968
(value in millions of U.S. dollars)

Year	Total	U.S.	% of Total Exports	Industrial Europe	% of Total Exports	Japan	% of Total Exports
1961	118,600	21,037	(17.7)	40,770	(34.4)	4,236	(3.6)
1962	124,700	21,715	(17.4)	43,260	(34.7)	4,917	(3.9)
1963	136,000	23,389	(17.2)	47,490	(34.9)	5,453	(4.0)
1964	152,600	26,652	(17.5)	53,760	(35.2)	6,674	(4.4)
1965	165,400	27,532	(16.6)	60,230	(36.4)	8,452	(5.1)
1966	180,900	30,430	(16.8)	65,990	(36.5)	9,776	(5.4)
1967	190,500	31,622	(16.6)	70,500	(37.0)	10,442	(5.5)
1968	213,100	34,636	(16.3)	79,920	(37.5)	12,971	(6.1)

Source: *International Financial Yearbook*, International Monetary Fund, Selected Volumes.

Table VI
Gross National Product, 1961-1968
With Average Annual Increases Over Selected Periods, Quarterly Figures at Seasonally Adjusted Annual Rates
(billions of dollars)

Year		Gross National Product	Average Annual Increase	Average Annual Percent Increase	
1961		520.1			
1962		560.3			
1963		590.5			**Period I:**
1964		632.4	41.2	7.9%	**1961-1964**
1965		684.9			
1966		747.6			
	I	728.4			**Period II:**
	II	740.4	53.1	8.0%	**1965-mid 1966**
1966	III	753.3			
	IV	768.2			
1967	I	772.2			
	II	780.2			**Period III:**
	III	795.3			**mid 1966-**
	IV	811.0			**March 1968**
1968	I	831.2	44.5	5.9%	

Source: *Economic Report of the President to Congress*, Selected Years.

312

Table VII

Gross National Product in Constant 1958 Dollars, 1961-1968

With Average Annual Increases Over Selected Periods, Quarterly Figures at Seasonally Adjusted Annual Rates
(billions of dollars)

Year		Gross National Product	Average Annual Increase	Average Annual Percent Increase	
1961		497.2			
1962		530.0			**Period I:**
1963		550.0			**1961-1964**
1964		577.9	29.9	6.0%	
1965		616.7			
1966		652.6			**Period II:**
1966	I	645.4			**1965-mid 1966**
	II	649.3	30.0	5.0%	
1966	III	654.8			
	IV	661.1			
	I	660.7			
	II	664.7			**Period III:**
	III	672.0			**mid 1966**
	IV	679.0			**March 1968**
1968	I	689.7	19.9	3.0%	

Source: *Survey of Current Business,* Selected Issues.

313

Table VIII
Corporate Profits Before Taxes, 1961-1968
All Industries, With Average Annual Increases Over Selected Periods,
Quarterly Figures at Seasonally Adjusted Annual Rates
(billions of dollars)

Year		Corporate Profits	Average Annual Increase	Average Annual Percent Increase	
1961		50.3			
1962		55.7			
1963		58.9			**Period I:**
1964		66.3	6.5	12.8%	**1961-1964**
1965		76.1			
1966		83.9			
1966	I	82.7			**Period II:**
	II	83.4	6.8	9.3%	**1965-mid 1966**
1966	III	84.2			
	IV	85.3			
1967	I	79.5			
	II	79.6			**Period III:**
	III	80.2			**mid 1966-**
	IV	82.3			**March 1968**
1968	I	83.8	-0.2	-0.3%	

Source: *Economic Report of the President,* Selected Volumes.

314

Table IX
Industrial Production Index, 1961-1968
**With Average Annual Increases Over Selected Periods, Quarterly Figures
at Seasonally Adjusted Annual Rates**
(1957-1959 = 100)

Year		Index	Average Annual Increase	Average Annual Percent Increase	
1961		109.7			
1962		118.3			**Period I:**
1963		124.3			**1961-1964**
1964		132.3	8.4	7.7%	
1965		143.4			
1966		156.3			**Period II:**
1966	I	150.7			**1965-mid 1966**
	II	156.5	11.8	8.5%	
1966	III	158.1			
	IV	159.5			
1967	I	157.2			
	II	155.9			
	III	157.4			**Period III:**
	IV	159.7			**mid 1966- March 1968**
1968	I	162.0	2.7	1.7%	

Source: *Economic Report of the President,* Selected Volumes.

Table X
Capacity Utilization Rate, 1961-1968, All Industries

Year	Capacity Utilization Rate
1961	78.5
1962	82.1
1963	83.3
1964	85.7
1965	88.5
1966	90.5
1967	85.3
1968	84.4

Source: *Economic Report of the President,* Selected Volumes.

315

Table XI
Labor Productivity Index, 1961-1968

With Average Annual Increases Over Selected Periods, Quarterly Figures at Seasonally Adjusted Annual Rates
(1957-1959 = 100)

Year	Output per Man-hour Private Nonfarm	Average Annual Increase	Average Annual Percent Increase	
1961	107.9			
1962	114.3			
1963	118.9			**Period I:**
1964	124.6	5.2	4.8%	**1961-1964**
1965	125.7			
1966	127.7			
1966 I	127.3			**Period II:**
II	127.2	1.5	1.2%	**1965-mid 1966**
1966 III	127.5			
IV	128.7			
1967 I	127.8			
II	128.9			
III	129.5			**Period III:**
IV	130.0			**mid 1966-**
1968 I	131.9	2.5	2.3%	**March 1968**

Source: *Monthly Labor Review,* October 1967 and October 1968.

Table XII
Percentage Change Per Year in Compensation[1], Productivity, and Unit Labor Costs

	1961-1965	1965-1966	1966-1967
Total Private			
Average hourly compensation	4.4	6.9	6.0
Output per man-hour	3.8	3.1	1.4
Unit labor cost	0.5	3.7	4.5
Manufacturing			
Average hourly compensation	3.6	4.9	6.1
Output per man-hour	4.6	2.2	0.9
Unit labor cost	-1.0	2.7	5.1

[1]Wages and salaries of all employees and supplements to wages and salaries such as employee contributions for social insurance and for private pension, health, unemployment, and welfare funds, compensation for injuries, pay of the military reserve, etc. Also includes an estimate of wages, salaries, and supplemental payment of income of the self-employed.

Source: Committee for Economic Development, *The National Economy and the Vietnam War,* p. 20.

Table XIII
Consumer Price Index, 1963-1968
With Average Annual Increases Over Selected Periods, Quarterly Figures at Seasonally Adjusted Annual Rates
(1963 = 100)

Year	Consumer Price Index	Average Annual Increase	Average Annual Percent Increase	
1963	100.0			**Period I:**
1964	101.3	1.7	1.7	**1963-1964**
1965 I	102.1			
II	102.8			
III	103.2			
IV	103.7			**Period II:**
1966 I	104.5			
II	105.6	3.0	2.9	**1965-mid 1966**
1966 III	106.6			
IV	107.4			
1967 I	107.6			
II	108.4			**Period III:**
III	109.5			**mid 1966-**
IV	110.4			
1968 I	111.6	2.9	2.7	**March 1968**

Source: *Economic Report of the President,* Selected Volumes.

Table XIV
Federal Government Receipts, Expenditures, and Surplus, 1961-1968
With Average Annual Increases Over Selected Periods, Quarterly Figures at Seasonally Adjusted Annual Rates[1]
(billions of dollars)

Year		Receipts	Expenditures	Surplus or Deficit
1961		98.3	102.1	- 3.8
1962		106.4	110.3	- 3.9
1963		114.3	114.0	.3
1964		114.5	118.3	- 3.8
1965		124.8	123.4	1.4
1966		143.2	142.9	.3
1966	I	137.0	134.8	2.2
	II	141.6	138.4	3.2
	III	145.6	146.3	- .7
	IV	148.6	151.9	- 3.3
1967		151.8	164.3	-12.5
1967	I	149.1	160.9	- 11.9
	II	148.1	162.8	- 14.7
	III	152.7	165.9	- 13.2
	IV	157.3	167.9	-10.7
1968	I	164.5	175.6	- 11.1

[1]Minus sign indicates deficit.

Source: *Survey of Current Business,* Selected Volumes.

Table XV
Changing Geographic Distribution of Defense Contracts
(Percentage Distribution of Dollar Volume)

Census Region	Korean War (Fiscal Year 1952)	Cold War (Fiscal Year 1962)	Vietnam (Fiscal Year 1966)
Northeast:			
New England	8	11	12
Middle Atlantic	25	19	17
Subtotal	33	30	29
Midwest:			
East North Central	27	12	15
West North Central	7	7	8
Subtotal	34	19	23
South:			
South Atlantic	8	10	13
South Central	6	8	12
Subtotal	14	18	25
Far West:			
Mountain	1	5	3
Pacific	18	28	20
Subtotal	19	33	23
Total	100	100	100

Source: Murray L. Weidenbaum, *Peace in Vietnam: Possible Economic Impacts and the Business Response,* September, 1967, p. 6.

NOTES

Introduction

1. Indochina Resource Center, "A Statistical Fact Sheet on the Indochina War," (27 September 1972).
2. See Noam Chomsky and Edward Herman, *The Washington Connection and Third World Fascism,* Boston, South End Press, 1979, pp. 304-313.

I: Five Interpretations of U.S. Intervention in Vietnam

1. Harry Magdoff, *The Age of Imperialism*, New York, Monthly Review Press, 1969. See also the collection of editorials coauthored with Paul Sweezy and published as *The Endless War*, New York, Monthly Review Press, 1972. This section has benefitted from a reading of Tom Burke's unpublished manuscript, "Radical Theories of Intervention in Vietnam."
2. The domino theory holds that the "loss" of any particular country, in this case Vietnam, threatens the immediately adjacent countries. Extreme versions of the domino theory extend the threat to more and more countries.
3. Examples of the Pacific Rim approach include Martin Murray, "The United States' Continuing Economic Interests in Vietnam," *Socialist Revolution*, nos. 13 and 14, January-April 1973, pp. 11-68; and Peter Wiley, "Vietnam and the Pacific Rim Strategy," *Leviathan*, June 1969 (available from New England Free Press).
4. Felix Greene, *The Enemy*, New York, Random House, 1970.
5. Doug Dowd, "The Political Economy of the American War Against Indochina" (Unpublished paper, 1971). Quoted by Burke, *op. cit.*
6. On the role of Japan for U.S. decision-making in Vietnam, see John Dower, "The Superdomino in Postwar Asia: Japan in and out of the Pentagon Papers," *The Pentagon Papers*, vol. V., Beacon Press, Boston, 1972, pp. 101-142; and Carl Oglesby and Richard Shaull, *Containment and Change*, New York, Macmillan, 1967.
7. Francis Fitzgerald, *Fire in the Lake*, Boston, Little, Brown and Co., 1972.
8. Aspects of Fitzgerald's argument, particularly those focused on the failure of Americans to understand Vietnam, are classified more properly in the quagmire position. Her stress on the cultural imperative sometimes creates the impression that she is characterizing the intervention as blind or unknowing. In the final analysis, her anger, total opposition to U.S. involvement in Vietnam, and her sensitivity to the revolutionary character of the Vietnamese resistance dictate classification in the radical perspective.
9. *Roots of American Foreign Policy*, Boston, Beacon Press, 1969, p. 85. See also Kolko's "American Goals in Vietnam," *Pentagon Papers*, Beacon Edition, vol. V, pp. 1-15.
10. See Michael Klare, *War Without End*, New York, Vintage, 1972; and "The Great South Asian War," *The Nation*, March 9, 1970.

11. Noam Chomsky and Edward Herman, *The Washington Connection and Third World Fascism*, Boston, South End Press, 1979. Chomsky and Herman use the term "subfascism" to stress the similarities between U.S. supported client regimes and Nazi Germany with one exception: the Third World regimes lack Hitler's popular support.

12. Kolko, *op. cit.*, p. xv.

13. William A. Williams, "Multinational Corporations and Cold War Ideology," in David Horowitz (ed.), *Corporations and the Cold War*, New York, Monthly Review Press, 1971, p. 103.

14. Noam Chomsky, *For Reasons of State*, New York, Random House, 1973.

15. Frequently referred to as the conflict between Yankees, representing the Northeast, and Cowboys, representing the Southern Rim. See Stephen Johnson, "Who Rules the Defense Companies: A Test of the Yankee-Cowboy Theory," *Insurgent Sociologist*, Fall, 1975. For a discussion of the same issues from a non-Marxist viewpoint, see Kirkpatrick Sale, *Power Shift*, New York, Random House, 1975.

16. For the impact of the antiwar movement see Thomas Powers, *The War At Home*, New York, Grossman Publishers, 1973; and James O'Brien, "The Antiwar Movement and the War," in *Radical America*, vol. 8, no. 3, May-June, 1974.

17. See especially Chomsky and Herman, *op. cit.*

18. Examples of the state intervention approach include: Richard Barnet, *Roots of War*, Baltimore, Penguin, 1973; Ralph Stavens, Richard Barnet, and Marcus Raskin, *Washington Plans An Aggressive War*, New York, Random House, 1971; and Seymour Melman, *Pentagon Capitalism*, New York, McGraw Hill, 1970.

19. The economic impact of the war, on both society as a whole and the "industrial" and "multinational" corporations, will be treated more extensively in Chapter Six.

20. See the *Power Elite*, New York, Oxford University Press, 1956.

21. Melman, *op. cit.*

22. According to the concept of "mass society," the American public is fragmented, atomized, broken down into passive individuals, who are incapable of overcoming the insecurity of economic and personal life, and are unable to find any alternative sources of information than the increasingly homogeneous media. There is little room for free debate and exchange of ideas in the mass society.

23. See Richard Barnet, *Intervention and Revolution*, New York, New American Library, 1969, pp. 16-18.

24. See William Fulbright, *The Arrogance of Power*, New York, Random House, 1966; and Richard Hofstadter, "Uncle Sam Has Cried 'Uncle' Before," *New York Times Magazine*, May 19, 1968.

25. *The Logic of World Power*, New York, Pantheon, 1974.

26. Examples of the quagmire approach include David Halberstam, *Best and the Brightest*, New York, Random House, 1972; Hannah Arendt, "Lying in Politics: Reflections on the Pentagon Papers," *New York Review of Books*, November 18, 1971; and Arthur Schlesinger, "Eyeless in Indochina," *New York Review of Books*, October 21, 1971.

27. David Halberstam, in particular, refers continually to Vietnam as a "tarbaby."

28. For an example of this approach see the "organizational process" model presented by Graham Allison, *Essence of Decision*, Boston, Little, Brown, 1971, esp. pp. 67-100.

29. Harold Wilensky's book by the same title focuses on the various limits on "organizational intelligence." New York, Basic Books, 1967.

30. See Ralph White, *Nobody Wanted War: Misperception in Vietnam and Other Wars*, Garden City, Doubleday, 1970.

31. Adopted from Leslie Gelb, "The System Worked," *Foreign Policy* #3, Summer, 1971.

32. See Richard Betts, "Analysis, War and Decision: Why Intelligence Failures Are Inevitable," *World Politics*, vol. xxxi, no. 1, October 1978, pp. 61-89.

33. See Richard Holbrooke, "Presidents, Bureaucrats, and Something In-Between," in Anthony Lake (ed.), *The Vietnam Legacy*, New York University Press, 1976, p. 154.

34. See Betts, *op. cit.*

35. See *The Bitter Heritage: Vietnam and American Democracy 1941-1966*, quoted by Daniel Ellsberg, *Papers on the War*, New York, Harper and Row, 1972, pp. 48-50.

36. This approach began with studies conducted by Roberta Wohlstetter on U.S. intelligence failures in Pearl Harbor and continued through numerous Congressional hearings and Presidential panels.

37. See Leslie Gelb, *op. cit.*; "The Pentagon Papers and the Vantage Point," *Foreign Policy*, Spring 1972; "Dissenting on Consensus" in Lake (ed.), *op. cit.*; and his major work (co-authored with Richard Betts), *The Irony of Vietnam: The System Worked*, Washington, Brookings Institution, 1979. Daniel Ellsberg's position is outlined in *Papers on the War* and in an interview in *Rolling Stone*, November 8, December 6, 1973.

38. Lake, *op. cit.*, p. 104.

39. As outlined below, however, Ellsberg has recently come closer to the radical position.

40. For an elaboration of this argument, see Betts, *op. cit.*

41. Herbert Schandler, a military historian who also worked on the Pentagon Papers, combines the quagmire and "system worked" models. U.S. goals in South Vietnam are found to be consistent with the national interest. Washington's intervention was even successful, in Schandler's view, for the "threat" of Communist-inspired wars of national liberation in Asia subsided as a result. U.S. intervention gave surrounding countries, most noticeably Indonesia and Thailand, a chance to prepare stable governments capable of providing an effective bulwark against Communism. Within South Vietnam, however, Schandler paints a picture which is a little more complicated. Between 1965 and early 1968 U.S. policy was handicapped by the absence of a strategic concept to guide the ground war and by an inability to conduct a rational calculation of costs and benefits based on the capacity of North Vietnam to frustrate early American efforts. This much fits into the quagmire emphasis on the failure of the U.S. to understand the nature of the Vietnam war.

Hostile public reaction in the U.S. following the TET Offensive produced a turning point. The last years of the Johnson Administration culminated in what

Nixon and Kissinger called Vietnamization, a policy that brought the costs and benefits and the domestic constraints on U.S. intervention into clear focus. Thereafter U.S. policy reflected such calculation and successful peace negotiations, after a long and difficult path, were the result. This much is close to the "system worked" approach in its recognition of the pull and tug of domestic political forces on U.S. decisions in Vietnam. *The Unmaking of a President*, Princeton, Princeton University Press, 1977.

42. During the fifties and sixties, the "China lobby" was a powerful group of Congressmen, lobbyists and companies especially concerned with maintaining U.S. control over the Pacific.

43. See *Papers on the War*, pp. 134-141.

44. Interview with Daniel Ellsberg, April, 1975.

45. New York Times edition of the *Pentagon Papers*, p. 426.

46. Quoted in Jeffrey Milstein, *Dynamics of the Vietnam War*, Columbus, Ohio, Ohio State University Press, 1974, p. 182.

47. Gelb has left the State Department for a research position at the Brookings Institution.

48. Two recent collections of rightwing views on the Vietnam war are W. Scott Thompson and Donaldson Frizzell (eds.), *The Lessons of Vietnam*, New York, Crane, Russak and Co., 1977; and Anthony Bouscaren (ed.), *All Quiet on the Eastern Front*, Greenwich, Connecticut, Devin-Adair Company, 1977. Other studies of particular aspects of the war from a conservative perspective include Peter Braestrup, *Big Story*, New York, Doubleday, 1978 (on the press); Frank Snepp, *Decent Interval*, New York, Vintage, 1978 (on the final defeat for the U.S.); and Douglas Kinnard, *The War Managers*, Hanover, University Press of New England, 1977 (on the ground war).

49. Douglas Kinnard, for example, conducted a detailed survey of more than a hundred and seventy Army generals who held operational command in Vietnam. Over seventy percent of those responding felt that U.S. objectives were not clear. And over half felt that in the final analysis the war was not worth the effort. The generals harbored no illusions about the success of the "search and destroy" tactics that relied heavily on the use of U.S. combat troops in vulnerable positions. About two-thirds believed that the official body count was inflated. The generals claim that they knew that Johnson's reliance on wearing the enemy down through the sheer weight and mass of American resources ("attriting the Viet Cong to death") was not working.

Anyone who thought that the U.S. fought the war with selectivity and discrimination in the choice of targets will be disillusioned by the *War Managers*.

50. For an elaboration of the political significance of tactical differences see Chapter Three.

51. See the exchange on U.S. objectives in Vietnam in Thompson and Frizzell, *op. cit.*, pp. 1-17.

52. See Drew Middleton, *Retreat From Victory: A Critical Appraisal of American Foreign and Military Policy from 1920 to 1970's*, Hawthorn, 1974.

53. "We Could Have Won in Vietnam Long Ago," *Reader's Digest*, May, 1969, p. 1.

54. Thompson and Frizzell, *op. cit.*, p. 15.

55. See Chapter Four on the triangular relationship among Moscow, Peking and Washington and its impact on the Vietnam War.

56. Quoted in Bouscaren, *op. cit.*, p. 20.

57. Thompson and Donaldson, *op. cit.*, p. 105. Of course Thompson's account is a tissue of lies. In fact, it was the regional B-52 fleet that was in danger of depletion, not the SAM arsenal. In fact, when compared to the October 1972 draft, the January Peace Treaty did not contain any significant concessions from North Vietnam. In fact, the U.S. bombing of Hanoi was for Thieu's benefit, to demonstrate continued resolve, and to show the world that military force was producing the Treaty. The critical point is that the conservatives are attempting to rewrite history to demonstrate that massive armed force can bring useful results.

58. *America in Vietnam*, New York, Oxford University Press, 1978, p. vii (emphasis in the original). For a powerful argument that the U.S. intervention was in fact immoral see Chomsky and Herman, *op. cit.*

59. In Thompson and Donaldson, *op. cit.*, p. 7.

II: Policy Currents and the Capitalist State

1. Emphasis added. For an excellent treatment of Marx's theory of the state see Ralph Miliband, *Marxism and Politics,* Oxford, Oxford University Press, 1977.

2. *Roots of American Foreign Policy,* Boston, Beacon Press, 1969, p. 5.

3. *Ibid,* p. 6.

4. *Ibid,* pp. 16-23.

5. Richard Barnet, *Roots of War,* Baltimore, Penguin, 1972, p. 179.

6. *Men Who Govern,* quoted by Barnet, *op. cit.* p. 179.

7. Laurence Shoup and William Minter, *Imperial Brain Trust,* New York, Monthly Review, February 1970.

8. William Appleman Williams remains central to this school of thought. His books include *Roots of the Modern American Empire,* New York, Random House, 1969; *The Tragedy of American Diplomacy,* New York, Dell, 1961; and *The Contours of American History,* Cleveland, The World Publishing Co., 1961. See as well David Horowitz, *Corporations and the Cold War,* New York, Monthly Review Press, 1970.

9. Quoted by Barnet, *op. cit.* p. 139.

10. For a summary of the record see Harry Magdoff, *Militarism and Imperialism,* Monthly Review, Feb. 1970.

11. "The Council on Foreign Relations and American Policy in Southeast Asia, 1940-73," *The Insurgent Sociologist,* vol. VII, no. 1, Winter, 1977, pp. 19-30. Also see Christopher Lasch, "The Making of the War Class," *Columbia Forum,* Winter, 1971.

12. *Ibid,* p. 25.

13. Anthony Lukas, *New York Times Magazine,* Nov. 21, 1971, p. 34.

14. "Business Ideology and Foreign Policy: The National Security Council and Vietnam," *Pentagon Papers,* Beacon Press, 1972, vol. V., pp. 16-31.

15. *Ibid,* p. 20.

16. *Ibid*, p. 28.

17. Subtle differences exist among conspiracy theorists. Principal areas of contention include the rationale for the assassination of President Kennedy, the magnitude of the power of organized crime, the allocation of responsibility for government cover-ups and the degree of conscious government duplicity *vis a vis* the American public.

18. *The War Conspiracy,* New York, Bobbs-Merrill, 1972, p. xxii.

19. Gabriel Kolko contends that an argument based on a "ruling class which makes its policies operate" through a pervasive "business-defined consensus" is an argument that rejects conspiracy theories. *op. cit.* p. xii-xiii. It is this position that Scott explicitly opposes.

20. Scott rejects the image of Nixon as "omnipotent Machiavellian" or a "slavish puppet of hidden economic interests." *op. cit.* p. 168. But he also holds Nixon responsible for many of the covert programs, including carpet-bombing, against Cambodia. Franz Schurmann has suggested that Nixon ordered the invasion of Cambodia in order to avert drastic escalations against North Vietnam. Speech before University of California, Berkeley, assembled gathering (unpublished transcript), May 20, 1970.

21. *Pentagon Papers*, vol. V, p. 231.

22. Nicos Poulantzas, "The Problem of the Capitalist State," *New Left Review*, no. 58 (1969), p. 73. The opposite position is best represented by William Domhoff. His books include: *Who Rules America?*, Englewood Cliffs, Prentice-Hall, 1967; *The Higher Circles*, New York, Vintage, 1971; and the special issue of the *Insurgent Sociologist*, "New Directions in Power Structure Research" (Spring 1975).

23. See Fred Block, "The Ruling-Class Does Not Rule: Notes on the Marxist Theory of the State," *Socialist Revolution*, #33, vol. VII, no. 3, May-June 1977, pp. 6-28.

24. My concept of policy currents has been influenced by Franz Schurmann's discussion of "politically significant currents." My presentation locates policy currents within ruling groups and includes both interests and ideology under the same umbrella. Schurmann's discussion of politically significant currents applies to the population as a whole and counterposes the "realm of interests" with the "realm of ideology." See his *Logic of World Power*, New York, Pantheon, 1974, especially pp. 33-39.

25. Four useful summaries of this debate are: Alan Wolfe, "New Directions in the Marxist Theory of Politics," *Politics and Society,* Winter, 1974, pp. 131-160; Erik Olin Wright, Clarence Lo and David Gold, "Some Recent Developments in the Marxist Theory of the State," *Monthly Review*, October, November, 1974; John Mallenkopf, "Theories of the State and Power Structure Research," *Insurgent Sociologist*, vol. V. no. 3, Spring, 1975; and Bob Jessop, "Recent Theories of the Capitalist State," *Cambridge Journal of Economics*, 1977, 1, pp. 353-373. Michael Useem's "The Inner Group of the American Capitalist Class," *Social Problems*, Spring 1978, pp. 225-240, is a criticism of the proposition that the capitalist class contains a sophisticated core conscious of long-range interests.

26. Nicos Poulantzas, *Political Power and Social Classes,* London, New Left Books, 1969.

27. For an example of this argument see Robert Fitch and Mary Oppenheimer, "Bank Control over Corporations," *Socialist Revolution*, nos. 1-3, January-February, March-April, May-June, 1970.

28. For an application of this argument to Chile see Maurice Zeitlin, W. Laurence Neuman, and Richard Earl Ratcliff, "Class Segments: Agrarian Property and Political Leadership in the Capitalist Class of Chile," *American Sociological Review*, 1976, vol. 41 (December): 1006-1029.

29. See "The 18th Brumaire of Richard Nixon," working paper of the *Kapitalistate*, California collective (unpublished).

30. See the summary in Jessop, *op. cit.* pp. 361-364.

31. See Carl Olgesby, *The Yankee-Cowboy War*, New York, Berkeley Medallion Books, 1977. Also relevant here is Kirkpatrick Sale, *Power Shift*, New York, Random House, 1975.

32. David Vogel, "Why Businessmen Mistrust Their State: The Political Consciousness of American Corporate Executives." Thesis, School of Business Administration, University of California, Berkeley, 1975.

33. The executive branch is not fundamentally divided between the civilians and the military (one way that the issue of power in the executive branch is sometimes posed). Civilian state managers and military officers may adhere to the same policy current. Moreover, the outcome of interservice rivalries among specific interests in the military are better explained by the conflict between policy currents than by a more narrow bureaucratic framework.

34. See the excellent summary of Poulantzas' views by George Ross, "Nicos Poulantzas, Eurocommunism, and the Debate on the Theory of the Capitalist State," *Socialist Review*, No. 44, pp. 143-58.

35. See Block, *op.cit.;* and Jessop, *op. cit.*

36. See Carl Boggs, *Gramsci's Marxism*, London, Pluto Press, 1977; and Perry Anderson, "The Antinomies of Antonio Gramsci," *New Left Review*, No. 100, November 1976, pp. 5-80.

37. Account drawn from Charles Mee, *Meeting at Potsdam*, New York, Dell, 1975.

38. Joseph Davies, *Mission to Moscow*, New York, Simon and Schuster, 1941, p. 74.

39. *Ibid*, p. 95.

40. See Block, *op.cit.*

41. Quoted by Dan Gilbarg, "United States Imperialism," in Tom Christoffel, et al. (eds.), *Up Against the American Myth*, New York, Holt, Rinehart, Winston, 1970, p. 245.

42. Characteristics taken from Istvan Meszaros, "Dictatorship and Dissent," *New Left Review*, #108, p. 19.

43. Poulantzas, *New Left Review*, No. 58, p. 70.

44. Claus Offe, "The Theory of the Capitalist State and the Problem of Policy Formation," (unpublished manuscript).

45. Summary drawn from *Pentagon Papers*, vol. II, pp. 201-76.

46. Quoted by Irving Kristol,"Consensus and Dissent in U.S. Foreign Policy," in Anthony Lake (ed.), *The Vietnam Legacy*, New York, New York University Press, 1976, p. 109.

47. August, 1969.
48. Interview with the author, Summer, 1974.
49. Interview with Daniel Ellsberg, *Rolling Stone,* November 8, December 6, 1973.

III: Policy Currents and the U.S. in Vietnam: 1943-1967

1. Nguyen Khac Vien, *Vietnamese Studies*, no. 26.

2. Studies of the "Pacific Rim" include Martin Murray, "The United States' Continuing Economic Interests in Vietnam," *Socialist Revolution* nos. 13-14; Banning Garrett, "Post-War Planning for South Vietnam," *Pacific Research and World Empire Telegraph*, July-August 1972; and Peter Wiley, "Pacific Rim Strategy," New England Free Press Reprint.

3. Victor Marchetti and John Marks, *The CIA and the Cult of Intelligence*, New York, Dell, 1975, p. 72. At the peak of Washington's efforts, Tatsuzo Mizukami, President of Mitsui and Co., Ltd., oldest and largest trading company in Japan, estimated that between 550 million and one billion of Japan's ten billion dollars of exports were tied to the war. See "How Vietnam Affects World Business," *Business Abroad*, August, 1967, p. 9.

4. The World Bank projected its role in South Vietnam ahead to 1985. See *International Bulletin*, March 11-24, 1974.

5. *The Wall Street Journal*, April 29, 1975.

6. Two important analyses are Fred Block, *The Origins of International Economic Disorder*, Berkeley, University of California Press, 1977; and Gabriel Kolko, *The Politics of War*, New York, Random House, 1968.

7. R. Harris Smith, *OSS: The Secret History of America's First Intelligence Agency*, New York, Dell, 1973, pp. 320-360.

8. The reemergence of the multilateral current reflects two kinds of changes: global political conditions in which national liberation movements played an increasing role, and the ideological proclivities of the top leaders of the new Administration.
   The only real exception to the dominance of the containment current during the Eisenhower Administration was Cuba; a debate over the nature of U.S. policy towards the Castro-led forces developed in the State Department. This debate largely reproduced alternatives that had been posed in similar situations.

9. See Leslie Gelb with Richard Betts, *The Irony of Vietnam: The System Worked*, Washington, The Brookings Institution, 1979, p. 35.

10. *Memoirs of Cordell Hull*, p. 1598; quoted by Gelb, *op. cit.* p. 35.

11. Edward Drachman, *United States Policy Toward Vietnam*, 1940-1945, Fairleigh Dickinson University Press, 1970, pp. 54-5.

12. See Joyce and Gabriel Kolko, *The Limits of Power*, New York, Harper and Row, 1972; and Richard Freeland, *The Truman Doctrine and the Origins of McCarthyism*, New York, Schocken, 1974.

13. See Joseph Buttinger, *Vietnam: A Political History*, New York, Praeger Publishers, 1968, pp. 108-116.

14. *Pentagon Papers*, Beacon Press Edition, 1972, Vol. I, p. 4. Hereafter referred to as *PP*, I, p. 4.

15. For details of U.S. support for the French, see *PP*, I, pp. 55-107. See also Philippe Devillers, " 'Supporting' the French in Indochina?" in Noam Chomsky and Howard Zinn (eds.) *The Pentagon Papers: Critical Essays*, Boston, Beacon Press, 1972. For a parallel argument, namely that the U.S. role in Southeast Asia helped secure Japan's participation in the postwar capitalist economy, see John Dower, "The Superdomino in Postwar Asia: Japan in and out of the Pentagon Papers" in Chomsky and Zinn (eds.), *op. cit.*

16. *PP*, I, p. 4.

17. *PP*, I, p. 34.

18. For a discussion of the rightwing in the Pacific in the postwar period see Franz Schurmann, *The Logic of World Power*, New York, Pantheon, 1974, pp. 149-200.

19. On the economic impact of the Korean War see Block, *op. cit.* and Joyce and Gabriel Kolko, *op. cit.*

20. See John Spanier, *The Truman-MacArthur Controversy and the Korean War*, New York, W. W. Norton & Co., 1965.

21. See Hanson Baldwin, "The Never Again School," *New York Times*, June 25, 1964.

22. *Full Circle: The Memoirs of Anthony Eden*, Boston, Houghton Mifflin, 1960, p. 92; quoted by Leslie Gelb, *op. cit.* p. 46.

23. For specifics of U.S. aid to the French see *PP*, I, pp. 408-9. For the argument that Washington's leverage over the French actually declined with greater amounts of aid see Gelb, *op. cit.* pp. 46-7.

24. *PP*, I, pp. 471-2.

25. See Chalmers Roberts, *Washington Post*, October 24, 1971; quoted by Gelb, *op. cit.* p. 57.

26. For Dulles' willingness to use an atomic bomb at Dien Bien Phu, see and hear the testimony of Georges Bidault in the film documentary "Hearts and Minds."

27. See Chapter Four.

28. *PP*, I, p. 162.

29. Kennedy quoted by David Horowitz, *Free World Colossus*, New York, Hill and Wang, 1965, p. 151.

30. *Mandate for Change*, New York, Doubleday, 1963, pp. 337-8.

31. *Ibid.*, p. 372.

32. Gabriel Kolko, *Roots of U.S. Foreign Policy*, Boston, Beacon, 1968, p. 110.

33. For a discussion of various doctrines covering the use of nuclear weapons see Samuel Huntington, *The Common Defense*, New York, Columbia University Press, 1961, p. 299.

34. A *conventional war* is fought with non-nuclear weapons by the regular armed forces of a nation; a *limited war* is generally conceived to be a war fought for less than the complete subordination of one state to another. The implication is that one nation is mobilizing less than its total available forces and does not seek to impose full capitulation on its opposition. A war that is limited for one side might be total for the other. An *unconventional war* involves paramilitary or irregular military outfits. For further details see Michael Klare, *War Without End*, New York, Vintage, 1972. Taylor's book is the *Uncertain Trumpet*, New York, Harper and Row, 1960.

35. See Michael Mandelbaum, *The Nuclear Question*, New York, Cambridge University Press, 1979, esp. pp. 69-98.

36. New York Times edition of the *Pentagon Papers*, New York, Bantam, 1971, p. 89. Hereafter referred to as *NYT*, p. 89.

37. *Ibid.*, p. 86.

38. *Ibid.*, p. 90.

39. See Bernard Fall, *The Two Viet-Nams*, New York, Praeger, 1963, p. 332.

40. See National Security Action Memorandum (NSAM) 111. *PP*, II, p. 111.

41. See Gelb, *op. cit.* p. 84.

42. *NYT*, pp. 667-69. Taylor's assessment was written in 1964. The *Pentagon Papers* contain many examples of assessments that the NLF controlled the countryside and that only U.S. intervention could stave off victory. McNamara's memorandum for the President of March 16, 1964 is an especially good example. See *PP*, III, pp. 499-510. For examples of clear intentions to intervene, even without the prospect of immediate victory, see *PP*, II, p. 204; *PP*, III, pp. 598, 622-28, 657-59, 712, 713, 714.

43. The details of the Diem coup and Washington's complicity can be found in *PP*, II, pp. 201-76. Also see Ralph Stavins account in *Washington Plans An Aggressive War*, New York, Vintage, 1971, pp. 57-90.

44. *PP*, III, p. 103.

45. Three exposes of the Gulf of Tonkin incident are Peter Scott, *The War Conspiracy*, Bobbs-Merrill Publishers, 1972; Eugene Windchy, *Tonkin Gulf*, Doubleday, 1971; and Joseph Goulden, *Truth is the First Casualty: The Gulf of Tonkin Affair—Illusion and Reality*, Rand McNally, 1969.

46. See the cable from William Bundy cited in *PP*, III, p. 9. Bundy also admitted that the Congressional resolution had been prepared before the attack. See Gelb, *op. cit.* p. 104.

47. Some commentators have argued that Kennedy would not have taken these steps and that he was in the process of extricating the United States from Vietnam. But these arguments do not confront the implications of the rapidly deteriorating situation in South Vietnam that developed after Diem's—and Kennedy's—death. With the NLF in "control of virtually the entire countryside," Kennedy told Ted Sorenson in the few days between the Diem coup and his own death, talk of abandoning so unstable an ally and so costly a commitment "only makes it easy for the Communists." Kennedy said, "I think we should stay." Quoted by Leslie Gelb, "The System Worked," *Foreign Policy*, Summer 1971.

48. *PP*, III, p. 221.

49. See Ross Koen, *The China Lobby in American Politics*, New York, Harper and Row, 1974.

50. *PP*, III, p. 131.

51. Interview with the author.

52. *PP*, III, p. 727.

53. Chester Cooper, "The Complexities of Negotiations," *Foreign Affairs*, April 1968, vol. 46, no. 3, pp. 454-66. Cooper's efforts to outline a "minimal" goal in a campaign for a less costly policy did not prevent him from exhibiting a good dose of the racism shared by all of the state managers. Cooper found "Hanoi's demeanor towards the west [to] reflect an amalgam of old-style Marxist contempt for

'degenerate capitalism,' Asian xenophobia, Buddhist obsurantism, the emotional scars of Western colonialism, an innate sense of oriental superiority, and an almost pathological feeling of inferiority and insecurity." Such is the left current's fear of governments that appear to be genuinely revolutionary.

54. *PP*, III, pp. 223-34.

55. *Ibid.*

56. See David Halberstam, *Best and the Brightest*, New York, Random House, 1972, p. 369.

57. *PP*, III, p. 67.

58. Consider the following episode reported by Phil Goulding: "I had been present a few weeks earlier at a colloquy between the Secretary [McNamara] and one of the nation's highest ranking officers, who was arguing the case for mining Haiphong harbor. McNamara asked him whether he would still press for that option if he were given the intelligence judgment that such an act would bring serious retaliatory action from the U.S.S.R. The officer declined to answer. He would only say that he did not think the U.S.S.R. would respond in any way. McNamara pursued the point: 'if that were the intelligence estimate,' he asked again, 'would you nonetheless recommend mining the harbor?' Again the officer responded only by stating his position that the Soviets would not react in this fashion. He refused to meet head on this most critical question." Phil Goulding, *Confirm or Deny: Informing the People on National Security*, New York, Harper and Row, 1970, p. 207.

59. Cy Vance believed that either an invasion of North Vietnam or mining the ports would provoke Chinese intervention. (*PP*, IV, p. 188.)

The center knew that ROLLING THUNDER produced many civilian deaths. McNamara and Johnson were well aware of the various technical and meteorological limits on bombing accuracy. But as Johnson used to say about the Air Force: "If they hit any civilians, I'll bust their asses." The statement signifies that Johnson ruled out the deliberate bombing of civilian centers. Civilian deaths as a consequence of erratic bombing of military targets or at critical junctures in secret diplomatic exchanges were "acceptable" since they did not constitute a change in policy.

60. *PP*, IV, p. 185. Interviews with Rusk and Sharp confirmed the assumption among state managers that China and North Vietnam did have an agreement whereby North Vietnamese MIGs could use airfields in southern China if their home bases became inoperable.

61. U. S. Grant Sharp, "We Could Have Won in Vietnam Long Ago," *Reader's Digest*, May 1969, p. 2.

62. Interview on file at the Institute of Oral History, Columbia University.

63. Interview with the author.

64. McGeorge Bundy, "The End of Either/Or," *Foreign Affairs*, January 1967, vol. 45, no. 2, p. 197.

65. Under Secretary of State Katzenbach also sided with the civilians in the Pentagon. But his ties with RFK, and LBJ's dislike for the former President's younger brother, helped minimize his effectiveness as a left current advocate.

66. Interview with the author.

67. *Ibid.*

68. *Ibid.*

69. Allan Goodman, *The Lost Peace*, Stanford, Hoover Institution Press, 1978, p. 28.

70. The Pugwash Conference was one of a series of meetings among international scientists organized by Cyrus Eaton to promote relations between East and West.

71. As reported by Marvin and Bernard Kalb, *Kissinger*, Boston, Little, Brown, 1974, pp. 66-77.

72. These raids were carried out in the context of the Stennis Hearings. See Chapter 7.

73. Marcovich and Aubrac later told Hanoi that Kissinger wanted to assure North Vietnam that the bombing of the dikes was accidental (thus indicating that the bombing had escalated and now included a range of targets that threatened the civilian population). No wonder the Vietnamese expressed alarm.

74. *PP*, IV, p. 207.

75. Goulding, *op. cit.* p. 210.

76. Interview with the author.

77. This distinction was made by DRV Foreign Minister Trinh in an October 20, 1967 interview with Wilfred Burchett.

78. *New York Times*, October 13, 1967.

79. Henry Brandon, *Anatomy of Error*, Boston, Little, Brown, 1969, p. 109.

80. Quoted in Halberstam, *op. cit.* p. 596.

81. Quoted by Herbert Schandler, *The Unmaking of a President*, Princeton, Princeton University Press, 1977, pp. 36-7.

82. For examples of pessimistic assessments see John McNaughton's memoranda, *PP*, III, pp. 46-48, 291, 346.

83. This transition is charted well by Schandler, *op. cit.* pp. 24-32.

84. See the exchange of view over the effectiveness of the attrition strategy in W. Scott Thompson and Donald Frizzell, *The Lessons of Vietnam*, New York, Crane, Russack and Company, 1977, pp. 73-93.

85. "How Not to Win a War" in Anthony Bouscaren (ed.), *All Quiet on the Eastern Front*, Old Greenwich, Devin-Adair, 1977, p. 17.

86. *PP*, IV, p. 313.

87. *PP*, IV, p. 188.

88. For further details of the reserves debate see Halberstam, *op. cit.*, Chapters 25-6.

89. A good account of the NLF is David Hunt's "Organizing for Revolution in Vietnam," *Radical America*, vol. 8, nos. 1 & 2.

90. See Wilfred Burchett, *Vietnam Will Win*, New York, Guardian, 1968.

91. For an excellent analysis of the antiwar movement see James O'Brien, "The Antiwar Movement and the War," in *Radical America*, vol. 8, no. 3, May-June 1974. For a more optimistic account see Thomas Powers, *The War At Home*, New York, Grossman Publishers, 1973. Useful information can be found in Milton Rosenburg, et. al., *Vietnam and the Silent Majority*, New York, Harper and Row, 1970.

92. For an example of Johnson and McNamara's efforts to prevent full public discussion of the war's economic impact see Halberstam, *op. cit.* p. 609.

IV: Playing Hardball: Sino-Soviet Aid to Vietnam, the Sino-Soviet Dispute, Vietnam and Nuclear Weapons

1. There are some exceptions: See "Vietnam-Kampuchea War," *Southeast Asia Chronicle*, No. 64, Sept.-Oct. 1978; Anthony Barnett, "China and the New Cold War," Institute for Policy Studies (pamphlet), 1979; Bill and Peggy Herod, "The Sino-Vietnamese Conflict and U.S. Policy," pamphlet available from Friendshipment, 1979; and "Vietnam-China War," *Southeast Asia Chronicle*, No. 68, December, 1979.

2. Michel Tatu, "Moscow, Peking and the Conflict in Vietnam," in Anthony Lake (ed.), *The Vietnam Legacy*, New York, New York University Press, 1976, p. 20.

3. Secretary of State Dean Rusk was so intrigued by the bargaining advantages of Vietnam *vis a vis* its stronger allies that he commissioned a study of the situation and its implications for U.S. relations with its allies. Interview with the author.

4. "We Should Have Won in Vietnam Long Ago," *Reader's Digest*, May, 1969.

5. Institute of Oral History, Columbia University Archives.

6. Statement by the Communist Party of the Soviet Union, July 14, 1963. Quoted by Walter Clements, *The Arms Race and Sino-Soviet Relations*, Stanford, Hoover Publications, 1968.

7. Donald Zagoria, *Vietnam Triangle: Moscow, Peking, Hanoi*, New York, Pegasus, 1967.

8. Criticism of the Soviet role in Geneva should be tempered by two facts: (a) *Washington* thought that the Accords were "disastrous" to their interests; and (b) the *Vietnamese* were comfortable with the general principles of the Accords, which did affirm the unity of their country.

9. For evidence of Ho's struggle with "leftist deviationism," members of the Vietminh who opposed Geneva, see Jean Lacouture, *Ho Chi Minh: A Political Biography*, New York, Random House, 1968, pp. 193-196.

10. See William Shawcross, *Sideshow*, New York, Simon and Schuster, 1979, pp. 237-8. During the nineteen-sixties the Vietnamese supported Sihanouk at the expense of their natural allies, the Khmer Rouge. In exchange Sihanoik did not complain about Vietnamese supply routes and staging areas that ran through Cambodia. Of course the Cambodian Communists who wished to overthrow Sihanouk were not too happy with this arrangement, thus furthering the tension between the Khmer and Vietnamese communists.

11. During the late fifties Chinese aid to Vietnam was greater than that offered by the Soviet Union. Bernard Fall places Soviet aid to Vietnam between 1955 and 1961 at 365 million dollars, compared to 662 million dollars from China over the same period. For the same years, Harry Eckstein places the relative amounts at 130 million and 457 million. See Joseph Whelen, "Soviet Aid to the Vietnamese Communists," Library of Congress Legislative Reference Service, JX 1435; F-211 (December 19, 1966); and Jan Prybyla, "Soviet and Chinese Economic Aid to North Vietnam," *China Quarterly*, No. 27, July-Sept. 1966. The Soviet Union places the amount of their military aid to Hanoi for 1965 alone at half a million roubles (Letter of CPSU Central Committee to Some Parties, quoted by John Gittings, *Survey of the Sino-Soviet Dispute, 1963-1967*, New York, Oxford University Press, 1968, p. 268.) A useful summary of Soviet-North Vietnamese relations between 1955 and 1968 can be found as an appendix in Charles McLane,

"The Russians and Vietnam," *International Journal*, No. 24, 1968, pp. 47-64.

12. Kosygin may have also tried to secure Vietnamese attendance at a conference of communist parties that the Soviet Union had been trying to organize for some years.

13. The 1965 figure is from the *New York Times*, March 23, 1966; the 1968 figure is from the *New York Times*, July 5, 1968.

14. The Japanese visit came in 1966.

15. Letter of CCP Central Committee to CPSU Central Committee, July, 1965. Quoted by Gittings, *op. cit.*, p. 263.

16. See David and Nancy Milton, *The Wind Will Not Subside*, New York, Pantheon, 1976, p. 82.

17. An interesting example of how Soviet technology, in this case modern communications, helped the Vietnamese is provided by Thomas Powers in his recent study of the CIA: "After the initiation of B-52 raids from an American air base on Guam . . . [the] CIA discovered that as many as 90 percent of the strikes were being compromised . . . The CIA discovered that the NLF was being warned of the strikes in the following way: Russian trawlers picked up the B-52s as they approached the South Vietnamese coast (an easy process because each B-52 mission involved the transmission of as many as a thousand separate radio messages), then radioed the information to Hanoi, which in turn relayed the warning to their headquarters in Cambodia . . . which passed on the word to local units." *The Man Who Kept the Secrets: Richard Helms and the CIA*, New York, Alfred Knopf, 1979, p. 185.

18. This interpretation explains the current hostilities between China and Vietnam in terms of the immediate history of the postwar period (and the domination of that history by the U.S.). The alternative is a broader, more far-reaching, and diffuse explanation based on long-standing ethnic antagonisms.

19. Miltons, *op. cit.*, p. 84.

20. *Peking Review*, February 12, 1965.

21. Zagoria, *op. cit.*, pp. 96-7.

22. *Peking Review*, May 13, 1966.

23. Quoted by Zagoria, *op. cit.*, p. 97.

24. *Ibid.*

25. Miltons, *op. cit.*, p. 87.

26. For more detail on the differences on military tactics that separated the two camps see Morton Halperin and John Lewis, "New Tensions in Army-Party Relations in China; 1965-1966," *China Quarterly*, April-June 1966.

27. Quoted by the Miltons, *op. cit.*, pp. 138-9.

28. A good discussion of the larger U.S.-China-Soviet triangle is Banning Garrett, "China Policy and the Strategic Triangle," in *The Eagle Entangled: American Foreign Policy in a Complex World*, Longman Publishers, 1979.

29. On the other hand the Chinese may have good reason to fear a tacit Washington-Moscow alliance. Moscow did mass troops against the border with China. Richard Nixon's Chief of Staff, H.R. Haldeman, now claims that the Soviet Union made overtures for joint U.S.-Soviet action against China's nuclear facilities during 1969 and 1970. *The Ends of Power*, New York, New York Times Books, 1978, pp. 89-94.

30. *Peking Review*, November 3, 1966.

31. Gittings, *op. cit.*, p. 257.

32. Moscow Radio Peace and Progress, January 16, 1967.

33. *Pravda*, October 14, 1966.

34. July 7, 1966.

35. Quoted by Gittings, *op. cit.*, p. 258.

36. *Ibid.*, p. 268.

37. On the other hand the left current argued that the Soviet installation of surface-to-air-missiles (SAM-2s) in North Vietnam had little military significance. Moscow was just demonstrating its support. The right thought that the purpose of the missile was to shoot down American planes. General Westmoreland later recalled an episode that illustrates the conflict between left and right on the issue: " 'You don't think the North Vietnamese are going to use them!' [John McNaughton, a member of the left current] scoffed to General Moore [a member of the right current]. 'Putting them in is just a political ploy by the Russians to appease Hanoi.'

It was all a matter of signals, said the clever civilian theorists in Washington. We·won't bomb the SAM sites, which signals the North Vietnamese not to use them." (*A Soldier Reports*, New York, Doubleday, 1976, p. 120.) The left current was wrong. The SAMs were used to shoot down U.S. jets.

Politics are complicated. In this case internal policy camps in each capital were attempting to signal to positions within the enemy camp who could serve as possible allies.

38. See the interesting account of the U.S. attack on Soviet shipping in Peter Dale Scott, *The War Conspiracy*, New York, Bobbs-Merrill, 1972.

39. See Chapter 7.

40. *Pravda*, August 8, 1966.

41. Gittings, *op. cit.*, p. 257.

42. Wilfred Burchett, "Vietnam Responds," *In These Times*, July, 1979.

43. Tad Szulc, "Behind the Vietnam Cease-Fire Agreement: How Kissinger Did It," *Foreign Policy*, Vol. 15, Summer 1974, p. 45.

44. Jeffrey Godsell, *Christian Science Monitor*, June 17, 1975.

45. Later Nixon and Kissinger attempted to defeat the Vietnamese through Moscow and especially Peking. They did not succeed but it does appear that at least some pressure was placed on Hanoi via Peking. Anthony Barnett reports the following incident between Mao and North Vietnamese leader Pham Van Dong:

"Before Nixon arrived in Peking, Kissinger made a second visit to finalize the arrangements. Afterwards Pham Van Dong was summoned from Hanoi for a briefing. One unimpeachable Vietnamese source reports that Mao told the Vietnamese Premier that Vietnam would be the main topic of discussion with Nixon. Mao quoted one of his famous proverbs — something to the effect that if your broom does not have a long handle, it cannot sweep away dirt from the furthest corners.

'Our broom is not long enough to sweep away the enemy from Taiwan,' Mao concluded, 'and yours is not long enough to reach Saigon.'

Pham Van Dong is said to have replied, 'Our broom is long enough to sweep away Thieu and his puppet army.' Mao flushed with anger, says the source, and clenched his fists." Barnett, *op. cit.*, p. 22.

On the other hand the Soviet Union was not particularly helpful in Cambodia, particularly after 1970 when they recognized the U.S.-supported Lon Nol government.

46. For a treatment of the hardline views against the Soviet Union see Daniel Yergin, *Shattered Peace*, Boston, Houghton Mifflin, 1977.

47. Quoted in a pamphlet written by American Security Council, *USSR vs. USA: The ABM and the Changed Strategic Military Balance*, Washington D.C., Acropolis Books, 1969.

48. *Ibid.*, p. 23. The accuracy of these figures is not the point here. Data concerning expenditures is frequently distorted for political purposes. In this case these figures reflect the logic of the rightwing current. For a critique of the premise that the Soviet Union is currently outspending the U.S. on defense see Frank Holzman, "Are the Soviets Really Outspending the U.S. on Defense?" *International Security*, Spring 1980.

49. Bernard Udis (ed.), *Adjustments of the U.S. Economy to Reductions in Military Spending*, U.S. Arms Control and Disarmament Agency, pp. 74-76.

50. Interview with the author.

51. National Security Council—68 was a significant policy statement, approved by President Truman in April 1950, which called for major increases in military spending in response to an alleged Soviet threat.

52. "Our Defense Needs: The Long View," *Foreign Affairs*, April 1964, pp.365-378.

53. The intelligence community was originally split on whether the "Tallin system" deployed across the northern part of the Soviet Union was in fact an ABM system. It later turned out to be part of the elaborate air defense system. According to Morton Halperin, there was no dispute at all that the new system being deployed around Moscow in 1966 was an ABM. See his *Bureaucratic Politics and Foreign Policy*, Washington, D.C., Brookings, 1974, pp. 297-8.

54. The history of Army involvement with the anti-ballistic missile is long and involved. The Army asserted that the anti-ballistic missile was "artillery," and therefore fell into its jurisdiction. As Army Chief of Staff, Maxwell Taylor stumped for the old Nike-Zeus antimissile. Out of the Nike-Zeus grew the Nike-Ajax with a conventional warhead and the Nike-Hercules with an atomic warhead. Finally came the Nike-X, the last generation of missiles.

55. Clark Murdock, *Defense Policy Formation*, Albany, SUNY Press, 1974, p. 122.

56. This is an example of McNamara's political tactic of turning Systems Analysis on and off to suit his own policies.

57. Halperin, *op. cit.*, p. 300.

58. A MIRVed (Multiple Independently-Targeted Reentry Vehicles) missile contains many different warheads on one launcher.

59. McNamara, *Essence of Security*, New York, Harper and Row, 1968, p. 57.

60. Quoted by Phil Goulding, *Confirm or Deny*, New York, Harper and Row, 1970, p. 226.

61. Henry Trewhitt quotes an unidentified Air Force General: "He (McNamara) was so determined to build his case against the ABM, that it wouldn't work, that he went for MIRV ... The Air Force thought MIRV was a splendid idea; it understood the implications fully," *McNamara*, New York, Harper and Row, 1971, pp. 127-128.

62. Goulding, *op. cit.*, pp. 215-16.

63. Managing editor Benjamin Bradlee and editorial writer Philip Geyelin of the WASHINGTON POST began the series of half hour interviews. They were

63. Managing editor Benjamin Bradlee and Editorial Writer Philip Geyelin of the *Washington Post* began the series of half hour interviews. They were followed by Richard Stolley of *Life*, Robert Donovan of the *Los Angeles Times*, columnist William White, Eric Severeid of CBS, Tom Wicker of the *New York Times*, Roscoe Drumond and columnist Marquis Childs. John Chancellor of NBC had been briefed the previous day. On the morning of the speech, Paul Nitze, McNamara's deputy, and Dan Henkin and Dick Fryklund, Goulding's two assistants, gave the same briefing to twenty-seven more newspeople. One of the goals of these interviews was to encourage the leading newspapers to print the full text of the speech. The other was to prevent stories that McNamara, long time opponent of the ABM had, in announcing a limited deployment, reversed his position. See Goulding, *op. cit.*, p. 218.

64. McNamara, *op. cit.*, p. 164.

65. Trewhitt, *op. cit.*, p. 131.

66. *Ibid.*, p. 289.

67. Edward Randolph Jayne, "The ABM Debate: Strategic Defense and National Security," Ph.D. thesis, MIT, 1969, cited by Halperin, *op. cit.*, p. 299.

68. *Ibid.*

69. *Ibid.*, pp. 227-8.

70. See Allan Goodman, *The Lost Peace*, Washington, Brookings, 1978.

V: Domestic Opposition

1. David Halberstam, *Best and the Brightest*, New York, Random House, 1972, p. 641.

2. Thomas Oliphant, "Harrington Says Admiral Discussed North Vietnam Invasion," *Boston Globe*, April 15, 1972; quoted by Noam Chomsky, *For Reasons of State*, New York, Vintage, 1973. (emphasis added)

3. *New Dimensions of Political Economy*, Cambridge, Harvard University Press, 1966.

4. Quoted in Lyndon Johnson, *The Vantage Point*, New York, Holt, Rinehart, Winston, 1971, p. 127.

5. Which is not to imply that the U.S. would have won if Johnson had met the levels recommended by the military. For an example of government deception regarding the change of mission for U.S. ground troops (now charged with initiating battles with the NLF) see Herbert Schandler, *The Unmaking of a President*, Princeton, Princeton University Press, 1977, p. 22.

6. For an interesting analysis of why the "need to deceive is inherent in the nature of limited war" see Philip Geyelin, "Vietnam and the Press: Limited War and an Open Society" in Anthony Lake (ed.), *The Vietnam Legacy*, New York, New York University Press, 1976, pp. 166-193.

7. Robert Smith, "Disaffection, Delegitimation and Consequences: Aggregate Trends for World War II, Korea and Vietnam," in Charles Moskos (ed.), *Public Opinion and the Military Establishment*, Beverly Hills, Sage Publications, 1971.

8. James O'Brien, "The Antiwar Movement and the War," *Radical America*, vol. 8, no. 3, May-June 1974.

9. Milton Rosenberg, et. al., *Vietnam and the Silent Majority*, New York, Harper and Row, 1970, p. 31.

10. News of these protests were carried in the *Wall Street Journal*, November 24, 1967.

11. The number of urban riots rose from sixteen in 1964 to sixty-five in 1968.

12. Smith, *op. cit.*, p. 235. For an analysis of the draft resistance see Michael Useem, *Conscription, Protest and Social Conflict. The Life and Death of a Draft Resistance Movement*, New York, Wiley, 1973.

13. "Fragging" originally referred to the practice of rolling a grenade under the tent flap of an officer's quarters. As used in the chart the term refers more generally to physical assaults in any form.

14. Also see Matthew Rinaldi, "The Olive-Drab Rebels," *Radical America*, vol. 8, no. 3, May-June 1974. Most estimates place the number of combat soldiers on heroin by the end of 1971 at thirty percent.

15. *Ibid.*

16. Quoted by Thomas Powers, *The War At Home*, New York, Grossman Publishers, 1973, p. 235.

17. Interview with the author.

18. See Lady Bird Johnson's account, *White House Diary*, New York, Holt, Rinehart, Winston, 1970, pp. 620-624.

19. This material will be covered in detail in Chapters Seven and Eight.

20. Jack Anderson column, *San Francisco Chronicle*, February 23, 1975. See as well Thomas Powers, *The Man Who Kept the Secrets: Richard Helms and the CIA*, New York, Alfred Knopf, 1979.

21. See Herbert Blumer, "Public Opinion and Public Opinion Polling," in *Symbolic Interaction*, Englewood-Cliffs, Prentice-Hall, 1969.

22. Herb Schiller, "The Polling Industry: The Measurement and Manufacture of Opinion." Paper delivered before the Society for the History of Technology, New York City, December 29, 1971.

23. *Gallup Opinion Index*, December 1967, p. 37.

24. *Ibid.*

25. Philip Converse and Howard Schuman, " 'Silent Majorities' and the Vietnam War," *Scientific American*, June 1970, vol. 222, no. 6, p. 21.

26. *Gallup Opinion Index*, May 1968, p. 18.

27. *Gallup Opinion Index*, December, 1967, pp. 39-40.

28. *Political Man*, New York, Doubleday, 1959.

29. For example see Harlan Hahn, "Dove Sentiment Among Blue-Collar Workers," *Dissent*, XVII, May-June 1970.

30. Rosenberg, *op. cit.*

31. Hahn, *op. cit.*

32. "A Research Note on the Mass Support for 'Tough' Military Initiatives," *American Sociological Review*, XXXIII, June 1968, pp. 439-445.

33. *Ibid.*

34. David Armor, et. al., "Professors Attitudes Towards the Vietnam War,"

Public Opinion Quarterly, Summer 1967, pp. 159-175.

35. Sidney Verba, et. al., "Public Opinion and the War in Vietnam," *American Political Science Review*, (61) 1967, pp. 317-33. See as well John Mueller, *War, Presidents and Public Opinion*, New York, Wiley, 1973.

36. Rosenberg, *op. cit.*, p. 66.

37. See Table 5.4.

38. Rosenberg, *op. cit.*, p. 37.

39. *Ibid.*, p. 49. Ironically the success of the antiwar movement helped stimulate less progressive tendencies. For a report of how leaders of a Washington D.C. suburb organized an antibusing drive which opposed the goals but adopted the tactics of the antiwar movement see Peter Osnos, "The War in Riverdale," in Lake, *op. cit.*, pp. 66-79.

40. Rosenberg, *op. cit.*, p. 45.

41. Quoted by Philip Foner, *American Labor and the Indochina War*, New York, International Publishers, 1971.

42. *Ibid.*, p. 7.

43. The state managers differ, naturally, from their extra-state counterparts, in their access to secret information, and in their elaboration of options on a more detailed level. But the logic of the political positions, especially as a response to forces of opposition, remains similar both inside and outside the state.

44. *Time* "switched" October 6th; *Life*, October 13th; Walter Cronkite in February 1968, following a post-TET visit to South Vietnam. The story of the *Wall Street Journal*'s change of editorial opinion is told in Don Oberdorfer, *Tet*, New York, Avon, 1971.

45. Interview with the author.

46. Min Yee, *Boston Sunday Globe*, February 18, 1968, p. A-2. Yee places the *Washington Post* in the category supporting the Administration. My reading of their post-TET editorials places them in the critical category. Certainly the reaction of national officials indicates that the *Post* was not considered supportive.

47. Noam Chomsky has consistently criticized the press for loyally serving the ideological needs of the state. He points out that even the "antiwar" newspapers such as the *New York Times* rarely strayed from the "system of state propaganda." By studiously avoiding a serious analysis of the basic tenets of anti-communism, by failing to examine the assumptions underlying the U.S. intervention in Vietnam, and limiting criticism to the failure of means to achieve already agreed-to ends, the press embraces the existing structure of economic and political power. See "Ten Years After TET: The Big Story That Got Away," *More*, June, 1978. His most recent study, in two volumes, written with Edward Herman, is a devastating analysis of press compliance in its treatment of foreign affairs. *The Washington Connection and Third World Fascism* and *After the Cataclysm*, Boston, South End Press, 1979. See as well James Aronson, *The Press and the Cold War*, Boston, Beacon Press, 1973.

Another interpretation is that the press was fundamentally irresponsible and, through its criticism of official reports, fueled domestic dissent, prolonged the war, and gave aid to the enemy. For an example of this point of view see Peter Braestrup, *Big Story*, New York, Doubleday, 1978.

48. William Bundy planned a major overhaul of the Administration's public relations treatment of the war. Ed Thompson, former managing editor of *Life* and, as

Bundy put it, "an old veteran of the intelligence business," was hired to get the Administration's point of view across. The TET Offensive cut off the last-minute effort to save the last vestiges of credibility. (Interview with the author)

49. See Todd Gitlin, *The Whole World is Watching*, Berkeley, University of California Press, 1980.

50. The twenty-one signatories were: Harding Bancroft, Lincoln Bloomfield, Charles G. Bolte, John Cowles, Daniel Ellsberg, Francis Fitzgerald, Ernest Gross, Roger Hilsman, Joseph Johnson, Milton Katz, George Kistiakowsky, Franklin Lindsay, Richard Neustadt, Matthew Ridgway, Marshall Shulman, Donald Straus, Kenneth Thompson, James Thomson, Stephen Wright, Adam Yarmolinsky and Charles Yost; from Townsend Hoopes, *Limits of Intervention*, New York, David McKay, 1969, p. 241.

51. Interview with the author.

52. The Fourteen Asian Scholars were: A. Doak Barnett, Leo Cherne, Chancellor Harry Gideonse, Oscar Handlin, William Lockwood, Richard Park, Guy Pauker, Lucian Pye, Edwin Reischauer, I. Milton Sacks, Robert Scalapino, Paul Seabury, Fred Von Der Mehden, and Robert Ward. Hoopes, *op. cit.*, p. 242.

53. In January a third group calling itself the Citizens Committee for Peace and Freedom in Vietnam published a statement critical of the "efficiency" of the bombing of the North. The members of the group, including former presidents Truman and Eisenhower, Omar Bradley and James Conant, also argued against any sharp increase in ROLLING THUNDER.

54. The American Security Council is an example.

VI: The Vietnam War, the Economy and the Capitalist Class

1. Testimony before the Joint Economic Committee, "Economic Effect of Vietnam Spending," 90th Congress, first session, I, (1967), pp. 253-54.

2. The War and Its Impact on the Economy," *Review of the Radical Political Economists*, August, 1970, p. 1.

3. A chart of the *Business Week* Index is included in the Economic Appendix.

4. See especially William Appleman Williams, *The Roots of the Modern American Empire*, New York, Random House, 1969.

5. These figures are drawn from Table I in the Economic Appendix.

6. In part the balance of trade deteriorated because prices for U.S. exports increased more rapidly than prices for exports from other industrial countries. Between 1960 and 1966 the index of export prices for U.S. products (1963 = 100) rose from 99 to 107, almost exactly equalling the rise from 99 to 106 for all industrial countries. But the index for U.S. exports jumped eight points to 115 in 1969, while only increasing three points to 109 for all industrial countries. Higher prices lowered the demand for U.S. products. And the problem began to emerge in full force in 1967.

7. For an interesting debate on the relative strength of the U.S. in the world arena see James Petras and Robert Rhodes, "The Reconsolidation of US Hegemony," *New Left Review*. #97, May-June 1976; the response by Fred

Block. "Communication," *New Left Review,* #99, September-October 1976; and the reply by Petras and Rhodes, *New Left Review,* Nos. 101-102, February-April 1977.

8. For U.S. financial transfers abroad see Table III, Economic Appendix; for military contributions to U.S. balance of payments problems see Table IV, Economic Appendix.

9. For U.S. exports as a percentage of world exports see Table V, Economic Appendix.

10. Testimony before the Senate Committee on Foreign Relations, 91st Congress, second session, April 15, 1970.

11. For the rate of capacity utilization see Table X, Economic Appendix.

12. Committee for Economic Development, *The National Economy and the Vietnam War: Statement by the Research and Policy Committee,* April 1968. Also see Table XII, Economic Appendix.

13. *Economic Report of the President,* 1975, p. 317.

14. See Tom Ridell, "The Economic Impact of the Vietnam War," Ph.D. dissertation, University of California, Berkeley, 1975, p. 234.

15. *Ibid,* p. 240.

16. Details can be found in Table XIV, Economic Appendix.

17. Quoted by Murray Weidenbaum, "Impact of the Vietnam War on the American Economy," background paper prepared for the Joint Economic Committee, "Economic Effect of Vietnam Spending," *op. cit.*

18. Individuals and organizations whose positions are synthesized include a report of the Georgetown University Center for Strategic Studies authored by Murray Weidenbaum, *The Economic Impact of the Vietnam War,* Special Report Series, no. 5 (New York, Renaissance Editions, 1967); the Committee for Economic Development, *The National Economy and the Vietnam War,* (April 1968); the Foreign Policy Association, *Vietnam: Issues for Decision* (April 1968); an Ad Hoc Committee of leading businessmen and economists of the Chamber of Commerce of the United States, *After Vietnam: A Report of the Ad Hoc Committee on the Economic Impact of Peace after Vietnam* (Washington, D.C. 1968); the National Association of Manufacturers in NAM Reports (selected issues); *Fortune; Business Week; The Wall Street Journal;* statements from Marriner Eccles, former chairman of the Federal Reserve Board; George Moore, Chairman, First National City Bank; Tom Watson of IBM; Louis Lundborg of the Bank of America; Pierre-Paul Schweitzer, Managing Director of the International Monetary Fund; and various bank newsletters including that of the First National City Bank of New York.

19. Noted in Peter Scott, "The Vietnam War and the CIA-Financial Establishment," in Selden (ed.), *Remaking Asia,* New York, Random House, 1974, pp. 135-6.

20. "Needed: Better War- and Peace-Aims," *Fortune,* vol. 73, no. 1, January 1966, pp. 116-7.

21. See David Halberstam, *Best and the Brightest,* New York, Random House, 1972, p. 609.

22. Statement to the Senate Foreign Relations Committee, U.S. Congress, *Hearings on the Impact of the War in Southeast Asia on the U.S. Economy,* 91st Congress, second session, April, 1970.

23. *Ibid.*

24. Eccles' speech is reprinted in *War/Peace Report*, October 1967, pp. 3-5.

25. *Ibid.*

26. Nitze's views are explored more completely in Chapter Four on Vietnam and nuclear weapons, and again in Chapter Eight.

Others who supported Eccles' point of view included interests within the capitalist class that stood to gain from a shift in defense priorities back to strategic weaponry. But these defense interests were articulated in the context of policy. One policy forum was *Aviation Week and Space Technology* where it was argued that "U.S. strategic security through the nineteen-seventies is being threatened by the vitiating dollar drain of the war in Vietnam coupled with impressive improvements in Soviet hardware and technology...." (March 18, 1968). A second story entitled "Long-Range Aerospace Research Sacrificed to Vietnam Demands" maintained "that long-range defense-oriented Pentagon budget restrictions are placing new burdens on the U.S. aerospace industry and scientific community." On the one hand the military can always be expected to push for a large budget. On the other it is important that special interests within the military and within the defense industry began to criticize the Vietnam War for draining funds away from stategic programs against the Soviet Union.

27. *The National Economy and the Vietnam War* (April 1968). Dissenting footnotes from portions of the Commitee's Research and Policy Group report contain disagreements falling within the framework of policy currents. Allan Sproul, Marvin Bower and C. Wrede Petersmeyer, representing the left current, felt "that it is not enough to say, as the Statement does, that the Vietnam War need not have caused the economic dislocations we have experienced. It has become the core of these dislocations." Their position was consistent with a call for quick reduction in U.S. commitments to Southeast Asia; however the Committee's rule against overt political stances prevented those dissenters from doing so explicitly (p. 68). A minority of the Committee took a harder line on the Vietnam War (the right current). Robert Kleberg of the King Ranch, argued that the "struggle against Communism is a continuing one that does not leave room for extravagance at home. It is important that the Administration should try as soon as possible to commit the necessary force to win the war and an estimate should be made of the force to be committed so that the people of the nation will know what they are asked to do" (pp. 62-3). Kleberg's views not only addressed the right current's economic views but its strategy for reducing domestic dissent as well.

The Report of the Committee on Economic Development thus illustrates the argument made in this chapter in two ways: First, that its main message concerns the Vietnam War and the overall performance of the economy. An explicit political stand on the war itself was not taken. Second, different political preferences, expressed in dissenting footnotes, fall within the framework of policy currents. If the Committee is taken to represent the capitalist class as a whole then the message is that only the Vietnam War is hurting the economy. Individual members do make recommendations with policy implications, but they also disagree with each other thus making it impossible for the Committee to serve as a forum for the general interests of the capitalist class on the Vietnam War.

28. Committee for Economic Development, *A Stabilizing Fiscal and Monetary Policy for 1970*, 1970.

29. A *Fortune* poll taken a year-and-a-half later reported a ten-to-one majority of businessmen favoring the continuation of the surtax (August 1969).

30. Examples include William Bowen, "The Vietnam War: A Cost Accounting," *Fortune*, April 1966; and Allan Demaree, "Defense Profits: The Hidden Issues," *Fortune*, August 1969.

31. "Business Round-Up," *Fortune*, February 1968.

32. *Business Week*, March 30, 1968.

33. *Wall Street Journal*, February 23, 1968.

34. Poll conducted by Daniel Yankelovich and reported in the August 1969 issue of *Fortune*.

35. Note the range of opinion on the Vietnam War within the business community.

36. Donald Snodgrass, San Francisco Federal Reserve Board, *Monthly News Letter*, September 1967, p. 181.

37. *Ibid.*

38. Alvin Hanson, "Inflation: Korea Versus Vietnam," *Washington Post*, November 30, 1969.

39. *Ibid.*

40. For a powerful argument that government spending on social programs comes only in response to social movements see Francis Piven and Richard Cloward, *Regulating the Poor: The Functions of Public Relief*, New York, Pantheon, 1971.

41. Quoted in Murray Weidenbaum, "Impact of the Vietnam War on the American Economy," Joint Economic Committee, *Economic Effect of Vietnam Spending*, Vol. I, pp. 205-6.

42. *Ibid.*, p. 217.

43. *Economic Report of the President*, 1967, pp. 61, 97.

44. U.S. Chamber of Commerce, Ad Hoc Committee, "The Economic Impact of Peace in Vietnam," Washington D.C., 1968. For example, the Chamber of Commerce Report argued that the multiplier effect of Vietnam spending had a strong impact on employment rates and the Gross National Product: "The Research Seminar on Quantitative Economics at the University of Michigan referred to by Professor Daniel Suits in his April 1967 testimony before the Joint Economic Committee has ascertained that each dollar of this kind of spending [defense] stimulates about 85 cents of additional consumer spending. By this reckoning, the $20 billion increased outlay on Vietnam from mid-1965 to mid-1967 added $37 billion to the GNP. Similarly, on the Seminar's estimate of one additional man-year of employment per each additonal $10,000 of GNP at today's prices, the $20 billion defense spending increment was responsible for about 3.7 million new jobs of the two-year period, compared to the induced primary employment of one million jobs estimated by the U.S. Department of Labor and of 1.4 million estimated by Dr. Leonard Lecht."

45. *The Business Cycle in a Changing World*, p. 317.

46. U.S. Congress, Joint Economic Committee, "Economic Effect of Vietnam Spending," 90th Congress, first session.

47. *The Economic Impact of the Vietnam War*, Special Report Series, no. 5, New York, Renaissance Editions, 1967, p. 210.

48. Weidenbaum was later named to the Nixon Administration and most recently to the Reagan Administration.

49. David Halberstam has President Johnson saying: "I don't know much about economics, but I do know Congress. And I can get the Great Society through right now — this is the golden time. We've got a good Congress and I'm the right President and I can do it. But if I talk about the cost of the war, the Great Society won't go through and the tax bill won't go through. Old Wilbur Mills will sit down there and he'll thank me kindly and send me back my Great Society, then he'll tell me that they'll be glad to spend whatever we need for the war." *op. cit.*, p. 606.

50. On the impact of popular movements on state decisions, see Chapter Two.

51. Statement to the Senate Foreign Relations Committee, *op. cit.*

52. "Inflation and Taxes: Herbert Stein Replies," *Washington Post*, July 14, 1974.

53. Betty Hanson and Bruce Russett, "Testing Some Economic Interpretations of American Intervention: Korean, Indochina, and the Stock Market" in Rosen (ed.) *Testing the Theory of the Military-Industrial Complex* (Lexington, D.C. Heath and Co., 1973).

Hanson and Russett also tested a fourth hypothesis which they call "neo-imperialist." The neo-imperialist perspective stresses the future benefits to be derived from Vietnam and the rest of Southeast Asia. The purpose of the war is to create an environment for investment opportunities, rather than defend existing ones, and to demonstrate the determination of the United States to hold the line against revolutionary movements.

This logic does underlie intervention in Vietnam. But the authors' operational hypothesis ("corporations with substantial overseas investments, especially in less developed countries, will support military intervention more strongly and for a longer period of time than will other corporations") is not a valid test of the theory (the expectation of future benefits is diffused throughout the multinational corporations and banking circles thus making the stock prices of particular corporations too limited a test). At any rate Hanson and Russett find little empirical support for the "neo-imperialist" hypothesis.

54. Quoted by Ridell, *op. cit.* p. 238.

VII: The Collapse of the Center: August 1967 to the TET Offensive

1. The most complete account of the Offensive is by Don Oberdorfer, *TET*, New York, Avon Books, 1971.

2. *Pentagon Papers*, Gravel Edition, Boston, Beacon Press, 1971 (hereafter referred to as *PP*), IV, pp.189-90.

3. *PP*, IV, p.208.

4. *PP*, IV, p.177.

5. *PP*, IV, pp.189-90.

6. *PP*, IV, p.208.

7. *PP*, IV, p.177.

8. McGeorge Bundy, "The End of Either/Or," *Foreign Affairs*, January 1967, Vol. 45, No. 2, pp.189-201.

9. The most important decisions regarding the war were taken at the Tuesday Cabinet. It was here that Secretary of State Rusk, often silent at larger meetings, exercised most of his influence. Henry Graff's *Tuesday Cabinet* gives some indication of its scope of operations (Prentice-Hall, 1970).

10. *PP*, IV, p.198.

11. *Ibid.*, p.199.

12. *New York Times*, August 16, 1967.

13. *PP*, IV, pp.203-4.

14. *Ibid.*, p.204.

15. *New York Times*, August 22, 1967.

16. The *Pentagon Papers* analyst for the period considers as the turning point the failure of the attack on the North Vietnam POL (Petroleum, Oil, and Lubricants) depots in June 1966 to produce any measureable effect on North Vietnam's will and capacity to fight. The POL were destroyed, but increased imports from the Soviet Union substituted for the lost facilities. After the attack McNamara attempted to stabilize the airwar. See his recommendations of August 1966 in Herbert Schandler, *The Unmaking of a President*, Princeton, Princeton University Press, 1977; p.43.

17. *New York Times*, August 26, 1967.

18. *PP*, IV, p.200.

19. *Ibid.*, p.201.

20. McNamara had the audacity to argue that "their [the leaders of North Vietnam] regard for the comfort and even the lives of the people they control does not seem to be sufficiently high to lead them to bargain for settlement in order to stop a heightened level of attack." As if Hanoi was responsible for the terror of United States bombs!

21. *PP*, IV, p.202-3.

22. McGeorge Bundy shared McNamara's views on the bombing. Although out of government at the time, Bundy attempted to affect the process with a letter to the *Washington Post* (September 11, 1967). He criticized the Committee with the following:

> The Senators appeal not to evidence but to authority. They set up a group of generals and admirals against Secretary McNamara, and their position is that the generals and admirals are right simply because they are professionals. The Subcommittee does not demonstrate the military value of the course it urges: it simply tells us that the generals and admirals are for it ... Nothing is less reliable in choices of this sort, than the unsupported opinion of men who are urging the value of their own chosen instrument — in this case military force. We must not be surprised, and still less persuaded, when generals and admirals recommend additional military action — what do we expect them to recommend?

23. *PP*, IV, p.221.

24. *PP*, IV, p.222.

25. *PP*, IV, p.224.

26. *PP*, IV, p.225.

27. *PP*, IV, p.136.

28. *PP*, IV, p.71.

29. For the Air Force defense of the bombing program see Robert Boles, "Bombing as a Policy Tool in Vietnam: Effectiveness," U.S. Senate Committee on Foreign Relations, U.S. Printing Office, Washington D.C., 1972. For a fuller debate, including an example of McNamara's cost effectiveness technique applied to ROLLING THUNDER, see the exchange of views in W. Scott Thompson and Donaldson D. Frizzell (eds.), *The Lessons of Vietnam*, New York, Crane, Russak, and Company, Inc., 1977; pp.125-149.

30. Townsend Hoopes, *Limits of Intervention*, New York, David McKay, 1969; p.77.

31. Colonel James Donovan, *Militarism, U.S.A.*, New York, Charles Scribner's and Sons, 1970.

32. For further evidence of distortions, including deliberately optimistic reports of destruction achieved through bombing, see Leslie Gelb with Richard Betts, *The Irony of Vietnam: The System Worked*, Washington, Brookings Institute, 1979; p.309.

33. David Halberstam, *Best and the Brightest*, New York, Random House, 1971; pp.149-50.

34. Quoted by Aaron Wildavsky, *Politics of the Budgetary Process*, Boston, Little, Brown and Co., 1964; p.140.

35. Robert McNamara, *The Essence of Security*, New York, Harper and Row, 1968; p.x.

36. Samuel Huntington (*The Common Defense*, New York, Columbia University Press, 1961) makes a similar distinction (p. 146). James Roherty also distinguishes between the "generalists'" style of decision-making and that of the "functionalists," represented by Robert McNamara. See his *Decisions of Robert McNamara*, Coral Gables, University of Miami Press, 1970.

37. Quoted in Walter Kaufman, *The McNamara Strategy*, New York, Harper and Row, 1964; p.171.

38. Phil Goulding, *Confirm or Deny*, New York, Harper and Row, 1970. Goulding feels that had McNamara not been removed from office, Wheeler would not have met Westmoreland in February and returned with the 206,000 troop request. McNamara would have bargained Westmoreland down and come back with a much lower figure. As a result the request would have been accepted and the policy review of March would not have taken place.

39. See *PP*, IV, pp.112-16.

40. Hoopes, *op. cit.*; p.108.

41. The McNamara memorandum and Johnson's response are in *The Vantage Point*, New York, Holt, Reinhart, Winston, 1971, pp.372-78. See as well Leslie Gelb, "The Pentagon Papers and *The Vantage Point*," *Foreign Policy*, Spring, 1973.

42. Only a little over five million were eligible to vote. Eighty-three percent of this total did vote.

43. Noted in the Keesing Research Report, *South Vietnam: A Political History 1954-1970*, New York, Charles Scribner's and Sons, 1970; p.130.

44. Thieu and Ky continued a feud which testified to the profound instability of the Saigon government. To compete with Thieu, Ky established a "National Reconstruction Committee" which virtually assumed the functions of the government. The Vice-President also launched a campaign to revise the Constitution in a manner guaranteed to increase his power. For his part, Thieu feared a Ky-inspired coup, and kept tanks and additional troops stationed around the Presidential Palace instead of fighting the NLF. Ky was forced to dissolve his committee on February 20. To keep track of such internecine squabbles the CIA had the Presidential Palace in Saigon bugged. See Thomas Powers, *The Man Who Kept the Secrets*, New York, Alfred Knopf, 1979; p.198.

45. *Pentagon Papers*, New York, Bantam Books, 1971; p.592.

46. *Washington Post*, February 6, 1968.

47. Dien Bien Phu was a remote valley that the French marched into in 1954 only to become surrounded by the Viet Minh. The humiliating defeat culminated in the Geneva Conference and the withdrawal of French armed forces from Vietnam.

48. General William Westmoreland, *A Soldier Reports*, New York, Doubleday and Co., 1976; p.338.

49. MAC 01586. Quoted by Schandler, *op.cit.*; p.90.

50. See the debate over the significance of Khe Sanh in Thompson and Frizzell, *op.cit.*

51. One of the most detailed accounts of the events surrounding the capture of the *Pueblo* is contained in Peter Scott's *The War Conspiracy*, Bobbs-Merrill, 1972. Scott hints that Admiral Sharp and other Commanders of the Pacific Fleet ignored a series of warnings from the Koreans and deliberately sent the *Pueblo* into North Korean territorial waters to heighten tensions throughout the Pacific, undermine diplomatic exchanges between Washington and Hanoi, and secure a mobilization of the reserves. Scott also situates the *Pueblo* incident in the context of eight bombing and strafing attacks by U.S. planes on Soviet and Chinese vessels between June 1966 and January 27, 1968 (p. 118).

52. *The Economist*, January 27, 1968.

53. Admiral Sharp also thought this was the case. Interview with the author.

54. Marvin Kalb and Elie Abel, *Roots of Involvement*, New York, Norton and Co., 1971; p.213.

55. Henry Brandon, *Anatomy of Error*, Boston, Gambit, 1969; p.125.

56. Shown on the CBS network, February 6, 1970.

57. Transcript, CBS News; p.1.

58. Schandler, *op.cit.*; p.83.

59. Oberdorfer, *op.cit.*; p.306.

60. John Henry, "February 1968," *Foreign Policy*, No. 4, Fall, 1971.

61. *PP*, IV, pp.541-2.

62. See Kalb and Abel, *op.cit.*; pp.209-210.

63. Schandler, *op.cit.*; p.97.

64. Kalb and Abel, *op.cit.*; p.210.

65. The logistical details of the troop request provides additional evidence that its origin was in Washington, not the military in Saigon. The magnitude of the request for additional airpower (17 tactical squadrons), the rationale as given by the Army

Chief of Staff (to maintain the existing air-to-ground ratio), and their specific missions, all reflect a compromise among the Marines, Air Force, and Army that could have only been worked out in Washington. See Hoopes, *op.cit.*; pp.161-66. In addition, a "top military authority" who had been in close contact with the Joint Chiefs was quoted in *U.S. News and World Report* immediately *prior* to Wheeler's departure for Saigon, saying "What is required is another 200,000 American ground troops, immediately" [exactly the size of the request that eventually emerged from Saigon]. See Oberdorfer, *op.cit.*; p.282. Westmoreland later claimed to not recognize the Joint Chiefs of Staff's elaborated request as his own. "I never dreamed of being accused of having asked for 206,000 men," Westmoreland later told one source. Brandon, *op.cit.*; p.124.

66. Brandon, *op.cit.*; p.123.

67. Schandler, *op.cit.*; p.106.

68. *Ibid.*, p.111.

69. Quoted by Kalb and Abel, *op.cit.*; pp.214-5.

70. Oberdorfer, *op.cit.*; p.209.

71. Henry, *op.cit.*; p.15. Although Rostow, as a member of the right current, generally favored expansion of the ground war into Laos and part of North Vietnam, he did not do so at this time. Rostow did, however, favor mobilization of the reserves. See Schandler, *op.cit.*; p.164.

72. An account of this transformation of intelligence is given in Oberdorfer, *op.cit.*; p.279.

73. *PP*, IV, pp.546-7.

74. For a fuller treatment of this issue see my "Politics of 'Good' and 'Bad' Intelligence," *Politics and Society*, 7 (1977): 105-26.

75. The order of battle is an estimate of the size of opposing forces.

76. Hubert Humphrey also attended the meeting.

77. Correspondence with the author.

78. Robert Kennedy, *Thirteen Days*, New York, W.W. Norton, 1969, pp.37-8.

79. *Pentagon Papars*, New York Times Books, pp.615-16.

80. Henry, *op. cit.* Wheeler told Henry that Westmoreland understood that he would receive only the first increment, or half of the 206,000, even if the entire request was approved. The other two increments were to be kept in the strategic reserve available for MACV if the situation demanded them. Wheeler's remark seems to be contradicted by the published text of his report, where the full 206,000 are slated for Vietnam. See *Pentagon Papers*, New York Times Books, p.518.

81. Rusk later stated that he realized that the troops would be used in Laos, Cambodia, and North Vietnam. Interview with the author.

82. Present besides Wheeler were Johnson, Humphrey, Rusk, McNamara, Clifford, Taylor, Nitze, Helms, Rostow, and Presidential aides Christian and Johnson.

83. Johnson, *op.cit.*; p.393.

84. *Ibid*, p.393.

85. *Ibid*, p.394.

86. Clark Clifford, "A Vietnam Reappraisal," *Foreign Affairs*, Vol. 47, no. 4, July 1969, p.609.

87. It is possible to exaggerate the importance of the directive itself. As Under Secretary of State Katzenbach later recalled, "You just can't control a man like Clifford with a directive." Quoted by Henry, *op.cit.*; p.26.

88. The precise status of the directive remains obscure. Johnson labels the directive sent to Defense and State a "draft." Clifford reports that his instructions were oral. His executive officer, Colonel Pursley, called the White House for a copy of the directive and was informed that no such paper existed. It appears that William Bundy did draft a set of operating questions that were sent to Warnke in the Pentagon. For more see Townsend Hoopes, "LBJ's Account of March 1968," *New Republic*, March 14, 1970.

VIII: The Crisis: February-March 1968

1. *Pentagon Papers*, Boston, Beacon Press, 1971, Vol. IV, p.551. (Hereafter *PP*).

2. *PP*, IV, p.558.

3. *Pentagon Papers*, New York, New York Times Books, 1971; p.602.

4. For the exchange between Warnke and Wheeler over possible changes in ground strategy see Herbert Schandler, *The Unmaking of a President*, Princeton, Princeton University Press, 1977; pp.157-58.

5. Admiral Sharp, a member of the right current, later called Warnke "as close as one could get to becoming a Communist without actually being one." Interview with author. (Warnke is actually a corporate lawyer.)

6. *PP*, IV, p.239.

7. *PP*, IV, p.247.

8. *PP*, IV, p.245.

9. *PP*, IV, p.258. For background see Chapter Four.

10. *PP*, IV, p.254.

11. *PP*, IV, p.250.

12. *PP*, IV, p.257.

13. Chester Cooper, *The Lost Crusade*, New York, Dodd, Mead, 1970; p.391.

14. Quoted in Townsend Hoopes, *Limits of Intervention*, New York, David McKay, 1969; p.221.

15. *PP*, IV, p.564.

16. Under the San Antonio formula the United States would halt the bombing of the North if "Hanoi promised to not take advantage of the pause." It required reciprocity from the Vietnamese. For the dispute over the definition of "not take advantage" see Chapter Three.

17. *PP*, IV, p.575.

18. In a separate assessment sent directly to Johnson, Taylor advocated the withdrawal of the San Antonio formula. This would have been a significant step · away from the chance of a negotiated settlement.

19. Don Oberdorfer, *TET*, New York, Avon, 1971; p.304. In an interview with the author, Sharp said that a feint towards North Vietnam was planned during the

period. He could not remember the exact date. Under the plan several divisions would head for the North Vietnamese coast. One possible result would be the withdrawal of some or all North Vietnamese divisions from I Corps in South Vietnam. Another would be a movement of Chinese troops into North Vietnam proper, thus giving the right further argument for escalation.

20. Lyndon Johnson, *The Vantage Point*, New York, Holt, Rinehart, Winston, 1971; p.400.

21. At that time Wheeler called the possible bombing halt below the 20th Parallel an "aerial Dien Bien Phu."

22. Documentation of the Johnson-Rusk rationale behind the partial bombing halt will be presented later in the chapter.

23. On March 1, Nitze gave Clifford a memorandum arguing for a reappraisal of Vietnam policy in the light of other national security interests, especially the deteriorating strategic balance with the Soviet Union.

24. Interviews with Paul Nitze and Paul Warnke conducted by the author. Also see Phil Goulding, *Confirm or Deny: Informing the People on National Security*, New York, Harper & Row, 1970; pp.310-12.

25. Clark Clifford, "A Vietnam Reappraisal," *Foreign Affairs*, Vol. 47, 1969, pp.35-49.

26. David Halberstam, *The Best and the Brightest*, New York, Random House, 1971; pp.596-97.

27. Clifford, *op.cit.*

28. Johnson, *op.cit.*; pp.374-75.

29. *Ibid.*, p.390.

30. Oberdorfer, *op.cit.*; p.191.

31. Clifford, *op.cit.*

32. David Kraslow and Stuart Loary, *The Secret Search for Peace in Vietnam*, New York, Random House, 1968; p.231.

33. *Ibid.*, p.230.

34. Schandler, *op.cit.*; p.132.

35. Clifford, *op. cit.*

36. *Ibid.*

37. *Ibid.*

38. Quoted in *PP*, IV, p.589.

39. *PP*, IV, p.583.

40. Johnson's plans to insert a withdrawal in the 1968 State of the Union Address are revealed by Lady Bird Johnson, *A White House Diary*, New York, Holt, Rinehart, Winston, 1970; pp.616-17.

41. As he had done in 1964. The material in this section is drawn from Oberdorfer, *op.cit.*; Theodore White, *The Making of a President: 1968*, New York, Atheneum, 1969; Chester Lewis, et.al., *An American Melodrama*, New York, Viking Press, 1969; Tom Powers, *The War at Home*, New York, Grossman, 1973; and the *New York Times*.

42. As reported by Chambers Roberts and Walter Pincus, *Washington Post*, March 18, 1968.

43. Nixon prepared a speech in which he outlined linkage with the Soviet Union as

the key to ending the war, intimating greater intensity of bombing if the North Vietnamese failed to capitulate. He never gave the speech, although he did later follow the strategy.

44. A split within the Democratic Party over Vietnam began to widen. George Kennan announced his support for McCarthy. Tiford Dudley, chairman of the Washington D.C. chapter of the Democratic Party, cited his opposition to the war and announced that he would not be on the regular party slate. Theodore McClelden, former governor of Maryland and mayor of Baltimore, stated that the United States should stop the bombing without restrictions. Johnson's record in the three most important states is indicative of the period. He lost all of the Massachusetts delegates after failing to file by the March 5th deadline. The Westchester Democratic County Committee reversed its earlier endorsement of Johnson, and in a new polling produced 17 votes for Kennedy, 13 for Johnson and 3 for McCarthy. A spokesman attributed the reversal to growing resentment over the war. Edwin Weisl arranged to have lawyer Louis Nizer defend Johnson at a meeting of Democrats in New York City; yet the vote was 129-26 to back McCarthy. Weisl's own Democratic club voted 249 to 48 to support McCarthy. After a meeting of forty large New York contributors to the party attended by Marvin Watson and Larry O'Brien, Weisl estimated that Johnson would only pick up one third of the New York votes.

In California, Jesse Unruh, the party's political leader in the state, was a staunch Kennedy supporter. The California Democratic Council condemned the war. Thirty of the forty-two Democratic state assemblymen and thirteen of the twenty Democratic state senators refused offers to run on the Johnson slate.

The Americans for Democratic Action were equally divided. In February the ADA voted 65 to 47 to support McCarthy after John Roche, another Presidential aide, attempted to put off the decision until May 17. Roche's subsequent resignation from the ADA was followed by a number of influential labor leaders including I.W. Abel of the Steelworkers, Louis Stulberg of the Garment Workers and Joseph Beinne of the Communication Workers, all of whom continued to back Johnson.

45. See Gordon Weil and Ian Davidson, *The Gold War*, New York, Holt, Rinehart, Winston, 1970; pp.98-100.

46. See Paul Enzig, "The Dollar and Sterling and a Vietnam Peace," *Commercial and Financial Chronicle*, February 22, 1968.

47. On March 28, three days before the speech, a Martin Luther King led march in support of a Memphis garbage workers' strike met violence. On April 4 King was assassinated in Memphis.

48. The 372 million figure and the one billion dollar estimate are Johnson's, *op.cit.*; p.318. Other estimates are much higher, including a loss of two billion on the 14th and an expected loss of five billion on the 15th! See Sidney Rolfe and James Burtle, *The Great Wheel: The World Monetary System*, New York, Quadrangle, 1973; p.94.

49. The seven were the United States, Britain, Italy, Belgium, Switzerland, Germany and the Netherlands. France withdrew from the Gold Pool the previous June.

50. For lunch on March 6. Lady Bird Johnson, *op.cit.*; p.635.

51. *PP*, IV, p.407.

52. The subsequent decision *not* to send the thirty thousand troops was made on

March 26, after the meeting of the Senior Advisory Group (see below). Johnson later claimed that he never made the decision on the thirty thousand because of their economic cost (Johnson, *op. cit.* ; p. 407). but the *Pentagon Papers* maintains that the "President decided to deploy the troops" (*PP*, IV, p. 589). A formal memorandum from Nitze to Wheeler on March 14 refers to the approval of the thirty thousand troops, as does a Systems Analysis memorandum of the 16th (*PP*, IV, p. 591).

53. *PP*, IV, p.591.

54. Westmoreland was originally promised some civilians to support the 10,500 troops decided on in mid-February. When these were not forthcoming the 13,500 pushed by Resor become mandatory. Everyone in the national security apparatus including Clifford and Warnke understood that the 13,500 were devoid of political significance, merely filling out decisions reached earlier.

55. Ambassador Chester Bowles sent a similar proposal from India three days later.

56. Quoted by Hoopes, *op.cit.*; p.185.

57. On March 21 the *New York Times* carried a front-page summary of a pessimistic article by Roger Hilsman ("Must We Invade the North," Vol. 46, April, 1968, no. 3, pp.425-441.) Hilsman argued that the U.S. must either modify its objectives or invade the North. Of the two an invasion seemed more likely. Hilsman's generally pessimistic analysis of ARVN's performance, the pacification program, and the lack of success in attempting to "bomb Hanoi to the conference table," also contained a devastating critique of the bombing's ability to stop men and supplies moving South. Hilsman likened the task to stopping one small coastal tanker, 4 or 5 junks, 14 army-type 6 x 6 trucks, 85 jeeps, 225 elephants, 340 reinforced bicycles, or 1,135 men with packs moving through an area the size of Connecticut (p.436). The annual cost of the bombing was estimated at six billion to the United States and 340 million to the North Vietnamese (which was more than made up by aid from the Soviet Union and China).

Foreign Affairs published a number of other important articles on Vietnam during this period. Almost all reflected the position that the war's costs outweighed its benefits. Editor Hamilton Fish Armstrong called for a negotiated settlement and an end to open-ended commitment. An article on gold and the dollar linked financial difficulties to Vietnam ("Gold and the Dollar" by William Butler and John Deaver 46 [1] October 1967, pp.181-192). Edward Landsdale bemoaned the military's influence in defining goals in South Vietnam ("Still the Search for Goals," 47 [1] October 1968, pp.92-98).

58. Interview with the author.

59. Interview with the author.

60. This was also a favorite argument of Dean Rusk's.

61. Johnson, *op.cit.*; p.419.

62. Quoted by Schandler, *op.cit.*; p.271.

63. *New York Times*, March 22, 1968.

64. Maxwell Taylor, *Swords and Plowshares*, New York, W.W. Norton, 1972; p.378.

65. *Ibid.*; p.391.

66. Halberstam, *op.cit.*; p.653.

67. Quoted by Hoopes, *op.cit.*; pp.215-16.

68. Taylor, *op.cit.*; pp.388-89.

69. Murphy did not voice this opinion in the immediate context of the Group's meetings. Thomas Powers recounts the following episode: "Later, in the 1960s, a member of the President's Foreign Intelligence Advisory Board, Robert Murphy, asked why the CIA didn't kill Ho Chi Minh, since he was giving us so much trouble. Murphy asked loudly, positively, and repeatedly: Ho is the problem, isn't he? Can't you fellows do something to get rid of him? You're supposed to be able to handle things; handle him!" *The Man Who Kept Secrets: Richard Helms and the CIA*, New York, Alfred Knopf, 1979; p.127. In a footnote, Powers says that "The Church Committee was also told about the PFIAB discussions concerning the possibility of assassinating Ho Chi Minh, but decided not to mention them in its final report because the CIA had never followed them up with concrete action. PFIAB is sometimes described as if it were an 'oversight' group intended to keep the Agency in line. It seems to have taken a more aggressive view of its responsibilities, and constantly urged the CIA to do more, rather than less" (p.336).

70. Henry Cabot Lodge, *The Storm Has Many Eyes*, New York, W.W. Norton, 1973; p.219.

71. Oberdorfer, *op.cit.*; p.327.

72. "Indochina: Disengaging," *Foreign Affairs*, Vol. 47, no. 4, July 1971; p.588.

73. Harry McPherson, *A Political Education*, Boston, Little, Brown and Co., 1972; p.433.

74. For example see Laurence Shoup, "The Council on Foreign Relations and American Policy in Southeast Asia, 1940-73," *The Insurgent Sociologist*, Vol. VII, No. 1, Winter 1977; pp.19-30.

75. Quoted by Schandler, *op.cit.*; p.264.

76. McPherson, *op.cit.*; pp.433-34.

77. Interview with the author.

78. The political significance of this omission will be discussed below.

79. The economic impact of the speech was successful. On the next day the stock market enjoyed its highest volume of trading since October 29, 1929. The Dow Jones average leapt twenty points as 17.33 million shares changed hands. Gold markets opened calmly at thirty-eight dollars an ounce, with the dollar and sterling strong against the continental currencies.

80. Schandler, *op.cit.*; p.312.

81. *Ibid.*, p.38.

82. *PP, New York Times* edition; p.622.

83. *Ibid.*

84. *Ibid.*

85. Schandler, *op.cit.*; p.236.

86. Quoted in *ibid.*; p.279.

87. *Ibid.*; pp.241-42; Also see comments by William Bundy, p.251.

88. Johnson, *op.cit.*; p.420.

89. McPherson, *op.cit.*; p.437.

90. Kalb and Abel, *op.cit.*; p.251. The steel bridge at Thanh Hoa was an extremely frustrating target. U.S. jets were unable to take it out until well into the Nixon Admininstation.

91. On March 30, McPherson looked over the speech for the last time. He was struck by the language announcing the partial bombing halt, particularly the possibility that the Administration would be opening itself to charges that it was duping the public. He called Clifford who said that he did not think that the North Vietnamese would quibble since the U.S. would no longer be bombing the areas where ninety percent of their people lived. Also, it would be difficult to retrieve the orders that had already gone out to CINCPAC. This struck McPherson as "peculiar" but he says no more about it.

92. The 20th Parallel was mentioned in messages to the North Vietnamese through diplomatic channels in Moscow, and in communications to Congress, to the military, and to U.S. Ambassadors.

93. For details see Leslie Gelb with Richard Betts, *The Irony of Vietnam: The System Worked*, Washington, Brookings Institute, 1979; p.169.

94. Goulding, *op.cit.*; Goulding also details Clifford's efforts to maintain the momentum built by the partial bombing halt (p.330ff.).

95. See Morton Halperin, *Bureaucratic Politics and Foreign Policy*, Washington, Brookings Institute, 1974.

96. Goulding, *op.cit.*; p.333.

97. Halperin, *op.cit.*

98. This episode is described by Powers, *op.cit.*; pp.197-200.

99. See Paul Joseph and Banning Garrett, "Thirty Years of U.S. Imperialism in Vietnam," *Socialist Review*, No. 25, July-September 1975.

100. See William Shawcross, *Sideshow*, New York, Simon and Schuster, 1979.

IX: The Permanence of Policy Currents: U.S. Policy Toward Post-Liberation Vietnam

1. *Foreign Policy*, No. 24, Fall, 1976.

2. A good example of this argument is Franklin Winstein, "U.S.–Vietnam Relations and the Security of Southeast Asia," *Foreign Affairs*, July 1978, Vol. 56, No. 4, pp. 843-56. Winstein argues that "although the U.S. strategic deterrent and naval presence obviously retain important roles, multi-alignment [among the Communist and ASEAN states] will further reduce demands on U.S. military power, which is appropriate in an era of diminished U.S. capacity to project its military power in Asia" (p. 845).

3. For a fascinating account of these events from the perspective of the right current see Frank Snepp, *Decent Interval*, New York, Vintage Books, 1978.

4. Much of the analysis that follows is based on Bill and Peggy Herod, "The Sino-Vietnamese Conflict and U.S. Policy," (pamphlet published by Friendshipment); and "The Vietnam-China War," *Southeast Asia Chronicle*, No. 68, December 1979.

5. Other members of the left current were appointed to important posts in the State Department.

6. *New York Times*, May 1, 1977.

7. See Elizabeth Becker, "The Chinese Invasion of Vietnam: Changing Alliances," *Indochina Issues*, No. 1, March 1979.

8. Richard Holbrooke, remarks at World Affairs Council of Northern California, Asilomar Conference, May 5, 1979.

9. Elizabeth Becker, "The Politics of Famine in Cambodia," *Washington Post*, November 18, 1979.

10. Elizabeth Becker, "If Politics Win Out in Cambodia, the People Will Be the Losers," *Los Angeles Times*, December 30, 1979.

11. Becker, "The Politics of Famine in Cambodia," *op. cit.*

12. *New York Times*/CBS Poll, July 29, 1977.

13. Winstein, *op. cit.*, p. 850.

14. Michael Morrow, "Vietnam's Embargoed Economy: In the U.S. Interest?" *Indochina Issues*, No. 3, August 1979.

15. As opposed to the deliberate—but not sustained—bombing of civilian targets that were ordered "to punish" the Vietnamese for their stubborness in negotiations and to threaten still greater destruction on the North Vietnamese population.

INDEX